Key to symbols used in route maps

————————	PCT	⋮⋮	marsh
------------	PCT variation	C	possible w~~~ ~~e
═══════════	paved road		
— — — — — —	majo~		
– – – – – –	dirt ro~		~x
···············	trail		
╫╫╫╫╫╫╫╫	railway	▪	building
—z—z—z—	power line	Ⓡ	restaurant
⌐⌐⌐⌐⌐	fence	▲	major summit
◯	lake or pond	△	minor summit
◌	good swimming	)(	saddle, col
——————	river	ᵐᵐ	crag
——————	year-round creek	♠	forest or semi-wooded
------------	seasonal creek	♠	burned forest
•	spring	⑦⑦ᴬ ㉓	links to other maps
●	hot spring	6	numbers for notes
Ⓦ	year-round water	⟨34⟩	start of section
Ⓦ	seasonal water	•265	miles from Mexico/US border
P	piped water		

THE PACIFIC CREST TRAIL

A LONG DISTANCE FOOTPATH THROUGH CALIFORNIA, OREGON AND WASHINGTON

About the Author

Since taking early retirement from his career as a physics and sports teacher, Brian Johnson has found time for three thru'-hikes of the Pacific Crest Trail, a 2700-mile round-Britain walk, two hikes across the Pyrenees from the Atlantic to the Mediterranean and a single summer compleation of the Munros (Scotland's 3000ft mountains).

He has also completed a 2200-mile cycle tour of Spain and France and done multi-week canoe tours in Sweden, France, Spain and Portugal.

In his younger days, Brian's main sport was orienteering. He competed at a high level and coached both Bishop Wordsworth's School and South-West Junior Orienteering squads.He also surveyed and drew many orienteering maps. A keen climber and hiker, he led school groups in Britain, the Alps, the Pyrenees and California.

As a fanatical sportsman and games player, Brian competed to a high standard at cricket, hockey, bridge and chess. His crowning achievement was winning the 1995/96 World Amateur Chess Championships.

Brian hikes under the trail name Ancient Brit.

THE PACIFIC CREST TRAIL

A LONG DISTANCE FOOTPATH THROUGH
CALIFORNIA, OREGON AND WASHINGTON

by
Brian Johnson

2 POLICE SQUARE, MILNTHORPE, CUMBRIA LA7 7PY
www.cicerone.co.uk

All maps and photographs by the author
Printed by MCC Graphics, Spain

Dedication

To all those trail angels who make life so much easier for the PCT hiker.

Warning

The Pacific Crest Trail is designed as a summer trail to be hiked when it is free of snow and the creeks are relatively low. You should be aware that navigation could be difficult and the trail could be dangerous when there is snow in the mountains or when the creeks are running high because of snowmelt. The maps in this guide will not be adequate for navigation when snow covers the trail. If you hike the PCT you will be going into high mountains, wilderness areas and deserts. You might be faced with severe storms, fording unbridged creeks and hiking through long waterless sections in high temperatures. Mountain and wilderness trekking can be dangerous, carrying the risk of personal injury or death.

While every effort has been made to check that the information in this guide is accurate at the time of going to press, neither the author nor the publisher accept responsibility for damage of any nature (including damage to property, personal injury or death) arising directly or indirectly from use of the information in this guide.

Advice to Readers

Readers are advised that, while every effort is made by our authors to ensure the accuracy of guidebooks as they go to print, changes can occur during the lifetime of an edition. Please check Updates on this book's page on the Cicerone website (www.cicerone.co.uk) before planning your trip. We would also advise that you check information about such things as transport, accommodation and shops locally. Even rights of way can be altered over time. We are always grateful for information about any discrepancies between a guidebook and the facts on the ground, sent by email to info@cicerone.co.uk or by post to Cicerone, 2 Police Square, Milnthorpe LA7 7PY, United Kingdom.

Front cover: Crabtree Meadows in the High Sierra (Section 30)

CONTENTS

Ladybird in Valle de San Jose (Section 4)

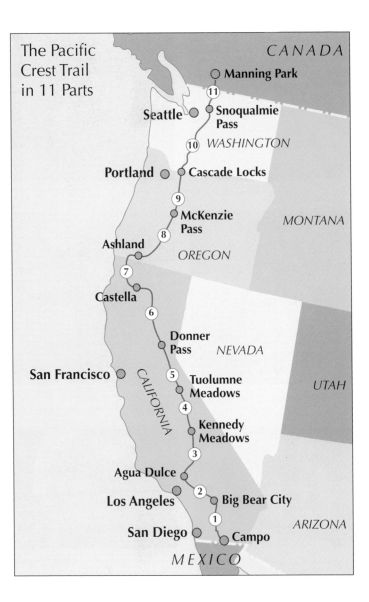

The Pacific Crest Trail in 11 Parts

CANADA

Manning Park

11

Snoqualmie Pass

Seattle

10 WASHINGTON

Portland

Cascade Locks

9

McKenzie Pass

8

Ashland

7

OREGON

Castella

6

Donner Pass

NEVADA

San Francisco

5

Tuolumne Meadows

4

CALIFORNIA

Kennedy Meadows

3

Agua Dulce

2

Big Bear City

Los Angeles

1

San Diego

Campo

MEXICO

MONTANA

UTAH

ARIZONA

Charger and his wife (Section 19)

Willie (Section 74)

Pockets above Carson Pass (Section 41)

A thru'-hiker descends from Kearsarge Pass (Section 31A)

Notorious BOB, a north-to-south thru'-hiker, in the Oregon Desert (Section 69)

Nicola and Huckleberry – don't forget your teddy bear (Section 100)

PREFACE

Potest quia posse videntur – He can because he thinks he can.

When you reach Manning Park at the end of the Pacific Crest Trail you will be tired and dirty – but you will feel great. You will have had the experience of a lifetime and be a changed person. You will have an intense feeling of personal satisfaction. You will be ready for other big ventures in life. You will have learnt not to give up and you will continue to feel great.

The Pacific Crest Trail (PCT) is the world's longest continuous footpath, running from the Mexican border to the Canadian border through California, Oregon and Washington. It is estimated that about 500 hikers, known as thru'-hikers, attempt a continuous hike of the entire PCT each year; of those perhaps forty per cent succeed. A much larger number, who hike short or long sections of the PCT, are known as section-hikers. This comprehensive but concise guide is intended to provide all the information and maps thru'-hikers or section-hikers will need to hike the PCT.

Hiking 2650 miles isn't something that just anyone can do, is it? Over the years I have become more and more astonished by the extraordinary things that people who regard themselves as 'ordinary' can do when they set their mind to it.

- In 2000 I met Dennis at 12,000ft, on snow-covered Muir Pass. He had had a heart and lung transplant in 1999.
- In 2002 I hiked with 63 year-old George 'Billy Goat' Woodard. After starting his thru'-hike he was hospitalised for two weeks with heart pains but that didn't prevent him reaching Canada. To date he has hiked more than 20,000 miles on the PCT.
- In 2004, Mary 'Scrambler' Chambers, a 10-year-old girl thru'-hiked the PCT with her parents, Gary Chambers and Barbara Egbert.
- Scott, in 2006, had one objective: to lose 120lb. He'd weighed 310lb when he set off but when I met him he was already down to 230lb, after just six weeks on the trail.
- In 2006, 22-year-old Ashley 'Ladybird' Ravenstein was bitten on the foot by a brown recluse spider and was off-trail for a month with an injury described as resembling a gunshot wound. Nevertheless she returned to the PCT and arrived in Canada in late October.

If these people can hike the PCT, so can you.

Brian Johnson

Early morning view of Mount Thielsen from Crater Lake Rim (Section 70)

INTRODUCTION

The 2650-mile PCT starts in California at the Mexican border, about 50 miles east of San Diego, and passes through California, Oregon and Washington to reach the Canadian border about 100 miles east of Vancouver, British Columbia.

It is a well-engineered and, for the most part, well-maintained trail. The trail itself is easy to hike: it is well-graded and never steep, as it is designed for horseriders as well as hikers. The PCT is for the exclusive use of hikers and riders and only a few miles, on paved or dirt roads, are shared with other users.

Europeans, accustomed to long distance paths designed to pass through towns and mountain villages with easy access to shops, hotels and commercial campsites, should realise that there is a completely different philosophy to such trails in the US. The PCT is very much a wilderness trail that only occasionally touches civilisation. Wilderness camping is an integral part of hiking the PCT.

The PCT is very varied. You will hike through deserts, forests, over snow-covered passes and along alpine ridges. The trail starts in the arid hills and mountains of Southern California,

Camp on descent from Forester Pass (Section 30)

and cuts across a corner of the Mojave Desert before heading into the Sierra Nevada, with its majestic mountains in a lake-studded landscape. The granite of the Sierra Nevada gives way to the volcanic rocks of the Cascade Mountains, with a succession of volcanoes that tower above the forests of Northern California, Oregon and Washington.

A GEOLOGIST'S DELIGHT

The PCT is a delight for the geologist. Continental drift and plate tectonics are the driving forces behind the geology of the Pacific West Coast. The cause is deep down in the Earth, where radioactive decay produces the heat that keeps the planet's core molten. Convection currents in that molten core cause relative motion between the Pacific and North American plates. That motion between tectonic plates creates stress along the fault lines. Stored elastic energy can be released catastrophically, producing large earthquakes such as that which destroyed San Francisco on April 18, 1906.

There have been many theories about how continental drift causes the formation of volcanoes. In the Pacific North-West it is thought that the Pacific Plate is descending beneath the Continental Plate. Water and gases from the porous oceanic crust are carried down and superheated, melting the surrounding rock to produce magma (the term given to molten rock, or lava, while it remains beneath the Earth's surface). A combination

Granite outcrops above Holcomb Creek (Section 11)

of magma and highly pressurised gas can cause explosive volcanic eruptions, such as that seen when Mount St Helens exploded in 1980.

The mountains of Southern California and the Sierra Nevada are primarily composed of granitic rocks, formed about 80–240 million years ago when magma cooled and solidified below the Earth's surface. Insulating layers of rock meant that that cooling process took place very slowly, allowing coarse-grained crystals to form. Continental drift has caused the rock to be lifted to heights above 20,000ft while the covering rocks have been eroded away, leaving granite as the predominant surface rock today. When granite is eroded, the large crystals tend to form the sandy and gravely soils that predominate in Southern California and the Sierra Nevada.

Over the last two million years, major glacial erosion has produced the fantastic rock scenery and the multitude of lakes we see today in the Sierra Nevada. Granite is an ideal rock for the formation of lakes; most of those you will see in Northern California and Oregon are actually on outcrops of granite in a primarily volcanic landscape.

The situation is further complicated by the San Andreas Fault System, which developed about 30 million years ago and resulted in some rocks being transported as much as 200 miles to the north-west. Hot magma is still present near the surface. Evidence appears in the form of hot springs, such as Deep Creek Hot Springs in San Bernardino National Forest, passed on the PCT. Water flowing underground is heated by the hot magma before coming to the surface.

North of Sonora Pass, in Central California, the rocks become predominantly volcanic although there are outcrops of granite and some of metamorphic rock, such as the limestone in Marble Mountain Wilderness. The northern end of the Sierra Nevada is further complicated in that much of it was buried in volcanic ash about 30 million years ago. Then, ten million years ago, massive lava flows caused metamorphosis of existing rocks, after which erosion left a very complicated geological story.

The Cascade Mountains start with Lassen Peak in Northern California. They continue through Oregon and Washington and into Canada with a succession of major volcanoes and associated lava flows and ashes. You will see many different types of volcano in the Pacific North-West. These developed over the past two million years and remain active today. The last major eruption was in 1980 when Mount St Helens blew its top off. About 7000 years ago, Mount Mazama, in what is now Oregon, exploded with about 40 times as much force, resulting in the formation of Crater Lake. Some of the large lava flows you will see in Oregon are only 200 years old. Volcanic activity

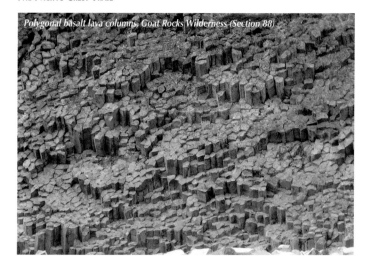
Polygonal basalt lava columns, Goat Rocks Wilderness (Section 88)

can be seen on a smaller scale on Lassen Peak, which suffered a major eruption in 1915. The PCT also passes Terminal Geyser and Boiling Springs Lake, which are evidence of magma very close to the surface there. The next eruption could occur at any time.

Four main types of volcano can be seen on the PCT.

- **Stratovolcanoes**, such as Mount Shasta, are tall conical mountains composed of alternating layers of lava flows and ejected material.
- **Lava domes**, such as Lassen Peak, are built up by slow eruptions of highly viscous lavas.
- **Cinder cones** result from the eruption of small pieces of scoria or pyroclastics, which resemble cinders. These are often relatively short-lived eruptions and build

up cones of between 100ft and 1000ft high. Most cinder cones erupt only once and often form as flank vents on the sides of larger volcanoes.

- Shield volcanoes are formed by the eruption of low viscosity lavas which can flow a great distance from the vent. They don't usually explode catastrophically or form volcanic cones but they can produce massive lava fields.

There is no agreed distinction between an active and a dormant volcano but the Smithsonian Institute defines a volcano as active if it has erupted within the last 10,000 years and many of the volcanoes in the Pacific North-West fall into this category. Volcanoes can be dormant for thousands of years and become eroded and worn down but magma remains close to the surface, which means they could erupt again. Often these eruptions will be violent, as pressure will have built up beneath the plug that has prevented lava escaping. Volcanoes are only considered extinct when they no longer have a lava supply.

Pumice is formed when frothy, escaping lava solidifies, trapping lots of bubbles. Pumice is very light and will float on water until it becomes waterlogged. In violent volcanic eruptions, escaping steam often tears magma and the solid rock surrounding the vent into small particles, resulting in volcanic ash.

In places along the PCT you will see polygonal basalt lava columns, the best-known being the Devil's Postpile at Reds Meadow. The Postpile was created about 100,000 years ago when a lava flow was impounded by a moraine and reached a thickness of 400ft. Because of its great thickness, much of the pooled lava mass cooled slowly and evenly, producing long, symmetrical columns. The mainly hexagonal joints developed when the lava contracted during the cooling process.

More recently, ice ages have eroded the volcanoes of the Cascade Mountains. Glaciers remain on many volcanoes, particularly Mount Rainier and Glacier Peak. You can gain an idea of the comparative age of volcanoes from their appearance. Younger ones, including many of the small

volcanoes that you see, tend to have the classical conic shape, whereas older volcanoes have been eroded during the ice ages, leaving only the towering crags of their more resistant cores.

There are three main types of glacial erosion.

- **Plucking**: glacial melt water freezes around lumps of cracked and broken rock. When the ice moves downhill, the rock is plucked from the back wall.
- **Abrasion**: rock frozen to the base and back of the glacier scrapes the bedrock.
- **Freeze-thaw**: melt water or rain penetrates cracks in the bedrock. At night it freezes, expands and enlarges the crack, eventually breaking the rock away.

Volcanic rocks are easily eroded but granite is very resistant. Only where it is highly fractured or has been subjected to deep weathering is it easily eroded. Such weakened rock is easily excavated by glaciers, which leave basins of resistant granite that fill with water as the glaciers retreat. These are the corrie lakes that make granite mountain landscapes so attractive. Volcanic mountains lack the resistant rocks that allow lakes to form but in places glaciers have peeled them right down to the granite beneath, allowing the formation of lakes.

There are very few sedimentary rocks in the mountains through which the PCT passes.

15

WEATHER PATTERNS

The mountains of Southern California, the Sierra Nevada and the Cascades form a highly effective rain shadow. Very little rain falls to the east of the mountains and desert conditions predominate as a result.

The PCT generally keeps to the crests or western slopes of the mountains to avoid the desert areas. This is epitomised by the long detour west of Mount Shasta, in Northern California, to avoid the dry, waterless hills east of the massive volcano. The main exception is the crossing of the western corner of the Mojave Desert, which has very little rainfall.

Rain and snow come either from frontal storms (often tropical storms developing well to the south-west) or from thunderstorms. Fortunately for PCT hikers, the frontal storms, which dump large quantities of snow in the mountains, occur mainly in winter. Storm frequency and the duration of the storm season increase as you head north. In Southern California most of the storms occur from January to March; by Northern California they have spread from late-September to May; and in Washington you can expect frontal storms at any time of year.

Thunderstorms develop mainly as a result of convection currents caused by the power of the sun and are concentrated in the summer months, with July being the peak. The frequency of thunderstorms diminishes as you head north. Storm clouds usually start to build in the early afternoon, with the storm arriving in the late afternoon or evening.

Debris from the storm of 2003 (Section 96)

Yucca at Vasquez Rocks (Section 18)

A thru'-hiker can expect hot, dry weather in Southern California and the High Sierra. Northern California is hiked at the peak of the thunderstorm season but there are fewer here than further south. Oregon in August is generally warm and dry but an occasional frontal storm or thunderstorm can be expected. In Washington in September you can expect periods of frontal rain but you can also get long sunny periods.

> ### The weather's boring!
>
> *Liz Willis, a British thru'-hiker in 2002, after weeks of continuous sunshine in California.*

The weather does not always follow these patterns. You must be prepared for rain or snow at any time in the mountains.

Vegetation

The mountain vegetation of California and Oregon has to deal with a difficult climate. Most of the precipitation at higher altitudes comes in winter, in the form of snow, and there is very little rain in summer. It has to survive high summer and low winter temperatures, as well as the poor quality soils in areas where granite is the predominant rock type.

The first thing Northern Europeans will notice on the PCT is the absence of grass and the poor quality of the meadows. Grass requires a lot of water and it isn't until you reach Washington that it seems to thrive.

The second feature Europeans will notice in Southern California is the absence of trees at lower altitudes, except along creeks. Only at higher altitudes are temperatures cool

Just some of the flowers and cacti you may see along the Trail

enough and water plentiful enough for trees to survive. Below tree-line chaparral predominates. Chaparral is composed of broad-leaved shrubs, bushes and small trees, usually below 8ft high, which have evolved to cope with hot dry conditions. At the lowest altitudes, in the drier areas, only true desert vegetation survives and you will see various species of cactus and yucca.

There are many different species of tree on the PCT and each seems to have evolved to fill a particular niche in the ecosystem. Deciduous trees predominate at lower altitudes where there is sufficient water but in the mountains you see a wide variety of pine.

There is also an upper limit to tree-line, above which conditions are too harsh for any tree to survive. In

Southern California the hardiest species eek out an existence at 9000ft on exposed ridges but in Washington you will find that trees struggle to survive on ridges at 6000ft.

You will see many dead or dying trees. In many areas they are suffering from beetle infestations, as well as problems caused by pollution and forest fires.

In Washington you will spend much of your time in what is described as temperate rainforest, with the profusion of vegetation you would expect when there is plenty of rain throughout the year.

For much of the PCT you will hike through areas of forest that are only very lightly managed. Often this consists of little more than keeping trails clear for hikers. Fallen trees are allowed to rot, providing habitat for insects and returning nutrition into the soil. Only in Northern California will you hike through areas of commercial forestry, and even here authorities try to ensure a ribbon of natural woodland remains along the route of the PCT.

The variety and abundance of flowers increases as you head north. In Southern California the desert flora waits for rain before producing flowers and if you arrive in a wet spell you can expect to see the desert bloom. In a dry spell, however, there will be few signs of flowers. As you head north you will see plenty of flowers in the damper meadows.

Animals and birds
Some of the animals you will see are mentioned in the Wilderness Hiking section of the introduction; others will be featured in the map sections.

Birds have generally evolved separately in the Americas, and Europeans will find few species with which they are familiar. Migration patterns are mainly north-to-south rather than east-to-west and the greatest species-overlap is among waterfowl and waders (shore birds). Notes on the birds you are most likely to see appear in the map sections.

Southern California
The distance between Campo and Kennedy Meadows is approximately 700 miles. The terrain is varied, with rolling hills and mountains rising to 9000ft separated by sections of desert. This is an arid landscape with desert vegetation at low altitudes and chaparral (brush) at intermediate altitudes; only in the mountains is it cool and damp enough for forests to thrive. The PCT goes right past Deep Creek Hot Springs in San Bernardino National Forest, possibly the best wilderness hot springs in California.

Spring is the best season for hiking this section of the PCT but you need to wait until the snow has melted in the higher mountains. Thru'-hikers will tackle this section in April, May and June and this is the best time for section-hikers as well. In a dry year most of the creeks and springs will have dried up by early spring and you will encounter long stretches without water. Fortunately this section is well provided for by trail angels, who maintain many water caches to help hikers through the drier parts. Despite their help, there could be times when you need to carry up to six litres of water. To be successful and enjoy the conditions, you must work out a strategy to cope with the heat.

Even in April temperatures can reach 90°F (32°C) but don't depend on it. You can get snow in the mountains and it can freeze at night. By May or June temperatures can exceed 100°F (38°C).

The ground is mainly sandy and finding somewhere to camp will rarely be a problem. You will see plenty of rattlesnakes but these are only really a danger to those who try to handle them. Any wild bears you encounter will run when they sense you and mosquitoes shouldn't pose any problems.

The High Sierra

The 450 miles from Kennedy Meadows to Donner Pass take you through a spectacular alpine landscape. You reach an altitude of 13,180ft at Forester Pass and cross a succession of passes above 11,000ft. For much of the time you will be above tree-line, where ice age glaciation has produced a landscape of crags and bare rock, dotted with

thousands of lakes. Between the high passes you drop into deep, forested valleys. The mountain ridges and summits are the realm of the rock climber and mountaineer, the valleys and high passes are for the walker.

Many hikers take a day off to scale 14,494ft Mount Whitney, the highest mountain in the US outside Alaska. For 200 miles the PCT coincides with the world famous John Muir Trail (JMT), which starts on the summit of Mount Whitney and ends in Yosemite Valley. The PCT leaves the JMT at the head of Yosemite and some hikers might want to take a few days off to explore this wonderland of rock domes and plunging waterfalls.

The High Sierra is the most exciting section of the PCT but also the part with most problems to overcome. Supply is a problem, with a 200-mile section without a single road. Any bears you meet might be after your food and mosquitoes can be a problem, especially just after the snow has melted.

You will probably enjoy days of endless sunshine but, in high mountains, fresh snow can fall in any month of the year and thunderstorms can be spectacular. Despite the altitude it can get very hot in the sun but you must be prepared for freezing temperatures at night.

The biggest problem is winter snow. The JMT is best hiked in late July, August or September but most PCT thru'-hikers pass through in June or early July when there is still snow

Summit ridge, Mount Whitney (Section 30A)

on the passes. Rapidly melting snow can produce high water levels in the many unbridged creeks that need to be crossed. Conditions vary from year to year. In 1996 there was substantial snow on the passes into August, while in 2006, a record snow year, there was almost continuous snowpack for 300 miles in June, together with dangerous or impossible creek crossings. In other years hikers wonder what all the fuss is about. Thru'-hikers would be advised to read the section in this guide on starting dates and decide, very carefully, the date on which they should leave Kennedy Meadows; section-hikers would be best to visit the area in late summer.

A number of the photos in this guide, taken in June 2006, show how fantastic the scenery can be before

the snow has melted but these are not safe conditions for hikers without extensive winter mountaineering experience.

Northern California

You've already hiked 1150 California miles but a further 550 remain before you reach Oregon. In the first half of the Northern California section, much of the PCT passes through forest on rolling hills. On entering the Cascade Mountains, large volcanoes, including Lassen Peak and Mount Shasta, dominate the landscape. Approaching Oregon, you return to alpine terrain as you enter the Klamath Mountains.

Thru'-hikers will pass through this section in July and August, which is a good time to hike these mountains. It is likely to be sunny most of the time but it is also the main season for thunderstorms, and torrential rain or hail is possible. There is also the risk of fire, started by lightning striking the often tinder-dry forests.

Several long sections, where forests were clear-felled in the last century or where they have been destroyed by fire, present very little shade. Water can become a problem again as the springs and creeks start to dry up through the summer.

The hiking is fairly easy and fast and remains so until you reach Northern Washington.

Oregon

There is generally less ascent in Oregon than elsewhere on the PCT and the 430 miles here are fast going; fit thru'-hikers should cover 20 miles comfortably each day.

In geological terms, the Cascade Mountains in Oregon are extremely young with unvegetated lava flows only 200 years old. The landscape is dominated by volcanoes, large and small. Crater Lake, one of the wonders of the natural world, was created a mere 7000 years ago, when Mount Mazama underwent a cataclysmic volcanic explosion which spread a thick layer of ash over hundreds of miles. The Three Sisters, Mount Washington, Three Fingered Jack, Mount Jefferson and Mount Hood are spectacular volcanoes that tower above tree-line. Thousands of lakes are dotted throughout the mountains.

When the PCT was under development it temporarily followed the fantastic Oregon Skyline Trail (OST). As the trail was designed to keep hikers and horses away from

Wizard Island, Crater Lake (Section 70)

Mount Jefferson, seen through a 'ghost forest' (Section 77)

environmentally sensitive areas, however, it was eventually routed through dry, viewless forests, avoiding far too many of the lakes. The author recommends that you follow the old OST rather than the PCT through large sections of Oregon; these alternatives are detailed in the map section of this guide.

Probably 99 per cent of PCT hikers follow an alternative route along the rim of Crater Lake, which has now become an official pedestrian variation to the official trail. Similarly, most hikers follow the spectacular Eagle Creek Trail down to Cascade Locks, with only horses taking the official PCT.

There will be some fairly long stretches without water, especially if you ignore the author's advice and

follow the official PCT all the way through Oregon. At lower altitudes you will hike through forest where there is plenty of shade from the sun.

Oregon is notorious for its mosquitoes. By August, when the first thru'-hikers will be passing through, they will have become only a minor nuisance; if you are hiking immediately after the snowmelt, however, you could find them extremely annoying.

Thru'-hikers will tackle Oregon in August and early September and can expect good weather to predominate. There will be the occasional thunderstorm and hikers must be prepared for rain and even snow. Forest fires have been a problem in recent years, so don't be surprised if a section of the PCT is closed for this reason.

Washington

Only 480 miles remain before you reach the Canadian border. Southern Washington is rather like Oregon and, assuming you are fit, you can manage high mileages. In Goat Rocks Wilderness, however, you return to a spectacular alpine landscape. Mount Rainier and Glacier Peak, both covered by large glaciers, dominate your hike through Northern Washington. You are back in terrain characterised by long steep climbs and descents, and your average hiking speed will be closer to two than three miles per hour.

Washington's Cascade Mountains have a reputation for rain and you will

THE EARLY DAYS OF THE PCT

The first documented hiker to complete the PCT was Martin Papendick in 1952, long before the trail was officially recognised. The impetus for the creation of the trail as we know it today was the passing of the National Trails Systems Act by the US Congress in 1968, which granted the PCT the status of National Scenic Trail.

The PCT was the main feature of the June 1971 edition of *National Geographic Magazine* and this, together with the publication by Wilderness Press of guidebooks to the trail, led to a spate of hikers attempting to thru'-hike it.

For the pioneers in the 1970s, there was little knowledge about how to tackle such a long wilderness route. Very little lightweight equipment was available and little was known about finding water or locating supplies. The PCT was simply regarded as a longer example of the backpacking trips to which hikers were then accustomed.

Hikers had to carry extremely heavy packs, often with more than ten days' food, and averaged about 15 miles a day, completing the trail in about six months. Then, in 1992, Ray Jardine wrote a best-selling handbook about how to hike the PCT. He advocated an ultra-lightweight hiking style that made distances of 20–30 miles a day achievable and his methods soon became the norm. They have been taken to the extreme by some: in 2009, for example, Scott Williamson completed a thru'-hike in 67 days, averaging 40 miles a day.

The methods publicised by Ray Jardine are outside the capabilities and inclinations of most hikers and the introduction to this book is designed to redress the balance by combining the advantages of the lightweight revolution with the traditional methods of the pioneers. The guide's map sections should be useful to all hikers, whatever their hiking style.

be hiking through temperate rainforest. In August and September you can expect long settled periods but must be prepared for periods of rain. Most thru'-hikers will be in Washington in September, a good month for these mountains. You could get snow but it shouldn't be too much of a problem and the first heavy snowfall of winter is unlikely to fall until well into October.

Few roads cross the Cascade Mountains so supply points are widely separated and you will often carry a heavy burden of food. The absence of roads makes it difficult for weekend hikers to tackle some of Washington's PCT sections.

PLANNING

Can the 'ordinary hiker' thru'-hike the PCT?
The most difficult thing about thru'-hiking the PCT is making the decision to attempt it. To most people, the idea of a continuous 2650-mile hike sounds such a daunting expedition that they assume it is only for the super-fit young person. It is actually a challenge that is achievable by the ordinary hiker.

My experience prior to my successful 2002 thru'-hike is worth relating, as there are lessons to be learnt. By 1997 a foot injury became so serious that my surgeon said he could do no more for me and recommended early retirement from teaching. By

2000 I was able to start walking again and I hiked a section of the PCT in the High Sierra, averaging eight miles a day. In April 2002 I arrived in Campo to thru'-hike the PCT. I only managed 10 miles on the first day before I had to camp, because I was exhausted and hurting. Yet five months later I stood at the Canadian border.

I hadn't done any training but I had done a lot of preparation. In particular, I had worked out a strategy to complete the hike and had prepared a detailed schedule, which recognised that I was very unfit. In fact I finished about 14 days ahead of my schedule. Most of all I succeeded because I had the mental strength to overcome the difficulties I encountered (others would say I was too stubborn and pig-headed to give up!).

> Billy Goat: **'How much training did you do for the PCT?'**
>
> Ancient Brit: **'None – I wasn't fit enough to train!'**

However, between 20 and 30 per cent of thru'-hikers give up in the first week. Many of those are ill-prepared 'ordinary' hikers; a good number of those succumb to injury. That means that between 30 and 50 per cent of those who fail to reach Canada actually give up in the first week!

Examples of mistakes made by hikers in 2006 include Ladybird, who set out from Campo carrying two bear boxes packed with enough food to last 12 days; Luigi, who had a 75lb load on his back; and Three Gallon, who set off carrying three gallons of water. That latter example might sound like good planning until you learn that it was a wet spring, it was raining and 10 creeks were running within the first 20 miles.

Despite those early errors, all three made it to Canada. Each started with an easy schedule, which meant that they got the most important part of their planning right. If you prepare properly and give yourself enough time you should be able to achieve a successful thru'-hike.

How long do you need for a thru'-hike?

The length of time you need to complete the PCT's 2650 miles will obviously depend on how many miles you walk each day and how many zero (rest) days you take. If you average 15 miles per day, you should complete the trail in 176 days, or just under six months. Upping your daily mileage by two miles will bring the number of days needed to reach Canada down to 154, or five months. If you were capable of averaging 20 miles per day, it would take you 132 days – just under four months – while a hiker capable of hitting 25 miles per day should be able to cover the entire distance in 106 days, just three and a half months.

To those figures, you would need to add the number of zero days you

might have in order to calculate the total time it might take to complete the hike. Most thru'-hikers take between four and six months. If you take few zero days, you can do a low daily mileage hike in five or six months. The data in appendices E, F, G and H illustrate how a thru'-hike can be completed with relatively low daily mileage. The longest realistic schedule to allow you to get through the High Sierra after the snow has melted and get through Washington before the winter snows is 180 days.

There are many reasons for doing relatively low daily mileages. The main one is the avoidance of injury. Many hikers are injured early during their hikes, primarily with blisters and repetitive strain injuries. Unless you are trail-fit before you start (and very few hikers are), you shouldn't be hiking for more than between five and seven hours each day in the first week. Even when fully fit, your body won't be able to cope with walking 25 miles or more a day, day-after-day, without a rest. Those exceptional hikers who set trail records have been building up their strength and stamina over years rather than weeks or months.

Do you want to enjoy your hike? Many people think the best parts of any hike are the rest periods! You've earned those rests and will appreciate the views, a mug of tea and the chance to chat to other hikers. You've earned that swim or soak in the hot springs. You can read that book you've never had time for at home, or even write your own book. You won't have time for long breaks if you plan to hike 20 or 30 miles every day. You should instead follow the example of the gentleman from Seattle who 'wanted time to smell the roses'.

Hiking schedules

It is possible to hike the PCT without a plan. People do so successfully but more of them will give up at some stage. You are more likely to succeed if you have a strategy to complete the hike and a detailed plan to fall back on in times of difficulty. Obviously circumstances might force you to adjust your plans as you go along.

The main reasons for a detailed schedule are to help you organise your food supplies and to ensure you

neither reach the High Sierra too soon nor Washington too late. If travellers from outside the US have confidence in their schedule they can book a return flight at the same time as their outbound flight, and save themselves a lot of money.

In 2006, a record snow year, most hikers started far too early and, despite all sorts of delaying tactics, reached Kennedy Meadows when there was almost continuous snowpack in the High Sierra. Of the early starters only a small minority, who were experienced winter mountaineers, got through the High Sierra.

There is a lot to be said for having a schedule that you can achieve fairly easily: you will feel good when you get ahead and it will give you flexibility in case of problems or injuries. If

Sun cups (Section 32)

your schedule is too demanding you will become demoralised when you fall behind, or injured if you try to keep up.

You will find all the information you need to produce a schedule in the appendices. Appendices D1 and D2 give hiking hours between recommended resupply points and outline schedules for 110, 120, 130, 140, 150, 160, 170 and 180 day thru'-hikes. All of these leave Kennedy Meadows on June 15, which would be an appropriate date in an average snow year. Appendix E gives a breakdown of the figures for miles, hiking hours and miles/hour between the five main regions of the PCT. Appendix F gives the precise daily schedule completed by Ancient Brit in 2002. Appendix G gives a detailed sample schedule for a 180-day though-hike. This is the type of schedule you should produce for yourself. Appendix H gives a schedule for a very slow start for those who are extremely unfit. Those hiking 160–180-day schedules might prefer to start a little earlier, if snow conditions allow, so that they finish a little earlier in October.

Zero days

'Zero day' is the term used on the trail for a rest day. Simply, you cover zero trail miles that day. Avoiding too many zero days is key to a low daily mileage hike. In 2006 EricD had taken 30 zero days by the time he reached Donner Pass and, despite hiking between 25 and 35 miles every day, still took

longer to reach that point than the author, whose longest day was about 20 miles. The thru'-hiker who completed the PCT in 1979 averaging 15 miles a day, with no zero days, had it much better worked out.

Why do you need zero days? Hikers in 2006 gave many reasons. Some said their body needed a break after covering too many miles in successive days. Others had blisters, repetitive strain injuries, were ill or simply needed to recover from the night before! Some had started their thru'-hikes too early and needed to wait for the Sierra snows to melt, while others waited in town for rain and snowstorms to pass through.

Resupplying was another reason for taking zero days. Some hikers had reached town on a Saturday to find the post office to which they had sent their resupply parcel didn't open until Monday. Even those who reached town mid-week sometimes needed time to organise supplies. Others spent a day with a husband or girlfriend, waited for another hiker to catch up or took time out to attend a family occasion including weddings and funerals, or to visit attractions such as Las Vegas or the Quincy Music Festival.

Other reasons to take a zero day might include the fact that you're reached a lovely place in the wilderness that you can't bear to leave in a hurry. Perhaps the comforts of town – hotel beds, showers and laundry – are too tempting. Or perhaps you want to take a zero day for no other reason than everyone else is doing the same.

There are plenty of reasons to avoid zero days. They can be very expensive: someone calculated that the average hiker spent $100 at Vermillion Valley Resort in the Sierra Nevada. Most people who quit the trail do so after a zero day, particularly at Warner Springs in Southern California, just 110 miles from the start. But the most important consideration is that every unscheduled zero day you take means that you have to hike an extra hour or more each day for the next week to make up the lost time.

Before you set off think carefully about your zero day policy. It is best to produce a schedule with very few zero days but one that is fairly easy to achieve. You can then earn your zero days by getting ahead of schedule and enjoy them with a clear conscience.

Annual Day Zero Pacific Crest Trail Kick-Off

A kick-off party is held every year, on the last or penultimate weekend in April, at Lake Morena campground, 20 trail miles from the Mexican border. The whole campground is booked for the weekend and the party is attended by past and future PCT hikers, as well as that year's aspirants. A large number of trail angels will also be present. The kick-off – known as ADZPCTKO – is a good chance to meet fellow hikers and pick up

information about conditions and things such as water caches on the trail. There will also be organised talks for your education or entertainment.

There are good reasons for attending the kick-off if it fits into your schedule. However, there are also dangers in attending. The timing of the kick-off is about right for those doing a relatively slow thru'-hike and for section-hikers. Faster thru'-hikers will, however, find that they reach the High Sierra much too early.

At Lake Morena, around kick-off time, it will be relatively easy to find someone willing to give you a lift to the Mexican border, tempting you to slack-pack the first 20 miles to the

Ladybug and Ancient Brit at the PCT's southern terminal, Campo (Section 1)

29

campground, either before or after the kick-off party. Covering that mileage on the first day, however, is a recipe for disaster even if you don't have to carry your pack. It's a great way to get blisters and there is the danger, if you are slack-packing, that you won't carry enough water. After the kick-off, when you leave Lake Morena, you will be with a large group of hikers. Do you have the discipline to go slow? Or will you find yourself dragged along at the excessive early speeds of others? If you are at the back of the pack, you might find that hikers just ahead of you have emptied the water caches.

Some hikers leave Campo well-before the kick-off and get a lift back from Warner Springs or even further up the trail, while others leave from Campo on Wednesday or Thursday and arrive at the kick-off party after a gentle start. Both strategies could upset your hiking routine too early in the journey.

If you intend to be at the kick-off, the best thing would be to get a lift to Campo after the party, to start your hike properly. That works best if the dates fit in with your schedule. For details of the kick-off, see www.siechert.org/adz.

Start date

Decide your start date as late as possible, so that you can adjust it depending on snow levels in the High Sierra. Websites given in Appendix B should enable you to keep a check on snow levels throughout the winter. In 2006

30

many hikers started at least a month too early in what was a record snow year.

The key date isn't when you begin but when you reach Kennedy Meadows at the start of the High Sierra. Ray Jardine's suggestion is that, in an average snow year, you should leave Kennedy Meadows on June 15, known as Ray Day. You will still find some snow on the higher passes but most of it will have melted and water levels in the creeks will have started to drop. Snow melts extremely quickly at that time of year and even a week's difference in start date can make a tremendous difference to the snowpack.

In a high snow year it would be best to leave Kennedy Meadows at a later date. In 2006, even the beginning of July was too early. Obviously the later you leave Kennedy Meadows, the later you will arrive in Canada. In 2006 hikers were still reaching Manning Park at the end of October though that was preferable to hitting the High Sierra too soon.

In a year of low snow levels, hikers who have opted for a schedule of between 160 and 180 days might prefer to leave Kennedy Meadows a little earlier so that they reach Canada a little earlier. Appendices D1 and D2 give finishing dates for different schedules assuming you leave Kennedy Meadows on June 15.

Once you have decided on your Kennedy Meadows departure date, work back to determine the date on which you should leave Campo. For

Fuller Ridge, in the San Jacinto Mountains,
on April 30 2006 – too early to start! (Section 8)

example, if you plan to take 50 days, including zero days, to reach Kennedy Meadows by June 15, you will start about April 26 – it isn't just coincidence that that is the approximate date of the kick-off party.

Another consideration will be snow conditions in the San Jacinto Mountains, which you reach during your second week. The trail contours on steep north- and east-facing slopes, where snow can persist into late April. Those who start the PCT in early to mid-April might find dangerous conditions on those steep slopes and navigation can be very difficult if the snowpack is continuous. However, in a low snow year, the trail could be clear by early April.

Hiking north-to-south

Only a few hikers attempt to thru'-hike from north to south each year. In an average snow year the PCT in Washington won't be free of snow until late June, even later in a high snow year. In North Washington the trail often contours on steep slopes, the most difficult and dangerous terrain to cross in snow conditions. Crossing creeks in North Washington can also be a serious problem if you start too early.

If you are considering hiking south, therefore, you should consider starting about July 1 so that you finish by the end of November. That means tackling Washington in July, Oregon in August and Northern California in September, which is fine. You would then pass through the High Sierra in October, a time when you might expect some storms. You would be unlucky to have the first heavy winter snow but you would be cutting it rather fine. You will have supply problems because most of the facilities in the High Sierra will have closed and you might need to hike into the night occasionally to get in your mileage, which will certainly test your navigational skills. November could be a good time for hiking in Southern California, as long as you've had rain to replenish the creeks and springs and as long as you haven't got deep snow in the higher mountains.

Basically a north-to-south thru'-hike is only for experienced long distance walkers who have good knowledge of the PCT or are super-fit and intend to do the trail in three or four months. There is an additional legal problem as there is no easy procedure for gaining permission to enter the US from Canada along the PCT. This guidebook assumes you are hiking from south to north.

Flip-flopping

Some thru'-hikers reach Kennedy Meadows too early. Rather than face deep snow conditions or wait for it to melt sufficiently, they decide to head to Northern California and return to the High Sierra later in their hike. That is not a good idea, however, as the High Sierra is the easiest PCT section to traverse in snow. If there is substantial snow there, there will also

be snow in the mountains of Northern California, Oregon and Washington where the PCT traverses many steep slopes, which are difficult and dangerous under snow.

The only section to which you might flip-flop is the short section from Hat Creek Resort to Castella, in Northern California. The other flip-flop some hikers choose is to hike through California from Campo to Ashland, then travel to Canada and hike south from Manning Park to Ashland. That can be a good plan if you reach Ashland rather late and don't want to risk being in Northern Washington for the first big winter storms.

Hiking 7–8 hours a day

A typical backpacker will hike between four and six hours a day. Even a relatively low-mileage thru'-hiker will need to hike between six and eight hours each day once they have built up their fitness. This takes discipline.

You could do what too many hikers seem to do: start fairly late, walk for seven or eight hours with minimal breaks and collapse into camp, exhausted, about teatime. However there are much better hiking patterns, patterns which will make your hike more enjoyable and easier to achieve.

Most hikers take short breaks. That might be fine for youngsters but for the older hiker a break of between 15 and 30 minutes is long enough to stiffen up yet not really long enough

Late start from Pioneer Mail Picnic Area for Hans (Section 3)

to recover. It also means you are hiking through the hottest part of the day!

In the hot conditions that predominate along the PCT, an early start is essential. Once you are fit, try hiking from 7am until 10am or 11am without any substantial break. Then stop for two hours before walking for an hour in the afternoon (not too long if it is hot), then take another long break before doing a two or three hours in the evening, once it has cooled down.

Many might consider 7am to be a late start. Billy Goat would start walking at first light and stop for breakfast between 7am and 8am. When it is hot, the earlier you start and the longer the morning session, the easier you'll find it. It can be uncomfortably hot by 10am.

One other thing to consider is having your evening meal before doing another hour or two before camping. That is certainly a good idea if you arrive at water between 4pm and 6pm. Have your meal, then do an evening session to a dry camp. That is also good practice in bear country. You could consider walking on after dark. That might sound a good idea in hot conditions but probably won't help much, as you might then make a later start the following morning. You would be better off getting up while it is still dark and getting away at, or even before, dawn.

On reaching Washington you will find the days getting shorter but the temperature will be comfortable for hiking. By then you should be fit enough to walk for four hours in the morning

RULE OF 11 AND 13

You can expect to spend 11 hours in camp: an hour in the morning, two hours at night and eight hours asleep. This leaves 13 hours for walking and resting during the day. If you are going to be walking for eight hours, that leaves five hours of breaks to scatter through the day. If you spend more than 11 hours in camp you probably aren't making the best use of the day!

before one long break and completing your mileage in the evening.

In bad weather you should consider having a lie-in but still get away between 9am and 10am, then keep walking with a few short breaks until you decide to camp. If you decide to have an easy (half) day, you are much better sticking to your morning hiking routine and then camping, rather than making a late start and walking when it is hot.

Early starts can be difficult to achieve after a night in town. By the time you've eaten breakfast in the restaurant or with your trail angel hosts, you might find it is already rather late. It is difficult to maintain good walking patterns if you spend many nights indoors. It takes more discipline than most hikers possess to get away from town between the hours of 6am and 7am. The author tries to arrive in town in time for a

late breakfast in a restaurant, spends the hottest part of the day in town and then hikes into the evening. If you follow that example, you can get a couple of meals in town, sort out supplies and still walk in the coolest part of the day, as well as saving yourself a lot of money.

The first week

It is estimated that between 20 and 30 per cent of thru'-hikers give up in the first week. How can you avoid becoming one of them? When you stand on the Mexican border it's no good thinking about the 2650 miles that lie ahead, it's much too great a distance to contemplate. Instead, focus on things that you can achieve in the first week on the trail.

In cool weather or after a damp spring, your first week will be a lot less demanding than what is described here but you must be mentally prepared for hot dry conditions.

Develop efficient hiking habits from the beginning. Start hiking in the cool of morning and in the evenings, and avoid taking unnecessary zero days. Develop efficient camping habits and, as you do so, decide how much equipment you can send home from Warner Springs. After all, almost everyone starts with things they don't need. Learn to interpret the maps and to use them for navigation. Assess the seasonal water sources you encounter to give you a better idea of which springs and creeks are likely to be running further along the trail.

During that vital week you should be starting to get fit while being careful to avoid injury. You should avoid sunburn and hopefully you'll start to build up a tan. Get a sense for how much water you need to drink to keep hydrated in hot conditions. Also learn to recognise and avoid poison oak (see section on Wilderness Hiking). You should not worry about how much progress you are making at this stage. If you are getting behind schedule, you will be able to catch up when you get fitter.

Your first resupply package will probably be at Warner Springs, so it would be helpful if your schedule gets you there when the post office is open.

Try to find out before you set off whether any water sources will be running before you reach Lake Morena. It varies greatly from year to year. In mid-April 2002 there were none but in 2009 there were several. In 2006 there were about 10.

Consider how you will hike the 20 miles to Lake Morena campground, which you can expect to take between nine and 10 hours of hiking. Let's assume it is a relatively dry year. Your first water will be piped at Morena campground but you should not consider getting there in one day. If you attempt nine or 10 hours of walking on that first day you are likely to end up with blisters and will risk other injuries. Therefore you will need a dry overnight camp before you reach Lake Morena.

How much water should you carry? If it is hot assume half a litre of

Approaching Hart Bar Creek Canyon (Section 9)

water per hour of hiking and two litres for the overnight camp. You should therefore be carrying six or seven litres of water.

You won't need to carry food to get you to Warner Springs as you could resupply at the well-stocked stores at Lake Morena and Mount Laguna. You could send a resupply package to Mount Laguna Post Office as an alternative to using the store. Make sure you have food that you will be able to eat in hot, dry conditions.

Before you start, drink plenty of water and make sure you have put sun cream on hands and face as well as your legs and arms if you have decided to start in shorts and short-sleeved shirt. Even if you've kept the weight of your equipment to a sensible level, which you probably haven't yet, with six litres of water your pack will feel too heavy.

What time should you set out? It doesn't really matter. Ideally you would leave Campo by 7am and walk five or six hours on your first day. At this stage you will probably need several long breaks. You will be hiking in the sun, so make sure you find shade for your breaks. Take a long break during the hottest part of the day and complete your hiking in the evening. Even if you are going well, don't try to hike for more than six hours.

If you camp on the trail, particularly at Hauser Creek, you might be disturbed during the night by illegal immigrants or drug smugglers crossing the border from Mexico, or

possibly even by US Border Patrol officers. It is very unlikely that they will be a danger to you as they will want to avoid contact but it would be a sensible precaution to camp out of sight of the trail.

Be away next morning before 7am; you must get into good habits at this stage. When you reach Hauser Creek take a good look at the underbrush beneath the oak trees, where there is a good growth of poison oak: learn to recognise and avoid it. Have a good break here in the shade and make sure you are fully hydrated before setting off on the shadeless climb around Morena Butte. You should be able to reach Lake Morena campground by lunchtime. When you have rehydrated and possibly resupplied there you could, if you are feeling good, continue a further three miles and camp at Cottonwood Creek, a reliable water source in April. If you made a later start from Campo you will probably want to spend your second night at Lake Morena campground.

Your next water on the trail is likely to be in Long Canyon, about 12 shade-free miles beyond Cottonwood Creek. You will need to carry plenty of water. In 2006, an elderly hiker suffered from heat exhaustion in this section and died from injuries caused during a fall above Kitchen Creek. This won't happen to you because, if it is hot, you will be carrying at least three litres of water. You might camp in Long Canyon but, if you have any

The San Gorgonio Mountains from Fuller Ridge (Section 8)

energy left, you could continue to Lower Morris Meadow where there is a reliable spring with good water. A little further on you will find good camping under the shade of some pine trees. From Long Canyon or Lower Morris Meadow you can reach the Mount Laguna Store by opening time the following morning (the post office doesn't open until later in the day).

Fill up with water at Mount Laguna as the next source is likely to be at the Pioneer Mail Trailhead Picnic Area, a further 10 miles up the PCT. Recent fire damage means that there is little shade on this section of the PCT but you must search it out for your breaks. The picnic area will be a good place to camp.

You will want to leave camp early in the morning as you have another shadeless day without water. In April 2002 a young lady section-hiker was helicoptered off this section of the PCT with heat exhaustion. It is possible that trail angels will have left a water cache in this section but you should not depend on it. Caches should be seen as a bonus, for topping up supplies, rather than as your principal source of water. They would soon run dry if every hiker took a gallon of water. Your next water is likely to be at Rodriguez Spur Truck Trail, a hot 16 miles away, where a large water tank is maintained by the fire service. Assuming there is water here, it is a good place to camp.

The next water source, in the San Felipe Valley, is about four shade-free hours ahead. The creek might be dry but you will probably find a water cache here. If both cache and creek are dry you will have to hitch to Banner or Julian. In the San Felipe Valley you will start to encounter real desert plants.

Your next challenge is the 25 miles over the exposed San Felipe Hills to Barrel Spring. You have a shadeless 2000ft climb up south-facing slopes ahead of you. If it is hot, it is probably best to wait for the cool of the evening before setting off from the San Felipe Valley, then camp and reach Barrel Spring the following afternoon or evening. Alternatively you could camp in the San Felipe Valley, leaving at dawn the following day before camping in the San Felipe Hills so that you arrive at Barrel Spring the next morning. I hope you aren't thinking of doing this section in one day! Trail angels try to maintain a cache in the San Felipe Hills but, again, you shouldn't depend on it.

You should camp in the shade of the oak trees at Barrel Spring. In the morning you have eight easy miles to Warner Springs, where most hikers collect packages they have sent to the post office. You can get a cheap meal at the Golf Club Grille, even if you are scruffily dressed! By the time you reach Warner Springs you should have started to develop good hiking habits and will also have identified some surplus items of equipment – now is time to send them home.

Warner Springs, a private spa resort, is a very dangerous place for thru'-hikers. Hikers can stay in bungalows, enjoy meals in a fine restaurant,

soak in the hot springs and have a massage. Apart from separating impecunious hikers from their money, the resort's attractions can distract hikers from their objectives. I have seen figures suggesting that 40 per cent of thru'-hikers give up here. While I don't believe that, many do indeed end their hikes here. While a lot do so because of injury after attempting too high a daily mileage early in their hike, others find civilisation's attractions too great and, after a few days at the resort, don't return to the trail.

If you have followed the advice in this guide you shouldn't be injured and you would be well-advised not to spend more than a few hours at Warner Springs. It is too early in your hike to get out of the good habits you're only just starting to adopt. If you continue you will find good camping beside the reliable Agua Caliente Creek about six miles up the PCT and you will be ready to start your second week.

> *Warner Springs is just like a Black Hole...Hikers enter but they don't seem to come out.*
>
> Ladybird

Trail angels

You will find that there are people on the trail who offer hospitality and help to hikers. The services they provide might include holding supply packages, offering showers, laundry, local transportation, bed space, camping, meals, zero day relaxation and trail information, along with telephone and internet access. The trail angels also maintain water caches.

Trail angel information given in this guide was checked in 2009. I have only included contact details and addresses where I have a trail angel's permission. Otherwise the information I have provided is minimal – you will have to use the internet and the trail grapevine to discover further information.

Many trail angels refuse any form of payment for their services though most will accept a contribution towards costs. You might feel you could make a donation towards ADZPCTKO, which organises the kick-off party, for which there is no charge to thru'-hikers, or to the Pacific Crest Trail Association, a non-profit making organisation dedicated to the promotion and maintenance of the trail.

One thing is common to all trail angels: they don't have to do it. You should remember that they give up a great deal of time, they welcome strangers on to their property or into their homes and often there is considerable expense involved. Give the trail angels the respect they deserve. In particular, under no circumstances should you take illegal drugs on to their properties. If you are going to drink alcohol, do so in moderation, and do not smoke unless the trail angels themselves are smokers.

Many of the stores and resorts along the PCT and many of the trail angels have a hiker box. This is a box, sometimes a barrel, into which hikers can place any surplus food, fuel, clothing or other equipment for the use of other hikers. It has been known for impecunious youngsters to resupply from hiker boxes but, since most people are putting in the food they find least appetising, this is a rather desperate way of saving money. A hiker box is a good place to leave books you have read on the trail.

Supplies along the trail

How you organise your supplies will vary depending on your personal circumstances but you need to plan carefully in advance what you are going to do. Poor organisation of supplies is a major cause of hikers failing on the PCT. A lucky few hikers have a supporter – usually the wife of a male hiker! – who will meet them at road crossings with supplies.

An increasing number are resupplying completely from stores on or near the trail, as more of the small stores and mini-marts improve the range of supplies suitable for hikers. Be aware, however, that the selection of food could be limited, as the main business of such stores is supplying snacks to the car-based tourist.

Before setting out on the PCT, a small number of hikers hire cars and drop off supplies along the trail, at stores and post offices, with trail angels and at private houses, sometimes even leaving wilderness caches (though that is not something to risk unless you know how to protect them from animals; bears and little mammals enjoy coming across your food as much as you do). You could try that method for the first part of your hike if you flew into LA and hired a car, which you could leave at San Diego. If you want to hire a car further north you will have to book it in advance as they tend to be fully booked during the main holiday season.

Other hikers organise their supplies in advance for the whole route and have a friend or relative post them out a couple of weeks before they are needed. You could call your helper to ask them to add anything you are missing or to send replacement equipment. The system is only really feasible if your helper lives in the US, as sending packages with food into the US is fraught with US customs difficulties. Some professional organisations offer a similar service but you will have to scour the internet to find them.

The majority of hikers will use a combination, buying supplies from stores and sending supply parcels ahead to post offices, stores and trail angels. When they head into town they will send supplies on ahead for the next few weeks. Remember that most post offices close at the weekend and are only legally required to hold parcels for two weeks before returning them to the sender. However,

most will hold hikers' parcels longer. State clearly on your parcel the fact that you are a PCT hiker, the date on which you expect to collect it and where to return it if you don't pick it up. Address your parcel to: [your name] (PCT hiker) c/o General Delivery, [post office address].

If possible use the package holding services of stores, resorts and trail angels rather than the post office, as your package will then be available for you to collect seven days a week. Some stores and resorts will charge a small holding fee for the service they offer.

The hiking schedule given in Appendix G gives a resupply system based on buying food from stores where it is sensible and using the postal system where necessary. Appendices D1 and D2 give the hiking time between recommended resupply points. Detailed information on resupply points is given in the section introductions. Note that this information was correct for 2009 and you should check that it is still accurate.

Some hikers post a 'drift box' ahead, containing items that they cannot easily obtain along the route such as spare equipment, clothing, shoes or other items that will not be needed until later in the hike. You should include packaging supplies in your drift box and send it to the next town where you will be organising and sending out resupply boxes.

Training for the PCT

How do you get fit for the PCT? The only effective way to train for hiking with a heavy pack is to hike with a heavy pack. Work in the gym, running or cycling might give you the idea that you are getting fit but, when you start hiking with a pack, you will find that you use different muscles. You will have gained cardio-vascular fitness, which is admirable, but that won't stop you getting blisters or repetitive strain injuries.

The people who will benefit most from training are those who are very overweight. They would be advised to try to lose some of that weight before starting their hike as the combination of pack and excess bodyweight will put a big strain on the knees and feet. You can manage the PCT without any training – the author certainly has – but you must be aware of your lack of fitness while planning the early stages of your hike. You will benefit from stretching exercises, both before and during your hike, to help overcome stiffness and reduce the risk of injury. Stretches should be done before and after exercise, as well as during breaks.

The few hikers for whom thru'-hiking the PCT will be their first experience of backpacking would be well-advised to do a backpacking trip as part of their preparation, if only to gain some experience of lightweight camping and to learn a little about their equipment.

Mental preparation

Any ultra-long challenge tends to be more of a mental than a physical challenge. On the PCT there will be times when you wonder why you have accepted the challenge. Walking between 15 and 20 miles any day is hard work and repeating that day after day is even harder. There will be times when you feel like giving up: you miss your girlfriend and home comforts; you are demoralised by heat, cold or rain; you have sore feet and your shoulders ache because your pack is too heavy. At such times you must be mentally strong. You must realise, in advance, that those times will occur and you must be prepared for them and have the strength of mind to keep going.

Statistically, you're most likely to give up during the first week. Read the section about that, so that you know what to expect, and be prepared for it. If you have the right equipment and a sensible schedule you will be better off than most hikers but the mental preparation is probably even more important. No-one can teach you to be mentally strong (though a lot of psychologists attempt to do so with sports teams). It is something you must think out for yourself before you set off, if you are to avoid giving up when the first difficulties occur.

Some people are happy, or even prefer, walking on their own though

The High Sierra (Section 28)

most prefer walking with a companion or in a group. Loose groups and pairs form on the trail and that can give a hiker a good mental boost. Conversely, it could be the reason why they give up. You should be aware of the dangers of walking in a group where one member isn't really committed to the completing the hike. A negative attitude is contagious. Once one member contemplates giving up, it is easy for the whole group to follow suit. If one member of a group displays a negative attitude you are better off leaving before your own is infected.

If you start as a pair or member of a group you must realise the problems of spending 24 hours a day with the same person for five months. You will have to happily put up with their idiosyncrasies and avoid conflict. It would probably be better to be independently equipped so that you have the option of splitting up en route (I hope this won't happen to husband and wife partnerships).

Cost

How much will it cost to thru'-hike the PCT? That depends how much money you spend! The main costs are:

- Travel: flights, trains or buses to get you to the PCT and home again, and possibly local transport. If you intend to hire a car or use taxis you must include that in your budget.
- Food and restaurants: food in supermarkets and eating out is

generally cheaper in the US than in much of Europe. Specialist backpacking food (freeze-dried meals) is relatively expensive but still cheaper and better quality than in Europe. Food bought in mountain stores will be considerably more expensive than food bought in supermarkets.

- Postage: if you are going to send lots of resupply packages you need to budget for postage. Internal postage in the US is very reasonably priced but international postage is rather expensive.
- Accommodation: staying in mountain hotels while off-trail could be a major expense. However it is possible to hike the PCT for very little. Ancient Brit's total accommodation cost in 2006 was $2, which was $2 more than in 2002 and 2009!
- Medical insurance: treatment in the US is very expensive so you should get medical insurance (see section on Required documentation)
- Equipment: it makes sense to start with the best equipment you can afford. New gear is more likely to last the distance than well-used equipment.
- Loss of income: this is probably the biggest cost to many hikers as you will need to be off work for up to six months.

One advantage of being in the wilderness is that there are very few places to spend money!

Getting to the PCT

You can use public transport to reach Campo from San Diego and to get from Manning Park to Vancouver at the end of the hike.

From Downtown San Diego you need to get to the El Cajon Transit Centre, via bus or trolley, then transfer to the San Diego Metropolitan Transit System bus to Campo (route 894). See www.transit.511.com/services for information on bus services to Campo.

There is a Greyhound bus service from Manning Park to Vancouver, BC: www.greyhound.ca, (800)-661-8747 (within US and Canada).

You can fly into San Diego but more international flights go to Los Angeles (LA) from where you can get to San Diego by plane, train or bus. An alternative idea is to fly to LA, hire a car and arrange to drop it off in San Diego after spending a few days organising supplies for the first sections of your hike.

At the end it is easiest to fly out of Vancouver in Canada. Seattle, in Washington in the US, is another possibility and could be a cheaper option if you are returning to a US destination.

Unless airlines change pricing policies, it is likely that all cheap flights will be for fixed dates and cannot be changed. Since it will probably cost about the same for a return flight as for a single you might as well book your return flight as well. If you want to book a return ticket from Vancouver cheaply you will have to use an

Railroad, Soledad Canyon (Section 18)

airline that also flies into San Diego or LA. Those unsure of their ability to complete the hike might opt to book a cheap return ticket to San Diego or LA then throw away the return ticket if it is unneeded. That option is bad mental preparation for the hike but the author did just that in 2002 simply because a return ticket to San Diego was cheaper than a one-way ticket.

Required documentation

Regulations regarding the documents necessary to enter the US and Canada are frequently revised. You must check the accuracy of the following information before depending on it. According on your circumstances you might need:

- **Passport with valid US visa**: non-US citizens will probably need a full US visa which must be obtained in advance from the

US embassy or consulate in their home country. A visitor's visa, which you can obtain on entry to the US, is only valid for three months. If you have a full visa you will be admitted to the US for a maximum of six months at a time. US immigration service staff might ask how you are intend to support yourself financially while in the US. At the time of writing, Canadians need a passport but not a visa. US citizens will need a passport to enter Canada.

- **Canadian border crossing document**: you will need a permit to cross into Canada along the PCT at the end of your hike. It is illegal for you to enter Canada without one. The document must be obtained in advance from the Canada Border Services Agency. The PCTA website has forms and details of how to obtain the permit. Note that even Canadian citizens require the document. The author's attempts to find out how you enter the US from Canada along the PCT have failed. All US officials contacted stated that crossing the border along the PCT is illegal. US and British nationals don't need a visa to enter Canada but citizens of some other countries do and should check this out. If you intend to fly home from Seattle, ensure that your visa allows you to re-enter the US.

• **PCT permit and fire permit**: many national parks and wilderness areas require that you obtain a permit in advance to camp in the wilderness or to light fires. Other areas require that you complete a form at the trailhead. Thru'-hikers and section-hikers planning to hike more than 500 miles can, for a nominal fee, obtain a single permit from the PCTA that covers the entire trail. If you intend to take the side-trip up Mount Whitney, you can obtain the necessary permit at the same time. Section-hikers covering fewer than 500 miles must obtain their permit from the authority in the first area they enter. Details about how to obtain such permits should be given on each area's website and these websites are listed in the Part introductions in this guide. You will need a fire permit if you intend to light fires during your hike.

• **Medical insurance**: you should have medical insurance. Make sure it covers wilderness hiking as some companies might exclude it as a hazardous activity. There is unlikely to be a charge for mountain rescue in case of accident but you could be charged if you abused the system.

Other important papers include your **travel documents** including **airline tickets**, your **hiking schedule** and a **contact sheet** containing useful addresses, telephone numbers, email and web addresses in case you lose credit cards or other important documents. Few Americans have passports and **driving licences** are the most commonly used forms of identification in the US. You will also need **money** – in the form of **US dollars, a credit card and a debit card** – and, of course, this **guidebook**.

Is it safe to walk alone?

Virtually every mountaineering textbook and mountaineering course will tell you never to go into the mountains alone. The people who write such books ignore their own advice.

Probably the majority of people who hike the PCT start on their own and a substantial number walk alone for much of the time. It is relatively safe to hike solo on the PCT as long as you stay on the trail. If you have an accident, other hikers coming

Erik the Red arrives at Forester Pass (Section 30)

down the trail will be able to help you. However, if you leave the trail and have an accident you could be in serious trouble. In the wilderness it could be years before you are found. The big advantage of hiking alone is that you can go at your own pace, get away early in the mornings and stop when you want to. Many hikers form into loose groups, camping together, often taking breaks together but hiking at their own rate.

An increasing number of single girls hike the PCT and are probably safer there than they would be in a city centre. Only near the Mexican border might you come across

unsavoury characters; if you are on your own for the first few nights it might be best to camp slightly away from the trail.

Unless you are an experienced mountaineer – and even if you are – you should seriously consider being part of a group for the section from Kennedy Meadows to Sonora Pass, especially if there is still a lot of snow on the passes and the creeks are running high.

> **Hike your own hike!**
>
> *Trail saying*

Water treatment

All the official information will tell you to treat all water you find in the wilderness and recommend that you carry a water filter. Many thru'-hikers choose not to follow this advice and there is no scientific evidence that they become ill any more often than those who do.

If you are going to carry a water filter make sure it will be effective against giardiasis (known as giardia), a diarrheal infection caused by an organism called giardia lamblia. Some cheaper filters do little more than make the water look clean and won't filter out the micro-organisms which can make you ill. You could treat your water with chemicals. Iodine tablets are effective but give water an unpleasant taste. Aquamira tablets and drops are the most popular as they are effective and fairly tasteless though they are more expensive.

The author carries neither filter nor chemicals but does boil any water whose purity gives cause for concern. The method is effective and is probably a sensible solution for those who drink most of their water in the form of tea, coffee or soup, though you will need to carry more fuel if you use this method.

Most water in mountain springs should be drinkable without treatment. Surface water is more of a problem and particular care is needed with water that might have been contaminated by cattle, horses or humans. Flowing water is likely to be safer than

water in lakes, while stagnant ponds should be avoided.

Sun and heat

Heat

First, a cautionary tale from the author's journal: 'In July 1996 I set off from Walker Pass for a section hike in the High Sierra with temperatures well over 100°F (38°C). I set off in late afternoon, intending a dry camp on Morris Peak before reaching Joshua Tree Spring, only 13 miles away, next morning. I thought I was carrying plenty of water but I was close to heat exhaustion by the time I reached the spring. On the third day I only managed five miles to Spanish Needle Creek. On the following day I was again close to heat exhaustion when I walked the 12 miles to Canebrake Campground. I had completed 30 miles in four days and I needed a day off before continuing my hike.'

By 2002 I had learnt how to cope with the conditions and completed the same section in similar conditions in two days. That year I hiked for a while with a super-fit youngster, Luke, who was covering 30 miles a day and carrying only a one-litre water bottle. When I met him at Cold Spring in Northern California he needed an eight-hour break to rehydrate before setting off again and walking into the night.

You could meet similar conditions anywhere in California or Oregon. Even in your first week on the trail it could be too hot for hiking. How do you cope? In hot conditions you will need about half a litre of water per hour of hiking, plus two litres for an overnight camp. You need to drink regularly, before you become thirsty and before you become dehydrated.

Try to walk in the cooler parts of the day – dawn and pre-dawn starts are advisable, as is walking in the late evening – and find shade for any rest periods. The Spanish have a siesta for a good reason and if you are hiking to a reasonably gentle schedule you should have plenty of time for a long siesta in the afternoon when it is hot.

Drinking tea, coffee or alcohol in the heat is not a good idea. All have diuretic properties. Keep an eye on the colour of your urine. A clear colour is a good sign but yellow urine suggests you aren't drinking enough water. Consider drinking sports drinks, such as Gatorade, instead of water, as they will replace some of the salts you sweat out. Gatorade, in powder form, is available in most US supermarkets.

If you can't cope with the heat you could consider hiking during the night and sleeping during the day. In 1996 I met a Swiss girl who set off from Campo at the beginning of July and hiked 25 miles every night through Southern California before completing the PCT in three months!

Sun

Consider carefully how you are going to avoid being burned by the sun. The degree to which you are able to cope

will depend, in part, on your skin-type and how easily you burn or tan. If you burn easily you will need to wear a long-sleeved shirt, long trousers and possibly thin gloves. If you tan easily you might be more comfortable in shorts and short-sleeved shirts but should still use a lot of sun cream in the first few weeks. A good sunhat is preferable to a cap as it protects your ears and neck, as well as shading your face.

There will be times when you want to wear sunglasses; some hikers prefer to wear them all the time. Don't follow the example of Grasshopper who, in 2006, wore sunglasses through the deserts of Southern California then sent them home, only to suffer snow-blindness on the snowfields of the High Sierra.

If you plan to read a lot during your hike and need reading glasses, consider getting a pair with reactive lenses, which can be used for reading in bright sunlight or at night in your tent. It makes sense to carry a hard protective case for sunglasses and glasses, especially prescription models. Soft cases leave too much chance that glasses might be broken.

Snow

You could encounter fresh snow at any time on your hike. Snow shouldn't present a problem as long as you have sufficient waterproofs and warm clothing, including gloves. Extra care will be needed with navigation as even a few inches of snow can

Mount Shakespeare (Section 32)

hide the trail in places. In these conditions hikers using a proper tent will be warmer than those using a tarp-tent.

The Pacific Crest Trail was designed to be hiked in summer conditions and can be extremely dangerous or impassable when buried under snow. Thru'-hikers who follow the advice about starting dates offered in this guide shouldn't encounter significant old winter snow until they reach Forester Pass in the High Sierra. Beyond, they are likely to find snow on a succession of high passes until they reach Tuolumne Meadows in Yosemite National Park. In high snow years section-hikers might encounter snow on passes into August or could find that it has all melted.

Thru'-hikers can expect to encounter small snow patches in the highest mountains of Southern California during the spring. These can be dangerous where they cross the trail on steep slopes and great care is needed, though they should not prove insurmountable obstacles.

Section-hikers walking in the spring could encounter substantial snowpack anywhere in Northern California, Oregon and Washington. Because of the way the trail is designed, snowpack in Southern California, Northern California, Oregon or Washington is much more difficult and dangerous to overcome than that in the High Sierra. In a high snow year, Washington trail sections might still be impassable at the end of June.

If you encounter significant winter snow in the San Jacinto Mountains, on Mount Baden-Powell and again at Cottonwood Pass at the start of the High Sierra, you have a serious problem: you are hiking the PCT too early and, unless you are a mountaineer experienced in winter conditions with the proper equipment and maps, you should wait for the snow to melt rather than risk your life in dangerous conditions that you don't understand.

You would be ill-advised to attempt the High Sierra on your own if significant levels of snow remain on the passes. If you decide to persevere into the Sierra, then you should wait until the snows soften in the morning before climbing to a pass, unless you are carrying crampons. While you might have little difficulty scaling the passes (with the exception of Mather Pass), descents in snow are much more dangerous. Descending is probably safest in late-morning when the snow has softened just enough to kick steps. In hot weather the snow could become unstable later in the day and you could sink into or even through the snow. You will find it much easier to follow the footsteps of an earlier group than create your own trail.

Pay particular attention to navigation when descending. The trail will be buried and most accidents are caused by people getting on to steep terrain. Do not attempt snow-covered passes in bad weather as navigation will be almost impossible, other than for experts with good contour maps.

The most dangerous descents are those from Forester, Glen and Sonora

Passes further north. If you are carrying an ice axe you shouldn't send it home from Tuolumne Meadows; wait until after Sonora Pass. As an absolute minimum you will need an ice axe or two walking poles to descend safely.

Snow equipment

You could experience fresh snow anywhere at any time on the trail. Two walking poles are much more useful than an ice axe for coping with fresh snow. There is always debate among thru'-hikers about what they need in the way of ice axe, crampons or even snowshoes when they leave Kennedy Meadows. Much of this debate is ill-informed, since most thru'-hikers are not mountaineers and don't understand the functions of the various pieces of equipment.

Ice axes have four main functions: use as a walking stick on snow slopes to prevent falls, cutting steps in snow and ice, controlling a glissade and arresting a fall down a steep snow slope. Let's examine each in turn.
- For a non-expert the main use of ice axe is as a walking stick, in which case you might as well carry two walking poles instead.
- You won't need to cut steps on the PCT. The trail takes relatively gentle slopes and the sun soon softens the snow enough for you to kick steps.
- You shouldn't glissade. It is dangerous. A glissade is a controlled slide down a snow slope, either standing or sitting. Assuming

that many hikers will ignore this advice, the only time you should even consider a glissade is on a concave slope with a gentle run-off, where you can see the entire way down and be sure that there are no rocks. Even then you shouldn't glissade.

- Unless you have trained and practised ice axe arrest you can't rely on stopping a fall and you could easily stab yourself with the ice axe.

Despite following the advice and setting out after the bulk of the snow has melted, the higher passes will probably still hold some snow. If you learn that this is the case, then you should use a pair of walking poles or carry an ice axe. That advice also applies to section-hikers in July and August, especially in high snow years.

Crampons are designed for use on hard snow and ice but can be dangerous if you are not experienced. You won't need crampons unless you leave Kennedy Meadows too early. If you have crampon experience and have left Kennedy Meadows relatively early, you will find walking poles and crampons make an excellent combination in the High Sierra terrain covered by the PCT. Make dawn starts and ascend passes before the snow starts to soften, to save wasting energy later in the day.

Crampons are designed to be fitted to stiff climbing boots but they can be used on walking shoes on the relatively gentle slopes on the PCT.

Ten-point crampons will be as good as 12-point crampons as you won't be able to front-point using walking shoes. Check that they fit and that the straps are not worn before you set out.

Various forms of mini-crampons are coming on to the market. They are not as effective as full-size crampons and should only be used to follow tracks created by other hikers, not in virgin snow. They will give you more confidence on snow-covered passes and will enable you to climb the passes earlier in the morning before the snow softens too much. There is no need to consider snowshoes or cross-country skis as they would only be useful at times when creek crossings would make the trail virtually impassable.

On his thru'-hikes the author has entered the High Sierra early, when there has been substantial snowpack, and considers two walking poles with crampons to be the best combination.

In the record snow year of 2006 the author set out early from Kennedy Meadows to traverse the High Sierra in deep snow. It proved fine as far as the snow was concerned but creek crossings posed horrendous problems. Lengthy diversions had to be made to avoid creeks that were unsafe to ford. Tuolumne Meadows was reached in very hot weather and the section from there to Sonora Pass proved impassable because of snowmelt. There was the added problem that potential resupply points Muir Trail Ranch, Reds Meadow and Tuolumne Meadows were still closed as their access roads had only just re-opened. Substantial snowpack remained until Donner Pass was reached on Independence Day (July 4).

A winter traverse of the High Sierra would be an interesting proposition for an experienced mountaineer but is outside the scope of this book.

Creek crossings

Most creeks should be crossable in relative safety if you follow the advice about starting dates but it is inevitable that some will still prove difficult. Don't be afraid to turn back or look for a safer crossing.

If a creek is running strongly it is worth looking upstream or downstream for a log to cross on. Creeks are always deeper than they look and if you can't see the bottom you might find holes in the riverbed, especially in bouldery creeks. Any fast-moving, bouldery creek above knee-deep ought to be regarded as dangerous, as should any smooth-flowing creek above waist-deep.

You should wear boots for all but the easiest creek crossings. By the time you get into difficulties when wearing sandals or with bare feet it will be too late. You can always take your socks off before crossing (unless they need a wash).

Some of the creek crossings in the High Sierra in June and possibly Washington, later, require the use of two walking poles to provide the stability for a safe crossing. In fast-moving water you should face upstream and shuffle across the creek using the

Holcomb Creek (Section 11)

walking poles so that you always have three points of contact.

If you don't have walking poles you should form a triangle with two other hikers to give you stability. If you are hiking solo, therefore, you need to be carrying walking poles. Poles are also essential for safely crossing wet logs or slippery boulders across creeks. Walking poles and crampons, if you are carrying them, make an excellent combination for crossing wet or icy logs.

If the creeks in the High Sierra look too dangerous and there are no logs to cross on, you could wait until the morning. As most creeks are carrying snowmelt, water levels could be lower in the morning. The difficult creek crossings in Washington are also easier in the mornings as their water is flowing from melting glaciers.

The High Sierra has two notorious creek crossings, Bear Creek and Evolution Creek. Both are dangerous when running high. You would be better crossing the three main tributaries of Bear Creek higher up the hill where you should be able to cross them on logs. Evolution Creek is better crossed in the deep-but-slow-flowing water at the west end of Evolution Meadow than at the official crossing place.

Campsites and campgrounds

Some explanation of the terms campsite and campground is needed. A campsite is just a patch of ground where you can pitch one or two tents.

A campground is an organised collection of campsites.

Wilderness campgrounds might have no facilities at all: no warden, no toilets, no garbage cans and possibly not even water. Wilderness campgrounds with vehicle access will often – not always – have toilets and piped water. There might be a resident warden and a small fee to pay. Many resorts have commercial campgrounds with full facilities. In the popular tourist areas, most campgrounds are operated by the national park authorities or the US Forest Service (USFS) and often have a separate backpackers' area.

When you hike the PCT you will camp in wilderness campsites most of the time rather than at official campgrounds. Where possible you should use existing campsites, cleared by earlier hikers. Often, however, you will clear a patch of ground in the forest and put up your tent.

Europeans, accustomed to camping on grass, should appreciate that meadows in California and Oregon are very fragile and should not be used as campsites. You should camp at least 100ft from creeks and lakes unless reusing existing campsites.

In Southern California you will often camp in the open on sandy soil but for the remainder of the PCT most of your campsites will be in forest. They will be less exposed than in the European mountains, which is why many American hikers prefer to use tarp-tents rather than proper mountain

This is how forest fires can start (Section 46)

tents. In good weather many thru'-hikers prefer to sleep out rather than erect their tents.

It is often inconvenient to find a campsite near a water source so you should be prepared to carry water to a dry camp. That is one of the main differences between a thru'-hiker and an ordinary backpacker and is one of the ways that you can achieve the higher daily mileages required. Camping away from water can be a good idea during the main mosquito season.

Fires

The entire PCT is vulnerable to bush and forest fires. In a typical year you will find that lighting campfires is banned along extensive sections, other than at designated fire sites. There is a good reason: many forest fires are started by hikers. If you do light a fire, ensure there is no risk of it

spreading and that it is completely out before you leave the site. Never leave fires unattended or burning when you go to sleep.

If no ban is in place and you intend to light a fire, use an existing fireplace if possible. Ensure that the surrounding ground is clear of anything that will burn and that there are no branches overhanging the fire. There is usually plenty of dead wood on the ground; never cut branches from trees.

Some hikers burn their rubbish. If you do so you need to take full precautions against starting a forest fire. Much food packaging contains aluminium foil, which must be removed and packed out when you have finished with the fire. Burning plastic is not a good idea as the fumes are poisonous. The massive Manter Fire, near Kennedy Meadows in 2000, was started by an environmentally minded hiker burning toilet paper. Smokers should be particularly careful not to start wildfires. A cigarette end, thrown away, is all that is needed to start a forest fire. Cigarette ends are garbage and should be packed out.

You should use a commercially manufactured cooking stove. There has been a fad for hikers to use homemade stoves derived from soda cans. In 2006, a large fire was started by a pair of Israeli hikers using a homemade stove and, in 2002, Rogue started a small fire in the evening with a leaking stove. He thought he had put it out but in the morning discovered roots were burning underground. It took him half an hour to get it fully out. Such homemade stoves are illegal to use when there is a fire ban as

the exception is usually only for commercially produced stoves with a stop valve for the fuel.

Unless you are very lucky you will find sections of the PCT closed by the authorities because of an active fire. Hopefully they will post an alternative route but you might have to bypass a section. Follow any instructions given to you by the fire service: you could be arrested for entering an area closed due to fire.

For environmental reasons the fire service is increasingly allowing wildfires to burn rather than fight them, if they pose no danger to property. Wildfires will often appear to die down overnight but will get going again during the day as the wind picks up. It is inadvisable to go anywhere near a wildfire in strong winds.

Falls Creek Burn, 21 years after the devastating fire of 1988 (Section 90)

Altitude

You will climb to 13,180ft at Forester Pass and 14,496ft if you climb Mount Whitney, so there is scope for getting altitude sickness. A few people can suffer altitude sickness as low as 10,000ft but the vast majority can cope with the altitudes on the PCT. With acclimatisation you can increase your tolerance to altitude considerably.

At 13,000ft, only 60 per cent of the oxygen that you get at sea level is present, so you will find walking harder and you should ascend slowly to the high passes. The first symptom of mild altitude sickness is headaches, which should soon go away as you descend. A few individuals will suffer more severe symptoms for which the only effective treatment is to drop to lower altitudes as soon as possible.

The gradual ascending, eight-week approach to the Sierra Nevada's high country should provide thru'-hikers with the perfect acclimatisation regime. Section-hikers, however, could face problems. If you intend to hike the John Muir Trail (JMT) from Mount Whitney to Yosemite without first acclimatising, you are asking for trouble. Either hike from north to south, as recommended by Alan Castle in his Cicerone guide to the JMT, or do as the author has done and start your section hike at Walker Pass to give yourself a better period of acclimatisation before reaching Mount Whitney (it is also much easier to get a permit starting from Walker

Mount McLoughlin, from Fourmile Lake (Section 67B)

Pass than from Yosemite or Whitney Portal, which can be booked-up months in advance).

Lightning

Afternoon thunderstorms are not uncommon on the PCT, especially in July and August. You can see them building and should ensure you are not an exposed ridge when the storm hits, because of the danger of lightning. If the weather trend becomes thundery you should try to plan your days so that high passes are crossed and alpine ridges traversed in the morning, as thunderstorms will nearly always occur in the afternoon or evening.

If you are on an exposed ridge when a storm develops you should get off and preferably be below tree-line before it hits. If you are approaching a pass or ridge as a thunderstorm develops you should take a break. It might be sensible to put up your tent and ride out the storm in comfort.

If you are caught out and cannot descend safely you should at least try to get off the ridgeline. It is safest to crouch or sit on an insulating mat on a scree slope. Place metal objects such as walking poles away from you.

Be careful where you shelter. Cave entrances, rock overhangs or isolated trees might keep you dry but they are not safe places in a storm. You are usually relatively safe below tree-line but should not shelter too close to trees in case one is struck. Many forest fires in Northern California and Oregon are started by lightning.

Hail is fairly common during thunderstorms and you could experience hailstones as big as golf balls (fortunately not very often). Then, it is safer to get right under a tree for shelter and ignore the lightning risk.

Wet weather backpacking

Since you are being advised to keep the weight of your pack to a minimum you won't have much in the way of spare clothing. How do you cope if you get a succession of wet days?

The most important thing is to keep your sleeping bag and any spare clothing in your pack dry. Try to avoid wearing all your clothing in wet weather. When it starts to rain, unless it is very cold, you should remove a layer of clothing before putting on your waterproofs and wear as little as you need to keep warm. When you have put your tent up, change into your dry clothing and put any damp clothing on top and your body heat will help dry it. You can expect to be warm and comfortable in camp if you've got a dry pair of socks, dry trousers, dry fibre-pile top and dry sleeping bag.

The problem comes with the second and subsequent days of rain. In the morning you need to set off in damp clothing and put the dry clothing back into your pack.

It helps if you can cook and produce hot drinks under the flysheet of your tent, only really feasible if your tent has a fairly large flysheet and you are using a propane/butane stove. Cooking inside a tent with a liquid fuel stove is far too dangerous. Stoves should only be used in a ventilated area because of the risk of carbon monoxide poisoning from the fumes.

In wet weather you can get cold very quickly during stops, so you need to change your hiking pattern and take very short breaks. If there's a let-up in the rain, stop and spread all your damp equipment and clothing out to dry.

Garbage and human waste

The regulations for wilderness areas are very simple: 'Pack it in, pack it out.' You must carry all your rubbish out and dispose of it in town or in trailhead garbage cans. If there is no fire ban you can burn paper and other combustible material. You must not bury any rubbish.

Disposal of human waste and toilet paper is more problematic as there are few toilets along the trail. It is recommended (required in some areas) that you carry a plastic trowel for burying human waste and used toilet paper, which must be buried at least eight inches deep to make it difficult for animals to dig up. It must not be deposited within 100ft of creeks, lakes, trails or campsites. An alternative to carrying a trowel is to carry a couple of snow stakes. These large tent pegs, designed for erecting tents on snow, are also very useful securing your tent on sandy soil in windy conditions.

In the wilderness it is against regulations to discharge soap wastes within 100ft of creeks and lakes. If you need to use soap or detergents, you should only use biodegradable detergents which you can purchase at equipment stores in the US.

National park rangers

National park rangers in the US have much greater powers than their counterparts in most European countries. Some have police powers such as the power of arrest and, like the police, carry guns. Their principle function is to protect the fragile environment. The national park permit system controls the numbers impacting on the environment and one of the rangers' duties is to enforce that system. There are heavy fines for not having the required permit in a national park.

Rangers are generally courteous towards hikers and can be helpful with advice. They are well trained in first aid and can help in an emergency.

Navigation

There is a serious problem with navigation on the PCT: it's too easy so a lot of hikers don't take it seriously enough. Most of the trail is well-marked but there are unmarked trail junctions and places where the trail is indistinct, and there will be times when the trail has been washed away or is under snow.

Because so many hikers hike the PCT without any maps it was felt necessary to provide a useable sketch

Pacific Crest Trail sign (Section 11)

map for the entire trail in this guidebook. That is difficult to achieve in a guide that is lightweight enough for the weight-conscious thru'-hiker to carry and there have had to be compromises. The three major compromises are the scale of 1:100,000, the production of a strip map and the omission of contours. The 1:100,000 scale is possible because the trail is easy to follow most of the time. The absence of contours means you won't find the maps useful for navigation when the trail is under snow. If you intend to hike when there is significant snowpack you should obtain 1:50,000 scale maps that show contour detail. The strip maps provided in this book are useful only when you are on trail. If you get lost they won't help very much, so it is important not to get lost!

The main reason for navigational errors is not using the map. Many hikers hide their maps away in their rucksacks. People walking in groups tend to assume someone else is paying attention to the navigation and few therefore refer to their maps often enough, only digging them out when they are lost or don't know which way to go, by which time it can be very difficult to correct a mistake. The secret of good navigation is to prevent mistakes rather than have to correct them after they have been made.

Make sure you have easy access to your map. The usual British method of storing a map in the pocket of your waterproof jacket won't work as your waterproofs will spend most of the time in your rucksack. You could store it in a small waist pack (also known as a bumbag, or fanny pack in the US) worn in addition to your rucksack, on your front, in which you could also carry compass, camera, trail food, notebook and water. You can use any method you like as long as the map is readily available. To ensure your map is useable when it is tipping down with rain you will need some form of map case. A good quality transparent plastic bag will do.

When referring to the map you should always orientate it. That means north on the map should be aligned with north on the ground. With experience you should be able to do this accurately enough using the sun but initially you will need to use your compass. The maps in the guide are all aligned with true north at the top of the page. You will need to make a correction for the difference between magnetic north and true north (see section on Magnetic variation). Orientating the map in this way gets rid of 180° errors, such as turning left rather than right, or going back down the trail.

No attempt has been made to map every twist and turn of the trail or to map the many switchbacks the PCT takes while ascending and descending hills. Features are only included on the map when they are likely to be helpful to your navigation or planning.

When you look at the map you should try to visualise the terrain for the next section of trail and identify the next feature on the route. You should also note your direction of travel. When walking, keep an eye on

that direction of travel, either using the sun or keeping an eye on your compass. Refer to the map again if the features or the direction in which you are walking don't agree with what you have visualised. Study the map whenever you come to a feature that should appear on it or when you come to a trail junction, even if it is signposted, so that you keep constant track of your progress.

An altimeter, if carried, might be helpful as the guide gives the heights of significant points on the trail. Remember to set your altimeter to give readings in feet rather than metres. You might also keep an eye on your watch, because one of the most common navigational errors is to overshoot a junction. Timing your progress should alert you to keep an eye out for the junction.

You should get used to the style of the map in the first week while the trail is quite easy to follow and the weather is likely to be good.

The guide gives GPS (UTM) coordinates for some points along the trail. If you are carrying a GPS receiver it is not worth having it on constantly as the batteries will quickly run down. If you become lost or aren't sure where you are, however, a GPS unit could be very helpful, especially if you manage to walk off the strip map.

Remember that the map is your main navigational tool. The GPS, like your compass, is an aid that makes it easier to use the map, not a substitute for using the map.

Keep your eyes open for creatures large and small on the Trail

Animals

Bears

What do you do if you see a bear? Get out your camera! That isn't as silly as it sounds. You should have nothing to fear from bears on the PCT if you take sensible precautions.

You will meet only black bears on the trail, not the more dangerous grizzly bear. Of the two subspecies that you might meet, neither is black. Dark brown bears are the more common but you will also encounter cinnamon (light-brown) coloured black bears.

Wild bears, encountered away from popular tourist areas and unaccustomed to human presence, are not really a problem. When they see or hear you they will run away. If they fail to oblige initially, making a noise such as banging your walking poles together should see them scarper. The only time a wild bear might pose a problem is when mama bear thinks you are threatening her cubs. If you find yourself between mother and cubs you should get out of the way.

Camp bears, which frequent areas often used by visitors, are a much bigger problem. They are not after you, they are after your food. In popular tourist areas, such as Yosemite National Park, bears have lost their fear of humans and have become accustomed to feeding off our food

61

and garbage. They can cause a lot of damage when obtaining that food. Bears have an acute sense of smell and will break into food containers, garbage cans, rucksacks, tents and even cars – anywhere they smell food. If a bear does get hold of your food, it is no longer your food; if you try to recover it you could be seriously injured. The most likely area you will meet camp bears on the PCT is within 20 miles of Tuolumne Meadows in Yosemite National Park. In particular you should try to avoid camping in Lyell Canyon on the approach to Tuolumne Meadows.

In parts of the High Sierra you are required to store your food in a special container called a bear canister or bear barrel. Into this you should place not only your food but also all smelly items – such as garbage, toiletries and medicines – which bears will identify as food. Hanging food bags in trees, once recommended, is now illegal in some areas for the simple reason that it doesn't work. The regulations seem to change regularly so it is important to check with the Yosemite National Park and Sequoia and Kings Canyon National Park websites to check the latest regulations. You will probably need to carry the bear canister from Kennedy Meadows to Sonora Pass.

At the time of writing, the only places in these areas where you are legally entitled to camp without a bear canister are campgrounds where secure metal bear boxes have been provided for you to store your food

and other aromatic items at night. Bear boxes are placed at popular camping sites by the park authorities but you will pass through areas that do not have bear boxes.

Failure to use an approved canister where they are required is considered improper food storage and could result in a citation and property impoundment. You could also be requested to leave the backcountry.

BearVault (www.bearvault.com) sells bear resistant food canisters. The company will ship barrels to Kennedy Meadows, Tuolumne Meadows or Echo Lakes ($65 in 2008).

The Sierra Nevada Wilderness Education Project gives details of approved bear canisters and other suppliers, as well as detailing the areas in which bear canisters are required, at www.sierrawildbear.gov/foodstorage.

There are other precautions you can take in bear country to lessen the chances that your food will be raided. You could seal your food and garbage in airtight plastic bags. If you are unwise enough to carry smelly foods such as cheese you could double seal them, then place them in a new airtight canoe drybag.

Do not camp in the same place that you cook your evening meal. After eating, walk a bit further before camping so that your campsite doesn't smell of food. Avoid camping at popular campsites (unless they have a bear box) as bears know these sites and visit them regularly.

Most thru'-hikers pass through the High Sierra early in the season, when the majority of bears are still in the valleys. It is a good idea, therefore, to camp as high as possible, away from the trail, and to avoid places with fireplaces. Bears associate smoke with food so you should avoid lighting your own fires. Never store food in your tent or leave your rucksack unattended and remember that hanging food bags is a waste of time.

If a bear visits your camp, make a lot of noise and it will usually retreat.

Mountain lions

It is possible – though unlikely – that you will see a mountain lion. The author has only had one encounter, when one of the big cats stalked around his tent at night but wandered off as he prepared to get out to scare it away. Also known as puma or cougar, mountain lions should not present a problem to adult hikers who behave correctly. Face the lion, look big, make a lot of noise and back away slowly. If you are with others, group together and make sure any children are with you.

Don't panic and run away. Running is behaviour the lion will associate with prey – and it can run a lot faster than you. In the extremely unlikely event that you are attacked you will have to defend yourself.

Rattlesnakes

You will see many rattlesnakes, often basking in the sun on the trail. Be alert and do not surprise them. Be particularly careful at water sources. Snakes tend to live among rocks beside springs and your hand will present an

Protect the squirrels – Vermilion Valley Resort (Section 35)

inviting target. Rattlesnakes don't have eyelids so tend to retreat if you kick up dust. You might feel safer sleeping in a tent rather than sleeping out or using a tarp-tent.

The vast majority of those who get bitten by rattlesnakes have tried to handle them. If you are bitten, treat it as an emergency and seek medical help as quickly as possible.

Mice, squirrels, marmots and chipmunks

These smaller mammals are likely to be after your food. Food left outside your tent or under the flysheet tends to be the main target. If you are unlucky they will nibble your food bag, your pack, your tent or even your hat. Outside bear country you could hang food or keep it in your tent. Do not be tempted to feed these animals because it encourages them to see man as a source of food.

Mosquitoes and other biting insects

Mosquitoes should not present a problem until June, when they are at their peak immediately after the snowmelt. The problem then diminishes as summer progresses. In June and July, below tree-line, you need to be prepared for them swarming in the morning and evening. In those months it is best to camp high, away from water. When you decide between tent and tarp-tent, mosquito protection should be high on your list of priorities. Mosquitoes are rarely a

problem when you are on the move but you need to choose rest stops carefully. Breezy, open areas are usually free of mosquitoes during the day.

You might want to wear a long-sleeved shirt and long trousers in the mosquito season and will need a good supply of insect repellent. A mosquito hood will provide protection for your head. Carry some anti-histamine cream to treat bites. Overuse of burnable mosquito coils is not recommended as you could poison yourself as well as the bugs. If you cook outside your tent, you need to work out how to do so when mosquitoes are present. You might find it best, at times, to have your evening meal in a mosquito-free area before carrying on to your overnight camp spot, and to start hiking early in the morning then stop for breakfast at a suitable spot.

Thru'-hikers will find the biggest mosquito problem is in the High Sierra but section-hikers should be able to avoid major problems by tackling the High Sierra, Oregon and Washington sections in August or September.

Other biting insects you might meet later in the summer will be in smaller numbers and shouldn't cause serious problems. It might be a good idea to have hydrocortisone cream to treat the more serious bites.

There are a few spiders with a nasty bite, including the brown recluse spider, and you should treat spider bites as seriously as rattlesnake bites. Again you might feel safer

Trail riders (Section 72B)

sleeping in a tent. You will have to tolerate the many ants you find in the forest.

Horses

The PCT is intended for the use of equestrians as well as pedestrians. You are most likely to meet riders in the High Sierra, Oregon and Washington though they won't be on the trails until they are free of snow. Thru'-hikers won't meet many horses until they reach Oregon. The peak season for horses on the trail is September, with the start of the hunting season.

When horses and mules pass, you need to get off the trail and keep very still. This isn't for your benefit, it's for the protection of the riders. Many are tourists, inexperienced on horseback, and the animals can be very sensitive to sudden movement.

Llamas

Llamas, South American relatives of the camel, are used as pack animals on the PCT and other US trails.

Dogs

Most dogs on the trail will be well-trained. Should you meet one of the few that are not, stop, face it, and use your walking poles as a deterrent. The owner will then usually take control of his dog. Off-trail, you will find many properties are protected by noisy dogs. Most, fortunately, are well fenced in.

Don't try to thru'-hike with your dog. Dogs cannot cope with the heat and dehydration. You might be aware that it's 25 miles to the next water source but your dog cannot know that. There are also long sections, in the national parks, in which it is illegal to take a dog. Section-hikers will be able to do some stretches with their dogs but they are advised to check the regulations with the national park and wilderness authorities before doing so.

Coyote

You might see and hear the howls of coyotes – wild dogs that resemble Alsatians – but they are very unlikely to be a problem.

Poison oak

Poison oak is the only poisonous plant you are likely to encounter on the PCT. It is a shrub rather than a tree and tends to grow in shaded spots, particularly under oak trees, in arid regions. It is common in the chaparral belt of Southern California and you will meet it at low altitudes further north.

It is simple to deal with: don't touch any part of the plant at any time. Learn to identify it early on your hike (you will find it under the

Learn to recognise poison oak

oak trees at Hauser Creek) and if you stay alert you should be able to avoid contact. If you are careless enough to touch poison oak and suffer an allergic reaction (not everyone is allergic to it) do not rub it. Wash the effected area immediately with soap. You might find that alcohol (on the skin, not drunk) helps. In the case of a severe reaction – breathlessness, dizziness and swelling around the mouth and eyes – you should seek immediate medical attention.

Never burn poison oak as the smoke can damage your lungs.

EQUIPMENT

Lightweight backpacking

While the equipment section is written with thru'-hikers in mind, much of the advice will be just as valid for section-hikers.

There is no intention to tell you what equipment to buy and carry on your hike. Certain product names are mentioned to illustrate points rather than to suggest that you buy a particular brand. Rapid developments in lightweight hiking equipment mean any detailed advice on brands would soon be out of date. This section is intended to guide you in examining the equipment you carry and to enable you to discuss your requirements sensibly with your supplier.

Equipment choice is a balance between carrying as light a pack as possible and having enough

East Vidette Peak (Section 30)

equipment to be safe and comfortable. Monty Tam claimed to have reduced the base weight of his pack (weight excluding food and water) to 5lb, while Luigi admitted to setting off from Campo with 75lb on his back. There must be a balance somewhere between those extremes. The author's base weight in 2009 including boots, all clothing and walking poles was 20lb. With the addition of food and water that would have risen to 45lb, as much as anyone might want to carry. Most thru'-hikers carried lighter packs, most section-hikers had heavier.

Let's assume you hike for eight hours every day, sleep eight hours every night and relax for a further eight. The ultra-lightweight hiker's efforts to be comfortable when hiking come at the expense of the other two-thirds of the day. Is that why they hike for between 12 and 15 hours? You might prefer to sleep well at night and enjoy your time in camp and during rest periods, which will also aid recovery and make the hiking easier.

You also need to consider how you will cope with snow, wind, rain, cold and heat. Are you going to be safe in the High Sierra or Washington in a storm? You want your pack weight to be as low as possible but how much do you want to compromise comfort and safety? After the ultra-lightweight hiker has added water and food to their load, they sometimes still have quite a heavy pack.

You will want equipment that will withstand 2650 miles of trail and around 150 nights of camping. The cheapest equipment could be of too low a quality to survive the use you inflict on it, so it is worth buying the best equipment you can afford.

Basic equipment

Rucksack
Before purchasing a rucksack gather together the rest of your gear, a week's supply of food and a day's supply of water. Take these with you to your outdoor store to ensure the pack you choose is big enough to hold everything (it can be amusing to watch thru'-hikers at Kennedy Meadows try to pack supplies for the High Sierra into their small rucksacks). Try the rucksacks on fully loaded and ask store staff to help adjust them correctly. Rucksacks need to fit your body, so you should try to buy from a store rather than by mail order.

The cheapest rucksacks on the market won't last 2650 miles so it is worth paying for a good quality model. Unfortunately most good quality rucksacks are rather heavy but some firms, such as GoLite and ULA from the US, produce quality lightweight equipment.

All good rucksacks should enable you to carry most of the load on the hip-belt. It is important that the belt is comfortable. When hiking you could try putting extra padding under the

hip-belt to prevent any bruises from developing. This is one use of a camp towel.

Rucksack liners
You need to ensure the contents of your rucksack remain dry. So-called waterproof rucksacks might be waterproof when new but are unlikely to remain so all the way to Washington. The rain cover that comes with some rucksacks won't be 100 per cent efficient and can give you problems in strong wind. Many hikers use bin-liners (garbage sacks) that will need replacing frequently, as they soon gather holes. The most important thing is to ensure that your sleeping bag and spare clothing remain dry and a good solution is to store them in a lightweight canoe dry-bag.

Waist pack
You might consider wearing a small waist pack on your front to carry items such as camera, guidebook, water, snack food, compass, insect repellent, sting relief, sun cream, sunglasses, notebook and gloves. This will enable you to get at these items without removing your rucksack. If you have the opportunity to slack-pack you can use the waist pack for essentials.

Sleeping bag
You could really do with a sleeping bag rated to 12°F (-11°C). It can be very cold at night in the deserts of Southern California in spring or in the High Sierra in June. If supply

arrangements allow, you could swap it for a lightweight summer bag for Northern California and Oregon in July and August. You would, however, want your warm sleeping bag back for September in Washington

Assuming your sleeping arrangements will keep you dry at night, you should opt for a down bag. Down bags don't work well when damp, so if you aren't going to be dry at night it would be better to opt for a good quality artificial fibre bag, which will work as well as a down bag and be better when damp, as well as being cheaper and easier to wash. However, a down bag will be considerably lighter than a synthetic one. Some hikers carry lightweight liners for their sleeping bags as they are easier to wash.

Be wary of buying a sleeping bag online or by mail order if you are tall or overweight, as you might find it is too small.

Sleeping mat
A good sleeping bag is useless without a decent sleeping mat. The main purpose of the sleeping mat is to provide insulation but it should also provide some comfort.

Hikers who appreciate a little more comfort might prefer a Therm-a-Rest style mat to a closed-cell foam mats. Therm-a-Rests are self-inflating mats, designed for backpacking. They come in a variety of weights and sizes. Heavier models are better insulators and provide more comfort but lightweight models are adequate.

You could carry a short mat though a standard-size mat will help you avoid having cold feet at night.

A closed-cell foam mat will provide excellent insulation at a lower price and weight but won't provide as much comfort as a Therm-a-Rest. If you decide to go for a Therm-a-Rest you should carry a repair kit in case it gets punctured.

Therm-a-Rest chairs
Cascade Designs, the company that manufactures Therm-a-Rests, also produces accessories with which you can turn the mats into seats to use in camp or during rest stops. They weigh very little and, if you are going to spend up to eight hours each day sitting down, you might appreciate the chair. It works best with a standard width, standard length Therm-a-Rest but it might also be possible to use one with other styles of sleeping mats, including the closed-cell foam mats, if they are the right size.

Tents
Before you decide what type of tent to carry, define what you want it to achieve.
- Protection from rain
- Protection from rain in the wind
- Keeping out groundwater
- Warmth
- Keeping out mosquitoes
- Keeping out snakes and spiders
- Enough space to sit up in
- Enough space to store your gear
- A safe cooking area

Gollywobbler in camp (Section 69)

If you need all of those functions you need a good tent. You might, however, decide to forego a few to save weight. It is also worth considering whether the tent will still be useable if something goes wrong with it. Zips are the main weakness in lightweight tents but what happens if you break a pole? You might be able to improvise using your hiking poles.

The main alternative to a tent is a tarp-tent. Tarp-tents were originally simple homemade shelters made with a tarpaulin, supported by one or two hiking poles. Now you can purchase purpose-built tarp-tents, including models with mosquito netting. They came into prominence because they were a lot lighter and cheaper than tents and seem to be favoured by American hikers. Tarp-tents don't

always come with sewn-in floors so you will probably need to carry a lightweight groundsheet in addition to your sleeping mat for use in damp conditions.

A few hikers carry neither tarp nor tent and instead choose to sleep out under the stars. That might be possible for a weekend hiker in Southern California with a good weather forecast but it is not safe for a thru'-hiker or for someone hiking long sections.

You can buy a good one-person tent weighing 2lb so there is very little difference in weight compared with a good tarp-tent with groundsheet though the tent will be considerably more expensive. UK company Terra Nova produces an excellent one-person tent which should meet all your requirements. It is designed for British conditions, so is probably to a higher specification than you might need for the PCT. It comes down to a matter of preference. You should be able to order a tarp-tent from the US on the internet.

In Southern California you will be camping on sandy soil. It is also likely to be windy, especially around the Mojave Desert, and you could have problems anchoring your tent. You might carry a couple of small snow stakes to use in sand. One could be kept throughout the hike to use as a trowel to bury toilet waste. Count your pegs as you take your tent down to ensure that none are lost.

Dust can get into the tent zips when camping on sandy terrain. You will prolong their lives by washing them occasionally.

Kitchen equipment

Stove
Cooking on an open wood fire is not an option because fire bans are likely to be in operation over much of the trail.

You need to decide how you will use your stove and obtain fuel and try to calculate in advance how much fuel you might use each day. That is better done on a camping trip than theoretically, at home.

If you intend to cook under the flysheet of your tent you should use a butane/propane cylinder-powered stove. Hose-fed models, which sit on the ground, are much more stable

– and therefore safer – than those that screw directly on to the top of a gas cylinder. Availability of cylinders can be problematic on the trail although they should be readily available in towns. Gas cylinders can be sent through the US mail service but parcels must be properly labelled and sent only by surface mail.

Availability of fuel for Trangia-type stoves, which burn methylated spirits or methanol – known in the US as denatured alcohol – can also be problematic on the trail. In their absence, other fuels such as HEET (methyl alcohol, used as a fuel-line anti-freeze) is widely available in gas stations and could be used as an alternative. It is sold in yellow bottles and must not be confused with Iso-Heet, which comes in similar red bottles and which makes a very poor fuel. In the past many thru'-hikers have used homemade meths stoves. Don't follow their example. They are dangerous and probably illegal when there is a fire ban.

Many Americans use MSR multi-fuel stoves, which burn white gasoline, petrol or kerosene. Their big advantage is that suitable fuel should be obtainable at most stores and resorts along the trail but they tend to be much heavier than cylinder or meths stoves. If you chose such a liquid fuel stove you will need sufficient fuel bottles. Use a specifically designed fuel bottle that is compatible with your stove and which is strong enough to withstand the pressures

71

generated when priming liquid fuel stoves. Do not use plastic bottles, which are not designed for such pressurisation and which could melt from the stove's heat.

Cooking inside the tent itself, with any type of stove, risks carbon monoxide poisoning, setting fire to the tent and spilling hot water or food all over your gear.

Modern cigarette lighters are reliable and more convenient than matches for lighting your stove.

Cooking pot and mug

Titanium cooking pots, though expensive, are lightweight and can withstand mistreatment. You can manage without a lid but this will result in a small increase in fuel consumption when boiling water. You should carry a pot-grab to avoid burning your hands. The use of aluminium pots is not recommended for extended periods as there are concerns about the metal's effect on your health. You could chose a cooking pot that doubles as a mug but most hikers prefer a separate mug made of an unbreakable plastic such as Lexan.

Tableware

Many backpackers manage without a plate, eating instead from the cooking pot or from the tough bag in which their freeze-dried meal is prepared. If you do carry a plate make sure that, like the mug, it is made of unbreakable plastic. Spoons – you won't need a fork – are available in such plastics as well as in lightweight, strong titanium. For a knife, use the blade on your

Tooks and the Majgals at Golden Oaks Spring (Section 23)

pocketknife. As well as being part of your cooking kit, a Swiss Army-style penknife with scissors, tin opener, bottle opener and perhaps other tools such as corkscrew, tweezers, saw and toothpick will be useful in your repair and first aid kits.

Washing up
You might be able to manage without washing up liquid. If not, use a bio-degradable detergent available from camping stores. You might need a scourer and a tea towel.

Food containers
See the bear section for requirements in the High Sierra.

When organising your food and resupply parcels, dispose of all unnec-essary packaging and repack the food into sealable plastic bags. Items that are particularly vulnerable, such as powders (Gatorade, sugar etc) and food that is likely to need containing if it melts, such as butter or chocolate, should be double-bagged. As you use your food, the bags can be used for garbage.

Miscellaneous equipment

Water bottles
You will need sufficient water bot-tles to carry about two gallons (eight litres) of water. Consider having a cou-ple of half- or one-litre Nalgene-style bottles for immediate use, with your remaining water stored in water bags, also known as bladders, such as those

manufactured by Platypus, MSR and Ortlieb, which are much stronger than they look.

Wide-mouthed bottles are bet-ter for drinks such as Gatorade and fruit juice, as narrow-mouthed bottles are awkward to clean and can attract fungal growths. For that reason, you should store only water in water bags.

A lot of hikers like to drink as they walk, from a hydration system. These consist of a water bladder stored inside your rucksack. An attached hose carries water from that to an external mouthpiece from which you drink. Many modern rucksacks feature an internal hydration bag sleeve and a hose exit, specifically for this purpose. The method does not suit everyone; you might prefer to drink from a water bottle or even a mug.

Water filter
See the section on Water treatment.

Trowel
See the section on Garbage and human waste.

Towel
A small camp towel from a specialist outdoor store can be used for drying and as padding for your rucksack hip-belt or shoulder straps.

Torch (flashlight)
Most hikers carry a head-torch for use in camp. Head-torches are more convenient than hand-held torches, especially if you want to hike after

dark using walking poles. Light-emitting diode (LED) head-torches have replaced traditional filament bulb models as they are not as heavy, offer more economic battery usage and their bulbs seem to last for ever. A single-LED head-torch will provide enough light for reading but you will want something brighter if you plan to do a lot of night hiking.

Glasses and sunglasses

See section on Sun and heat.

Navigation tools

A compass is a necessity though a simple model will suffice as it will generally be used only to orientate the map, not for taking bearings. A GPS receiver might be useful if you became lost but will not be needed for basic navigation on the PCT.

Wristwatch and altimeter

A watch with an alarm might be useful for making early morning starts. An altimeter is useful though not essential for navigation. Many hikers' wristwatches feature an altimeter.

Whistle

You should carry a whistle to attract attention in an emergency. Many rucksacks have a whistle incorporated into the chest strap buckle.

Umbrella

Some hikers walk with umbrellas, as much for shade from the sun as for protection against rain. It is difficult to use an umbrella when using walking poles but it would be useful during breaks and especially when cooking in rain. As you can expect fine weather most of the time, an umbrella represents extra weight that must be carried.

Toilet roll

Take plenty; it can be used for many purposes.

Notebook

You will probably want to carry a small notebook and pencil to record details of photos, other hikers' addresses and email details, and possibly to keep a journal.

Guns

A handgun is not necessary for protection from animals. There are legal problems with carrying them on some sections of the trail.

Walking poles

Walking poles have many advantages. During descents they absorb a lot of impact, considerably reducing pressure on the knees. They make those descents safer, as well as making ascents easier. They also help prevent trips and falls, a very important consideration on the PCT, which frequently crosses steep slopes where a fall could be fatal.

Poles provide a lot of additional stability during creek crossings and are suitable for the type of snow conditions you are likely to encounter on the PCT. They are useful if you need to

Olancha (Section 29)

defend yourself from dogs or wild animals, can be used to erect tarps and
tarp-tents and can serve as or emergency poles for tents.

It is strongly recommended that
you carry two poles. Walking poles
aren't very useful on their own. If you
are new to walking poles it will only
take a few days to get used to using
them.

Experiment with poles at different lengths. Many hikers would benefit from using them shorter than they
actually do. You can shorten them for
ascents, lengthen them when going
downhill and have them even longer
for creek crossings. Always use the
wrist straps, which are designed to
take some of the strain off your hands,
and will prevent you dropping a pole
down a steep slope.

It is highly likely that you will
need at least one set of replacement

pole tips during a thru'-hike. You will
not find them readily available on the
trail and outdoor gear stores often
seem to have run out, so keep a set
in your drift box or with your helper.
Plenty of force is needed to pull the
old tips off before you can replace
them.

Snow equipment
See 'Wilderness hiking' above.

Footwear

Trail footwear
Heavy boots are designed for rock and
ice climbing, not walking. Lightweight
walking boots are better but most PCT
thru'-hikers opt for running shoes or
walking shoes, also known as trail or
approach shoes. Trails shoes look like
trainers but are designed for walking
rather than running and are probably

the best choice for the PCT. You might expect to wear out two pairs of walking boots, three pairs of trail shoes or five pairs of running shoes during a thru'-hike.

Chose shoes with good tread patterns. All walking shoes ought to have a good tread but some trainers are designed for running on paved surfaces and are unsuitable for mountain trails. You will probably suffer fewer blister problems with fabric rather than leather shoes but leather models will last longer and you might even get away with just one pair. Many hikers choose shoes with Gore-Tex or similar waterproof/breathable linings but they are not really necessary on the PCT and are a disadvantage in desert conditions.

The most important thing is that the boots fit you – an excellent reason why you should not buy them online or by mail order. To say they should fit might seem obvious but how often have you bought a pair of shoes that really do? Don't go to the store with the idea of getting a particular brand or model of shoe. Go through all the suitable shoes on the shelves and, if none really fits, find another store. Try the shoes on with the socks you will wear on the trail.

Three points to consider:
• Your feet will expand when you walk all day in hot conditions.
• Try to find shoes with a low, or preferably no heel tab. They serve no useful purpose and can cause Achilles problems.

• If you have a foot problem such as metatarsalgia – which causes pain in the ball of the foot – or fallen arches, it is worth getting expert advice. Such problems can often be solved or alleviated cheaply with suitable insoles in your shoes.

Camp shoes
In the days when hikers walked in heavy boots, they usually carried a second pair of footwear for use in camp. That's no longer really necessary if you wear lightweight shoes. The main uses for a second pair are creek crossings, wearing in camp and in town – especially in motels – and for walking in if you find you're getting blisters from your trail shoes.

Camp footwear is unnecessary weight but, if you decide to carry some, a pair of lightweight rubber sandals would seem to make sense.

Socks
Good socks are as important as boots that fit. Socks designed for hiking should be seamless, or have flat-sewn seams that don't rub, be hardwearing and wash well in cold water on the trail. Many walkers believe that wearing two pairs of socks will lessen friction between their feet and shoes, helping to minimise blisters. However there is no need to wear two pairs at a time: if you have one good pair and well-fitting boots you are less likely to get blisters.

Socks made by Northern Irish company Bridgedale meet the necessary criteria. Its socks are available in more than 40 countries, including the US. Its website, www.bridgedale.com, has links to stockists and you can safely buy mail order. The product section on its website will tell you which models from its large range are the most suitable.

You should have two pairs of socks, one to wear and the other hanging on your pack drying after you have washed them. In the High Sierra and Washington you might prefer three pairs so you can keep a pair dry for camp. An extra spare pair is a good idea to replace socks that wear out and to use as emergency gloves!

Gaiters
There is no point wearing full-length gaiters designed for mountaineering in snow. However ankle gaiters might be useful to keep stones and sand from getting into your shoes and to prevent foxtails – burr-like seeds found on several sections of the trail, which disperse by clinging to the fur of passing animals – from sticking to your socks.

Clothing
Think carefully about the function of each item of clothing and how you might use them in combination to avoid carrying unnecessary weight and an overfull rucksack.

What is the function of your clothing? It protects you from the wind and rain, the cold and the sun, the heat and from mosquitoes. It protects your modesty and might be regarded as a fashion item.

Lower body clothing
It is essential that the clothing you wear is comfortable, especially around the groin as soreness and chafing could make your hike an excruciating process.

You need to carry waterproof overtrousers, not so much to protect you from the rain as to prevent hypothermia in wet and cold, or wet and windy conditions. Since you won't wear them often, buy the lightest pair that fits rather than the best pair. It is more important that they are wind-resistant than that they are 100 per cent waterproof. It will be useful, though not essential, if the ankles have openings so that you can remove the trousers without having to take your shoes off.

When the weather is warm and wet, you will probably be best wearing shorts and not bothering with the overtrousers. If it's cold and wet, try wearing just underpants and overtrousers so that you can keep your shorts and trousers dry for camp.

Your main decision will be whether to wear shorts or long trousers most of the time. If you opt for shorts, you might think you can get away without long trousers by carrying overtrousers. However, on the rare occasions when it is wet, cold and windy you would be risking

77

hypothermia. At least consider carrying a pair of tracksters (very lightweight tracksuit trousers) to wear in camp and as protection from mosquitoes.

If you intend to wear long trousers most of the time check what's available in specialist outdoor stores. Most trousers sold for general wear aren't suitable for hiking in hot or wet conditions. You might find that a pair of good quality running shorts is better than the shorts available in High Street stores. They are comfortable, lightweight, easy to wash and can be worn without underpants in sweaty conditions or when underpants are on your pack drying after being washed.

Try to use underpants that are comfortable when you are hot and sweaty, and wash them as often as possible.

Upper body clothing

Shirts

A specialist hiking shirt, made from a wicking material such as Dryflo, will be more comfortable in hot and sweaty conditions than cotton or nylon shirts bought on the High Street. Cotton shirts provide little warmth when damp and do little to prevent hypothermia in wet and windy conditions. You must choose between long and short sleeves depending on how sensitive your skin is to sunburn.

Overshirts/fleece tops

Although it will often be very hot during the day, it can be very cold at night and there will be days when the temperature barely gets above freezing. Minimum clothing would be some form of overshirt, such as a sweatshirt,

Siberian Outpost (Section 29)

and a lightweight fleece jacket or two thinner layers. The fleece jacket will mainly be worn in camp and can be used as a pillow overnight.

Bras
Most women hiking the trail will want to wear a bra and should probably opt for a quality sports bra for maximum comfort.

Waterproof top
Some hikers try to get away without carrying proper waterproofs but in doing so take a big gamble, risking hypothermia. You will need waterproofs when it is raining or snowing but even more importantly on the rare days with cold windy conditions. A good quality lightweight waterproof with a hood would be best. Some hikers have been seen with a poncho that covers the upper body and the rucksack. Though not as good as a conventional waterproof, such a garment will probably be adequate for the conditions likely to be encountered on the PCT. An alternative is to carry a cheap lightweight 'waterproof-when-new' jacket obtainable from some supermarkets or general stores. You will need to replace it when its waterproof qualities expire, which could be after just a few days' use.

Hats
A sunhat is essential in Southern California and for unforested sections of the trail further north. A good quality sunhat, such as an expensive Tilley

Hat, can be effective in rain as well as sun. You could take an additional hat for warmth, such as a woolly hat or balaclava, especially if you plan to cook outside your tent when it is cold.

Gloves
You won't need gloves very often but when you need them – on days with damp, freezing conditions – you will need them! Those with sensitive skin might need gloves to prevent sunburn during the early stages of their hike.

Scarf
Scarves seem to have gone out of fashion but a lightweight scarf is worth considering and could be used as an emergency bandage if your first aid kit is fairly meagre.

Sweatbands
You might consider sweatbands for your head – to stop sweat and possibly sunscreen running into your eyes – and wrists.

Alternative clothing
Conventional clothing isn't really designed for hot, sweaty conditions and there seems to have been a revival in lower body clothing, such as skirts and hiking kilts, that provides increased ventilation while still providing protection from the sun. If you plan to wear a skirt or kilt, you should buy models produced by outdoor gear companies, made from specialised hiking fabrics, rather than fashion items from High Street stores. Skirts

and kilts might not be such a good idea on exposed mountain ridges in bad weather but such conditions don't occur very often on the PCT.

Swim costumes

Swim costumes weigh little but are unnecessary. Either wear shorts or underclothes or follow the wilderness tradition of skinny-dipping.

Spare clothing

If it's spare, you don't need it! Some hikers carry a lot of spare clothing but the only spare clothing you need is a spare pair of socks. American attitudes to clothing are fairly informal compared to those in the UK and your trail clothing will be acceptable in restaurants and hotels. Hopefully you will wash it as often as possible, even if only in streams and lakes.

Entertainment

Books

You might put a paperback in each supply package. When you have finished with it give it to another hiker or put it in a hiker box.

Electronic devices

A lot of youngsters carry a variety of electronic devices, either to play music or as electronic notepads. If you are to carry any such device, consider how you are going to power it. You should only consider equipment that runs off more readily available AA or AAA batteries, rather than

rechargeable batteries, though solar chargers are becoming lighter and more robust and could soon be a viable option.

Cameras

Most hikers will want to carry a camera. Unless you need the photographs for professional purposes, the best option is a compact digital camera that runs off AA or AAA batteries. Remember to take plenty of memory cards. Keep your camera dry; resealable food bags should be adequate. In cold conditions, to help prevent condensation, don't remove the camera from the bag until it is at the same temperature as the surroundings.

Other options

A bird book and pair of binoculars would be nice to have but would also be rather heavy. Likewise a guitar: in 2002, Joe and Joe, walking together, each carried a guitar on their thru'-hike. They didn't reach Canada.

Communication

Mobile phones

Only a minority of thru'-hikers carry mobile phones. They could be helpful in an emergency or for contacting trail angels, as well as for keeping in touch with friends and relatives. There are, however, two major problems for cell phones on the PCT.

First, you cannot get a signal on large sections of the trail. Second, you won't have ready access to recharging

Marie Lake (Section 34)

facilities and no manufacturer makes a mobile phone that takes AA or AAA batteries. You would have to leave the phone switched off, only turning it on to check text messages or make calls. Even then, you could run into trouble with battery life. A few hikers carry satellite phones but they are heavy and expensive.

Internet access
Several trail angels *en route* will allow you to check emails. Many hotels also offer internet access.

Mail
You could give friends and relations a list of post office addresses on your route, along with estimated times of arrival, so they can send letters, news, press cuttings, sports results and more.

Information sheet
Before leaving home produce a sheet that includes addresses, telephone numbers, email and web addresses. Include any information you will need if important documents such as credit cards and passports are lost or stolen. Carry one copy with you and leave another with a contact. One 2006 hiker carried a USB memory stick containing all the relevant details, including photographs of pages from his passport, credit card and other documents. It proved very useful when his wallet was stolen in San Diego before he had even reached the trail.

You could even buy any folk left at home a copy of this guidebook! It not only provides them with contact addresses but also makes it easier for them to follow your hike.

Medical and first aid

If you have any particular health problems or haven't taken exercise for a long time, consult your doctor for advice before setting out on a serious backpacking trip.

Painkillers

Ibuprofen, sold under a number of brand names, has two main properties: it is both a painkiller and an anti-inflammatory. Its anti-inflammatory properties are the most helpful for hikers as they can reduce tissue damage and help recovery from minor aches and pains. The painkilling aspects can, however, be dangerous because they can mask injuries and allow you to continue hiking, perhaps unaware that you are aggravating a minor injury and turning it into a major problem. Remember that pain is the body's way of telling you that something is wrong.

A minority of thru'-hikers take Ibuprofen throughout their hike to help them hike high mileages. Ibuprofen has fewer side-effects than many drugs but isn't as free of them as some people think. The small minority of people who might suffer serious side effects probably know they should avoid Ibuprofen already. Long-term moderate use increases the risk of stomach bleeding and, for people with worn joints, it can increase the rate of wear on the joints such as hips.

Some hikers take more than the recommended dose for injuries, such as shin splints, which really require rest. All they are doing is aggravating the injury and putting off the time when they will need a break, as well as increasing the risk of side-effects.

Ibuprofen is more effective than aspirin or paracetamol for a hiker's aches and pains and there is less risk of side effects. However, be aware that there are risks, just as there are for people who continue smoking or drinking alcohol despite the associated risks. Before you decide to take Ibuprofen routinely it would be sensible to discuss it with your doctor.

Ice

Ice is usually a better treatment for strains than drugs. The anti-inflammatory properties of ice make it effective. In the mountains of Southern California and the High Sierra, and possibly further north, you can use old snow patches. If you seal ice in food bags, then wrap them in your camp towel and put them in your rucksack, it will take several hours to melt. You will also find ice readily available in cafés and stores in the US.

Vitamins

Some thru'-hikers' trail diets are poor. That can, after a few months, lead to health problems. Following a sensible balanced diet, however, might not be easy when eating lightweight hiking meals, which might be deficient in some vitamins. It might be sensible to take a multi-vitamin supplement each day.

Drugs

If you have a medical problem that requires the use of prescription drugs, you should discuss the hike with your doctor and make sure you have an adequate supply.

European youngsters might be surprised that the legal minimum age for buying and consuming alcohol in most American states, including California, is 21 and that enforcement of the laws is likely to be stronger than it is in some European countries.

You will meet youngsters (and some not-so-youngsters) on the trail smoking illegal substances. While this is not a good idea, nothing written here will change that reality. What is imperative is that hikers do not take illegal drugs on to the premises of trail angels. If you are carrying such substances, get rid of them before crossing the border from the US into Canada. Drug smuggling will be treated very seriously by the Canadian authorities.

If you are going to set yourself the challenge of hiking the PCT perhaps it is a good time to set yourself the more difficult task of giving up smoking?

Hygiene

Many of the stomach and other problems that hikers can have on the trail, which tend to be blamed on water or food, are in fact the result of poor hygiene. A lack of water might prevent you being able to wash your hands after a toilet stop or before meals but you can often do a reasonable cleaning job by rubbing your hands with leaves. You could carry sanitary wipes, which don't require water, but these represent additional weight and are not used by many hikers. Another possibility is antibacterial hand gels.

You don't have to reach civilisation before washing or having a shower. On the drier parts of the trail you can have a towel bath whenever you reach water. If you do this on a regular basis you can keep reasonably clean without hot water or soap. Further up the trail you should be able to take regular swims. Many hikers don't wash properly because of the lack of privacy on the trail and a sense of modesty that is more suitable for civilisation than the wilderness.

If clothes are washed regularly, even in cold water, you can keep them reasonably clean.

Prevention of blisters

Almost every thru'-hiker and many section-hikers gets blisters on their feet, often so painful that they make walking difficult or even impossible. They can cause hikers to take unwanted zero days or even give up their hike. Yet it is possible to manage a thru'-hike without suffering any blisters.

• Make sure your shoes or boots fit really well – remember that your feet will expand on the hike – and wear top quality socks.
• Do not cover more than 15 miles on any day during the first week

or when you change into new shoes or boots.
- Do not hike more than 100 miles during the second week.
- During the first two weeks don't hike more than two hours without taking a break of at least an hour with your shoes and socks off.
- Stop as soon as you feel any sand or gravel in your shoes.
- Stop immediately to apply tape or other treatment if you feel any soreness.
- Change socks frequently and wash them whenever possible.
- Avoid walking on paved roads and take frequent breaks if you do.
- Try using Vaseline (petroleum jelly) or anti-chafing products such as Bodyglide on your feet to reduce friction.
- Many shoe insoles curve up at the edges or back and can apply pressure to the edges of the sole of the foot. Try trimming the insoles so that they are flat.

Treatment of blisters

Treat early to prevent blisters developing.
- Blisters on the toes usually just need taping. Fabric tape, designed for first aid kits, is best but many hikers seem to use duct tape.
- Blisters on the back or side of the heel are best treated with Compeed plasters which are more effective than moleskin.

- Blisters on the base of the feet are the hardest to treat. Try padding all around the blister but not over the blister itself – try to relieve the pressure on the blistered areas.
- Doctors usually advise against popping blisters because of the risk of infection. Assuming you follow the example of most hikers and ignore this advice, you should wash thoroughly, sterilise needles using a lighter flame and apply antiseptic before bandaging or taping.

Tetanus

Check that your tetanus inoculations are up-to-date before departure

First aid

Anyone who spends a lot of time in the wilderness would be wise to get themselves trained in first aid. In case of serious accidents, you need to be able to do what is necessary to preserve life, such as preventing bleeding, ensuring a patient can breath and arranging protection against the weather. It is usually best, however, to give minimal additional treatment unless you know what you are doing.

Injuries to which you should definitely give immediate treatment are burns and scalds. A lot of damage can be prevented by immediate submersion in cold water or by treatment with an ice pack.

Ensure that the contents of your first aid kit remain dry.

The following list is much more extensive than most hikers will need but can be used as a checklist from which you can select what is appropriate to you.

First aid kit
Antiseptic cream
Antiseptic wipes
Antifungal cream
Antibiotic cream
Antibiotic tablets
Antihistamine cream
Hydrocortisone cream
Ibuprofen cream
Ibuprofen tablets
Anti-diarrhoea tablets (Imodium)
Metronidazole (for giardia)
Insect repellent
Mosquito coils
Mosquito net
Sunscreen
Lip salve
Iodine or Aquamira tablets
Fabric plasters
Fabric strapping tape
Dressings
Corn pads
Blister gel packs, such as Compeed
Felt padding
Steristrips

Elastic bandages
Handkerchiefs or bandanas (can be used for bandaging and padding)
Disposable gloves
Mirror
Safety pins
Penknife with scissors and tweezers
Cigarette lighter
Whistle

Hygiene kit
Toothbrush, paste and dental floss
Comb
Toilet roll, trowel and antibacterial gel
Camp towel
Shaving kit
Biodegradable detergent
Contraceptives
Sanitary towels/tampons

Repair kit
Needle and thread
Parachute cord
Walking pole tips
Duct tape

Most of your first aid kit's contents will be for dealing with minor injuries such as cuts and blisters and will, in the main, be put together with that in mind. Most hikers will have a combined first aid kit, repair kit and hygiene kit.

Food
Your diet is unlikely to be well-balanced so you should supplement it with multi-vitamin tablets (see section on Medical and first aid).

There will be times when you are carrying more than a week's supply of food. The food you carry, therefore,

Hogback Mountain (Section 88)

needs to be lightweight and dehydrated. Some Americans produce their own backpacking meals on home dehydrators but that won't be possible for non-Americans because of difficulties importing food.

For the first week you won't need much more food than you normally eat. By the second week, however, you will start to need greater quantities. Later in the hike, as your mileages increase, you will need even more. The amount needed varies considerably from person to person and is also dependent on your mileage. For that reason, there is no point in saying how many calories you will need each day.

Unless you start with a lot of excess fat you can assume, if you are losing weight, that you aren't eating enough. Try to be aware early in the

hike of whether or not you are losing weight so that you can adjust food quantities further up the trail. You will certainly lose body fat but you will also put on muscle and might even gain a little weight!

Remember, the calorific value of food you can't eat is zero. It's no good carrying food that is 'good for you' if you find it inedible. Be aware that some foods are difficult to eat when temperatures are high and go with food that is easy to eat. Furthermore, over a period of five to six months you can become bored with eating the same food all the time and should try to ensure you have as much variety as possible.

Any cooking has to be achieved with the limited cooking equipment you are carrying. You will often have dry camps so your food should not require a lot of water to be cooked. It should also be low-bulk, as it has to fit into your rucksack.

The ideas that follow are only suggestions. Everyone will have their own ideas about what food to carry and there is no standard system of food for backpacking.

- Cereal bars (granola bars) are a good – but expensive – alternative to breakfast muesli or cereals. They have the advantage that they don't need milk and can be eaten throughout the day as snacks.

- Trail mix – essentially dried fruit, nuts and possibly M&Ms – makes a good snack throughout the day. You can buy trail mix but it is cheaper to make up your own, buying the ingredients separately.

- Carrying chocolate presents a problem because it is difficult to prevent it melting. Try M&Ms, as the chocolate is enclosed in a sugary capsule and will therefore survive higher temperatures.

- Your staple diet will probably be based on pasta, rice or possibly dehydrated potato. You will find you get sick of them unless you have plenty of variety among the sauces and other ingredients with which you combine them. The freeze-dried meals manufactured by Backpacker's Pantry, Mountain House and other companies in the US are much more edible than similar dehydrated meals sold in Europe and a large selection is available. They require only the addition of boiling water and can be eaten out of the packet. You will sometimes find them in large superstores but they are primarily sold by outdoor gear retailers.

- Many hikers eat ramen noodle soups. These are good supplements to your diet but should be seen as snacks, not main meals.

- Remember tea bags. You can also get coffee bags, which are preferable to instant coffee. Those teas such as Earl Grey or herbal teas, which are intended to be drunk without milk, are preferable to putting powdered milk into standard tea. Consider drinking plenty of Gatorade – sold in powder form in supermarkets – or other electrolyte drinks on the hotter parts of the trail. You might prefer to drink it more dilute than is suggested on the packaging.

- In addition to backpacking food, why not include luxury items in each food package to eat straight away or not far up the trail. These could include such items as tins of stew, fish or fruit, cans of beer or soda, and cartons of fruit juice.

- Where possible, supplement your backpacking diet with 'real food'. Have a meal at the few cafés and restaurants you pass. Buy fruit, bread rolls, salads and cakes when you pass a store.

It is best to avoid foods that involve frying. You have only limited cooking equipment and facilities for washing up.

Remember, you will live off this diet for months on-end so need variety and food you can look forward to.

USING THIS GUIDE

Structure and direction

This guide is intended for those who want to hike the PCT in relative comfort at a reasonably sedate pace. The trail divides naturally into five **regions**, each taking about a month to cross. These have been further divided into

11 **parts** to provide hikes of between two and three weeks each and then into 100 smaller **sections** for two- or three-day hikes. Where possible, these sections end at roads but occasionally they end at trail junctions from which you could hike to a road.

The guide and maps assume that you are hiking from south-to-north since this is the way the vast majority of thru'-hikers travel, so that they can hike the desert sections in the relative cool of the spring and because snow in the mountains of Washington could make the PCT impassable into July. Section-hikers will find the guide easier to use if they also travel south-to-north.

TRAIL OVERVIEW

	Distance (miles)	Time (hours)	Ascent (feet)
Southern California			
1 Campo–Van Dusen Canyon (Big Bear City)	275	122	35,000
2 Big Bear City–Agua Dulce	181	80	21,000
3 Agua Dulce–Kennedy Meadows	248	111	32,000
The High Sierra			
4 Kennedy Meadows–Tuolumne Meadows	241	121	41,000
5 Tuolumne Meadows–Donner Pass	217	102	31,000
Northern California			
6 Donner Pass–Castella	348	150	40,000
7 Castella–Ashland	220	100	28,000
Oregon			
8 Ashland–McKenzie Pass	263	108	24,000
9 McKenzie Pass–Cascade Locks	167	70	21,000
Washington			
10 Cascade Locks–Snoqualmie Pass	249	114	33,000
11 Snoqualmie Pass–Manning Park	264	132	48,000

The trail description

Each of the 11 parts starts with an **overview map** of the route covered. The key information that follows includes a table showing the **sections** covered (with mileage, timing and ascent for each), a brief route **summary**, the **best time** to hike, any **permits** required (and where to get them) and details of **facilities** available in any towns and resorts en route.

The route description is then presented around a sequence of route maps, running continuously without breaks for sections in order to make this part of the guidebook as compact as possible – and to keep the weight in your rucksack down. Also for compactness, the maps are drawn at a scale of 1:100,000. At that scale it is not possible to show every twist and turn of the trail but the maps will enable you to follow the trail from south to north without getting lost.

Each map also features a small elevation profile to give you a feel for how much ascent you will face on that stretch. The horizontal axis is in miles and the vertical axis is in feet.

All the maps are oriented with north at the top of the page. Magnetic north will be about 12° east of true north at Campo, gradually increasing to 16° east of true north by the time you reach Manning Park (see table below). The annual change in magnetic variation is only 5'–10' each year and can be ignored.

The **notes** about the main route on the map pages are numbered from the beginning of each section (up the page, as you walk south-to-north) and always refer to the page on which they are situated (notes on major variations are numbered in green). Each note starts with the approximate **hiking time** from the beginning of the section. These estimates are conservative. A fit hiker can expect to better these times, so a thru'-hiker can expect to beat these times once they gain fitness. In particular, a fit hiker might expect to climb hills at a faster rate than allowed by the figures. The other figures on the maps, in green by a green dot, give the **distance from Campo**, at five-mile intervals.

Points of interest along the trail are described in italics. Where

MAGNETIC VARIATION (to the nearest full degree)			
	annual change	*Dec 31, 2010*	*Dec 31, 2014*
Mexican/US border	0°5'W	12°E	12°E
Yosemite National Park	0°6'W	14°E	13°E
California/Oregon border	0°7'W	15°E	15°E
Oregon/Washington border	0°9'W	17°E	16°E
US/Canadian border	0°10'W	17°E	16°E

possible the section summaries appear on the map page for the beginning of that section but will occasionally be on the preceding or following map page owing to space constraints.

Some of the notes also cite **GPS coordinates**. These are based on the Universal Traverse Mercator-based (UTM) system (map datum WGS 84) and were measured by the author in 2009.

- Maps 1–69: zone 11S
- Maps 70–83: zone 10S
- Maps 84–157: zone 10T
- Maps 158–166: zone 10U

Altitudes of peaks, cols and spot heights are in black italics, sometimes with a black dot, and are given in feet. They are based on best available evidence from measurements the author made with GPS and altimeter in 2009 and values derived from topo maps. Measuring altitude accurately is very difficult (GPS gives a much more accurate horizontal than vertical position) and you shouldn't expect absolute precision in the readings.

Water sources vary greatly from year to year and depend on snowpack, spring and early summer temperatures and summer rainfall. Where a year-round creek is shown with a seasonal water source symbol, it might dry up in a particularly dry summer.

- Parts 1–3: you can expect most seasonal creeks to be dry, unless the notes suggest times when they might be running. They are mainly mapped to show the shape of the land.

- Parts 4 and 5: only major creeks are mapped. There will also be a multitude of seasonal creeks and snowmelt creeks.
- Parts 6–11: expect most mapped seasonal creeks to have water in the main thru'-hiking season in an average year (July in Northern California, August in Oregon and September in Washington). Where a seasonal water source symbol is shown, there was water during the author's 2009 thru'-hike, probably an average year for water. You can expect some seasonal water sources to run throughout a wet summer.

In California you can usually find stealth campsites at regular intervals so only the major **campsites** are mapped. Mention is only made of camping when sites are likely to be difficult to find. As you reach Northern Oregon and Washington, stealth camping becomes more difficult due to the increasing underbrush in the forest and you are likely to be camping only at sites shown on the maps.

Symbols used in the overview maps and **abbreviations** used in the facilities information in the part introductions are explained at the front and back of this book, as are the symbols used on the **route maps**.

Facilities are listed and shown on the maps where they have been confirmed. There will often be more facilities than are listed, especially in bigger towns.

SOUTHERN CALIFORNIA

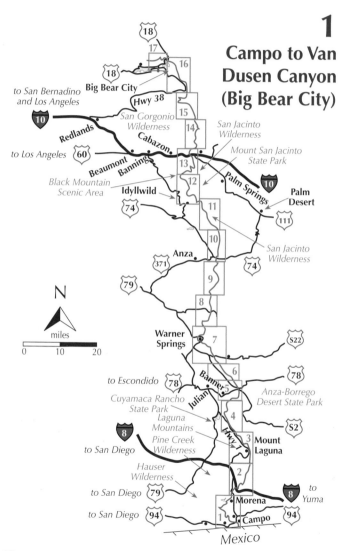

1

Campo to Van Dusen Canyon (Big Bear City)

to San Bernadino and Los Angeles

Big Bear City

Hwy 38

San Gorgonio Wilderness

Redlands

to Los Angeles

Beaumont

Banning

Cabazon

Black Mountain Scenic Area

Idyllwild

San Jacinto Wilderness

Mount San Jacinto State Park

Palm Springs

Palm Desert

San Jacinto Wilderness

Anza

Warner Springs

to Escondido

Banner

Anza-Borrego Desert State Park

Cuyamaca Rancho State Park

Julian

Laguna Mountains

Pine Creek Wilderness

to San Diego

Mount Laguna

Hauser Wilderness

to San Diego

Morena

to San Diego

Campo

Mexico

N

miles

0   10   20

to Yuma

PART 1: CAMPO TO VAN DUSEN CANYON (BIG BEAR CITY)

Section	Distance (miles)	Time (hours)	Ascent (feet)	Maps
1 Campo–Lake Morena	20	9	2000	1
2 Lake Morena–Mount Laguna	22	10	3000	1–3
3 Mount Laguna–Scissors Crossing	35	13	1000	3–5
4 Scissors Crossing–Warner Springs	33	13	3000	5–7
5 Warner Springs–Chihuahua Rd	17	8	2000	7, 8
6 Chihuahua Rd–Highway 74	25	11	3000	8–10
7 Highway 74–Saddle Junction	28	15	6000	10–12
8 Saddle Junction–San Gorgonio Pass	30	12	3000	12, 13
9 San Gorgonio Pass–Cienega Seca Creek	40	21	10,000	13–16
10 Cienega Seca Pass–Van Dusen Canyon	25	10	2000	16, 17
Part total	**275**	**122**	**35,000**	

This is a very varied section with an altitude range from 1000–9000ft. You must be prepared for 100°F (38°C) in the deserts and freezing conditions and even snow showers at night and in the mountains. Assuming you start once the winter snows have melted, the section's only real problem will be dealing with the heat and making sure that you have enough water as sources are infrequent, especially in drought years.

You should read carefully the chapter on the first week. It will give you a feel for what the section will be like in a dry year. The terrain is predominantly sandy and you should have no problem finding wilderness campsites. If you encounter significant snow before reaching Saddle Junction in the San Jacinto Mountains (Sections 7 and 8), the section from Saddle Junction to the Black Mountain Road will have substantial snowpack on steep north- and east-facing slopes. Navigation could be extremely difficult and ice could make conditions dangerous. You should consider dropping to Idyllwyld, regaining the PCT via the Black Mountain Road.

Best time to hike
Late April or early May. The section will be very hot by late May and most water sources will be dry. If you start any earlier you could run into snow flurries and winter weather, and might still encounter snow in the San Jacinto

93

Ladybug and Morena Butte (Section 1)

Mountains, which will make that section extremely difficult. Autumn might be a good time as far as temperatures are concerned but all the springs and creeks could be dry. Section-hikers could attend the kick-off party in late April and start the PCT with the thru'-hikers, and might like to hike Sections 1–6 in the winter.

Permits
Permits are required for Sections 1, 7 and 8.

Section 1: Hauser Wilderness
Cleveland National Forest, 10845 Rancho Bernado Rd, Suite 200, San Diego CA92127
(858)-673-6180,
www.fs.fed.us/r5/cleveland

Sections 7 & 8: San Jacinto National Forest Wilderness
Idyllwild Ranger Station, 54270 Pine Crest, Box 518, Idyllwild CA92549
(909)-382-2921, www.fs.fed.us/r5/sanbernardino/contact/sanjacinto.shtml
Mon–Fri: 8.00am–12.00noon, 1.00pm–3.30pm,
Sat & Sun: 8.00am–4.30pm

Section 8: Mount San Jacinto State Park Wilderness
Mount San Jacinto State Park Wilderness, Box 308, 25905 Hwy 243, Idyllwild CA92549
(951)-659-2607, www.parks.ca.gov
No dogs or fires are allowed in the state park and camping is only allowed at designated sites.

Parking permits

All cars parked in the Angeles, Cleveland, Los Padres and San Bernardino National Forests in Southern California require a permit under the National Forest Adventure Pass System. Passes can be purchased from the USFS, outdoor stores and local stores.
www.fs.fed.us/r5/sanbernardino/ap

Facilities

It is suggested that you resupply at Mount Laguna, Warner Springs, Paradise Corner Café, Cabazon and Big Bear City.

Campo (PO, small G, L) (Section 1) (0 hours)
Campo PO, 951 Jeb Stuart Rd, Campo CA91906
(619)-478-5466.

Mon–Fri: 8.30am–11.30am & 12.30pm–4.30pm,
Sat: 9.00am–12.00noon
Details of buses from San Diego are given in the section on getting to the PCT. There is a restaurant at Cameron Corner, 1½ miles north along Highway 94. http://california. hometownlocator.com/CA/San-Diego/Campo.cfm

Morena Village (small G, R, C, Sh, B) (Sections 1, 2) (9 hours)
There is a small store just east of the PCT and a good mini-mart with ATM and hot snacks in the centre of the village.
El Rancho Restaurant:
Tue–Thur: 4.00pm–8.00pm,
Fri–Sun: 11.00am–8.00pm
www.sdcounty.ca.gov/parks/Camping/lake_morena.html

The Warner Springs stage coach (Section 4/5)

Approaching Saddle Junction (Section 7)

Mount Laguna (PO, G, R, A, C)
(Sections 2, 3) (19 hours)
Mount Laguna PO, 810 Sunrise Hwy,
Mount Laguna CA91948
(619)-473-8341
Mon–Fri: 12.00noon–4.00pm,
Sat: 9.00am–11.00am
Laguna Mountain Lodge and Store,
10678 Sunrise Hwy, PO Box 146,
Mount Laguna CA91948
(619)-473-8533, www.laguna
mountain.com. 9.00am–5.00pm
Cabins, well-stocked store and hot
snacks. Package service ($5 in 2009).
The restaurant is only open for lim-
ited hours at the weekend.

Banner (P, small G, C) (from Scissors
Crossing) (Sections 3, 4) (32 hours)
Banner Store, 36342, Hwy 78, Julian
CA92036
(760)-765-0813. 8.00am–6.00pm
Banner Store will accept packages.
Camping $10 in 2009

Julian (PO, G, R, A, O, B) (from
Scissors Crossing) (Sections 3, 4) (32
hours)

Julian PO, 1785 Hwy 78, Julian
CA92036
(760)-765-3648. Mon–Fri: 9.00am–
4.00pm, Sat: 10.00am–12.00noon
Julian is a small town with good
facilities for hikers.

Warner Springs (PO, minimal G, R,
A, B) (Sections 4, 5) (45 hours)
Warner Springs PO, 31650, Hwy 79,
Warner Springs CA92086
(760)-782-3166. Mon–Fri: 8.00am–
4.00pm, Sat: 8.00am–1.30pm
The Golf Club Grill (6.30am–3.00pm)
serves cheap meals and there is a
mini-mart at the gas station for snacks
and minimal resupply.
Warner Springs Ranch, 31652, Hwy
79, PO Box 10, Warner Springs
CA92086
(760)-792-4200,
www.warnersprings.com
Warner Springs Ranch is a private spa
resort where hikers can find accommodation, restaurant, hot tubs and
massage. The sale of the resort in
2010 could lead to changes in provi-
sion of facilities for hikers.

Anza
Three well-separated facilities in the Anza area might be of use to hikers: Kamp Anza Kampground, Anza and the Paradise Corner Café. www. anza-valley.com

Kamp Anza Kampground (small G, C, L, Sh) (from Coyote Canyon Rd) (Section 6) (56 hours)
Kamp Anza Kampground, 41560, Terwilliger Rd, Anza CA92539
www.hikercentral.com/ campgrounds/101873.html

Paradise Corner Café (P, R) (Hwy 74) (Sections 6, 7) (64 hours)
Paradise Corner Café, 61721, State Hwy 74 CA92539
(951)-659-0730,
duqueisabell@aol.com
Wed: 11.00am–3.00pm,
Thur: 11.00am–7.00pm,
Fri–Sun: 8.00am–8.00pm
Paradise Corner Café will hold packages for hikers. Water is available from a tap when the store is closed.

Anza (PO, G, R, A, B) (from Hwy 74) (Sections 6, 7) (64 hours)
Anza PO, 39755, Contreras Road, Anza CA92539
(951)-763-2074, Mon–Fri: 9.00am–5.00pm, Sat: 10.00am–1.00pm
Anza has the facilities you would expect for a small town.

Idyllwild (PO, G, R, A, C, L, Sh, O, B) (from Saddle Junction) (Sections 7, 8) (79 hours)

Idyllwild PO, 54391, Village Centre Drive, Idyllwild CA92549
(951)-659-9719, www.idyllwild.com.
Mon–Fri: 9.00am–5.00pm
Idyllwild is a mountain resort with good facilities for hikers.

Cabazon (PO, G, R, A, B) (from San Gorgonio Pass) (Sections 8, 9) (91 hours)
Cabazon PO, 50360, Ramona Rd, Cabazon CA92230
(888)-275-9543. Mon–Fri: 8.30am–4.00pm
Cabazon has full town facilities.

Palm Springs (PO, G, R, A, B) (from San Gorgonio Pass) (Sections 8, 9) (91 hours)
Palm Springs PO, 333, E Amanda Rd, Palm Springs CA92262
(760)-322-4111. Mon–Fri: 9.00am–5.00pm, Sat: 9.00am–3.00pm (there are several POs)
Palm Springs is a large town.
www.palm-springs.org

Big Bear City (PO, G, R, A, L, Sh, O, B) (from Van Dusen Canyon) (Sections 10, 11) (125 hours)
Big Bear City PO, 120 W Country Club Blvd, Big Bear City CA92314
(909)-585-7132. Mon–Fri: 9.00am–4.30pm
Sat: 1.00pm–2.00pm (package collection only)
Big Bear City has full town facilities. The fire station offers showers to hikers. www.city-data.com/city/ Big-Bear-City-California.html

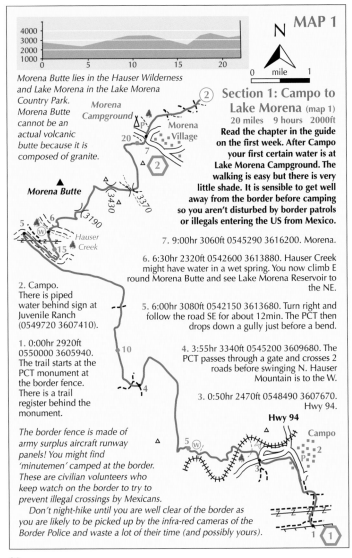

MAP 1

N

4000
3000
2000
1000

0   5   10   15   20

0   mile   1

Morena Butte lies in the Hauser Wilderness and Lake Morena in the Lake Morena Country Park.

Section 1: Campo to Lake Morena (map 1)

20 miles   9 hours   2000ft

Morena Butte cannot be an actual volcanic butte because it is composed of granite.

Morena Campground

Morena Village

Morena Butte

▲ **Morena Butte**

3430
3370
3190

Hauser Creek

Read the chapter in the guide on the first week. After Campo your first certain water is at Lake Morena Campground. The walking is easy but there is very little shade. It is sensible to get well away from the border before camping so you aren't disturbed by border patrols or illegals entering the US from Mexico.

7. 9:00hr 3060ft 0545290 3616200. Morena.

6. 6:30hr 2320ft 0542600 3613880. Hauser Creek might have water in a wet spring. You now climb E round Morena Butte and see Lake Morena Reservoir to the NE.

5. 6:00hr 3080ft 0542150 3613680. Turn right and follow the road SE for about 12min. The PCT then drops down a gully just before a bend.

4. 3:55hr 3340ft 0545200 3609680. The PCT passes through a gate and crosses 2 roads before swinging N. Hauser Mountain is to the W.

3. 0:50hr 2470ft 0548490 3607670. Hwy 94.

2. Campo. There is piped water behind sign at Juvenile Ranch (0549720 3607410).

1. 0:00hr 2920ft 0550000 3605940. The trail starts at the PCT monument at the border fence. There is a trail register behind the monument.

The border fence is made of army surplus aircraft runway panels! You might find 'minutemen' camped at the border. These are civilian volunteers who keep watch on the border to try to prevent illegal crossings by Mexicans.

Don't night-hike until you are well clear of the border as you are likely to be picked up by the infra-red cameras of the Border Police and waste a lot of their time (and possibly yours).

Hwy 94

Campo

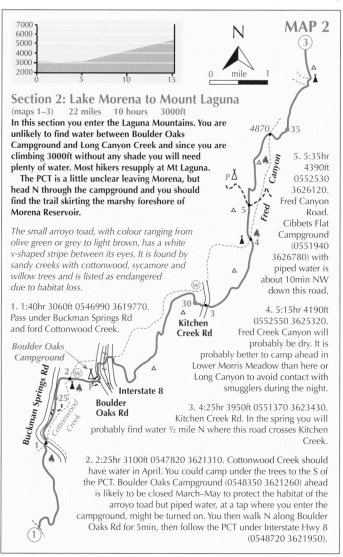

MAP 2

Section 2: Lake Morena to Mount Laguna
(maps 1–3)   22 miles   10 hours   3000ft

In this section you enter the Laguna Mountains. You are unlikely to find water between Boulder Oaks Campground and Long Canyon Creek and since you are climbing 3000ft without any shade you will need plenty of water. Most hikers resupply at Mt Laguna.

The PCT is a little unclear leaving Morena, but head N through the campground and you should find the trail skirting the marshy foreshore of Morena Reservoir.

The small arroyo toad, with colour ranging from olive green or grey to light brown, has a white v-shaped stripe between its eyes. It is found by sandy creeks with cottonwood, sycamore and willow trees and is listed as endangered due to habitat loss.

1. 1:40hr 3060ft 0546990 3619770. Pass under Buckman Springs Rd and ford Cottonwood Creek.

5. 5:35hr 4390ft 0552530 3626120. Fred Canyon Road. Cibbets Flat Campground (0551940 3626780) with piped water is about 10min NW down this road.

4. 5:15hr 4190ft 0552550 3625320. Fred Creek Canyon will probably be dry. It is probably better to camp ahead in Lower Morris Meadow than here or Long Canyon to avoid contact with smugglers during the night.

3. 4:25hr 3950ft 0551370 3623430. Kitchen Creek Rd. In the spring you will probably find water ½ mile N where this road crosses Kitchen Creek.

2. 2:25hr 3100ft 0547820 3621310. Cottonwood Creek should have water in April. You could camp under the trees to the S of the PCT. Boulder Oaks Campground (0548350 3621260) ahead is likely to be closed March–May to protect the habitat of the arroyo toad but piped water, at a tap where you enter the campground, might be turned on. You then walk N along Boulder Oaks Rd for 5min, then follow the PCT under Interstate Hwy 8 (0548720 3621950).

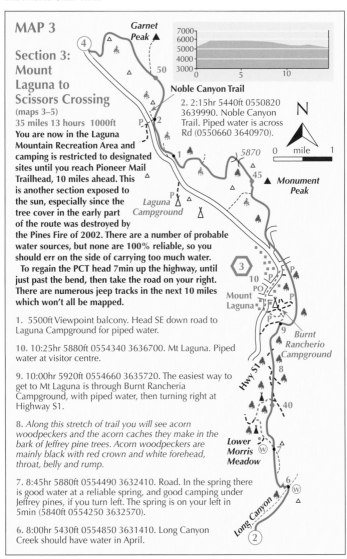

MAP 3

Section 3:
Mount
Laguna to
Scissors Crossing
(maps 3–5)

35 miles 13 hours 1000ft

You are now in the Laguna Mountain Recreation Area and camping is restricted to designated sites until you reach Pioneer Mail Trailhead, 10 miles ahead. This is another section exposed to the sun, especially since the tree cover in the early part of the route was destroyed by the Pines Fire of 2002. There are a number of probable water sources, but none are 100% reliable, so you should err on the side of carrying too much water.

To regain the PCT head 7min up the highway, until just past the bend, then take the road on your right. There are numerous jeep tracks in the next 10 miles which won't all be mapped.

Garnet Peak ▲

Noble Canyon Trail
2. 2:15hr 5440ft 0550820 3639990. Noble Canyon Trail. Piped water is across Rd (0550660 3640970).

N

0   mile   1

5870

45

▲ Monument Peak

3

10

Mount Laguna

Laguna Campground

9

Burnt Rancheria Campground

8

40

Lower Morris Meadow

6

Hwy S1

Long Canyon

2

1. 5500ft Viewpoint balcony. Head SE down road to Laguna Campground for piped water.

10. 10:25hr 5880ft 0554340 3636700. Mt Laguna. Piped water at visitor centre.

9. 10:00hr 5920ft 0554660 3635720. The easiest way to get to Mt Laguna is through Burnt Rancheria Campground, with piped water, then turning right at Highway S1.

8. *Along this stretch of trail you will see acorn woodpeckers and the acorn caches they make in the bark of Jeffrey pine trees. Acorn woodpeckers are mainly black with red crown and white forehead, throat, belly and rump.*

7. 8:45hr 5880ft 0554490 3632410. Road. In the spring there is good water at a reliable spring, and good camping under Jeffrey pines, if you turn left. The spring is on your left in 5min (5840ft 0554250 3632570).

6. 8:00hr 5430ft 0554850 3631410. Long Canyon Creek should have water in April.

MAP 4

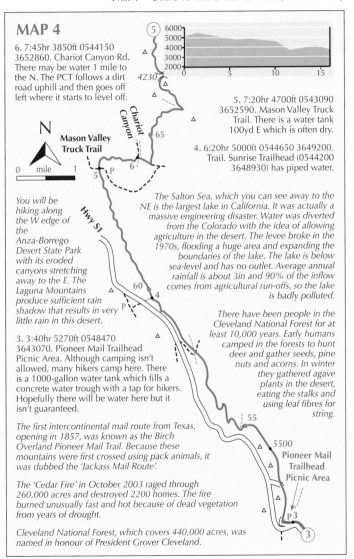

6. 7:45hr 3850ft 0544150 3652860. Chariot Canyon Rd. There may be water 1 mile to the N. The PCT follows a dirt road uphill and then goes off left where it starts to level off.

5. 7:20hr 4700ft 0543090 3652590. Mason Valley Truck Trail. There is a water tank 100yd E which is often dry.

4. 6:20hr 5000ft 0544650 3649200. Trail. Sunrise Trailhead (0544200 3648930) has piped water.

You will be hiking along the W edge of the Anza-Borrego Desert State Park with its eroded canyons stretching away to the E. The Laguna Mountains produce sufficient rain shadow that results in very little rain in this desert.

The Salton Sea, which you can see away to the NE is the largest lake in California. It was actually a massive engineering disaster. Water was diverted from the Colorado with the idea of allowing agriculture in the desert. The levee broke in the 1970s, flooding a huge area and expanding the boundaries of the lake. The lake is below sea-level and has no outlet. Average annual rainfall is about 3in and 90% of the inflow comes from agricultural run-offs, so the lake is badly polluted.

There have been people in the Cleveland National Forest for at least 10,000 years. Early humans camped in the forests to hunt deer and gather seeds, pine nuts and acorns. In winter they gathered agave plants in the desert, eating the stalks and using leaf fibres for string.

3. 3:40hr 5270ft 0548470 3643070. Pioneer Mail Trailhead Picnic Area. Although camping isn't allowed, many hikers camp here. There is a 1000-gallon water tank which fills a concrete water trough with a tap for hikers. Hopefully there will be water here but it isn't guaranteed.

The first intercontinental mail route from Texas, opening in 1857, was known as the Birch Overland Pioneer Mail Trail. Because these mountains were first crossed using pack animals, it was dubbed the 'Jackass Mail Route'.

The 'Cedar Fire' in October 2003 raged through 260,000 acres and destroyed 2200 homes. The fire burned unusually fast and hot because of dead vegetation from years of drought.

Cleveland National Forest, which covers 440,000 acres, was named in honour of President Grover Cleveland.

MAP 5
Section 4: Scissors Crossing to Warner Springs (maps 5–7)
33 miles   13 hours   3000ft

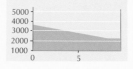

The 24-mile section to Barrel Spring over the San Felipe Hills is the most demanding so far on the PCT. You start by climbing 2000ft on a shadeless S-facing slope. Trail angels try to maintain a water cache on the top of the ridge but you should never depend on water caches. Unless the weather is cool, you should set off from Hwy 78 in the early morning or in the evening. It is too far at this stage for most hikers to walk in one day so you will need a dry camp in the San Felipe Hills. Once you reach Barrel Spring the going is easy to Warner Springs.

9. 13:10 hr 2280ft 0549500 3662400. Hwy 78. Banner is 5 miles SW along Hwy 78. Julian is about 13 miles away, SW down Hwy 78 then S down Hwy 79.

8. 13:00hr 2260ft 0549230 3662060. Hwy S2. You will probably find a water cache here. If you don't you might find water in San Felipe Creek in the spring but it might be of dubious quality.
  Stagecoach Trails, which offers a chance of shower and pool (9am–5pm), as well as accommodation, is about 2 miles SE.

You can never be certain of the reliability of water sources. San Felipe Creek was running well in April of the drought year of 2002 but was completely dry in 2006, when there seemed to be water everywhere, and in 2009 which was an average year for water!

Wildfire has been an essential part of the lifecycle of the region's native forests for thousands of years. Fire clears out underbrush and allows pines and oak woodlands to flourish at higher elevations. At lower elevations, chaparral plants such as manzita, scrub oak and chamise grow back quickly as sprouts or seeds awaken after fire.

San Felipe Valley
Hwy S2

Scissors Crossing

Hwy 78

Hwy S2

N

0   mile   1

Rodriguez Spur Truck Trail

3360

70

75

7. 9:45hr 3630ft 0544440 3656980. Rodriguez Spur Truck Trail. On your left, just before the junction with this jeep track, is a big water tank which is filled by the fire service. Water can be accessed from a pipe valve about 30m below the tank. There will be no more water before Scissors Crossing. Granite Mountain is to the E and Grapevine Mountain and the San Felipe Hills are to the N.

MAP 6

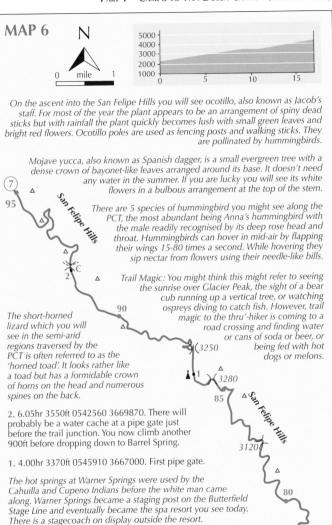

On the ascent into the San Felipe Hills you will see ocotillo, also known as Jacob's staff. For most of the year the plant appears to be an arrangement of spiny dead sticks but with rainfall the plant quickly becomes lush with small green leaves and bright red flowers. Ocotillo poles are used as fencing posts and walking sticks. They are pollinated by hummingbirds.

Mojave yucca, also known as Spanish dagger, is a small evergreen tree with a dense crown of bayonet-like leaves arranged around its base. It doesn't need any water in the summer. If you are lucky you will see its white flowers in a bulbous arrangement at the top of the stem.

There are 5 species of hummingbird you might see along the PCT, the most abundant being Anna's hummingbird with the male readily recognised by its deep rose head and throat. Hummingbirds can hover in mid-air by flapping their wings 15-80 times a second. While hovering they sip nectar from flowers using their needle-like bills.

Trail Magic: You might think this might refer to seeing the sunrise over Glacier Peak, the sight of a bear cub running up a vertical tree, or watching ospreys diving to catch fish. However, trail magic to the thru'-hiker is coming to a road crossing and finding water or cans of soda or beer, or being fed with hot dogs or melons.

The short-horned lizard which you will see in the semi-arid regions traversed by the PCT is often referred to as the 'horned toad'. It looks rather like a toad but has a formidable crown of horns on the head and numerous spines on the back.

2. 6.05hr 3550ft 0542560 3669870. There will probably be a water cache at a pipe gate just before the trail junction. You now climb another 900ft before dropping down to Barrel Spring.

1. 4.00hr 3370ft 0545910 3667000. First pipe gate.

The hot springs at Warner Springs were used by the Cahuilla and Cupeno Indians before the white man came along. Warner Springs became a staging post on the Butterfield Stage Line and eventually became the spa resort you see today. There is a stagecoach on display outside the resort.

MAP 7

Section 5: Warner Springs to Chihuahua Valley Road (maps 7,8)   17 miles   8 hours   2000ft

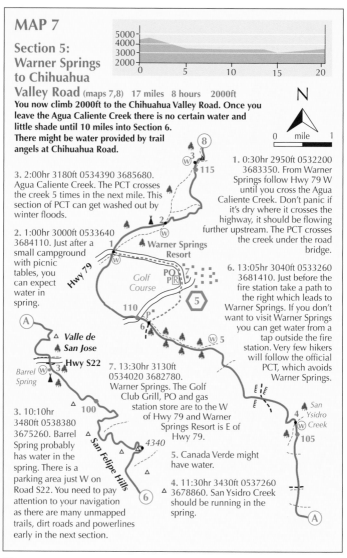

You now climb 2000ft to the Chihuahua Valley Road. Once you leave the Agua Caliente Creek there is no certain water and little shade until 10 miles into Section 6. There might be water provided by trail angels at Chihuahua Road.

N

0   mile   1

3. 2:00hr 3180ft 0534390 3685680. Agua Caliente Creek. The PCT crosses the creek 5 times in the next mile. This section of PCT can get washed out by winter floods.

2. 1:00hr 3000ft 0533640 3684110. Just after a small campground with picnic tables, you can expect water in spring.

1. 0:30hr 2950ft 0532200 3683350. From Warner Springs follow Hwy 79 W until you cross the Agua Caliente Creek. Don't panic if it's dry where it crosses the highway, it should be flowing further upstream. The PCT crosses the creek under the road bridge.

6. 13:05hr 3040ft 0533260 3681410. Just before the fire station take a path to the right which leads to Warner Springs. If you don't want to visit Warner Springs you can get water from a tap outside the fire station. Very few hikers will follow the official PCT, which avoids Warner Springs.

Warner Springs Resort

Golf Course

PO
PR

Valle de San Jose

Hwy S22

Barrel Spring

3. 10:10hr 3480ft 0538380 3675260. Barrel Spring probably has water in the spring. There is a parking area just W on Road S22. You need to pay attention to your navigation as there are many unmapped trails, dirt roads and powerlines early in the next section.

7. 13:30hr 3130ft 0534020 3682780. Warner Springs. The Golf Club Grill, PO and gas station store are to the W of Hwy 79 and Warner Springs Resort is E of Hwy 79.

5. Canada Verde might have water.

4. 11:30hr 3430ft 0537260 3678860. San Ysidro Creek should be running in the spring.

San Ysidro Creek

San Felipe Hills

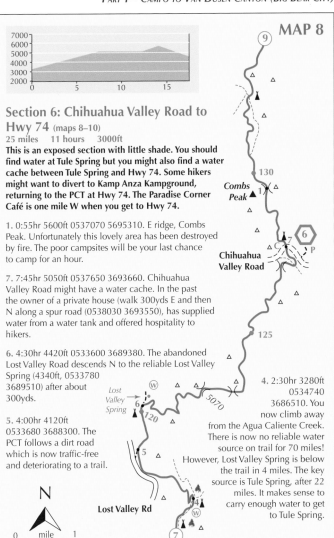

MAP 8

Section 6: Chihuahua Valley Road to Hwy 74 (maps 8–10)
25 miles   11 hours   3000ft

This is an exposed section with little shade. You should find water at Tule Spring but you might also find a water cache between Tule Spring and Hwy 74. Some hikers might want to divert to Kamp Anza Kampground, returning to the PCT at Hwy 74. The Paradise Corner Café is one mile W when you get to Hwy 74.

1. 0:55hr 5600ft 0537070 5695310. E ridge, Combs Peak. Unfortunately this lovely area has been destroyed by fire. The poor campsites will be your last chance to camp for an hour.

7. 7:45hr 5050ft 0537650 3693660. Chihuahua Valley Road might have a water cache. In the past the owner of a private house (walk 300yds E and then N along a spur road (0538030 3693550), has supplied water from a water tank and offered hospitality to hikers.

6. 4:30hr 4420ft 0533600 3689380. The abandoned Lost Valley Road descends N to the reliable Lost Valley Spring (4340ft, 0533780 3689510) after about 300yds.

5. 4:00hr 4120ft 0533680 3688300. The PCT follows a dirt road which is now traffic-free and deteriorating to a trail.

4. 2:30hr 3280ft 0534740 3686510. You now climb away from the Agua Caliente Creek. There is now no reliable water source on trail for 70 miles! However, Lost Valley Spring is below the trail in 4 miles. The key source is Tule Spring, after 22 miles. It makes sense to carry enough water to get to Tule Spring.

Combs Peak

Chihuahua Valley Road

Lost Valley Spring

Lost Valley Rd

N

0   mile   1

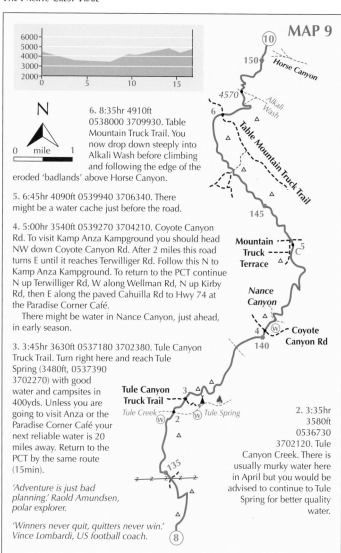

MAP 9

6000
5000
4000
3000
2000

0   5   10   15

N

0   mile   1

6. 8:35hr 4910ft 0538000 3709930. Table Mountain Truck Trail. You now drop down steeply into Alkali Wash before climbing and following the edge of the eroded 'badlands' above Horse Canyon.

5. 6:45hr 4090ft 0539940 3706340. There might be a water cache just before the road.

4. 5:00hr 3540ft 0539270 3704210. Coyote Canyon Rd. To visit Kamp Anza Kampground you should head NW down Coyote Canyon Rd. After 2 miles this road turns E until it reaches Terwilliger Rd. Follow this N to Kamp Anza Kampground. To return to the PCT continue N up Terwilliger Rd, W along Wellman Rd, N up Kirby Rd, then E along the paved Cahuilla Rd to Hwy 74 at the Paradise Corner Café.

There might be water in Nance Canyon, just ahead, in early season.

3. 3:45hr 3630ft 0537180 3702380. Tule Canyon Truck Trail. Turn right here and reach Tule Spring (3480ft, 0537390 3702270) with good water and campsites in 400yds. Unless you are going to visit Anza or the Paradise Corner Café your next reliable water is 20 miles away. Return to the PCT by the same route (15min).

'Adventure is just bad planning.' Raold Amundsen, polar explorer.

'Winners never quit, quitters never win.' Vince Lombardi, US football coach.

Horse Canyon

4570   Alkali Wash

6

Table Mountain Truck Trail

145

Mountain Truck Terrace   5   C

Nance Canyon

4   W   **Coyote Canyon Rd**

140

Tule Canyon Truck Trail   3
Tule Creek   W   2   W   *Tule Spring*

135

8

2. 3:35hr 3580ft 0536730 3702120. Tule Canyon Creek. There is usually murky water here in April but you would be advised to continue to Tule Spring for better quality water.

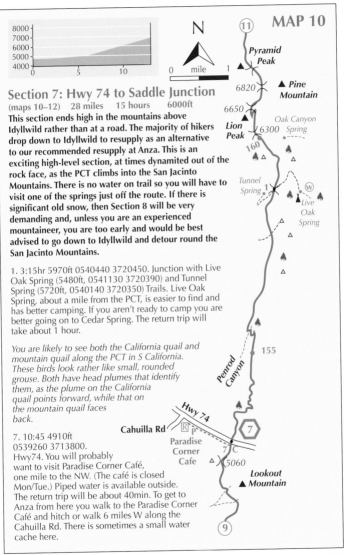

MAP 10

N

0   mile   1

Pyramid Peak

▲ Pine Mountain

6820

6650

Oak Canyon Spring

Lion Peak ▲ 6300

160

Tunnel Spring ⚡ 1

Ⓦ Live Oak Spring

155

Penrod Canyon

Hwy 74

Ⓡ Ⓟ

Cahuilla Rd

Paradise Corner Cafe   7 Ⓒ ▲ 5060

⬡ 7

Lookout ▲ Mountain

⑨

⑪

Section 7: Hwy 74 to Saddle Junction
(maps 10–12)   28 miles   15 hours   6000ft

This section ends high in the mountains above Idyllwild rather than at a road. The majority of hikers drop down to Idyllwild to resupply as an alternative to our recommended resupply at Anza. This is an exciting high-level section, at times dynamited out of the rock face, as the PCT climbs into the San Jacinto Mountains. There is no water on trail so you will have to visit one of the springs just off the route. If there is significant old snow, then Section 8 will be very demanding and, unless you are an experienced mountaineer, you are too early and would be best advised to go down to Idyllwild and detour round the San Jacinto Mountains.

1. 3:15hr 5970ft 0540440 3720450. Junction with Live Oak Spring (5480ft, 0541130 3720390) and Tunnel Spring (5720ft, 0540140 3720350) Trails. Live Oak Spring, about a mile from the PCT, is easier to find and has better camping. If you aren't ready to camp you are better going on to Cedar Spring. The return trip will take about 1 hour.

You are likely to see both the California quail and mountain quail along the PCT in S California. These birds look rather like small, rounded grouse. Both have head plumes that identify them, as the plume on the California quail points forward, while that on the mountain quail faces back.

7. 10:45 4910ft 0539260 3713800. Hwy74. You will probably want to visit Paradise Corner Café, one mile to the NW. (The café is closed Mon/Tue.) Piped water is available outside. The return trip will be about 40min. To get to Anza from here you walk to the Paradise Corner Café and hitch or walk 6 miles W along the Cahuilla Rd. There is sometimes a small water cache here.

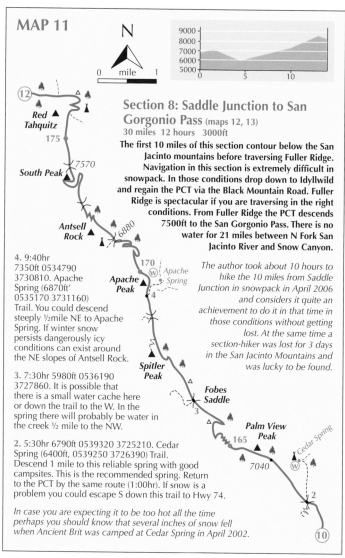

MAP 11

N

0 — mile — 1

9000
8000
7000
6000
5000
0   5   10

(12)

Red Tahquitz ▲

175

7570

South Peak ▲

Antsell Rock ▲

6880

170

Apache Peak ▲   (W) Apache Spring

4

Spitler Peak ▲

Fobes Saddle

3

Palm View Peak ▲

165

7040   Cedar Spring   (W)

2

(10)

Section 8: Saddle Junction to San Gorgonio Pass (maps 12, 13)

30 miles 12 hours 3000ft

The first 10 miles of this section contour below the San Jacinto mountains before traversing Fuller Ridge. Navigation in this section is extremely difficult in snowpack. In those conditions drop down to Idyllwild and regain the PCT via the Black Mountain Road. Fuller Ridge is spectacular if you are traversing in the right conditions. From Fuller Ridge the PCT descends 7500ft to the San Gorgonio Pass. There is no water for 21 miles between N Fork San Jacinto River and Snow Canyon.

The author took about 10 hours to hike the 10 miles from Saddle Junction in snowpack in April 2006 and considers it quite an achievement to do it in that time in those conditions without getting lost. At the same time a section-hiker was lost for 3 days in the San Jacinto Mountains and was lucky to be found.

4. 9:40hr
7350ft 0534790
3730810. Apache
Spring (6870ft'
0535170 3731160)
Trail. You could descend
steeply ½mile NE to Apache
Spring. If winter snow
persists dangerously icy
conditions can exist around
the NE slopes of Antsell Rock.

3. 7:30hr 5980ft 0536190
3727860. It is possible that
there is a small water cache here
or down the trail to the W. In the
spring there will probably be water
in the creek ½ mile to the NW.

2. 5:30hr 6790ft 0539320 3725210. Cedar
Spring (6400ft, 0539250 3726390) Trail.
Descend 1 mile to this reliable spring with good
campsites. This is the recommended spring. Return
to the PCT by the same route (1:00hr). If snow is a
problem you could escape S down this trail to Hwy 74.

*In case you are expecting it to be too hot all the time
perhaps you should know that several inches of snow fell
when Ancient Brit was camped at Cedar Spring in April 2002.*

MAP 12

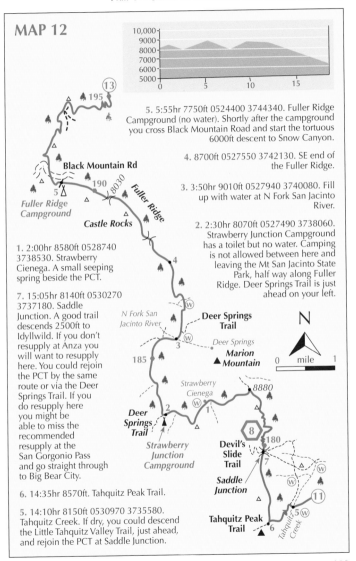

5. 5:55hr 7750ft 0524400 3744340. Fuller Ridge Campground (no water). Shortly after the campground you cross Black Mountain Road and start the tortuous 6000ft descent to Snow Canyon.

4. 8700ft 0527550 3742130. SE end of the Fuller Ridge.

3. 3:50hr 9010ft 0527940 3740080. Fill up with water at N Fork San Jacinto River.

2. 2:30hr 8070ft 0527490 3738060. Strawberry Junction Campground has a toilet but no water. Camping is not allowed between here and leaving the Mt San Jacinto State Park, half way along Fuller Ridge. Deer Springs Trail is just ahead on your left.

1. 2:00hr 8580ft 0528740 3738530. Strawberry Cienega. A small seeping spring beside the PCT.

7. 15:05hr 8140ft 0530270 3737180. Saddle Junction. A good trail descends 2500ft to Idyllwild. If you don't resupply at Anza you will want to resupply here. You could rejoin the PCT by the same route or via the Deer Springs Trail. If you do resupply here you might be able to miss the recommended resupply at the San Gorgonio Pass and go straight through to Big Bear City.

6. 14:35hr 8570ft. Tahquitz Peak Trail.

5. 14:10hr 8150ft 0530970 3735580. Tahquitz Creek. If dry, you could descend the Little Tahquitz Valley Trail, just ahead, and rejoin the PCT at Saddle Junction.

109

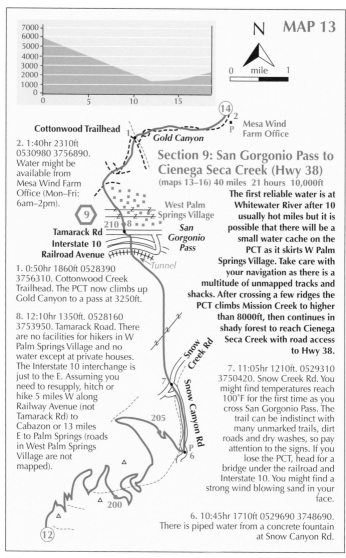

MAP 13

7000
6000
5000
4000
3000
2000
1000
0

0   5   10   15

N

0   mile   1

Cottonwood Trailhead

2. 1:40hr 2310ft
0530980 3756890.
Water might be
available from
Mesa Wind Farm
Office (Mon–Fri:
6am–2pm).

Gold Canyon

Mesa Wind
Farm Office

Section 9: San Gorgonio Pass to Cienega Seca Creek (Hwy 38)

(maps 13–16) 40 miles 21 hours 10,000ft

**The first reliable water is at
Whitewater River after 10
usually hot miles but it is
possible that there will be a
small water cache on the
PCT as it skirts W Palm
Springs Village. Take care with
your navigation as there is a
multitude of unmapped tracks and
shacks. After crossing a few ridges the
PCT climbs Mission Creek to higher
than 8000ft, then continues in
shady forest to reach Cienega
Seca Creek with road access
to Hwy 38.**

**Tamarack Rd
Interstate 10
Railroad Avenue**

*West Palm
Springs Village*

*San
Gorgonio
Pass*

Tunnel

1. 0:50hr 1860ft 0528390
3756310. Cottonwood Creek
Trailhead. The PCT now climbs up
Gold Canyon to a pass at 3250ft.

8. 12:10hr 1350ft. 0528160
3753950. Tamarack Road. There
are no facilities for hikers in W
Palm Springs Village and no
water except at private houses.
The Interstate 10 interchange is
just to the E. Assuming you
need to resupply, hitch or
hike 5 miles W along
Railway Avenue (not
Tamarack Rd) to
Cabazon or 13 miles
E to Palm Springs (roads
in West Palm Springs
Village are not
mapped).

Snow Creek Rd

Snow Canyon Rd

7. 11:05hr 1210ft. 0529310
3750420. Snow Creek Rd. You
might find temperatures reach
100°F for the first time as you
cross San Gorgonio Pass. The
trail can be indistinct with
many unmarked trails, dirt
roads and dry washes, so pay
attention to the signs. If you
lose the PCT, head for a
bridge under the railroad and
Interstate 10. You might find a
strong wind blowing sand in your
face.

6. 10:45hr 1710ft 0529690 3748690.
There is piped water from a concrete fountain
at Snow Canyon Rd.

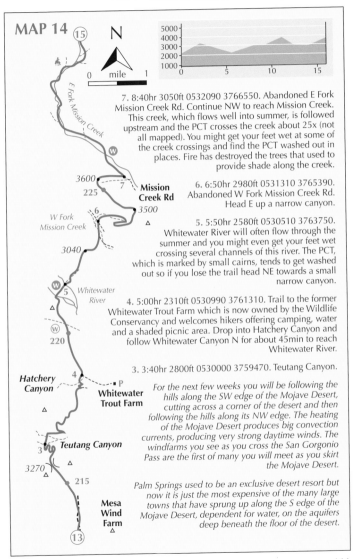

MAP 14

N

0   mile   1

E Fork Mission Creek

3600
225
7   **Mission Creek Rd**
3500

W Fork Mission Creek
6
3040

W
5   *Whitewater River*

W
220

Hatchery Canyon
4

■ P
Whitewater Trout Farm

3   *Teutang Canyon*

3270
215

Mesa Wind Farm

(13)

(15)

7. 8:40hr 3050ft 0532090 3766550. Abandoned E Fork Mission Creek Rd. Continue NW to reach Mission Creek. This creek, which flows well into summer, is followed upstream and the PCT crosses the creek about 25x (not all mapped). You might get your feet wet at some of the creek crossings and find the PCT washed out in places. Fire has destroyed the trees that used to provide shade along the creek.

6. 6:50hr 2980ft 0531310 3765390. Abandoned W Fork Mission Creek Rd. Head E up a narrow canyon.

5. 5:50hr 2580ft 0530510 3763750. Whitewater River will often flow through the summer and you might even get your feet wet crossing several channels of this river. The PCT, which is marked by small cairns, tends to get washed out so if you lose the trail head NE towards a small narrow canyon.

4. 5:00hr 2310ft 0530990 3761310. Trail to the former Whitewater Trout Farm which is now owned by the Wildlife Conservancy and welcomes hikers offering camping, water and a shaded picnic area. Drop into Hatchery Canyon and follow Whitewater Canyon N for about 45min to reach Whitewater River.

3. 3:40hr 2800ft 0530000 3759470. Teutang Canyon.

For the next few weeks you will be following the hills along the SW edge of the Mojave Desert, cutting across a corner of the desert and then following the hills along its NW edge. The heating of the Mojave Desert produces big convection currents, producing very strong daytime winds. The windfarms you see as you cross the San Gorgonio Pass are the first of many you will meet as you skirt the Mojave Desert.

Palm Springs used to be an exclusive desert resort but now it is just the most expensive of the many large towns that have sprung up along the S edge of the Mojave Desert, dependent for water, on the aquifers deep beneath the floor of the desert.

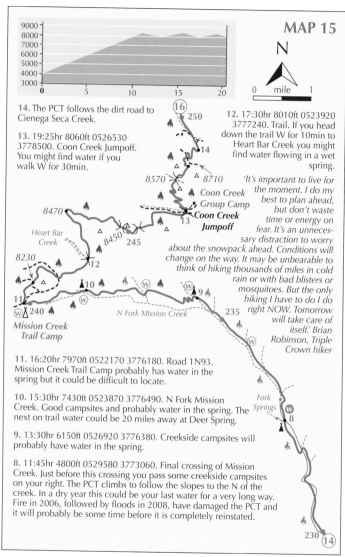

MAP 15

N

0   mile   1

14. The PCT follows the dirt road to Cienega Seca Creek.

13. 19:25hr 8060ft 0526530 3778500. Coon Creek Jumpoff. You might find water if you walk W for 30min.

12. 17:30hr 8010ft 0523920 3777240. Trail. If you head down the trail W for 10min to Heart Bar Creek you might find water flowing in a wet spring.

250

16

14

8570

8710

8470

Coon Creek Group Camp

Coon Creek Jumpoff

13

Heart Bar Creek

8230

8450   245

12

10

11

240

Mission Creek Trail Camp

W   9

235

N Fork Mission Creek

'It's important to live for the moment. I do my best to plan ahead, but don't waste time or energy on fear. It's an unnecessary distraction to worry about the snowpack ahead. Conditions will change on the way. It may be unbearable to think of hiking thousands of miles in cold rain or with bad blisters or mosquitoes. But the only hiking I have to do I do right NOW. Tomorrow will take care of itself.' Brian Robinson, Triple Crown hiker

11. 16:20hr 7970ft 0522170 3776180. Road 1N93. Mission Creek Trail Camp probably has water in the spring but it could be difficult to locate.

10. 15:30hr 7430ft 0523870 3776490. N Fork Mission Creek. Good campsites and probably water in the spring. The next on trail water could be 20 miles away at Deer Spring.

9. 13:30hr 6150ft 0526920 3776380. Creekside campsites will probably have water in the spring.

Fork Springs

W   8

8. 11:45hr 4800ft 0529580 3773060. Final crossing of Mission Creek. Just before this crossing you pass some creekside campsites on your right. The PCT climbs to follow the slopes to the N of the creek. In a dry year this could be your last water for a very long way. Fire in 2006, followed by floods in 2008, have damaged the PCT and it will probably be some time before it is completely reinstated.

230   14

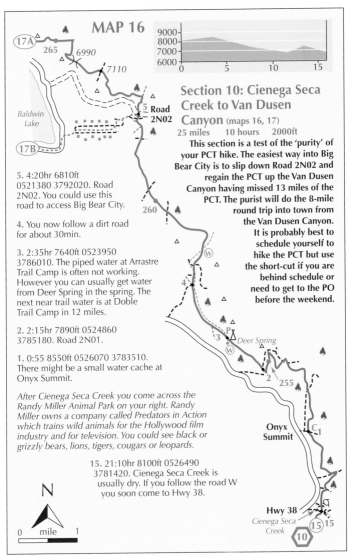

MAP 16

17A 265 6990
7110

Baldwin Lake

17B

5 Road 2N02

Section 10: Cienega Seca Creek to Van Dusen Canyon (maps 16, 17)
25 miles   10 hours   2000ft

This section is a test of the 'purity' of your PCT hike. The easiest way into Big Bear City is to slip down Road 2N02 and regain the PCT up the Van Dusen Canyon having missed 13 miles of the PCT. The purist will do the 8-mile round trip into town from the Van Dusen Canyon. It is probably best to schedule yourself to hike the PCT but use the short-cut if you are behind schedule or need to get to the PO before the weekend.

5. 4:20hr 6810ft 0521380 3792020. Road 2N02. You could use this road to access Big Bear City.

4. You now follow a dirt road for about 30min.

260

3. 2:35hr 7640ft 0523950 3786010. The piped water at Arrastre Trail Camp is often not working. However you can usually get water from Deer Spring in the spring. The next near trail water is at Doble Trail Camp in 12 miles.

W

4

2. 2:15hr 7890ft 0524860 3785180. Road 2N01.

1. 0:55 8550ft 0526070 3783510. There might be a small water cache at Onyx Summit.

P
3 *Deer Spring*
W

255
2

After Cienega Seca Creek you come across the Randy Miller Animal Park on your right. Randy Miller owns a company called Predators in Action which trains wild animals for the Hollywood film industry and for television. You could see black or grizzly bears, lions, tigers, cougars or leopards.

Onyx Summit

C 1

15. 21:10hr 8100ft 0526490 3781420. Cienega Seca Creek is usually dry. If you follow the road W you soon come to Hwy 38.

N

0   mile   1

Hwy 38
Cienega Seca Creek

15 15

10

MAP 17

The author walked across the middle of Baldwin Lake in 2002 but you might find it full of water. The lake is named after Elias Baldwin, owner of the Doble Gold Mine.

Gold rushes were normally started by prospectors finding small flecks of gold (placer gold) in the gravel in the creeks. Prospectors then rushed in to pan the gravel but, more importantly, to try to find the 'mother lode' from which the placer gold had eroded. Placer gold was found in Van Dusen Canyon in the 1860s which soon led to a gold rush. Doble Mine was just one of many sunk on Gold Mountain to search for the mother lode.

9. 9:50hr 7220ft 0510710 3794190. Van Dusen Canyon Rd. Caribou Creek should have water in the spring. There could also be a small water cache. Head S to Big Bear City to resupply and return by the same route (3:00hr).

8. 7:00hr 6900ft 0521690 3790140. Trail on the left down to Doble Trail Camp (6880ft, 0516190 3795060) with toilet and unreliable piped water.

7. 6:50hr 6910ft 0516270 3795680. Doble Rd, 3N08.

6. 6:05hr 6890ft 0518150 3794410. Hwy 18. There could be a small water cache here. You could hitch 5 miles down to Big Bear City. The road isn't good for hiking, but you could walk across the dry lakebed.

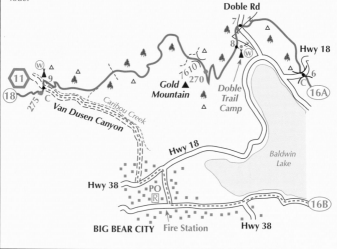

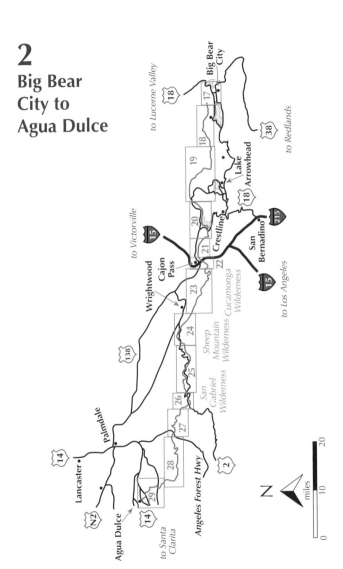

2
Big Bear City to Agua Dulce

to Lucerne Valley

Big Bear City

18

17

to Redlands

38

18

19

Lake Arrowhead

18

20

Crestline

215

21

San Bernadino

22

to Victorville

15

Wrightwood

Cajon Pass

23

Cucamonga Wilderness

15

to Los Angeles

Sheep Mountain Wilderness

24

138

25

San Gabriel Wilderness

26

27

Palmdale

28

Angeles Forest Hwy

2

14

Lancaster

29

N2

14

Agua Dulce

to Santa Clarita

N

miles

0   10   20

PART 2: BIG BEAR CITY TO AGUA DULCE

Section	Distance (miles)	Time (hours)	Ascent (feet)	Maps
11 Van Dusen Canyon–Highway 173	39	14	1000	17–20
12 Highway 173–Highway 138	15	6	1000	20
13 Highway 138–Cajon Pass	13	6	1000	20–22
14 Cajon Pass–Highway 2 (Inspiration Point)	27	14	6000	22–24
15 Inspiration Point– Highway 2 (Islip Summit)	17	9	3000	24, 25
16 Islip Summit–Mill Creek Summit	34	15	5000	25–27
17 Mill Creek Summit–North Fork Ranger Stn	18	8	2000	27, 28
18 North Fork Ranger Stn–Agua Dulce	18	8	2000	28, 29
Part total	**181**	**80**	**21,000**	

This is another varied section, following the line of hills along the southern edge of the Mojave Desert with mountains, rising to 9000ft, separated by sections of chaparral and desert. It is an easy section for hikers who have learnt to cope with the heat but water remains a problem and you must be prepared to carry sufficient quantities between sources.

You pass Deep Creek Hot Springs, possibly the best wilderness hot springs in the country, and Deep Creek and Silverwood Lake offer your first swims on the PCT. Scouts and former scouts will appreciate the ascent of Mount Baden-Powell and at the end of the section you pass through Vasquez County Park, the setting for numerous Hollywood films.

The terrain is predominantly sandy and you can easily find wilderness campsites.

At the time of writing Donna and Geoff Saufley host hikers at Hikers Heaven in Agua Dulce. Most thru'-hikers and many section-hikers visit Hikers Heaven and many take a rest day there.

Best time
May. Earlier if the snow in the San Bernadino, Mount Baden-Powell and the San Gabriel Mountains has melted. By June you will have temperatures in excess of 100°F (38°C) in the lowlands and the creeks and springs might well have dried up.

Permits

No wilderness permits are required. See Part 1 for details about parking permits for cars.

Facilities

It is difficult to resupply in this section without a lot of hitching or hiking well-away from the PCT. It is suggested you top up at the convenience store at Cajon Pass and resupply at Wrightwood and Agua Dulce.

Big Bear City (PO, G, R, A, L, Sh, O, B) (from Van Dusen Canyon) (Sections 10, 11) (0 hours)
See Part 1 for details.

Lake Arrowhead (PO, G, R, A, B) (from Hwy 173) (Section 11, 12) (14 hours)
Cedar Glen PO, 28982 Hook Creek Rd, Cedar Glen CA92321 (909)-337-4614. Mon–Fri: 8.30am–5.00pm, Sat: 9.00am–11.00am
Lake Arrowhead is a mountain resort with town facilities. Smaller Cedar Glen is reached first if you follow Highway 173 from the PCT.
http://lakearrowheadvillage.com

Silverwood Lake Marina (small G, R, C, Sh) (from Hwy 138) (Sections 12, 13) (20 hours)

Bottom pool, Deep Creek Hot Springs (Section 11)

Crestline (PO, G, R, A, L, B) (from Hwy 138) (Sections 12, 13) (20 hours)
Crestline PO, 23921 Lake Dr, Crestline CA92325
(909)-338-5489. Mon–Fri: 9.00am–5.00pm, Sat: 11.00am–1.00pm
Small town facilities

Cajon Pass (P, small G, R, A) (Sections 13, 14) (26 hours)
Cajon Pass has McDonalds and Del Taco Restaurants, two gas stations with mini-marts and a Best Western Hotel. The hotel will hold packages if you book a room.
Best Western Hotel, 8317 US Hwy 138, Phelan CA92371
(760)-249-6777

Wrightwood (PO, G, R, A, O, B) (from Acorn Canyon Trail) (Section 14) (32 hours)
Wrightwood PO, 1440 State Hwy 2, Wrightwood CA92397
(760)-249-8882.
Mon–Fri: 8.45am–5.00pm
Wrightwood is a mountain resort with good facilities for hikers.
www.wrightwoodcalif.com

Agua Dulce (G, R, B) (Sections 18, 19) (83 hours)
Agua Dulce has a good store and three restaurants. In addition, at the time of writing, trail angels run Hikers Heaven.

Hikers Heaven (P, A, C, L, Sh) (Sections 18, 19) (83 hours)

The PCT follows a drainage tunnel under Antelope Highway (Section 18)

Hikers Heaven c/o The Saufleys, 11861 Darling Rd, Agua Dulce CA91390
www.hikerheaven.com, dsaufley@sprynet.com (include PCT in subject line)
Apr 1–Jun 30 and Sept 15–Oct 31 for PCT hikers
Maximum two nights stay. Hikers Heaven offers a package service and is a gathering point for PCT hikers and a source of trail information.

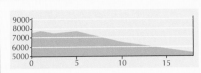

MAP 18

Section 11: Van Dusen Canyon to Hwy 173

(maps 17–20)

39 miles 14 hours 1000ft

After an undulating start you will reach Holcomb Creek and then, for the next 30 miles, you will be descending Holcomb Creek and Deep Creek. The PCT passes Deep Creek Hot Springs, which is an excellent place to take a break. The first reliable water is after 10 miles, after which you will have occasional access to the creeks. This is an easy section but it is exposed in places because of fire damage.

The massive Willow Fire in August 1999, started by a careless camper, burnt much of the hillside between Holcomb Creek and Mojave River Forks Reservoir Dam. Unfortunately most of the trees along Holcomb Creek and Deep Creek that were spared the 1999 fire were destroyed by another in 2008.

4. 6:45hr 5480ft 0495320 3792690. The PCT crosses Holcomb Creek and then Road 3N16 and follows a rocky path before crossing back to the N bank of the creek.

3. 4:35hr 6500ft 0501630 3795460. Holcomb Creek might run through the summer. Little Bear Springs Trail Camp has been destroyed by fire and it might be a long time before it is reinstated. After crossing Holcomb Creek the PCT stays on the slopes above the creek for 6 miles.

2. 2:50hr 7670ft 0505020 3794990. Road 3N12.

1. 1:40hr 7440ft 0507640 3793620. Road 2N09.

Mojave River Forks Reservoir Dam on Map 19 is another engineering disaster. The dam was built with irrigation of the surrounding land in mind, but it was then discovered that there wasn't enough water so the dam was never used for that purpose. The dam is now part of a flood control system in case the Cedar Springs Dam fails.

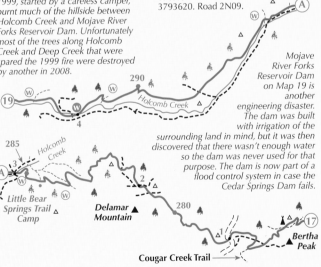

119

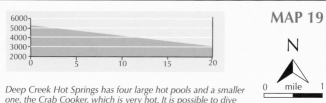

Deep Creek Hot Springs has four large hot pools and a smaller one, the Crab Cooker, which is very hot. It is possible to dive into Deep Creek from rocks into a pool which is warmed from the springs. The springs are costumes-optional and skinny-dipping is traditional. Before the USFS discouraged misuse of the area, the springs were frequented by hippies and were regularly used by the cult leader Charles Manson.

The rare arroyo southwestern toad is found at the hot springs.

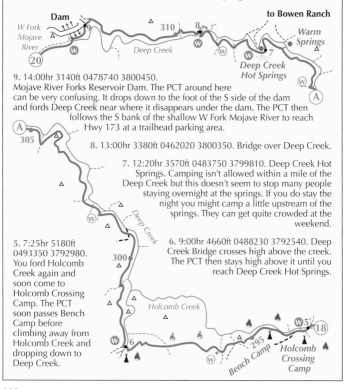

9. 14:00hr 3140ft 0478740 3800450.
Mojave River Forks Reservoir Dam. The PCT around here can be very confusing. It drops down to the foot of the S side of the dam and fords Deep Creek near where it disappears under the dam. The PCT then follows the S bank of the shallow W Fork Mojave River to reach Hwy 173 at a trailhead parking area.

8. 13:00hr 3380ft 0462020 3800350. Bridge over Deep Creek.

7. 12:20hr 3570ft 0483750 3799810. Deep Creek Hot Springs. Camping isn't allowed within a mile of the Deep Creek but this doesn't seem to stop many people staying overnight at the springs. If you do stay the night you might camp a little upstream of the springs. They can get quite crowded at the weekend.

6. 9:00hr 4660ft 0488230 3792540. Deep Creek Bridge crosses high above the creek. The PCT then stays high above it until you reach Deep Creek Hot Springs.

5. 7:25hr 5180ft 0493350 3792980. You ford Holcomb Creek again and soon come to Holcomb Crossing Camp. The PCT soon passes Bench Camp before climbing away from Holcomb Creek and dropping down to Deep Creek.

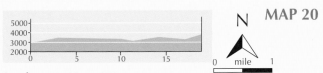

MAP 20

N

0   mile   1

Section 12: Hwy 173 to Hwy 138 (map 20)

15 miles   6 hours   1000ft

A short, easy low-level section which has little shade and can get very hot. Silverwood Lake has sandy beaches which are good for a refreshing swim.

3. 4:35hr 3330ft 0469530 3795770. The small beach where you first drop down to Silverwood Lake is your best spot for a swim before the PCT climbs well above the W shore of the lake.

4. Officially the PCT stays above the Cleghorn Picnic Area (3370ft, 0467980 3794100), but hikers will drop down for the piped water, toilets and possibly a swim. Descend the dirt road just after going under the pylons. This is your last water for 13 miles. Follow the entrance road W and it will take you to Hwy 138.

10. 14:30hr 3120ft 0477390 3799520. There might be a small water cache here. You could hitch E along Hwy 173 to Cedar Glen and Lake Arrowhead.

1. 1:35hr 3300ft 0475590 3796870. Grass Valley Creek usually has water in the spring. The PCT now winds in and out of gullies as it parallels Hwy 173. The only water before the Cleghorn Picnic Area is in Silverwood Lake.

2. 3:50hr 3170ft 0470620 3796460. Cedar Springs Dam, S of you, is 250ft high. Walk along Hwy 173 for about 10min, then the PCT angles up to your left.

5. 6:00hr 3410ft 0467300 3794130. Hwy 138. The PCT passes under Hwy 138. You could hitch SE to Crestline or walk 2 miles SE to the Silverwood Lake Marina.

Hwy 138

A

Cleghorn Picnic Area

325

Silverwood Lake

10 19

12 C

21

13

5

4

P

315

3520

W

330

to Silverwood Lake Marina

W

Grass Valley

W 1

Spillway

2

Hwy 173

A

3 Silverwood Lake

Cedar Springs Dam

320

Tracks and powerlines not mapped

MAP 21

Section 13: Hwy 138 to Cajon Pass (maps 20–22)

13 miles   6 hours   1000ft

This is another short, exposed section with little shade. Your first reliable water will be at Crowder Canyon near the end of the section. The start of the section can be a little unclear but it goes parallel to Road 2N47 before climbing steeply to the Cleghorn Ridge.

Horsethief Canyon, to the N, and Little Horsethief Canyon are named to commemorate the pursuit by Captain Gabriel Moraga of a group of Indians accused of horse rustling in 1819.

4. 5:25hr 3130ft 0457530 3797060. Crowder Canyon Creek usually has water in the spring. This is the last on-trail water for too long to contemplate! Fill up with water here or at the interchange on Interstate 15.

Section 14: Cajon Pass to Hwy 2 (Inspiration Point)

(maps 22–24)

27 miles   14 hours   6000ft

This is a tough section. The first reliable water will be after about 26 miles, early in Section 15. However, most hikers will drop down to Wrightwood to resupply, when the first water will still be 26 miles away. Resupplying at Wrightwood will add about 9 miles and 2500ft of ascent to your hike. If you are lucky trail angels will be maintaining a water cache in Swarthout Canyon, 5 miles into the section, but you should not depend on it. There is little shade until you reach the lightly wooded ridge. It is sensible to do the bulk of the 5000ft climb to Blue Ridge in the cool of the morning.

After heading under Interstate 15, the route is complex so you will have to pay attention to the navigation.

'Foot care is critical. At the first sign of a problem, I stop and find a solution. Even if the only solution is to rest 15 minutes every hour, that's much more efficient than having to recuperate for days.' Brian Robinson, Triple Crown hiker

3. 4:10hr 3830ft 0460170 379720. Road under powerline. You soon begin descending through eroded badlands.

2. 3:05hr 3570ft 0462280. Little Horsethief Canyon is usually dry.

1. 1:40hr 4130ft 0465210 3794910. Cleghorn Ridge. The creek ahead might have water in early season.

MAP 22

The San Andreas Fault cuts through Cajon Pass. Over the past 30 million years the rocks to the W of the fault have migrated hundreds of miles to the NW. The San Andreas Fault is still active today and has caused many earthquakes in S California, including the San Francisco Earthquake of 1906 when the fault line moved 20ft in places.

In 2010 there was a 15-mile detour in section 14 because of damage from the 2009 Sheep Fire on Lytle Creek Ridge.

Cajon Pass is the major communication link between Los Angeles and the rest of the US. It has Interstate 15, the Southern Pacific Railroad and the Atchison-Topeka and Santa Fe Railroad, as well as major powerlines carrying electricity from the Colorado River hydro-electric power stations. It is also a major route for exporting pollution from LA into the Mojave Desert and you shouldn't be surprised to see a yellow smog in the pass. The vegetation has enough problems coping with the desert conditions without having to put up with the pollutants. The lack of vegetation has contributed to widespread erosion, mainly caused by flash floods.

A Mojave Indian trail, which has existed on Cajon Pass for centuries, was used by the Spanish when they settled in Southern California. Then, in 1849, Jefferson Hunt led seven Mormon wagons over the pass and camped at Salt Creek where they discovered gold and started a gold rush in Southern California. The Santa Fe and Salt Lake Trail (also known as the Mormon Road) developed. The Mormon Rocks are also named after the Mormons – the first white settlers to colonise the San Bernadino Valley. They used the Cajon Pass to communicate with Salt Lake City.

'On the trail, aches and pains are my friends. The real enemy is an injury that could end my hike. Pain is an early warning system. I neither mask it nor curse it.' Brian Robinson, Triple Crown hiker

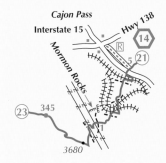

1. 1:15hr 3360ft 0456090 3794840. Road.

5. 5:40hr 3100ft 0457100 3796160. Interstate 15, Cajon Pass. Most hikers visit the facilities at the interchange on Interstate 15, taking a road to the right to reach the interchange in about 10min. The interchange has fast food restaurants, mini-marts and a hotel. Return to the PCT by the same route (20 min).

MAP 23

N

0 mile 1

8. 12:35hr 8260ft 0439730 3800230. Guffy Campground. There is a spring 200yd N down Flume Canyon (8060ft, 0439770 3800400). A faint trail leads to the spring from about 50yd E of the campground. Hikers have had difficulty finding the spring.

'Hike your own hike. The trail experience is more mental than physical, as your body will strengthen along the way.' Tom Caggiano, Appalachian Trail thru'-hiker

7. 12:00hr 8250ft 0440980 3799670. Acorn Canyon Trail is fairly obvious, but not signed (2009). It is suggested that you descend this trail to Wrightwood to resupply. Stay overnight and return by the same route in the morning. The round trip is about 9 miles with 2500ft of ascent (5 hours).

6. 8:10hr 6430ft 0445760 3797080. The road-end E of Gobblers Knob has poor campsites.

5. 7:40hr 6270ft 0446660 3796870. Road 3N31.

4. 5:10hr 5150ft 0451290 3794760. Road 3N29.

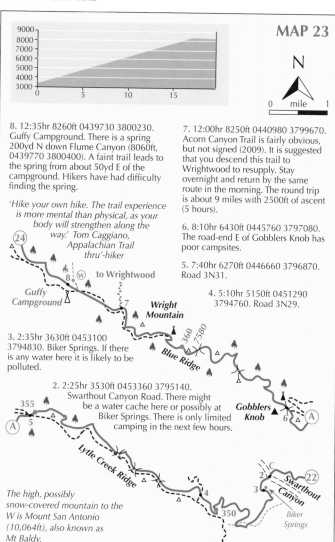

3. 2:35hr 3630ft 0453100 3794830. Biker Springs. If there is any water here it is likely to be polluted.

2. 2:25hr 3530ft 0453360 3795140. Swarthout Canyon Road. There might be a water cache here or possibly at Biker Springs. There is only limited camping in the next few hours.

The high, possibly snow-covered mountain to the W is Mount San Antonio (10,064ft), also known as Mt Baldy.

MAP 24

4. 3:25hr 7770ft. Unsigned 100yd spur trail to Lamel Spring (0430400 3803180), which is reliable in the spring. You can camp beside the PCT just after the spring.

3. 1:40hr 6590ft 0430830 3803790. Hwy 2 at Vincent Gap. There is only limited camping until you reach Little Jimmy Campground.

2. 7480ft 0432560 3804840. Spur to Jackson Flat Group Campground with toilets and piped water.

1. 0:20hr 7340ft 0433600 3804030. Grassy Hollow Visitor Centre is worth a visit but is only open at weekends from 10.00am–4.00pm. Piped water and toilets are available when the centre is closed.

10. 14:15hr 7380ft 0434570 3803620. Hwy 2 at Inspiration Point. Toilets but no water. You could hitch NE down to Big Pines and E to Wrightwood. There are good views of Mt Baden-Powell to the W. The PCT now stays close to Hwy 2 until Three Points, over 30 miles away.

Section 15: Hwy 2 (Inspiration Point) to Hwy 2 (Islip Saddle) (maps 24, 25)
17 miles   9 hours   3000ft

The main feature of this section is the ascent of 9400ft Mt Baden-Powell and the gradual descent down its W ridge. There are two well-placed springs which are reliable in the spring.

Mt Baden-Powell is named after Lord Baden-Powell, the founder of the Boy Scout movement. There is a memorial on the summit with 4 plaques commemorating his life and the scouting movement. Mt Baden-Powell is the E terminus of the Silver Moccasin Trail, Scouting's 53-mile challenge walk through the San Gabriel Mountains, which the PCT follows for 23 miles.

Grassy Hollow Visitor Centre has a superb display of the animals and birds of the mountains of Southern California.

'Blessed is the man who expects nothing, for he shall never be disappointed.' Alexander Pope.

Black oaks spread their branches below ponderosa pines at altitudes between 5000–7000ft.

9. 13:30hr 7920ft 0436790 3802230. Blue Ridge Campground.

MAP 25

0 mile 1

7. 8:40hr 6620ft 0421730 3802070.
Hwy 2 at Islip Saddle.

6: 7:55hr 7470ft 0423700 3800780.
Little Jimmy Spring runs well into
the summer. Little Jimmy
Campground, with toilets, is a little
further up the PCT.

5. 6:00hr 9240ft 0429760 3802310.
Mt Baden-Powell Spur Trail. You are
best to ignore the PCT here and
continue to the summit of Mt
Baden-Powell (9399ft), then regain
the PCT by descending the NW
ridge. In snowpack you will find the
summit route is much easier than
the PCT. The PCT now skirts Mt
Burnham and Throop Peak to arrive
at Windy Gap. Shortly after, you will
see reliable Little Jimmy Spring on
your right.

*Wally Waldron Tree, on the bare
summit ridge of Mt Baden-Powell, is
a limber pine, reckoned to be over
1500 years old. It has been
dedicated to the memory of Wally
Waldron for his efforts on behalf of
the Boy Scouts of America.*

Section 16: Hwy 2 (Islip Summit) to Mill Creek Summit

(maps 25–27) 34 miles 15 hours 5000ft
(by official diversion)

**Initially the trail parallels Hwy 2, crossing it
occasionally. Once you leave Hwy 2 you
wind in and out of gullies on N facing
slopes until you reach Mill Creek Summit
Ranger Station. The section starts with a
1200ft climb of the S ridge of Mt
Williamson before regaining Hwy 2. At the
time of writing (2009) the PCT is closed
after Eagles Roost Picnic Area. It is unlikely
that the PCT will reopen, so the official
diversion is the main route described.**

*You are now walking round the Los Angeles
Basin. You can expect to be in bright
sunshine, above the cloud and smog you
can see to the SW. A combination of the hills
surrounding LA and frequent temperature
inversions in the atmosphere prevent smoke
from escaping from the LA Basin, and LA
had a pollution problem from campfires
long before the modern city was built!*

*Question: 'What were you most afraid of?'
Answer: 'Failure!'
Ken Haddow, Arctic Explorer.*

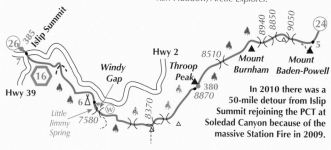

In 2010 there was a
50-mile detour from Islip
Summit rejoining the PCT at
Soledad Canyon because of the
massive Station Fire in 2009.

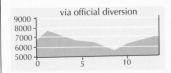

MAP 26

6. 6:40hr 7040ft 0414020 3801540.
Cloudburst Summit (4:20hr via Hwy 2).

5. 5:20 6260ft 0415320 3802560. Cooper
Canyon Trail Camp.

4. 4:30hr 5760ft. Regain the PCT in
Cooper Canyon. Water is likely well into
summer.

3. 3:35hr 6560ft. Take the paved minor dirt
road, which is the exit from Buckthorn Flat
Campground, to the campground (piped
water) and follow signs to the Buckhart
Trail, which you follow to regain the PCT.

2. 2:35hr 6630ft 0419260 3801820. Eagles
Roost Picnic Area. The next section of the
PCT is likely to be closed to protect the
habitat of the rare mountain yellow-legged
frog. Follow Hwy 2 until Buckthorn Flat
Campground. The official diversion then
descends the spectacular Buckhart Trail to
regain the PCT in Cooper Canyon. It is
possible to continue along Hwy 2 and
regain the PCT at Cloudburst Summit.

1. 2:05hr 6710ft 0419990 3802630.
Hwy 2.

Section 17: Mill Creek Summit to N Fork Ranger Station (maps 27, 28)
18 miles   8 hours   2000ft

The PCT goes parallel to Road 3N17 for most of this easy section. Water can be a problem as there are no totally reliable water sources until the piped water at the end of the section but there might be water at Messenger Flats Campground.

100 years ago the mountain yellow-legged frog was one of the most common vertebrates in the area but now it is close to extinction. In S California it is restricted to fewer than 10 sites with fewer than 100 adult frogs. There are also small populations in the Sierra Nevada.

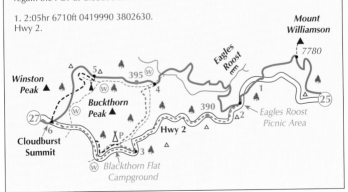

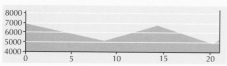

MAP 27

0   mile   1

9. 14:40hr 5000ft 0400630 3805920. There is piped water and toilets at the picnic area at Mill Creek Trailhead, just above Mill Creek Ranger Station. If the water is off there you can get water from hoses outside the ranger station.

8. 12:30hr 6750ft 0405030 3805750. Ridgetop. There is camping about 15min ahead but then camping is very limited until Mill Creek Summit.

7. 9:50hr 5230ft 0408900 3803260. Trail to Sulphur Springs Campground. If you haven't been able to get water on the PCT, you should find water at Sulphur Springs (5220ft, 0409030 3803350) in the spring. You will pass Fiddleneck Spring (6240ft, 0405960 3804320) and Fountainhead Spring (6420ft, 0405570 3804850), both of doubtful quality if they aren't dry, but the next reliable water is at Mill Creek Summit.

6. 8:30hr 5860ft 0409520 3800590. Hwy 2 at Three Points. Take care to follow the PCT and not the Silver Moccasin Trail, which separate here. There could be a small water cache here. Newcomb's Ranch Restaurant is just over 1 mile W.

5. There is good camping and possible water down this creek, as well as a possible trickling spring (6240ft, 0411060 3800840) beside the trail.

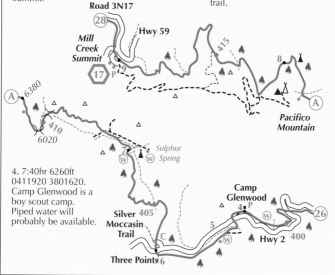

Road 3N17

Hwy 59

Mill Creek Summit

415

8

A   6380

410

6020

Pacifico Mountain

Sulphur Spring

Camp Glenwood

4. 7:40hr 6260ft 0411920 3801620. Camp Glenwood is a boy scout camp. Piped water will probably be available.

Silver 405 Moccasin Trail

5

Hwy 2   400

Three Points 6

MAP 28

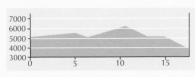

N

0 mile 1

Section 18: North Fork Ranger Station to Agua Dulce

(maps 28, 29)   18 miles   8 hours   2000ft

This exposed low-level section starts with a dusty descent to Mattox Canyon and crosses a number of low ridges before entering Vasquez Rocks County Park just before Agua Dulce.

The striped skunk, a black animal about the size of a badger with a white stripe along either side of its back that makes it look like a comic book animal, can be seen in these parts. A close encounter is not a good idea as, if threatened, it gives off a fine spray of yellow odoriferous liquid. The author, who saw one in Mattox Canyon, was advised that the only way to hide the odour of the skunk was to take a bath in tomato sauce!

4. 7:30hr 4210ft 0384890 3805840. N Fork Ranger Station has a picnic area with toilets. There is piped water at the ranger station.

3. 5:25hr 5880ft 0390610 3805070. Trail to Messenger Flats Campground. Toilets. The piped water is often off but you might find water at Moody Canyon Rd about a mile ahead.

2. 3:35hr 5460ft. The PCT approaches road at a trail junction. There is no campsite until the top of the climb.

1. 1:30hr 5580ft 0398260 3806620. Road 3N17. There are no camping opportunities before Big Buck Trail Camp.

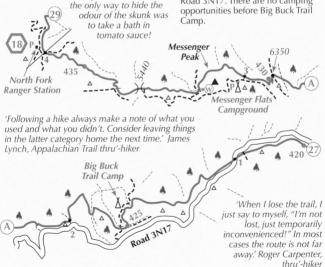

'Following a hike always make a note of what you used and what you didn't. Consider leaving things in the latter category home the next time.' James Lynch, Appalachian Trail thru'-hiker

'When I lose the trail, I just say to myself, "I'm not lost, just temporarily inconvenienced!" In most cases the route is not far away.' Roger Carpenter, thru'-hiker

129

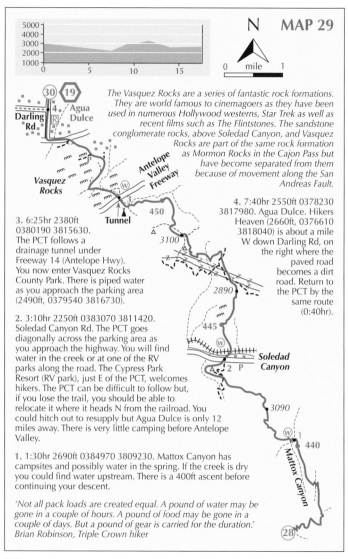

N   MAP 29

0   mile   1

The Vasquez Rocks are a series of fantastic rock formations. They are world famous to cinemagoers as they have been used in numerous Hollywood westerns, Star Trek as well as recent films such as The Flintstones. The sandstone conglomerate rocks, above Soledad Canyon, and Vasquez Rocks are part of the same rock formation as Mormon Rocks in the Cajon Pass but have become separated from them because of movement along the San Andreas Fault.

4. 7:40hr 2550ft 0378230 3817980. Agua Dulce. Hikers Heaven (2660ft, 0376610 3818040) is about a mile W down Darling Rd, on the right where the paved road becomes a dirt road. Return to the PCT by the same route (0:40hr).

3. 6:25hr 2380ft 0380190 3815630. The PCT follows a drainage tunnel under Freeway 14 (Antelope Hwy). You now enter Vasquez Rocks County Park. There is piped water as you approach the parking area (2490ft, 0379540 3816730).

2. 3:10hr 2250ft 0383070 3811420. Soledad Canyon Rd. The PCT goes diagonally across the parking area as you approach the highway. You will find water in the creek or at one of the RV parks along the road. The Cypress Park Resort (RV park), just E of the PCT, welcomes hikers. The PCT can be difficult to follow but, if you lose the trail, you should be able to relocate it where it heads N from the railroad. You could hitch out to resupply but Agua Dulce is only 12 miles away. There is very little camping before Antelope Valley.

1. 1:30hr 2690ft 0384970 3809230. Mattox Canyon has campsites and possibly water in the spring. If the creek is dry you could find water upstream. There is a 400ft ascent before continuing your descent.

'Not all pack loads are created equal. A pound of water may be gone in a couple of hours. A pound of food may be gone in a couple of days. But a pound of gear is carried for the duration.'
Brian Robinson, Triple Crown hiker

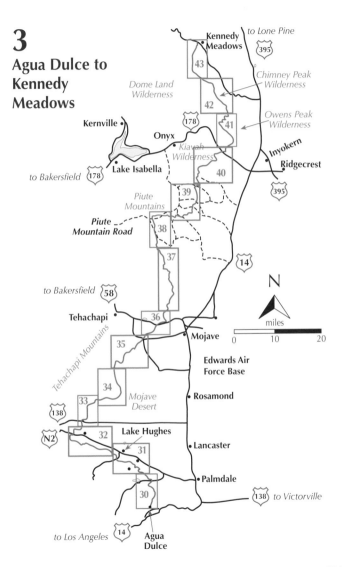

3
Agua Dulce to Kennedy Meadows

to Lone Pine

Kennedy Meadows

395

43

Chimney Peak Wilderness

Dome Land Wilderness

42

178

41

Owens Peak Wilderness

Kernville

Onyx

Kiavah Wilderness

Inyokern

Ridgecrest

40

to Bakersfield 178

Lake Isabella

395

Piute Mountains

39

Piute Mountain Road

38

37

to Bakersfield 58

14

N

miles

0   10   20

Tehachapi

36

Mojave

35

Edwards Air Force Base

Tehachapi Mountains

34

Mojave Desert

Rosamond

33

138

Lake Hughes

N2

32

31

Lancaster

30

138 to Victorville

Palmdale

to Los Angeles 14

Agua Dulce

PART 3: AGUA DULCE TO KENNEDY MEADOWS

Section	Distance (miles)	Time (hours)	Ascent (feet)	Maps
19 Agua Dulce–Elizabeth Lake Canyon Rd	31	14	4000	29–31
20 Elizabeth Lake Canyon Rd–Highway 138	32	14	4000	31–33
21 Highway 138–Cottonwood Creek	18	6	400	33, 34
22 Cottonwood Creek–Tehachapi Pass	31	15	5000	34–36
23 Tehachapi Pass–Piute Mountain Rd	42	19	5000	36–38
24 Piute Mountain Rd–Bird Spring Pass	23	10	2000	38, 39
25 Bird Spring Pass–Walker Pass	21	9	2000	39, 40
26 Walker Pass–Canebrake Rd	29	14	5000	40–42
27 Canebrake Rd–Kennedy Meadows	21	10	5000	42, 43
Part total	**248**	**111**	**32,000**	

The PCT completes its traverse of the mountains along the south-west edge of the Mojave Desert before cutting across its western corner and following the mountains along its north-eastern edge. At Tehachapi Pass you enter the Sierra Nevada and head north but the terrain and climate in this southern section of the range are similar to that of Southern California.

At the time of writing a major reroute is planned, to keep the PCT in the mountains to the west of the Mojave Desert. That is likely to add a day's hiking to this section. (See Map 31.)

The hiking is relatively easy as the mountains are lower than those to the south. This, however, is another section where heat and water shortages

present problems. Convection currents from the heating of the Mojave Desert can produce very strong winds and you will pass many wind farms. The soil is predominantly sandy and the only problem finding wilderness campsites is finding spots sheltered from strong winds.

For section-hikers intending to hike Part 4 from south to north, there is a case for starting at Walker Pass, in this section, to allow longer acclimatisation before reaching Forester Pass.

Best time

May. The earlier you hike this section, the cooler it will be and the more chance you have of finding water. Go as soon as the snow has melted

Joshua tree, Mojave Desert (Section 21)

in the Piute Mountains, which could be April in a low snow year. It will be too hot in summer for most hikers and water could be a serious problem.

Permits
See Part 1 introduction for information on parking permits for cars.

No wilderness permits are required but you need a fire permit if you intend to light fires in Sequoia National Forest.

Sequoia National Forest (Sections 23–27)
Sequoia National Forest, 1839, S Newcomb St, Porterville CA93257 (559)-784-1500, www.fs.fed.us/r5/sequoia

Facilities
Agua Dulce (G, R, B) and **Hikers Heaven** (P, A, C, L, Sh) (Sections 18, 19) (0 hours)
See Part 2 introduction.

Green Valley (small G, R) (from San Francisquito Canyon Rd) (Section 19) (11 hours)
Trail angels: Joe and Terrie Anderson in Green Valley maintain three water caches and provide hospitality and local transport to PCT hikers. (661)-270-0155, joedaddy44@aol.com

Lake Hughes (PO, G, R, A, C, Sh, B) (from Elizabeth Lake Canyon Rd) (Sections 19, 20) (14 hours)
Lake Hughes PO, 16817 Elizabeth Lake Rd, Lake Hughes CA93532 (661)-724-9281. Mon–Fri: 8.00am–12.30pm, 1.30pm–5.00pm
Good facilities for a small town.

Hikertown (P, C, L, Sh) (Hwy 138) (Sections 20, 21) (28 hours)
Hikertown, 26803, W Avenue C-15, Lancaster CA93536
www.hikertown.com, bobmayon@verizon.net

Hikertown, run by trail angels, is on the PCT where it crosses Highway 138 at 269th St W. You can camp on the lawn or stay in the bunkhouse (free but donations appreciated). Private rooms available for $20 donation. Transport available to Gil's Country store. Hikertown will hold packages for hikers.

Gils Country Store (P, small G, B) (Hwy 138) (Sections 20, 21) (29 hours)
Gils Feed Country Store, 28105 W Avenue C6, Lancaster CA93536
(661)-724-1028
This small store will hold packages for hikers.

Lancaster (PO, G, R, A, L, O, B) (from Hwy 138) (Sections 20, 21) (29 hours)
Lancaster PO, 43824 20th St W, Lancaster CA93534
(661)-948-7251,
Mon–Fri: 9.00am–5.00pm,
Sat: 9.00am–3.00pm
Lancaster is a large town.

Tehachapi (PO, G, R, A, L, B) (from Willow Springs Rd or Tehachapi Pass) (Sections 22, 23) (45 or 49 hours)
Tehachapi PO, 1085 Voyager Dr, Tehachapi CA93561
(661)-822-0279. Mon–Fri: 8.30am–5.30pm, Sat: 10.00am–2.00pm
Full town facilities.

Mojave (PO, G, R, A, L, B) (from Willow Springs Rd or Tehachapi Pass)

A PCT sign riddled with bullet holes (Section 19)

(Sections 22, 23) (45 or 49 hours)
Mojave PO, 2053 Belshaw St, Mojave CA93501
(661)-824-3502. Mon–Fri: 8.30am–5.30pm, Sat: 10.00am–4.00pm
Mojave is a small town.

Onyx (PO, small G) (from Walker Pass) (Sections 25, 26) (87 hours)
Onyx PO, 8275 Easy St, Onyx CA93255
(760)-378-2121. Mon–Fri: 9.30am–1.00pm, 1.45pm–4.00pm
Buses run west from Onyx to Lake Isabella and on to Bakersfield.

Lake Isabella (PO, G, A, R, L, B) (from Walker Pass) (Sections 25, 26) (87 hours)
Lake Isabella PO, Lake Isabella CA93240
(760)-379-2553.

Mayan Peak (Section 24)

Mon–Fri: 9.00am–4.00pm
Lake Isabella is a small town.

Ridgecrest (PO, G, R, A, L, O, B)
(from Walker Pass) (Sections 25,26)
(87 hours)
Ridgecrest PO, 101E Coso Avenue
CA93555
Mon–Fri: 8.30am–5.00pm,
Sat: 9.00am–2.00pm
Ridgecrest is a large town with all
facilities.

Kennedy Meadows (P, small G, C, L,
Sh) (Sections 27, 28) (111 hours)
Kennedy Meadows General Store,
PO Box 3A5, Inyokern CA93527
(559)-850-5647, Mon–Sun: 9.00am–
5.00pm
Kennedy Meadows Store offers a
package service for a nominal fee.
You should send packages at least

two weeks in advance. The store has
only a limited supply of backpacking food and is not really suitable for
supplying the long roadless section
ahead. However the store is very
hiker-friendly and is a gathering place
for hikers and does serve snacks.
You could camp at the store or at
Kennedy Meadows Campground.
There is a restaurant about three
miles to the south-east.

Resupply
It is suggested that you resupply
at Hikertown, Mojave, Onyx and
Kennedy Meadows. Gil's Country
Store and Kennedy Meadows Store
are the only stores in this section and
neither has a good selection of food
for backpackers. There are no other
facilities on the route.

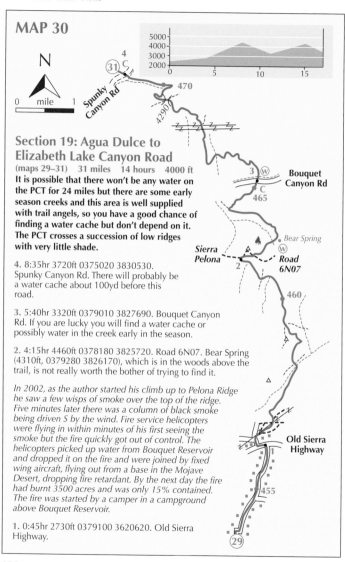

MAP 30

N

0   mile   1

Spunky Canyon Rd

4   C   31

470

4290

3   W   **Bouquet Canyon Rd**

C   465

Bear Spring

Sierra Pelona

2   **Road 6N07**

W

460

455

Old Sierra Highway

1

29

Section 19: Agua Dulce to Elizabeth Lake Canyon Road

(maps 29–31)   31 miles   14 hours   4000 ft

It is possible that there won't be any water on the PCT for 24 miles but there are some early season creeks and this area is well supplied with trail angels, so you have a good chance of finding a water cache but don't depend on it. The PCT crosses a succession of low ridges with very little shade.

4. 8:35hr 3720ft 0375020 3830530. Spunky Canyon Rd. There will probably be a water cache about 100yd before this road.

3. 5:40hr 3320ft 0379010 3827690. Bouquet Canyon Rd. If you are lucky you will find a water cache or possibly water in the creek early in the season.

2. 4:15hr 4460ft 0378180 3825720. Road 6N07. Bear Spring (4310ft, 0379280 3826170), which is in the woods above the trail, is not really worth the bother of trying to find it.

In 2002, as the author started his climb up to Pelona Ridge he saw a few wisps of smoke over the top of the ridge. Five minutes later there was a column of black smoke being driven S by the wind. Fire service helicopters were flying in within minutes of his first seeing the smoke but the fire quickly got out of control. The helicopters picked up water from Bouquet Reservoir and dropped it on the fire and were joined by fixed wing aircraft, flying out from a base in the Mojave Desert, dropping fire retardant. By the next day the fire had burnt 3500 acres and was only 15% contained. The fire was started by a camper in a campground above Bouquet Reservoir.

1. 0:45hr 2730ft 0379100 3620620. Old Sierra Highway.

MAP 31

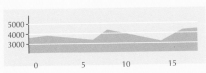

Section 20: Elizabeth Lake Canyon Road to Hwy 138
(maps 31–33)

32 miles   14 miles   4000ft

In a dry spring the only water in this section could be water provided by trail angels. The PCT runs parallel to dirt roads along the long ridge of Sawmill Mountain before dropping down to Pine Canyon Rd. Then an unsatisfactory section of trail brings you to Hwy 138 at Neenach. A major reroute is planned that will continue 3 miles NW from Liebre Mountain, before going down to the Mojave Desert and rejoining the PCT in the Tehachapi Hills. This will involve building 60 miles of new trail so it could be some time before it is open. It will add about a day to the trail.

1. 1:05hr 3700ft 0365640 3837070. You might find a little spring dripping from a tree-root to the left of the PCT.

7. 14:30hr 3050ft 0366180 3836270. Elizabeth Lake Canyon Rd. There might be a water cache on the approach to this road. Lake Hughes is 2 miles N.

6. 12:35hr 4290ft 0371270 3834150. Grass Mountain Rd.

5. 11:10hr 3390ft 0372600 3833390. San Francisquito Canyon Rd. You should walk 3min SW to Green Valley Ranger Station, with a picnic area where you will probably find water. If there isn't any you will have to follow the road 2 miles SW to Green Valley. You might find the only water in the next 40 miles is that provided by trail angels. Return to PCT by the same route.

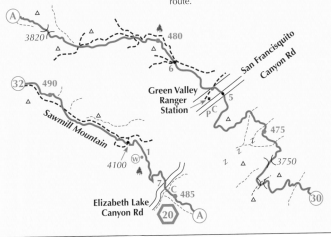

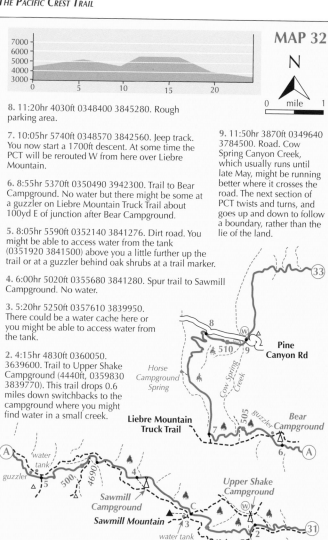

MAP 32

N

0 — mile — 1

8. 11:20hr 4030ft 0348400 3845280. Rough parking area.

7. 10:05hr 5740ft 0348570 3842560. Jeep track. You now start a 1700ft descent. At some time the PCT will be rerouted W from here over Liebre Mountain.

6. 8:55hr 5370ft 0350490 3942300. Trail to Bear Campground. No water but there might be some at a guzzler on Liebre Mountain Truck Trail about 100yd E of junction after Bear Campground.

5. 8:05hr 5590ft 0352140 3841276. Dirt road. You might be able to access water from the tank (0351920 3841500) above you a little further up the trail or at a guzzler behind oak shrubs at a trail marker.

4. 6:00hr 5020ft 0355680 3841280. Spur trail to Sawmill Campground. No water.

3. 5:20hr 5250ft 0357610 3839950. There could be a water cache here or you might be able to access water from the tank.

2. 4:15hr 4830ft 0360050. 3639600. Trail to Upper Shake Campground (4440ft, 0359830 3839770). This trail drops 0.6 miles down switchbacks to the campground where you might find water in a small creek.

9. 11:50hr 3870ft 0349640 3784500. Road. Cow Spring Canyon Creek, which usually runs until late May, might be running better where it crosses the road. The next section of PCT twists and turns, and goes up and down to follow a boundary, rather than the lie of the land.

33

8

510

W

9

Pine Canyon Rd

Horse Campground Spring

Cow Spring Creek

Liebre Mountain Truck Trail

7

505

guzzler

Bear Campground

6

A

A

water tank

guzzler

5

500

4600

4

Sawmill Campground

Sawmill Mountain

3

water tank

495

C

Upper Shake Campground

W

2

31

MAP 33

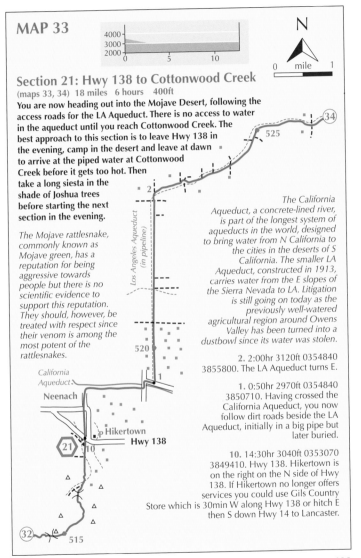

N

Section 21: Hwy 138 to Cottonwood Creek
(maps 33, 34)   18 miles   6 hours   400ft

You are now heading out into the Mojave Desert, following the access roads for the LA Aqueduct. There is no access to water in the aqueduct until you reach Cottonwood Creek. The best approach to this section is to leave Hwy 138 in the evening, camp in the desert and leave at dawn to arrive at the piped water at Cottonwood Creek before it gets too hot. Then take a long siesta in the shade of Joshua trees before starting the next section in the evening.

The Mojave rattlesnake, commonly known as Mojave green, has a reputation for being aggressive towards people but there is no scientific evidence to support this reputation. They should, however, be treated with respect since their venom is among the most potent of the rattlesnakes.

The California Aqueduct, a concrete-lined river, is part of the longest system of aqueducts in the world, designed to bring water from N California to the cities in the deserts of S California. The smaller LA Aqueduct, constructed in 1913, carries water from the E slopes of the Sierra Nevada to LA. Litigation is still going on today as the previously well-watered agricultural region around Owens Valley has been turned into a dustbowl since its water was stolen.

2. 2:00hr 3120ft 0354840 3855800. The LA Aqueduct turns E.

1. 0:50hr 2970ft 0354840 3850710. Having crossed the California Aqueduct, you now follow dirt roads beside the LA Aqueduct, initially in a big pipe but later buried.

10. 14:30hr 3040ft 0353070 3849410. Hwy 138. Hikertown is on the right on the N side of Hwy 138. If Hikertown no longer offers services you could use Gils Country Store which is 30min W along Hwy 138 or hitch E then S down Hwy 14 to Lancaster.

139

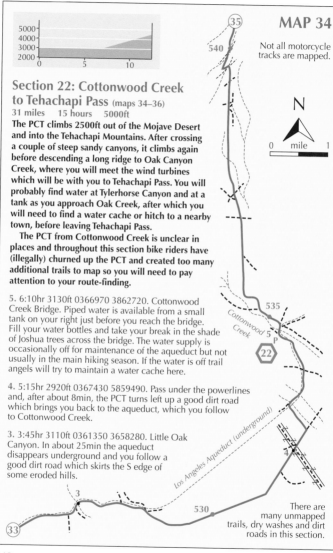

MAP 34

Not all motorcycle tracks are mapped.

N

0   mile   1

Section 22: Cottonwood Creek to Tehachapi Pass (maps 34–36)
31 miles   15 hours   5000ft

The PCT climbs 2500ft out of the Mojave Desert and into the Tehachapi Mountains. After crossing a couple of steep sandy canyons, it climbs again before descending a long ridge to Oak Canyon Creek, where you will meet the wind turbines which will be with you to Tehachapi Pass. You will probably find water at Tylerhorse Canyon and at a tank as you approach Oak Creek, after which you will need to find a water cache or hitch to a nearby town, before leaving Tehachapi Pass.

The PCT from Cottonwood Creek is unclear in places and throughout this section bike riders have (illegally) churned up the PCT and created too many additional trails to map so you will need to pay attention to your route-finding.

5. 6:10hr 3130ft 0366970 3862720. Cottonwood Creek Bridge. Piped water is available from a small tank on your right just before you reach the bridge. Fill your water bottles and take your break in the shade of Joshua trees across the bridge. The water supply is occasionally off for maintenance of the aqueduct but not usually in the main hiking season. If the water is off trail angels will try to maintain a water cache here.

4. 5:15hr 2920ft 0367430 5859490. Pass under the powerlines and, after about 8min, the PCT turns left up a good dirt road which brings you back to the aqueduct, which you follow to Cottonwood Creek.

3. 3:45hr 3110ft 0361350 3658280. Little Oak Canyon. In about 25min the aqueduct disappears underground and you follow a good dirt road which skirts the S edge of some eroded hills.

Cottonwood Creek

Los Angeles Aqueduct (underground)

There are many unmapped trails, dry washes and dirt roads in this section.

MAP 35

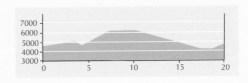

0   mile   1

4. 10:05hr 4980ft 0374080 3877700. Tiger Tank might have water requiring considerable treatment. If the shower is working it should have better quality water.

3. 7:45hr 6200ft 0369350 3874520. Shallow saddle.

2. 5:15hr 4640ft 0368130 3871050. Gamble Spring Canyon is usually dry. You now climb to 6280ft.

1. 3:40hr 4850ft 035960 3871740. Tylerhorse Canyon. You can expect to find water here into early summer but you need a reserve in case it is dry. You now contour round to Gamble Spring Canyon.

'Don't expect. Don't expect anything regarding comfort, weather, water, food, rest etc. Most of all, don't expect to quit.' Mike Lowell, thru'-hiker.

There are many unmapped motorcycle trails in this section.

5. 11:15hr 4090ft 0376280 3879430. The PCT crosses Oak Creek which used to be a reliable water source but now seems to dry up in early season. You shortly reach the Tehachapi–Willow Springs Rd. Tehachapi is 9 miles to the NW and is much easier to get to from here than from the Tehachapi Pass. However, most hikers prefer to resupply at Mojave to the E. The next on-trail water is at Golden Oak Spring, 23 miles away. You are climbing to Cameron Ridge, where camping can be very difficult because it can be extremely windy, before going down to Cameron Canyon. There are numerous unmapped dirt roads and powerlines, associated with the windfarms, on the ridge.

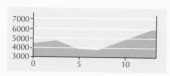

MAP 36

N

0 mile 1

Section 23: Tehachapi Pass to Piute Mountain Road
(maps 36–38)   42 miles   19 hours   5000ft

This section is easy to plan. There are 2 reliable springs after 17 and 36 miles and these are the only possible water sources until the end of the section. You start with a S-facing climb of more than 2000ft, exposed to wind and sun, after which it is much more comfortable as you will have shady forest for much of the section.

As you climb out of Tehachapi Pass you have magnificent views of the Mojave Desert. Across the desert you can see the mountains you have been hiking through for the past few weeks. The isolated hills in the desert, Soledad Mountain and Elephant Butte, are riddled with the shafts of gold and silver mines. Edwards Air Base, which is a base for experimental aircraft and has provided a landing strip for the space shuttle, is visible in the distance. Nearer is Mojave with its airfield, used for mothballing aircraft, as the dry desert area is good for storage. In 2002 there were over 100 large passenger aircraft parked on the airfield due to the reduction in air traffic following the Twin Towers attack in 2001.

In the area of Tehachapi Pass, one of the windiest places on Earth, each wind turbine will produce the same amount of electricity annually as burning 1000 barrels of oil in an oil-fired power station.

Tehachapi Pass is a major communication link with a 4-lane highway, railroad and powerlines.

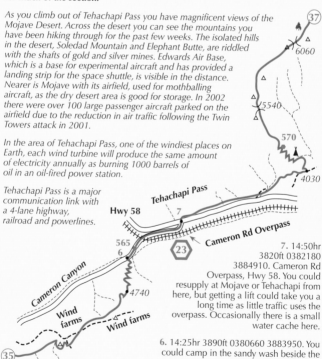

7. 14:50hr 3820ft 0382180 3884910. Cameron Rd Overpass, Hwy 58. You could resupply at Mojave or Tehachapi from here, but getting a lift could take you a long time as little traffic uses the overpass. Occasionally there is a small water cache here.

6. 14:25hr 3890ft 0380660 3883950. You could camp in the sandy wash beside the Cameron Canyon Rd.

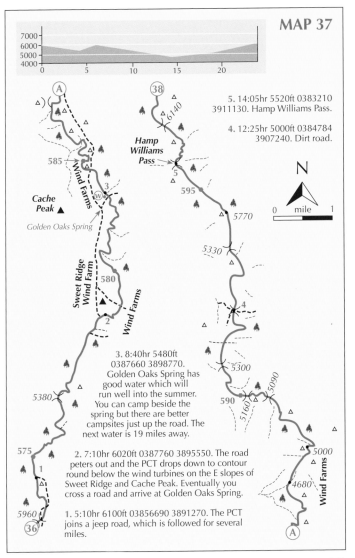

MAP 37

5. 14:05hr 5520ft 0383210 3911130. Hamp Williams Pass.

4. 12:25hr 5000ft 0384784 3907240. Dirt road.

N

0   mile   1

Hamp
Williams
Pass

Cache
Peak ▲

Golden Oaks Spring

Wind Farms

Sweet Ridge
Wind Farm

Wind Farms

Wind Farms

3. 8:40hr 5480ft
0387660 3898770.
Golden Oaks Spring has
good water which will
run well into the summer.
You can camp beside the
spring but there are better
campsites just up the road. The
next water is 19 miles away.

2. 7:10hr 6020ft 0387760 3895550. The road
peters out and the PCT drops down to contour
round below the wind turbines on the E slopes of
Sweet Ridge and Cache Peak. Eventually you
cross a road and arrive at Golden Oaks Spring.

1. 5:10hr 6100ft 03856690 3891270. The PCT
joins a jeep road, which is followed for several
miles.

143

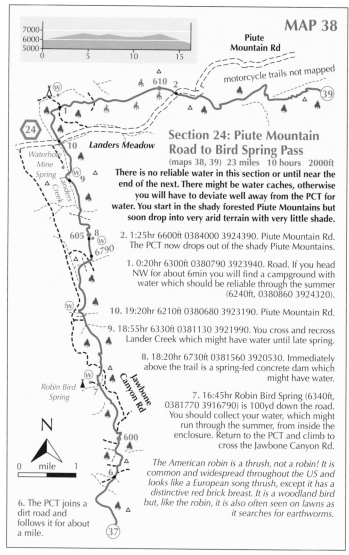

MAP 38

Piute
Mountain Rd

motorcycle trails not mapped

610

Landers Meadow

Waterhole
Mine
Spring

Section 24: Piute Mountain Road to Bird Spring Pass

(maps 38, 39) 23 miles 10 hours 2000ft

There is no reliable water in this section or until near the end of the next. There might be water caches, otherwise you will have to deviate well away from the PCT for water. You start in the shady forested Piute Mountains but soon drop into very arid terrain with very little shade.

2. 1:25hr 6600ft 0384000 3924390. Piute Mountain Rd. The PCT now drops out of the shady Piute Mountains.

1. 0:20hr 6300ft 0380790 3923940. Road. If you head NW for about 6min you will find a campground with water which should be reliable through the summer (6240ft, 0380860 3924320).

10. 19:20hr 6210ft 0380680 3923190. Piute Mountain Rd.

9. 18:55hr 6330ft 0381130 3921990. You cross and recross Lander Creek which might have water until late spring.

8. 18:20hr 6730ft 0381560 3920530. Immediately above the trail is a spring-fed concrete dam which might have water.

605

6790

Robin Bird
Spring

7. 16:45hr Robin Bird Spring (6340ft, 0381770 3916790) is 100yd down the road. You should collect your water, which might run through the summer, from inside the enclosure. Return to the PCT and climb to cross the Jawbone Canyon Rd.

Jawbone
Canyon Rd

600

The American robin is a thrush, not a robin! It is common and widespread throughout the US and looks like a European song thrush, except it has a distinctive red brick breast. It is a woodland bird but, like the robin, it is also often seen on lawns as it searches for earthworms.

N

0   mile   1

6. The PCT joins a dirt road and follows it for about a mile.

37

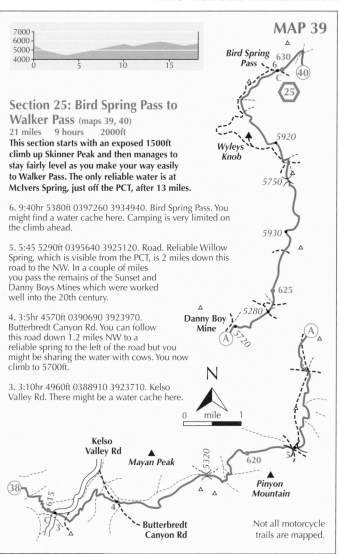

MAP 39

Bird Spring Pass

Section 25: Bird Spring Pass to Walker Pass (maps 39, 40)
21 miles   9 hours   2000ft

This section starts with an exposed 1500ft climb up Skinner Peak and then manages to stay fairly level as you make your way easily to Walker Pass. The only reliable water is at McIvers Spring, just off the PCT, after 13 miles.

6. 9:40hr 5380ft 0397260 3934940. Bird Spring Pass. You might find a water cache here. Camping is very limited on the climb ahead.

5. 5:45 5290ft 0395640 3925120. Road. Reliable Willow Spring, which is visible from the PCT, is 2 miles down this road to the NW. In a couple of miles you pass the remains of the Sunset and Danny Boys Mines which were worked well into the 20th century.

4. 3:5hr 4570ft 0390690 3923970. Butterbredt Canyon Rd. You can follow this road down 1.2 miles NW to a reliable spring to the left of the road but you might be sharing the water with cows. You now climb to 5700ft.

3. 3:10hr 4960ft 0388910 3923710. Kelso Valley Rd. There might be a water cache here.

Wyleys Knob

Danny Boy Mine

Kelso Valley Rd

▲ *Mayan Peak*

Butterbredt Canyon Rd

▲ *Pinyon Mountain*

N

0   mile   1

Not all motorcycle trails are mapped.

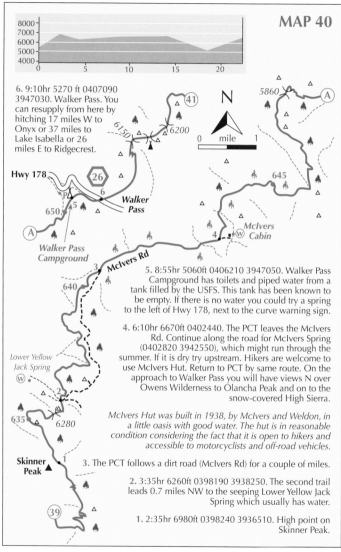

MAP 40

8000
7000
6000
5000
4000

0   5   10   15   20

6. 9:10hr 5270 ft 0407090 3947030. Walker Pass. You can resupply from here by hitching 17 miles W to Onyx or 37 miles to Lake Isabella or 26 miles E to Ridgecrest.

41
6150   6200

N

0   mile   1

5860   A

Hwy 178
26
645
P
650   45   6
Walker Pass
A
McIvers Rd
Walker Pass Campground
3
640
McIvers Cabin
4   W

5. 8:55hr 5060ft 0406210 3947050. Walker Pass Campground has toilets and piped water from a tank filled by the USFS. This tank has been known to be empty. If there is no water you could try a spring to the left of Hwy 178, next to the curve warning sign.

4. 6:10hr 6670ft 0402440. The PCT leaves the McIvers Rd. Continue along the road for McIvers Spring (0402820 3942550), which might run through the summer. If it is dry try upstream. Hikers are welcome to use McIvers Hut. Return to PCT by same route. On the approach to Walker Pass you will have views N over Owens Wilderness to Olancha Peak and on to the snow-covered High Sierra.

Lower Yellow Jack Spring
W
2
635
6280

McIvers Hut was built in 1938, by McIvers and Weldon, in a little oasis with good water. The hut is in reasonable condition considering the fact that it is open to hikers and accessible to motorcyclists and off-road vehicles.

Skinner Peak ▲
1

3. The PCT follows a dirt road (McIvers Rd) for a couple of miles.

2. 3:35hr 6260ft 0398190 3938250. The second trail leads 0.7 miles NW to the seeping Lower Yellow Jack Spring which usually has water.

39

1. 2:35hr 6980ft 0398240 3936510. High point on Skinner Peak.

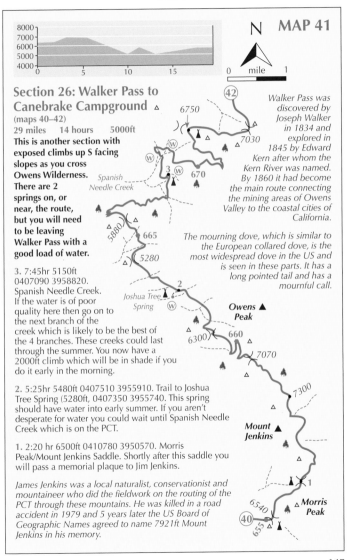

MAP 41

Section 26: Walker Pass to Canebrake Campground
(maps 40–42)

29 miles   14 hours   5000ft

This is another section with exposed climbs up S facing slopes as you cross Owens Wilderness. There are 2 springs on, or near, the route, but you will need to be leaving Walker Pass with a good load of water.

Walker Pass was discovered by Joseph Walker in 1834 and explored in 1845 by Edward Kern after whom the Kern River was named. By 1860 it had become the main route connecting the mining areas of Owens Valley to the coastal cities of California.

The mourning dove, which is similar to the European collared dove, is the most widespread dove in the US and is seen in these parts. It has a long pointed tail and has a mournful call.

3. 7:45hr 5150ft 0407090 3958820. Spanish Needle Creek. If the water is of poor quality here then go on to the next branch of the creek which is likely to be the best of the 4 branches. These creeks could last through the summer. You now have a 2000ft climb which will be in shade if you do it early in the morning.

2. 5:25hr 5480ft 0407510 3955910. Trail to Joshua Tree Spring (5280ft, 0407350 3955740. This spring should have water into early summer. If you aren't desperate for water you could wait until Spanish Needle Creek which is on the PCT.

1. 2:20 hr 6500ft 0410780 3950570. Morris Peak/Mount Jenkins Saddle. Shortly after this saddle you will pass a memorial plaque to Jim Jenkins.

James Jenkins was a local naturalist, conservationist and mountaineer who did the fieldwork on the routing of the PCT through these mountains. He was killed in a road accident in 1979 and 5 years later the US Board of Geographic Names agreed to name 7921ft Mount Jenkins in his memory.

MAP 42

N

0   mile   1

8000
7000
6000
5000
4000

0   5   10

Section 27: Canebrake Road to Kennedy Meadows

(maps 42, 43) 21 miles 10 hours 5000ft

This section starts with a climb to 8000ft then a gradual descent through woodland destroyed by the massive Manter Fire in 2000, before heading up the S Kern River to Kennedy Meadows. The first utterly reliable water source will be when you reach the Kern River but there will probably be water at Fox Mill Spring.

Look out for obsidian chips on the trail near to Fox Mill Spring. These Indian artifacts suggest obsidian, a natural glass, was being worked here for the production of arrow tips and other tools. The nearest obsidian outcrop is near Bishop, more than 100 miles away.

43
2

685

2. 4:10hr 7970ft 0402030 3972380. High point just before road.

1. 1:45hr 6540ft 0403910 3968400. The trail to Fox Mill Spring is just to the right of the trail. You might find water being piped into a horse trough but you will probably need to go to the creek. The spring should run through early summer. Once you enter the burnt area the next good campsite is at Manter Creek.

Fox Mill Spring

Chimney Creek Campground

Canebrake Rd

680

27

5. 13:30 5520ft 0405720 3966160. Chimney Creek, with reliable water through early summer, is followed by Canebrake Road. If you are ready to camp, head right to Chimney Creek Campground with piped water. Otherwise follow the PCT across the road.

4. 11:40 6840ft 0408830 3962570. Saddle SE of Lamont Peak.

Lamont Point

675
4

The Manter Fire was started by an environmentally minded hiker burning toilet paper. The author saw the first wisps of smoke from the fire on 23 July 2000 during a section-hike. The next day smoke had filled Owens Valley and spread 100 miles to the N. The fire was totally out of control before the fire service was able to put in resources to suppress it and it was still burning at the end of August.

41

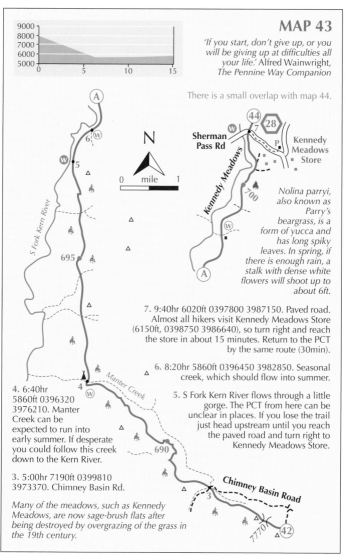

MAP 43

'If you start, don't give up, or you will be giving up at difficulties all your life.' Alfred Wainwright, The Pennine Way Companion

There is a small overlap with map 44.

Sherman Pass Rd

Kennedy Meadows Store

Nolina parryi, also known as Parry's beargrass, is a form of yucca and has long spiky leaves. In spring, if there is enough rain, a stalk with dense white flowers will shoot up to about 6ft.

7. 9:40hr 6020ft 0397800 3987150. Paved road. Almost all hikers visit Kennedy Meadows Store (6150ft, 0398750 3986640), so turn right and reach the store in about 15 minutes. Return to the PCT by the same route (30min).

6. 8:20hr 5860ft 0396450 3982850. Seasonal creek, which should flow into summer.

5. S Fork Kern River flows through a little gorge. The PCT from here can be unclear in places. If you lose the trail just head upstream until you reach the paved road and turn right to Kennedy Meadows Store.

4. 6:40hr 5860ft 0396320 3976210. Manter Creek can be expected to run into early summer. If desperate you could follow this creek down to the Kern River.

3. 5:00hr 7190ft 0399810 3973370. Chimney Basin Rd.

Many of the meadows, such as Kennedy Meadows, are now sage-brush flats after being destroyed by overgrazing of the grass in the 19th century.

Chimney Basin Road

THE HIGH SIERRA

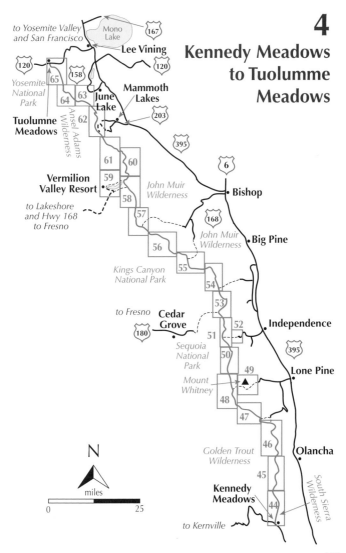

to Yosemite Valley
and San Francisco

Mono
Lake

167

Lee Vining

120

120

65

158

Yosemite
National
Park

63

64

Tuolumne
Meadows

62

Mammoth
Lakes

June
Lake

203

395

6

61

60

Vermilion
Valley Resort

59

58

John Muir
Wilderness

Bishop

to Lakeshore
and Hwy 168
to Fresno

57

168

56

John Muir
Wilderness

Big Pine

55

Kings Canyon
National Park

54

53

to Fresno

Cedar
Grove

52

51

Independence

180

50

Sequoia
National
Park

49

Mount
Whitney

Lone Pine

395

48

47

Golden Trout
Wilderness

46

Olancha

45

South Sierra
Wilderness

Kennedy
Meadows

44

to Kernville

N

miles

0   25

PART 4: KENNEDY MEADOWS TO TUOLUMNE MEADOWS

Section	Distance (miles)	Time (hours)	Ascent (feet)	Maps
28 Kennedy Meadows–Trail Pass	43	22	8000	44–46
29 Trail Pass–Crabtree Meadows	21	9	3000	46–48
30A Mount Whitney (optional)	17	9	4000	48, 49
30 Crabtree Meadows–Kearsarge Pass Trail	22	13	5000	48,50,51
31A Resupply over Kearsarge Pass (optional)	15	9	4000	51,52
31 Kearsarge Pass Trail–Taboose Pass Trail	21	13	5000	51,53,54
32 Taboose Pass Trail–Bishop Pass Trail	21	10	3000	54,55
33 Bishop Pass Trail–Piute Pass Trail	25	12	3000	55–57
34 Piute Pass Trail–Bear Ridge Trail	19	10	4000	57,58
35A Bear Ridge Trail–Reds Meadow (by PCT)	33	16	5000	58–62
See Section 35 introduction for variations				
36 Reds Meadow–Tuolumne Meadows	36	16	5000	62–65
Part total (via PCT)	**241**	**121**	**41,000**	
Part total (including Mount Whitney ascent, and resupplies over Kearsarge Pass and at VVR)	**281**	**143**	**49,000**	

This is a key section for PCT hikers. Much of the guide's introduction deals with the problems of hiking this section, so now is the time to reread that information, particularly the part on wilderness hiking.

The nature of the PCT changes dramatically as it climbs into a fantastic, roadless, alpine environment of rock, lakes, snow-covered passes, bare mountains, tumbling creeks

and waterfalls. You pass through the Sequoia and Kings Canyon and Yosemite National Parks. Eight passes above 11,000ft are crossed, including Forester Pass at 13,180ft. Between the passes you drop into steep forested canyons. Mount Whitney, the highest mountain in the US outside Alaska, is not part of the PCT but most hikers climb it as an optional extra (Section 30A). For much of the section

Forester Pass is the low point on the left, not the broad pass on the right (Section 30)

Mather Pass, June 16, 2006 (Section 32)

Helen Lake – Muir Pass is to the right of the highest peak (Section 33)

Three key passes to recognise in Part 4

153

the world-renowned John Muir Trail (JMT), which goes from the Yosemite Valley to Mount Whitney, is followed.

You are reminded that the maps in this guidebook are intended for use when the trail is free of snow and will not be adequate if substantial snowpack remains. For snowpack you will need 1:50,000 maps with contour detail (see Appendices B and C). Water symbols have not been included on maps in Sections 30-36.

The author checked the trail in June 2009 when there was substantial snowpack above 10,000ft, making it impossible to survey all the detail. The photographs were taken in June 2006 and 2009 and give a good impression of how the terrain would look if you hiked the High Sierra in early season.

The majority of thru'-hikers resupply at Independence over Kearsarge Pass (Section 31A). Most will also visit Vermilion Valley Resort to resupply. In addition you might like to take one of the variations given for Sections 35 and 36.

Best time
July–September. Early July would be good in a low snow year but in a high snow year there will be snow on the passes into August. By mid-September the limited resupply points might be closing down. This is the only section of the PCT that thru'-hikers will tackle at an inappropriate time of year. They will encounter more snow and more difficult creek crossings than was intended when the PCT was built.

154

It also means they will pass through when the scenery is at its most majestic.

Some of the photographs in this section were taken in June 2006, a record snow year with snowpack for most of the route between Trail Pass and Tuolumne Meadows. It is a fantastic hike in these conditions but it is also difficult and dangerous and not recommended for anyone other than experienced winter mountaineers.

Section-hikers: the only road in this section is at Reds Meadow so it is unsuitable for weekend hikers. The section boundaries have been chosen where there is trailhead within a day's hike of the PCT so the minimum time for a section-hike would be about four days. Section-hikers would be advised to hike north-to-south from Yosemite Valley, or to start this section at Walker Pass, so they become acclimatised to the altitude before reaching 13,000ft. The Cicerone guidebook to the JMT covers a north-to-south hike from Yosemite Valley to Whitney Portal.

Permits
Read the section on bears in the introduction. The regulations for protection of food from bears in the High Sierra change frequently so you should check the websites or contact Yosemite National Park and Sequoia and Kings Canyon National Park to find out the latest regulations.

At the time of writing, you do not need a separate permit if you intend to

Thru'-hikers enjoy the campfire's warmth, above Death Canyon (Section 29)

climb Mount Whitney from the PCT. However a permit is required to enter the Mount Whitney Zone, so you will need one if you intend to descend or ascend the trail to Whitney Portal. You can get your Mount Whitney permit at the same time as your wilderness permit.

You will need wilderness permits for virtually all of this section. Obtain them from the authority for the area where you enter the wilderness (or from the PCTA if you are hiking more than 500 miles on the PCT). A quota system controls the number of permits issued from each trailhead for each day. Popular trailheads, such as Whitney Portal and Yosemite Valley can reach their quota months in advance, particularly at weekends.

Section 28 & 29: Golden Trout Wilderness (from Kennedy Meadows)
Contact Sequoia National Forest: See Part 3 introduction.

Sections 30–33: Sequoia and Kings Canyon National Park
47050 Generals Hwy, Three Rivers CA93271
(559)-565-3341, www.nps.gov/seki

Sections 34 & 35: Mammoth Lakes Area
Inyo National Forest, 351Pacu Lane, Suite 200, Bishop CA93514
(760)-873-2400, www.//fs.fed.us/r5/inyo/recreation/wild
http://jrabold.net/mammoth/mamwild.htm

Section 36: Yosemite National Park
Yosemite National Park Wilderness Centre, Box 545, Yosemite CA95389
(209)-372-0740, www.nps.gov/yose/wilderness

Facilities
You must decide how you are going to supply the 240 miles of PCT between

Kennedy Meadows and Tuolumne Meadows. Most hikers send a resupply package to Kennedy Meadows Store. On leaving Kennedy Meadows, the next road you will meet will be at Reds Meadow 200 miles away in terrain where you cannot expect to average much better than two miles-an-hour with a heavy pack. Some hikers attempt to go from Kennedy Meadows to Vermilion Valley Resort (VVR) but this will require between 10 and 14 days' food to be carried, leaving no margin for delays due to storms.

Although most hikers base themselves at Kennedy Meadows to organise equipment and pick up bear canister and supplies for the High Sierra, you should consider continuing to Trail Pass, then dropping to Horseshoe Meadow Campground and hitching out to Lone Pine, a small town with good facilities for hikers, including a good outdoor store. This will put you about 20 hours of hiking closer to your first resupply in the High Sierra.

It is suggested you resupply at Independence, VVR and Tuolumne Meadows but study the section information and decide what is best for you.

Kennedy Meadows (P, small G, C) (Sections 27, 28) (0 hours)
See Part 3 introduction.

Lone Pine (PO, G, R, A, O, B) (from Trail Pass) (Sections 28, 29) (22 hours) or (from Crabtree Meadows) (Sections 29, 30) (31 hours)
156

Lone Pine PO, 121 E Bush St, Lone Pine CA93549
(760)-876-5681.
Mon–Fri: 9.00am–5.00pm
Full town facilities. Elevation Outdoor Store is very good (info@sierra elevation.com).
Trail Pass is only a couple of miles from Horseshoe Meadow Campground from where you should be able to get a lift to Lone Pine. Some hikers resupply at Lone Pine, hiking from Crabtree Meadows, over 13,560ft Trail Crest to Whitney Portal (small G, R). From there they hitch the 13 miles to Lone Pine. This is too far off the PCT unless you are climbing Mount Whitney, in which case it might make sense to take an additional day to resupply in Lone Pine, then aim to get through to Muir Trail Ranch or VVR without further resupply.

Independence (PO, small G, R, A, L, Sh, B) (from Kearsarge Pass Trail) (Sections 30, 31) (44 hours)
Independence PO, 101 S Edwards St, Independence CA93526
(760)-878-2210. Mon–Fri: 8.30am–12.30pm, 1.30pm–4.30pm
Small town facilities. Independence's store has closed but the mini-mart at the Chevron Gas Station has reasonable hiker supplies as well as laundry and showers.
It will take you at least 24 hours to resupply over Kearsarge Pass. There is enough tourist traffic driving up to the Onion Valley Roadhead (C) to have a

reasonable chance of hitching down to Independence. It is fairly easy to get from Independence to Lone Pine if you want better facilities.

Cedar Grove (small G, A, R, L, Sh) (from Woods Creek) (Section 31) (49 hours)
www.nps.gov/seki/cgvc.htm
It is a 14-mile hike down to Cedar Grove in Kings Canyon.

Bishop (PO, G, R, A, L, O, B) (from Bishop Pass Trail) (Sections 32, 33) (67 hours) or (from Piute Pass) (Sections 33, 34) (79 hours)
Bishop PO, 595 W Line St, Bishop CA93514
(760)-873-3526. Mon–Fri: 8.30am–4.00pm, Sat: 9.00am–1.00pm
Full town facilities.
It is 12 miles to South Lake by Bishop Pass Trail and 18 miles to North Lake by Piute Pass Trail, from where you can hitch to Bishop.

Muir Trail Ranch (P) (Section 34) (77 hours)
Muir Trail Ranch, PO Box 176, Lakeshore CA93634
(209)-966-3195 (reservations/information only; there is no phone at the ranch), www.muirtrailranch.com, resupply@muirtrailranch.com. 8.00am–5.00pm
Muir Trail Ranch is only about a mile from the PCT. It offers a package service. You might be able to stay overnight in a cabin if they aren't fully booked but this is only

likely at the beginning and end of the season. The ranch has a mini-store where you might be able to obtain items such as gas cylinders and fuel, film and batteries but not food. Computer time, with internet access, can be rented. The package service is expensive ($50 in 2008) because packages must be packed in by mule from the roadhead. You must send packages in a plastic barrel. See the website for details.

Vermilion Valley Resort (VVR) (P, small G, R, A, C, L, Sh) (from Bear Ridge Trail) (Sections 34, 35) (89 hours) (or from Mono Creek)
Vermilion Valley Resort, c/o Rancheria Marina, 62311, Huntington Lake Rd, Lakeshore CA93634
(559)-855-6558 (office), www.edisonlake.com.
Restaurant open 7.00am–8.00pm
VVR offers a package service. Check the website for latest details. Send at least two weeks in advance. Packages by UPS only to this address ($18 fee in 2009). Do not send US mail to this address. You could send by US mail to General Delivery, Mono Hot Springs PO, c/o VVR (your name) CA93642.
There is a ferry service from VVR to the eastern end of Lake Thomas A. Edison:
From VVR: 9.00am, 4.00pm. To VVR: 9.45am, 4.45pm ($18 return, $10 single in 2009)
VVR is about six miles from the PCT

but access is easy and most thru'-hikers visit VVR, which is hiker-friendly.

Mono Hot Springs (PO, small G, A, R) (from VVR)
Mono Springs PO, 72000 Hwy 168, Mono Hot Springs CA93642
(559)-841-3678,
www.monohotsprings.com.
Mon–Sat: 8.00am–6.00pm
Mono Hot Springs is seven miles west of VVR.

Reds Meadow (P, small G, R, C, A, Sh) (Sections 35, 36) (105 hours)
Reds Meadow, PO Box 395, Mammoth Lakes CA93546
(760)-934-2345, www.redsmeadow.com, rmps395@aol.com
Reds Meadow offers a package service ($25 in 2009). See its website for details of how to send packages. The store and café are open from 7.00am to 7.00pm but dinner reservations must be made by 3.00pm. Free showers, heated by hot springs, are available at a nearby campground.

Mammoth Lakes (PO, G, R, A, L, O, B) (from Reds Meadow) (Sections 35, 36) (105 hours)
Mammoth Lakes PO, 3330 Main St, Mammoth Lakes CA93546
(760)-934-2205.
Mon–Fri: 7.30am–4.00pm
Mammoth Lakes ski resort and Mammoth Lakes, with full town facilities, are linked by road with a shuttle bus to Reds Meadow.
www.visitmammoth.com

Tuolumne Meadows (PO, G, R, A, C, O, B) (Sections 36, 37) (121 hours)
Tuolumne Meadows PO, 14000 Hwy 120E, Yosemite National Park CA95389
(209)-372-4475.
Mon–Fri: 9.00am–5.00pm,
Sat: 9.00am–12.00noon
Facilities are open from early or late June, depending on snowpack, to mid–late September, 8.00am–8.00pm in high season and 8.00am–5.00pm at other times. Parcels are stored in Yosemite Valley's post office until Tuolumne Meadows opens. The store is well-stocked for backpackers. The post office and café are part of the store and you should be able to collect parcels during store opening hours. There is an outdoor store beside the gas station. There is a big campground with a backpacker section, a lodge and a ranger station with a visitor centre. There is a bus service between Tuolumne Meadows and Yosemite Valley.

Lee Vining (PO, G, R, A, B) (from Tuolumne Meadows) (Sections 36, 37) (121 hours)
Lee Vining PO, 121 Lee Vining Avenue, Lee Vining CA93541
(760)-647-6371.
Mon–Fri: 9.00am–2.00pm, 3.00pm–5.00pm
Full town facilities.

MAP 44

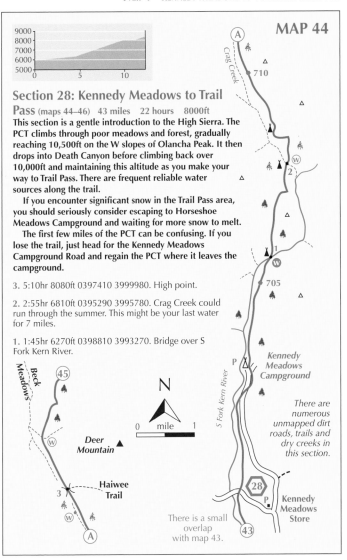

Section 28: Kennedy Meadows to Trail Pass (maps 44–46) 43 miles 22 hours 8000ft

This section is a gentle introduction to the High Sierra. The PCT climbs through poor meadows and forest, gradually reaching 10,500ft on the W slopes of Olancha Peak. It then drops into Death Canyon before climbing back over 10,000ft and maintaining this altitude as you make your way to Trail Pass. There are frequent reliable water sources along the trail.

If you encounter significant snow in the Trail Pass area, you should seriously consider escaping to Horseshoe Meadows Campground and waiting for more snow to melt.

The first few miles of the PCT can be confusing. If you lose the trail, just head for the Kennedy Meadows Campground Road and regain the PCT where it leaves the campground.

3. 5:10hr 8080ft 0397410 3999980. High point.

2. 2:55hr 6810ft 0395290 3995780. Crag Creek could run through the summer. This might be your last water for 7 miles.

1. 1:45hr 6270ft 0398810 3993270. Bridge over S Fork Kern River.

N
0 — mile — 1

There are numerous unmapped dirt roads, trails and dry creeks in this section.

There is a small overlap with map 43.

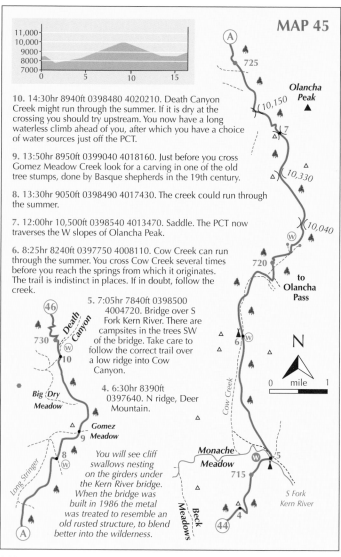

MAP 45

A

725

Olancha Peak ▲

(10,150

7
△

(10,330 △

(10,040

W

720

to
**Olancha
Pass**

N

0   mile   1

10. 14:30hr 8940ft 0398480 4020210. Death Canyon Creek might run through the summer. If it is dry at the crossing you should try upstream. You now have a long waterless climb ahead of you, after which you have a choice of water sources just off the PCT.

9. 13:50hr 8950ft 0399040 4018160. Just before you cross Gomez Meadow Creek look for a carving in one of the old tree stumps, done by Basque shepherds in the 19th century.

8. 13:30hr 9050ft 0398490 4017430. The creek could run through the summer.

7. 12:00hr 10,500ft 0398540 4013470. Saddle. The PCT now traverses the W slopes of Olancha Peak.

6. 8:25hr 8240ft 0397750 4008110. Cow Creek can run through the summer. You cross Cow Creek several times before you reach the springs from which it originates. The trail is indistinct in places. If in doubt, follow the creek.

46

Death Canyon

730

W

10

5. 7:05hr 7840ft 0398500 4004720. Bridge over S Fork Kern River. There are campsites in the trees SW of the bridge. Take care to follow the correct trail over a low ridge into Cow Canyon.

6 △ W
△
△

4. 6:30hr 8390ft 0397640. N ridge, Deer Mountain.

△

Big Dry Meadow

△ **Gomez Meadow**
9

8
W

Long Stringer

You will see cliff swallows nesting on the girders under the Kern River bridge. When the bridge was built in 1986 the metal was treated to resemble an old rusted structure, to blend better into the wilderness.

Cow Creek

Monache Meadow
W 5
715 △

S Fork Kern River

△
4

Beck Meadows

44

A

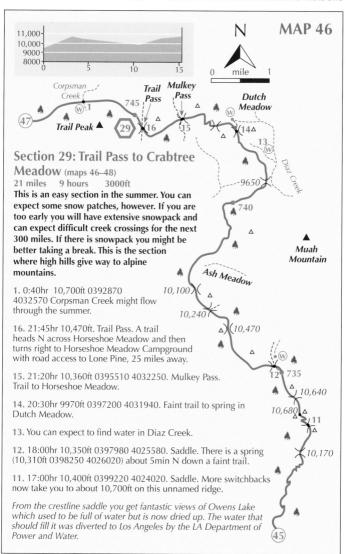

MAP 46

N

0 — mile — 1

Corpsman Creek

Trail Pass *Mulkey Pass*

745

Dutch Meadow

47

Trail Peak ▲

29 16 15 14

13

Section 29: Trail Pass to Crabtree Meadow (maps 46–48)

21 miles   9 hours   3000ft

This is an easy section in the summer. You can expect some snow patches, however. If you are too early you will have extensive snowpack and can expect difficult creek crossings for the next 300 miles. If there is snowpack you might be better taking a break. This is the section where high hills give way to alpine mountains.

9650

740

▲ *Muah Mountain*

Ash Meadow

10,100

10,240

10,470

1. 0:40hr 10,700ft 0392870 4032570 Corpsman Creek might flow through the summer.

16. 21:45hr 10,470ft. Trail Pass. A trail heads N across Horseshoe Meadow and then turns right to Horseshoe Meadow Campground with road access to Lone Pine, 25 miles away.

12 735

10,640

10,680

11

15. 21:20hr 10,360ft 0395510 4032250. Mulkey Pass. Trail to Horseshoe Meadow.

14. 20:30hr 9970ft 0397200 4031940. Faint trail to spring in Dutch Meadow.

13. You can expect to find water in Diaz Creek.

10,170

12. 18:00hr 10,350ft 0397980 4025580. Saddle. There is a spring (10,310ft 0398250 4026020) about 5min N down a faint trail.

11. 17:00hr 10,400ft 0399220 4024020. Saddle. More switchbacks now take you to about 10,700ft on this unnamed ridge.

From the crestline saddle you get fantastic views of Owens Lake which used to be full of water but is now dried up. The water that should fill it was diverted to Los Angeles by the LA Department of Power and Water.

45

MAP 47

6. 6:00hr 9570ft. Bear Box with camping at Rock Creek ford. In snowmelt you might prefer to cross on logs upstream.

5. 5:35hr 9960ft 0381740 4039540. Rock Creek Trail.

4. 4:00hr 11,040ft. Rock Creek Trail.

3. 2:20hr 11,240ft. Outlet, Chicken Spring Lake. There are good campsites by the SE shore of the lake. To visit the lake, as most hikers do, head up the E side of the creek. This, the first natural lake on the PCT, is a classic example of a corrie lake. In a dry year this might be your last water until Rock Creek.

Help maintain the trail system. Shortcutting and cutting switchbacks cause erosion, trail destruction and falling rock. Not only does it take more energy on your part but the damage it can cause is costly and might be impossible to rectify.

A corrie (combe, cwm, cirque) is an amphitheatre-like bowl situated high on a mountain. Corries are formed when glaciers hollow out a bowl by a combination of freeze, thaw and abrasion. The bowl is filled by water when the glacier melts, leaving a corrie lake. Corries often have steep crags on the headwall and sides. When two adjacent corries erode towards each other an arête can form, giving the spectacular steep-sided ridges charateristic of alpine terrain.

2. 2:05hr 11,150ft 0390970 4034910. Cottonwood Pass. The trail E leads to Horseshoe Meadow Campground (9930ft 0395100 4034310) with access to Lone Pine. Big Whitney Meadow is visible to the SW.

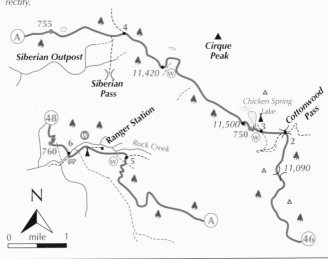

MAP 48

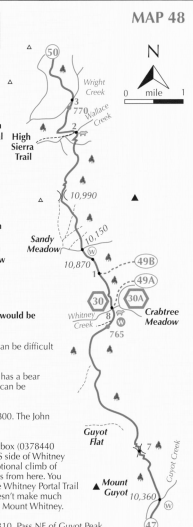

Section 30: Crabtree Meadows to Kearsarge Pass Trail (maps 48, 50, 51)

22 miles   13 hours   5,000ft

This is the first challenging section of the High Sierra. You ford several creeks which could be difficult when the snow is melting fast. Bighorn Plateau, with views of Mount Whitney and Kings Kern Divide, is a fantastic spot for those interested in mountain photography and would make a good but chilly campsite. You then have the crossing of 13,200ft Forester Pass, the highest point on the PCT. You could encounter snow on the N facing descent from Forester Pass into August and thru'-hikers in June will almost certainly encounter snow. Those unaccustomed to high mountains would be well advised to join into groups.

3. 2:45hr 10,720ft. Wright Creek can be difficult in early season.

2. 2:00hr 10,420ft. Wallace Creek has a bear box (0377380 4050680). The ford can be difficult in early season.

1. 0:50hr 10,760ft 0378130 4046800. The John Muir Trail (JMT) joins the PCT.

8. 9:30hr 10,330ft. There is a bear box (0378440 4046030) at the campsites on the S side of Whitney Creek in Crabtree Meadow. The optional climb of Mount Whitney (Section 30A) starts from here. You could also access Lone Pine by the Whitney Portal Trail but it will take you 2 days so it doesn't make much sense unless you are also climbing Mount Whitney.

7. 8:10hr 10,930ft 0379220 4042310. Pass NE of Guyot Peak.

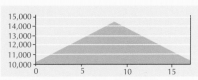

MAP 49

N

0   mile   1

This profile starts and ends at Crabtree Meadow on map 48.

Section 30A: Ascent of Mount Whitney (optional) (maps 48, 49)

17 miles   9 hours   4000ft

If you have time in your schedule, an ascent of Mount Whitney is certainly worthwhile. It is an easy climb on good trails provided that the trails are free of snow and the weather is good. Remember you will need an extra day's food if you are going to make the ascent.

The best option is to camp at Guitar Lake and climb Mount Whitney in the morning, before the risk of afternoon thunderstorms and before snow softens too much. Regain the PCT via the John Muir Trail (JMT).

3. 4:00hr 13,560ft 0394280 4046900. Whitney Portal Trail. There are some very exposed campsites at Trail Crest. It is a 5000ft descent to Whitney Portal and then a 13-mile hitch from here, if you intend to resupply at Lone Pine.

2. 2:00hr 11,480ft 0382480. Guitar Lake.

1. 0:35hr 10,620ft 0379260 4047300. Bear Box. The Crabtree Ranger Station is on the S side of Whitney Creek but you should cross the creek to join the JMT.

Mount Whitney is named after Josiah Whitney (1819-1896) who was chief of the California State Geological Survey. The stone cabin on the summit was built in 1909 by the Smithsonian Institute as an observatory. Be careful about using the cabin in a storm: in 1990 a hiker died here when the shelter was hit by lightning. The outhouse is the highest toilet in the US and probably the most expensive to maintain since it has to be emptied by helicopter.

The John Muir Trail (JMT) is arguably the finest long distance footpath in the world. The 230-mile trail starts (or ends) on the summit of Mount Whitney and coincides with the PCT for most of the way to Tuolumne Meadows before dropping into the spectacular Yosemite Valley.

4. 5:20hr 14,500ft 0384400 4048900. Mt Whitney. Return by the same route (2:30hr to Guitar Lake, then 1:25hr to JMT/PCT junction on map 48).

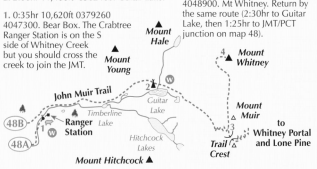

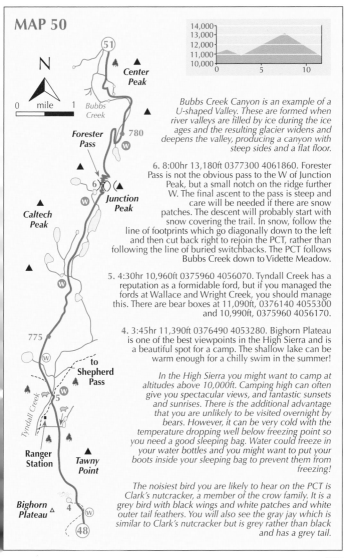

MAP 50

Bubbs Creek Canyon is an example of a U-shaped Valley. These are formed when river valleys are filled by ice during the ice ages and the resulting glacier widens and deepens the valley, producing a canyon with steep sides and a flat floor.

6. 8:00hr 13,180ft 0377300 4061860. Forester Pass is not the obvious pass to the W of Junction Peak, but a small notch on the ridge further W. The final ascent to the pass is steep and care will be needed if there are snow patches. The descent will probably start with snow covering the trail. In snow, follow the line of footprints which go diagonally down to the left and then cut back right to rejoin the PCT, rather than following the line of buried switchbacks. The PCT follows Bubbs Creek down to Vidette Meadow.

5. 4:30hr 10,960ft 0375960 4056070. Tyndall Creek has a reputation as a formidable ford, but if you managed the fords at Wallace and Wright Creek, you should manage this. There are bear boxes at 11,090ft, 0376140 4055300 and 10,990ft, 0375960 4056170.

4. 3:45hr 11,390ft 0376490 4053280. Bighorn Plateau is one of the best viewpoints in the High Sierra and is a beautiful spot for a camp. The shallow lake can be warm enough for a chilly swim in the summer!

In the High Sierra you might want to camp at altitudes above 10,000ft. Camping high can often give you spectacular views, and fantastic sunsets and sunrises. There is the additional advantage that you are unlikely to be visited overnight by bears. However, it can be very cold with the temperature dropping well below freezing point so you need a good sleeping bag. Water could freeze in your water bottles and you might want to put your boots inside your sleeping bag to prevent them from freezing!

The noisiest bird you are likely to hear on the PCT is Clark's nutcracker, a member of the crow family. It is a grey bird with black wings and white patches and white outer tail feathers. You will also see the gray jay which is similar to Clark's nutcracker but is grey rather than black and has a grey tail.

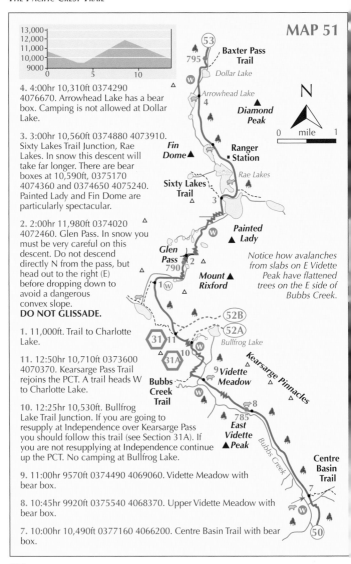

MAP 51

4. 4:00hr 10,310ft 0374290 4076670. Arrowhead Lake has a bear box. Camping is not allowed at Dollar Lake.

3. 3:00hr 10,560ft 0374880 4073910. Sixty Lakes Trail Junction, Rae Lakes. In snow this descent will take far longer. There are bear boxes at 10,590ft, 0375170 4074360 and 0374650 4075240. Painted Lady and Fin Dome are particularly spectacular.

2. 2:00hr 11,980ft 0374020 4072460. Glen Pass. In snow you must be very careful on this descent. Do not descend directly N from the pass, but head out to the right (E) before dropping down to avoid a dangerous convex slope.
DO NOT GLISSADE.

1. 11,000ft. Trail to Charlotte Lake.

11. 12:50hr 10,710ft 0373600 4070370. Kearsarge Pass Trail rejoins the PCT. A trail heads W to Charlotte Lake.

10. 12:25hr 10,530ft. Bullfrog Lake Trail Junction. If you are going to resupply at Independence over Kearsarge Pass you should follow this trail (see Section 31A). If you are not resupplying at Independence continue up the PCT. No camping at Bullfrog Lake.

9. 11:00hr 9570ft 0374490 4069060. Vidette Meadow with bear box.

8. 10:45hr 9920ft 0375540 4068370. Upper Vidette Meadow with bear box.

7. 10:00hr 10,490ft 0377160 4066200. Centre Basin Trail with bear box.

Baxter Pass Trail

Dollar Lake

Arrowhead Lake

Diamond Peak

Fin Dome

Ranger Station

Rae Lakes

Sixty Lakes Trail

Painted Lady

Glen Pass

Mount Rixford

Notice how avalanches from slabs on E Vidette Peak have flattened trees on the E side of Bubbs Creek.

Bullfrog Lake

Kearsarge Pinnacles

Bubbs Creek Trail

Vidette Meadow

East Vidette Peak

Bubbs Creek

Centre Basin Trail

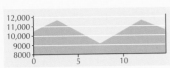

MAP 52

Profile begins and ends on the PCT on Map 51.

Section 31A: Resupply over Kearsarge Pass (optional)

(maps 51, 52)   15 miles   9 hours   4000ft

Many hikers resupply at Independence over the Kearsarge Pass. It is best to leave the PCT along the trail to beautiful Bullfrog Lake. Kearsarge Lakes are a good place to camp before the ascent of Kearsarge Pass and the 2500ft descent to the Onion Valley Trailhead, from which you will probably be able to get a lift down to Independence. This is a popular area with tourists which also means it tends to be an area where full bear precautions are essential.

4. 4:00hr 9160ft 0380410 4070480. Onion Valley Trailhead has a campground, parking area, toilets, piped water and bear boxes. You need to hitch 15 miles down to Independence. Return to Kearsarge Pass by the same route (7:40hr). You can then either retrace your route past Bullfrog Lake or take the contouring higher level trail to regain the PCT at the Kearsarge Pass Trail Junction (8:35hr).

Section 31: Kearsarge Pass Trail to Taboose Pass Trail

(maps 51, 53, 54)

21 miles   13 hours   5000ft

This section starts with the crossing of the awe-inspiring Glen Pass and the descent to Rae Lakes with their magnificent mountain scenery. The descent from Glen Pass is difficult and potentially dangerous if there is snow on the trail. There is an easy descent down S Fork Woods Creek and then up Woods Creek to cross the easy Pinchot Pass.

The ptarmigan is the grouse of the mountain tops. The rock ptarmigan with all white plumage in winter and a mottled brown plumage in summer, is adapted to live on high rocky slopes and in the tundra and can be found above 10,000ft in the High Sierra.

3. 2:00hr 11,760ft 0377160 4070590. Kearsarge Pass.

2. 11,360ft 0376690 4070650. Trail junction.

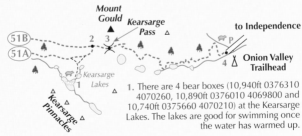

1. There are 4 bear boxes (10,940ft 0376310 4070260, 10,890ft 0376010 4069800 and 10,740ft 0375660 4070210) at the Kearsarge Lakes. The lakes are good for swimming once the water has warmed up.

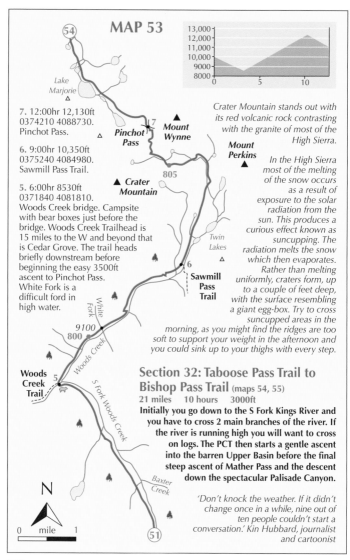

MAP 53

7. 12:00hr 12,130ft
0374210 4088730.
Pinchot Pass.

6. 9:00hr 10,350ft
0375240 4084980.
Sawmill Pass Trail.

5. 6:00hr 8530ft
0371840 4081810.
Woods Creek bridge. Campsite
with bear boxes just before the
bridge. Woods Creek Trailhead is
15 miles to the W and beyond that
is Cedar Grove. The trail heads
briefly downstream before
beginning the easy 3500ft
ascent to Pinchot Pass.
White Fork is a
difficult ford in
high water.

*Lake
Marjorie*

△ *Pinchot
Pass*

▲ *Mount
Wynne*

▲ *Mount
Perkins*

805

▲ *Crater
Mountain*

*Twin
Lakes*

**Sawmill
Pass
Trail**

*White
Fork*

9100
800

Woods Creek

**Woods
Creek
Trail**

S Fork Woods Creek

*Baxter
Creek*

*Crater Mountain stands out with
its red volcanic rock contrasting
with the granite of most of the
High Sierra.*

*In the High Sierra
most of the melting
of the snow occurs
as a result of
exposure to the solar
radiation from the
sun. This produces a
curious effect known as
suncupping. The
radiation melts the snow
which then evaporates.
Rather than melting
uniformly, craters form, up
to a couple of feet deep,
with the surface resembling
a giant egg-box. Try to cross
suncupped areas in the
morning, as you might find the ridges are too
soft to support your weight in the afternoon and
you could sink up to your thighs with every step.*

Section 32: Taboose Pass Trail to Bishop Pass Trail (maps 54, 55)

21 miles   10 hours   3000ft

Initially you go down to the S Fork Kings River and
you have to cross 2 main branches of the river. If
the river is running high you will want to cross
on logs. The PCT then starts a gentle ascent
into the barren Upper Basin before the final
steep ascent of Mather Pass and the descent
down the spectacular Palisade Canyon.

*'Don't knock the weather. If it didn't
change once in a while, nine out of
ten people couldn't start a
conversation.' Kin Hubbard, journalist
and cartoonist*

N

0   mile   1

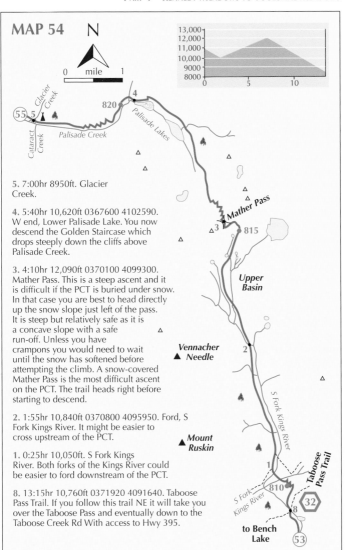

MAP 54   N

0   mile   1

5. 7:00hr 8950ft. Glacier Creek.

4. 5:40hr 10,620ft 0367600 4102590. W end, Lower Palisade Lake. You now descend the Golden Staircase which drops steeply down the cliffs above Palisade Creek.

3. 4:10hr 12,090ft 0370100 4099300. Mather Pass. This is a steep ascent and it is difficult if the PCT is buried under snow. In that case you are best to head directly up the snow slope just left of the pass. It is steep but relatively safe as it is a concave slope with a safe run-off. Unless you have crampons you would need to wait until the snow has softened before attempting the climb. A snow-covered Mather Pass is the most difficult ascent on the PCT. The trail heads right before starting to descend.

2. 1:55hr 10,840ft 0370800 4095950. Ford, S Fork Kings River. It might be easier to cross upstream of the PCT.

1. 0:25hr 10,050ft. S Fork Kings River. Both forks of the Kings River could be easier to ford downstream of the PCT.

8. 13:15hr 10,760ft 0371920 4091640. Taboose Pass Trail. If you follow this trail NE it will take you over the Taboose Pass and eventually down to the Taboose Creek Rd With access to Hwy 395.

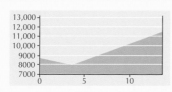

MAP 55

2. 4:45hr 11,600ft 0352500
4109290. Helen Lake. Helen and
Wanda Lakes were named after the
daughters of John Muir. Both lakes
could be covered in ice well into
summer.

1. 3:00hr 10,600ft. Creek crossing.

7. 10:00hr 8720ft. Bishop Pass Trail,
just after crossing the bridge over
the Dusy Creek (0358370
4106280). This trail will take you 12
miles over Bishop Pass and down to
S Lake from where you might be
able to hitch 24 miles to Bishop.

6. 8:10hr 8020ft. Middle Fork Kings
River.

Section 33: Bishop Pass Trail to Piute Pass Trail (maps 55–57)
25 miles   12 hours   3000ft

The pass in this section is Muir Pass. This
isn't as steep as the others, but it does
accumulate more snow so you could be
walking in snowpack, even into August.
Navigation can be difficult on the ascent,
so it would not be sensible to attempt the
pass in poor visibility if
there is snowpack.

*Helen Lake exemplifies the variability of
conditions in the High Sierra from year to year.
In August 1996 the author battled through a
blizzard to find Helen Lake still frozen, but in
August 2000 he managed his highest ever
swim in this lake.*

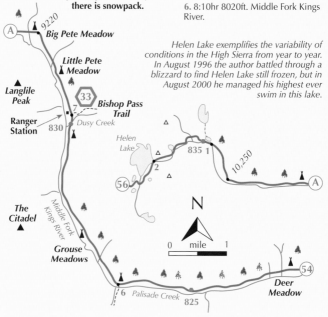

MAP 56

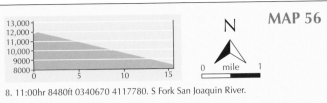

8. 11:00hr 8480ft 0340670 4117780. S Fork San Joaquin River.

7. 10:35hr 9180ft 0341860 4118070. Evolution Creek ford. The easiest place to cross is about 25yd upstream.

6. 10:25hr 9200ft. Evolution Meadow. The crossing of Evolution Creek, a little further down the PCT, can be difficult with fast-moving water and a bouldery ford. The author prefers to cross Evolution Creek at the bottom of Evolution Meadow. The water is deeper here, possibly waist-deep, but the water is slow-moving and the river has a sandy bed. A small path along the S bank of the river will return you to the PCT at the official crossing point.

5. 9:50hr 9650ft 0345620. McClure Ranger Station.

4. 7:30hr 11,890ft 0349780 4114020. Evolution Creek. There are stepping stones at this ford.

The peaks surrounding Evolution Basin, including Mount Darwin and Mount Huxley are named after the main protagonists in the debate on the evolution of Man.

John Muir was a Scottish immigrant, brought up in the E States before moving to San Francisco in 1868. He spent much of the next 6 years in the Yosemite Valley and started a campaign to preserve the wilderness. He even managed to persuade President Roosevelt to go on a 3-day camping trip with him into the wilderness. This campaign was successful in getting the Yosemite and Sequoia National Parks established. Muir Pass and the JMT are named in his memory.

3. 5:30hr 11,980ft 0351560 4108610. Muir Pass. There is a stone shelter on Muir Pass but overnight stays are prohibited except in a real emergency. The shelter seems to have a resident marmot.

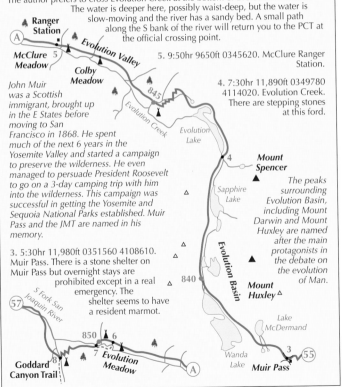

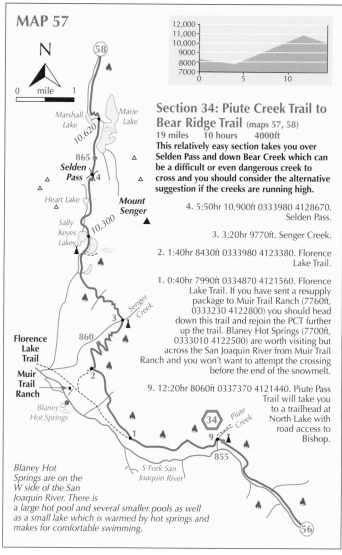

MAP 57

N

0 ——— mile ——— 1

Marshall Lake

Marie Lake

10,620

865
Selden Pass ✕ 4

Heart Lake

Mount Senger ▲

Sally Keyes Lakes
10,300

3
Senger Creek

860

2

Florence Lake Trail

Muir Trail Ranch

Blaney Hot Springs

1

855

S Fork San Joaquin River

34 *Piute Creek*

9

56

58

Section 34: Piute Creek Trail to Bear Ridge Trail (maps 57, 58)
19 miles   10 hours   4000ft
This relatively easy section takes you over Selden Pass and down Bear Creek which can be a difficult or even dangerous creek to cross and you should consider the alternative suggestion if the creeks are running high.

4. 5:50hr 10,900ft 0333980 4128670. Selden Pass.

3. 3:20hr 9770ft. Senger Creek.

2. 1:40hr 8430ft 0333980 4123380. Florence Lake Trail.

1. 0:40hr 7990ft 0334870 4121560. Florence Lake Trail. If you have sent a resupply package to Muir Trail Ranch (7760ft, 0333230 4122800) you should head down this trail and rejoin the PCT further up the trail. Blaney Hot Springs (7700ft, 0333010 4122500) are worth visiting but across the San Joaquin River from Muir Trail Ranch and you won't want to attempt the crossing before the end of the snowmelt.

9. 12:20hr 8060ft 0337370 4121440. Piute Pass Trail will take you to a trailhead at North Lake with road access to Bishop.

Blaney Hot Springs are on the W side of the San Joaquin River. There is a large hot pool and several smaller pools as well as a small lake which is warmed by hot springs and makes for comfortable swimming.

MAP 58

'Whether you believe you
can or you can't, you're
probably right.' Henry Ford

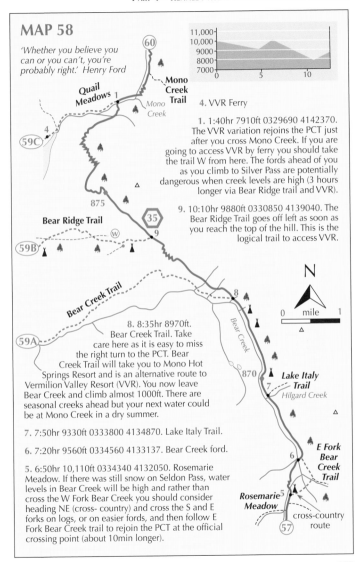

4. VVR Ferry

1. 1:40hr 7910ft 0329690 4142370.
The VVR variation rejoins the PCT just
after you cross Mono Creek. If you are
going to access VVR by ferry you should take
the trail W from here. The fords ahead of you
as you climb to Silver Pass are potentially
dangerous when creek levels are high (3 hours
longer via Bear Ridge trail and VVR).

9. 10:10hr 9880ft 0330850 4139040. The
Bear Ridge Trail goes off left as soon as
you reach the top of the hill. This is the
logical trail to access VVR.

8. 8:35hr 8970ft.
Bear Creek Trail. Take
care here as it is easy to miss
the right turn to the PCT. Bear
Creek Trail will take you to Mono Hot
Springs Resort and is an alternative route to
Vermilion Valley Resort (VVR). You now leave
Bear Creek and climb almost 1000ft. There are
seasonal creeks ahead but your next water could
be at Mono Creek in a dry summer.

7. 7:50hr 9330ft 0333800 4134870. Lake Italy Trail.

6. 7:20hr 9560ft 0334560 4133137. Bear Creek ford.

5. 6:50hr 10,110ft 0334340 4132050. Rosemarie
Meadow. If there was still snow on Seldon Pass, water
levels in Bear Creek will be high and rather than
cross the W Fork Bear Creek you should consider
heading NE (cross-country) and cross the S and E
forks on logs, or on easier fords, and then follow E
Fork Bear Creek trail to rejoin the PCT at the official
crossing point (about 10min longer).

173

Section 35: Bear Creek Trail to Reds Meadow (maps 58–62)

35A:	33 miles	15 hours	5000ft **(by PCT)**
35B:	41 miles	19 hours	5000ft **(by VVR, Silver Pass and PCT)**
35C:	36 miles	17 hours	5000ft **(by PCT, Silver Pass and Cascade Valley)**
35D:	42 miles	19 hours	5000ft **(by VVR, Silver Pass and Cascade Valley)**
35E:	41 miles	19 hours	5000ft **(by VVR, Goodale Pass and Cascade Valley)**

You now have a choice of routes. If you are not going to Vermilion Valley Resort (VVR) continue along the PCT. VVR is at the W end of Lake Edison and you have **three options** for access to VVR.
a) Head down Bear Ridge (recommended option).
b) Continue along the PCT to Quail Meadows and, after crossing the footbridge over Mono Creek, turn left to Lake Edison and either walk 4½ miles along the N shore or catch the ferry along the lake.
c) Follow the Bear Creek Trail to Mono Hot Springs Resort, then take the road to VVR.

From VVR you can:
a) regain the PCT by walking along the N shore of Lake Edison or taking the ferry to Quail Meadows, or
b) climb Goodale Pass, a mile W of Silver Pass. From Goodale Pass you drop down to Papoose Lake and rejoin the PCT or take the Minnow Creek Trail to Iva Bell Hot Springs and pick up the Cascade Valley variation to Reds Meadow.

Unless you take the Minnow Lake Trail, the PCT will bring you to the Cascade Lake Trail. Again you have 2 options.
a) Follow the PCT to Reds Meadow.
b) Follow the trail down Cascade Valley. This route follows Fish Creek, passes Iva Bell Hot Springs and drops further downstream before a climb takes you past Rainbow Falls to Reds Meadow.

The author checked the Goodale Pass–Minnow Creek route on his 2009 hike, so detail on the PCT and Cascade Valley routes was not checked. However you shouldn't encounter any problems once the snow has melted. During snowmelt there are a few tricky creek crossings and there is some awkward navigation over Silver Pass.

The author has done all these variations and would suggest that you follow the PCT in early season because creek crossings will make the Cascade Valley difficult and navigation on the Goodale Pass–Minnow Creek route will be difficult in snowpack. Once the snow has melted you might prefer to visit the Iva Bell Hot Springs by either of the alternative routes.

The Cascade Valley fords can be difficult or impossible during maximum snowmelt. In June 2006, the author continued down the S side of Fish Creek after the First Crossing, before crossing on a log before reaching the Second Crossing which would have been impossible to cross safely. The fords were easy in August 2000 and safe to cross in mid-June 2002.

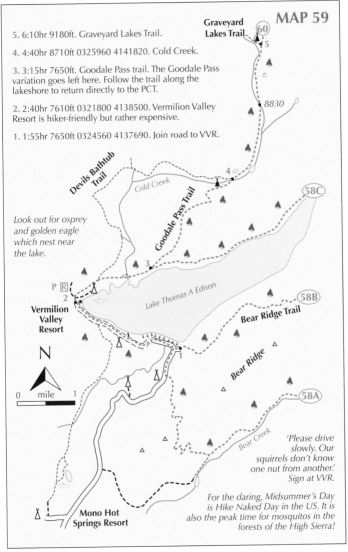

MAP 59

5. 6:10hr 9180ft. Graveyard Lakes Trail.

4. 4:40hr 8710ft 0325960 4141820. Cold Creek.

3. 3:15hr 7650ft. Goodale Pass trail. The Goodale Pass variation goes left here. Follow the trail along the lakeshore to return directly to the PCT.

2. 2:40hr 7610ft 0321800 4138500. Vermilion Valley Resort is hiker-friendly but rather expensive.

1. 1:55hr 7650ft 0324560 4137690. Join road to VVR.

Graveyard Lakes Trail

8830

Devils Bathtub Trail

Cold Creek

Goodale Pass Trail

Look out for osprey and golden eagle which nest near the lake.

Lake Thomas A Edison

P R
Vermilion Valley Resort

Bear Ridge Trail

Bear Ridge

N

0   mile   1

Bear Creek

Mono Hot Springs Resort

'Please drive slowly. Our squirrels don't know one nut from another.' Sign at VVR.

For the daring, Midsummer's Day is Hike Naked Day in the US. It is also the peak time for mosquitos in the forests of the High Sierra!

175

MAP 60

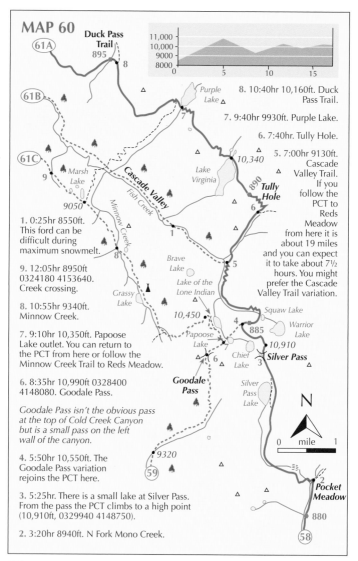

Duck Pass Trail
895

8. 10:40hr 10,160ft. Duck Pass Trail.

7. 9:40hr 9930ft. Purple Lake.

6. 7:40hr. Tully Hole.

5. 7:00hr 9130ft. Cascade Valley Trail. If you follow the PCT to Reds Meadow from here it is about 19 miles and you can expect it to take about 7½ hours. You might prefer the Cascade Valley Trail variation.

1. 0:25hr 8550ft. This ford can be difficult during maximum snowmelt.

9. 12:05hr 8950ft 0324180 4153640. Creek crossing.

8. 10:55hr 9340ft. Minnow Creek.

7. 9:10hr 10,350ft. Papoose Lake outlet. You can return to the PCT from here or follow the Minnow Creek Trail to Reds Meadow.

6. 8:35hr 10,990ft 0328400 4148080. Goodale Pass.

Goodale Pass isn't the obvious pass at the top of Cold Creek Canyon but is a small pass on the left wall of the canyon.

4. 5:50hr 10,550ft. The Goodale Pass variation rejoins the PCT here.

3. 5:25hr. There is a small lake at Silver Pass. From the pass the PCT climbs to a high point (10,910ft, 0329940 4148750).

2. 3:20hr 8940ft. N Fork Mono Creek.

MAP 61

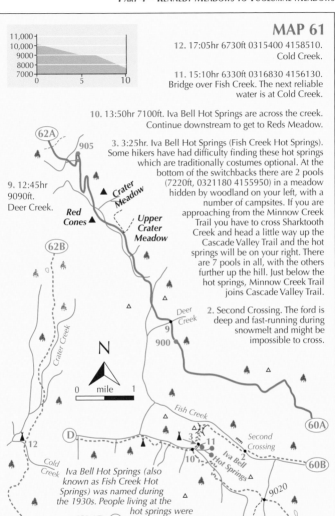

12. 17:05hr 6730ft 0315400 4158510.
Cold Creek.

11. 15:10hr 6330ft 0316830 4156130.
Bridge over Fish Creek. The next reliable
water is at Cold Creek.

10. 13:50hr 7100ft. Iva Bell Hot Springs are across the creek.
Continue downstream to get to Reds Meadow.

3. 3:25hr. Iva Bell Hot Springs (Fish Creek Hot Springs).
Some hikers have had difficulty finding these hot springs
which are traditionally costumes optional. At the
bottom of the switchbacks there are 2 pools
(7220ft, 0321180 4155950) in a meadow
hidden by woodland on your left, with a
number of campsites. If you are
approaching from the Minnow Creek
Trail you have to cross Sharktooth
Creek and head a little way up the
Cascade Valley Trail and the hot
springs will be on your right. There
are 7 pools in all, with the others
further up the hill. Just below the
hot springs, Minnow Creek Trail
joins Cascade Valley Trail.

2. Second Crossing. The ford is
deep and fast-running during
snowmelt and might be
impossible to cross.

62A
905
Crater
Meadow
9. 12:45hr
9090ft.
Deer Creek.
Red
Cones
Upper
Crater
Meadow
62B
Crater Creek
N
0   mile   1
Deer
Creek
9
900
Fish Creek
D
12
Cold
Creek
3
11
10
Second
Crossing
2
Iva Bell Hot Springs
60A
60B
9020
60C
D
11

*Iva Bell Hot Springs (also
known as Fish Creek Hot
Springs) was named during
the 1930s. People living at the
hot springs were
using illegal stills to beat
the prohibition and a baby,
Iva Bell, was born here.*

MAP 62

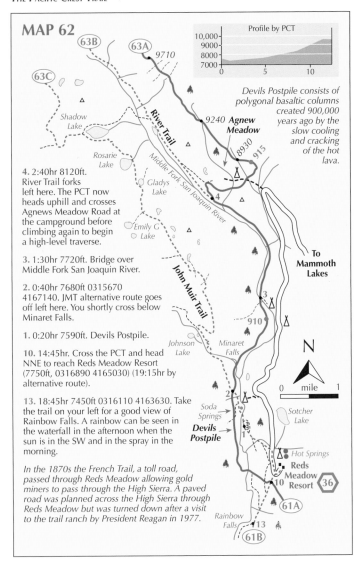

Profile by PCT

Devils Postpile consists of
polygonal basaltic columns
created 900,000
years ago by the
slow cooling
and cracking
of the hot
lava.

4. 2:40hr 8120ft.
River Trail forks
left here. The PCT now
heads uphill and crosses
Agnews Meadow Road at
the campground before
climbing again to begin
a high-level traverse.

3. 1:30hr 7720ft. Bridge over
Middle Fork San Joaquin River.

**2. 0:40hr 7680ft 0315670
4167140.** JMT alternative route goes
off left here. You shortly cross below
Minaret Falls.

1. 0:20hr 7590ft. Devils Postpile.

10. 14:45hr. Cross the PCT and head
NNE to reach Reds Meadow Resort
(7750ft, 0316890 4165030) (19:15hr by
alternative route).

13. 18:45hr 7450ft 0316110 4163630. Take
the trail on your left for a good view of
Rainbow Falls. A rainbow can be seen in
the waterfall in the afternoon when the
sun is in the SW and in the spray in the
morning.

*In the 1870s the French Trail, a toll road,
passed through Reds Meadow allowing gold
miners to pass through the High Sierra. A paved
road was planned across the High Sierra through
Reds Meadow but was turned down after a visit
to the trail ranch by President Reagan in 1977.*

MAP 63

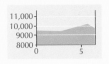

7. 8:30hr 10,200ft 0306680 4178880. Island Pass is more a high plateau than a pass.

6. 7:30hr 9840ft 0308650 4177910. Thousand Island Lake. Camping is prohibited at the eastern end of the lake. The JMT rejoins the PCT.

5. 7:00hr 9600ft. River Trail rejoins the PCT.

Fallen trees and branches provide habitat and shelter for other plants and wildlife and add essential nutrients to the soil. Vegetation grows very slowly at high elevations, so fires are only allowed below the alpine zone.

Approximately 400 black bears roam the Yosemite region. Dozens are killed each year in the Sierra Nevada after becoming aggressive in their pursuit of human food. When human food is unavailable, bears will return to their natural diet and no longer be aggressive.

Section 36: Reds Meadow to Tuolumne Meadows (maps 62–65)

36 miles   16hours   5000ft

There are 3 options to reach to reach Thousand Island Lake: the PCT, the JMT and River Trail. The JMT is the best route but it has more ascent and will be crowded in July and August. The low-level River Trail is the easiest route. Once these routes rejoin you cross the broad Island Pass and Donohue Pass before descending Lyell Canyon to Tuolumne Meadows. If possible, avoid camping in Lyell Canyon as it has a justified reputation for bear problems.

When you have finished with Reds Meadow Resort head along the main road to Bathhouse Campground (1st road on the right) where you can get a free shower heated by water from the hot springs. From here, head across the road and follow a trail to Devils Postpile. Continue N from the Devils Postpile, cross the bridge and continue N to a junction of the PCT and JMT, which separate for a few miles.

Ansel Adams Wilderness was named after photographer Ansel Adams (1902–1984) whose captivating photographic images contributed to the preservation of the wilderness.

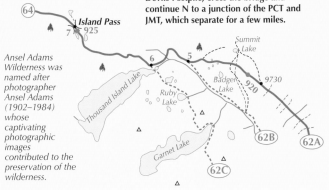

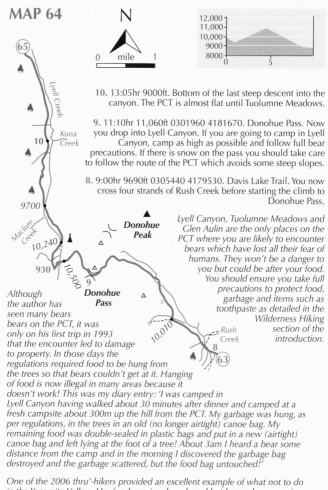

MAP 64

N

0   mile   1

12,000
11,000
10,000
9000
8000
0   5

10. 13:05hr 9000ft. Bottom of the last steep descent into the canyon. The PCT is almost flat until Tuolumne Meadows.

9. 11:10hr 11,060ft 0301960 4181670. Donohue Pass. Now you drop into Lyell Canyon. If you are going to camp in Lyell Canyon, camp as high as possible and follow full bear precautions. If there is snow on the pass you should take care to follow the route of the PCT which avoids some steep slopes.

8. 9:00hr 9690ft 0305440 4179530. Davis Lake Trail. You now cross four strands of Rush Creek before starting the climb to Donohue Pass.

Lyell Canyon, Tuolumne Meadows & Glen Aulin are the only places on the PCT where you are likely to encounter bears which have lost all their fear of humans. They won't be a danger to you but could be after your food. You should ensure you take full precautions to protect food, garbage and items such as toothpaste as detailed in the Wilderness Hiking section of the introduction.

Although the author has seen many bears on the PCT, it was only on his first trip in 1993 that the encounter led to damage to property. In those days the regulations required food to be hung from the trees so that bears couldn't get at it. Hanging of food is now illegal in many areas because it doesn't work! This was my diary entry: 'I was camped in Lyell Canyon having walked about 30 minutes after dinner and camped at a fresh campsite about 300m up the hill from the PCT. My garbage was hung, as per regulations, in the trees in an old (no longer airtight) canoe bag. My remaining food was double-sealed in plastic bags and put in a new (airtight) canoe bag and left lying at the foot of a tree! About 3am I heard a bear some distance from the camp and in the morning I discovered the garbage bag destroyed and the garbage scattered, but the food bag untouched!'

One of the 2006 thru'-hikers provided an excellent example of what not to do in the Yosemite Valley. Her food was in a bear barrel but her garbage was in her pack. A bear approached her camp so she backed away behind a campfire leaving her pack, which the bear duly ripped apart to get at the garbage.

Labels on map: Lyell Creek, Kuna Creek, 10, 9700, Maclure Creek, 10,240, 930, 10,500, 9, Donohue Pass, Donohue Peak, 10,010, Rush Creek, 8, 63, 65

MAP 65

Yosemite Valley, with its bare granite domes and plunging waterfalls, is one of the wonders of the natural world. If you have time to spare you could take a shuttle bus down there and join the crowds exploring the lower part of the valley. If you have a few days to spare it is worth hiking the JMT to the valley and taking the bus back to Tuolumne Meadows. (Your PCT permit will cover you for your hike down to Yosemite Valley.)

Half Dome in Yosemite Valley is one of the best-known mountains in the world. Half of the massive granite dome was carved away by the glacier flowing down Yosemite Valley. The vertical face is the realm of the rock climber but there is a chain up the steep curved side of the dome to help the ordinary hiker climb the mountain. You will see many smaller domes in the area of Tuolumne Meadows.

Look for evidence of glaciation, such as erratic boulders, glacial polish and striations in the bedrock. Only peaks such as Unicorn and Cathedral poked above the 2000ft of glacial ice 20,000 years ago.

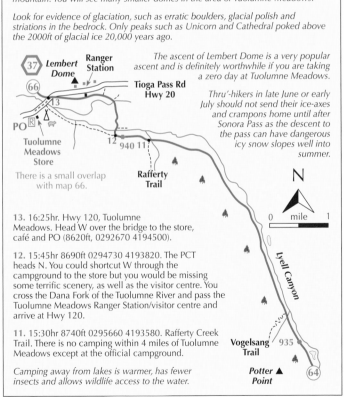

The ascent of Lembert Dome is a very popular ascent and is definitely worthwhile if you are taking a zero day at Tuolumne Meadows.

Thru'-hikers in late June or early July should not send their ice-axes and crampons home until after Sonora Pass as the descent to the pass can have dangerous icy snow slopes well into summer.

There is a small overlap with map 66.

13. 16:25hr. Hwy 120, Tuolumne Meadows. Head W over the bridge to the store, café and PO (8620ft, 0292670 4194500).

12. 15:45hr 8690ft 0294730 4193820. The PCT heads N. You could shortcut W through the campground to the store but you would be missing some terrific scenery, as well as the visitor centre. You cross the Dana Fork of the Tuolumne River and pass the Tuolumne Meadows Ranger Station/visitor centre and arrive at Hwy 120.

11. 15:30hr 8740ft 0295660 4193580. Rafferty Creek Trail. There is no camping within 4 miles of Tuolumne Meadows except at the official campground.

Camping away from lakes is warmer, has fewer insects and allows wildlife access to the water.

5

Tuolumne Meadows to Interstate 80 (Donner Pass)

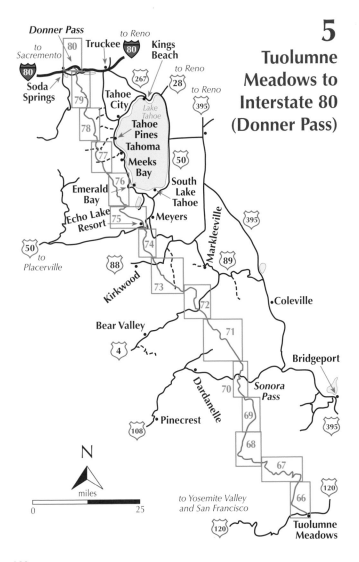

PART 5: TUOLUMNE MEADOWS TO INTERSTATE 80 (DONNER PASS)

Section	Distance (miles)	Time (hours)	Ascent (feet)	Maps
37 Tuolumne Meadows–Bear Valley Trail	38	19	7000	66–68
38 Bear Valley Trail–Sonora Pass	38	19	6000	68–70
39 Sonora Pass–Ebbetts Pass	32	15	5000	70–72
40 Ebbetts Pass–Carson Pass	29	12	3000	72, 73
41 Carson Pass–Echo Lakes	16	7	2000	73–75
42 Echo Lakes–Barker Pass	32	15	4000	75–77
43 Barker Pass–Interstate 80	32	15	4000	77–80
Part total	**217**	**102**	**31,000**	

The Sierra Nevada continues at a slightly lower altitude but is still a region of rugged alpine mountains. The 75-mile stretch to Sonora Pass is possibly the toughest on the PCT, crossing a succession of ridges and dropping to face difficult creek crossings before an exposed alpine ridge leads to Sonora Pass. The PCT then starts to become easier. There is still plenty of ascent but it feels gentler and there are no more difficult creek crossings.

Best time

Mid–July to mid-October. You should wait for the snow to melt as the section from Tuolumne Meadows to Sonora Pass has some extremely difficult creek crossings during snowmelt and snow patches can be dangerously icy on steep slopes. This section is actually much more difficult to hike under snowpack because of the time spent traversing steep slopes and the difficulties of navigation in the flatter parts. Mosquitoes are at their worst in late June and early July. In a dry year water sources could be few and far between by the end of the summer.

Permits

Bear canisters are needed until you leave Yosemite National Park at Dorothy Lake Pass in Section 38. Permits are required for Sections 39, 40 and 42.

Section 39: Carson-Iceberg Wilderness
Summit Ranger District, #1 Pinecrest Lake Rd, Pinecrest CA95364
(209)-965-3434

Lembert Dome, Tuolumne Meadows (Section 37)

Sections 39 & 40: Mokelumne Wilderness

Carson Ranger District, 1536 S Carson St, Carson City, NV89701 (775)-882-2766

Facilities

The 150 miles between Tuolumne Meadows and Echo Lake present a supply problem. Some hikers will manage without resupply but this is a tough section and could take up to 10 days. The serious creek crossings early in the section are best done without a very heavy pack. The only resupply option is Bridgeport, a 35-mile hitch from Sonora Pass. Many hikers take a zero day in South Lake Tahoe rather than resupplying at Echo Lake.

The suggested resupply is Bridgeport, Echo Lake and Truckee.

Tuolumne Meadows (PO, G, R, A, C, O, B) (Sections 36, 37) (0 hours)
See Part 4 introduction.

Bridgeport (PO, G, R, A, L, Sh, B) (from Sonora Pass) (Sections 38, 39) (38 hours)
Bridgeport PO, 29 Kingsley, Bridgeport CA93517
(760)-932-7991. Mon–Fri: 8.00am–12.00noon, 1.00pm–4.00pm
Facilities you would expect in a small tourist town.

Markleeville (PO, G, R, A, B) (from Ebbetts Pass) (Sections 39, 40) (53 hours)
Markleeville PO, 14845 State Route 89, Markleeville CA96120
(530)-694-2125. Mon–Fri: 8.15am–11.00am, 12.00noon–3.30pm, Sat: 8.30am–10.30am
Small town facilities.
www.markleeville-ca.com

Caples Lake Resort (small G, R, A) (from Carson Pass) (Sections 40, 41) (65 hours)
Mon–Sun: 7.00am–7.00pm

Little Norway (A, C, Sh) (Section 41) (71 hours)
(530)-659-7359, www.little-norway. net, norway@hughes.net
Little Norway has accommodation, camping, a coffee shop and very limited supplies.

Echo Lake (PO, G) (Sections 41, 42) (72 hours)
Echo Lake Resort PO, 9900 Echo Lakes Rd, Echo Lake CA95721
(530)-659-7207, www.echochalet. com. Mon–Sat: 11.00am–2.00pm
The small store is relatively well-stocked for hikers. The post office is inside the store and might be willing to serve hikers outside official post office hours.

Berkeley Camp (A, R, L, Sh) (Sections 41, 42) (72 hours)
(530)-659-7506, www.echocamp.org
Berkeley Camp, half a mile from Echo Lake store, is primarily a family camp but will take hikers if room is available.

South Lake Tahoe (PO, G, R, A, L, O, B) (from Echo Lake) (Sections 41, 42) (72 hours)
South Lake Tahoe PO, 1046, AL Tahoe Blvd, South Lake Tahoe CA96150
(530)-544-3462. Mon–Fri: 8.30am– 5.00pm, Sat: 12.00noon–2.00pm
Full town facilities.

Lichen on a volcanic outcrop, Leavitt Peak (Section 38)

Echo Lakes (Section 42)

Meyers (PO, G, R, A) (from Echo Lake) (Sections 41, 42) (72 hours)
Meyers PO, 1285 Apache Ave, S Lake Tahoe CA96150
(530)-577-5081. Mon–Fri: 9.00am–1.30pm, 3.00pm–4.45pm
Meyers is a suburb of South Lake Tahoe.

Soda Springs (PO, small G, R, L, B) (from Donner Pass) (Section 43) (102 hours)
Soda Springs PO, 21719 Donner Pass Rd, Soda Springs CA95728
(530)-426-3082. Mon–Fri: 9.00am–4.00pm

Truckee (PO, G, R, A, L, O, B) (from Donner Pass) (Section 43) (102 hours)
Truckee PO, 10050 Bridge St, Truckee CA96161
(530)-587-7158. Mon–Fri: 8.30am–5.00pm, Sat: 11.00am–2.00pm
Full town facilities.

Pooh Corner (P, R, A, L, Sh) (from Donner Pass) (Section 43) (102 hours)
(530)-587-4485, www.billperson.org/personal/PoohCorner.htm,
bill@billperson.org
Bill and Molly Person have provided free hospitality for PCT hikers at their chalet on Donner Lake. Open approximately June 25–July 25.

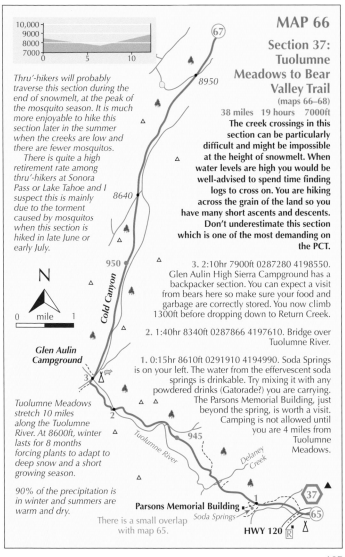

MAP 66

Section 37: Tuolumne Meadows to Bear Valley Trail
(maps 66–68)

38 miles   19 hours   7000ft

The creek crossings in this section can be particularly difficult and might be impossible at the height of snowmelt. When water levels are high you would be well-advised to spend time finding logs to cross on. You are hiking across the grain of the land so you have many short ascents and descents. Don't underestimate this section which is one of the most demanding on the PCT.

3. 2:10hr 7900ft 0287280 4198550. Glen Aulin High Sierra Campground has a backpacker section. You can expect a visit from bears here so make sure your food and garbage are correctly stored. You now climb 1300ft before dropping down to Return Creek.

2. 1:40hr 8340ft 0287866 4197610. Bridge over Tuolumne River.

1. 0:15hr 8610ft 0291910 4194990. Soda Springs is on your left. The water from the effervescent soda springs is drinkable. Try mixing it with any powdered drinks (Gatorade?) you are carrying. The Parsons Memorial Building, just beyond the spring, is worth a visit. Camping is not allowed until you are 4 miles from Tuolumne Meadows.

Thru'-hikers will probably traverse this section during the end of snowmelt, at the peak of the mosquito season. It is much more enjoyable to hike this section later in the summer when the creeks are low and there are fewer mosquitos.

There is quite a high retirement rate among thru'-hikers at Sonora Pass or Lake Tahoe and I suspect this is mainly due to the torment caused by mosquitos when this section is hiked in late June or early July.

Tuolumne Meadows stretch 10 miles along the Tuolumne River. At 8600ft, winter lasts for 8 months forcing plants to adapt to deep snow and a short growing season.

90% of the precipitation is in winter and summers are warm and dry.

There is a small overlap with map 65.

8950

8640

950

Glen Aulin Campground

Cold Canyon

N

0   mile   1

Parsons Memorial Building
Soda Springs

Tuolumne River

945

Delaney Creek

67

37

65

HWY 120

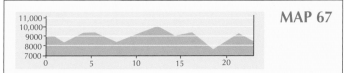

MAP 67

10. 17:05hr 9140ft 0278850 4214130. High point above Seavey Pass.

9. 14:50hr 7590ft. Piute Creek is deep but slow with a sandy bottom. You might be able to cross on logs downstream. The trail to Benson Lake, with its broad sandy beach, goes left immediately after Piute Creek. However, the best swimming is from the small lake two miles ahead which warms quickly.

8. 12:50hr 9220ft 0281840 4210130. Smedberg Lake. The PCT can be difficult to follow as it climbs 200ft over granite slabs before descending to Benson Lake.

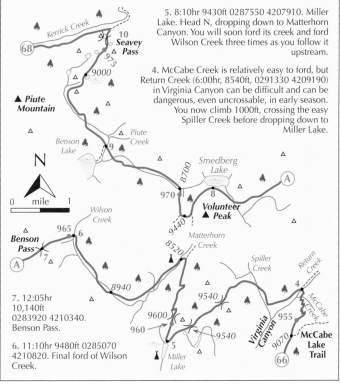

5. 8:10hr 9430ft 0287550 4207910. Miller Lake. Head N, dropping down to Matterhorn Canyon. You will soon ford its creek and ford Wilson Creek three times as you follow it upstream.

4. McCabe Creek is relatively easy to ford, but Return Creek (6:00hr, 8540ft, 0291330 4209190) in Virginia Canyon can be difficult and can be dangerous, even uncrossable, in early season. You now climb 1000ft, crossing the easy Spiller Creek before dropping down to Miller Lake.

7. 12:05hr 10,140ft 0283920 4210340. Benson Pass.

6. 11:10hr 9480ft 0285070 4210820. Final ford of Wilson Creek.

MAP 68

N

10,000
9000
8000
7000
0   5   10   15

0   mile   1

Section 38: Bear Valley Trail to Sonora Pass
(maps 68–70)   38 miles   19 hours   6000ft

Hopefully the creek crossings will now be a little easier. This section ends with a high level alpine traverse and a final descent to Sonora Pass, where the snow can be dangerously icy well into summer. After this section, unless it is an exceptionally high snow year, you can send your ice axe and crampons home, if you are carrying them. Once you leave Yosemite National Park at Dorothy Lake Pass, you are no longer required to store food in a bear canister, so it can be sent home at the next opportunity.

3. 4:45hr 7980ft. Falls Creek.

2. 4:00hr 8390ft. Tilden Canyon Creek.

1. 1:45hr 7790ft. Stubblefield Canyon Creek can be deep but flows slowly and has a sandy bed, so is easy to cross.

11. 19:00hr 7960ft 0274180 4213870. Bear Valley Trail junction. This trail will eventually take you to Hetch Hetchy Reservoir. The PCT now fords the often difficult Kerrick Canyon Creek but it might be possible to cross on a log upstream.

Although the main foods of black bears are fruit, nuts and insects, they will also eat human food and garbage. Leaving food and trash where a bear can find them could create a nuisance bear which might have to be destroyed.

Black bears mark trees by biting and clawing the bark as high as they can reach. If you see these marks on a tree, you can be sure you're in bear country.

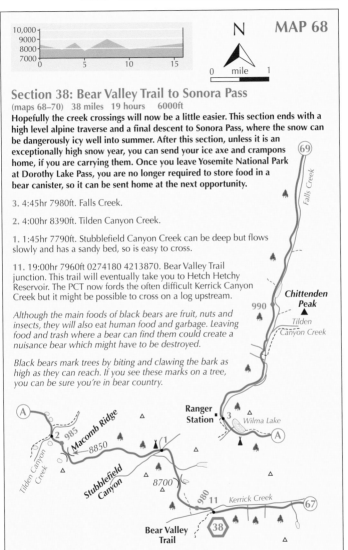

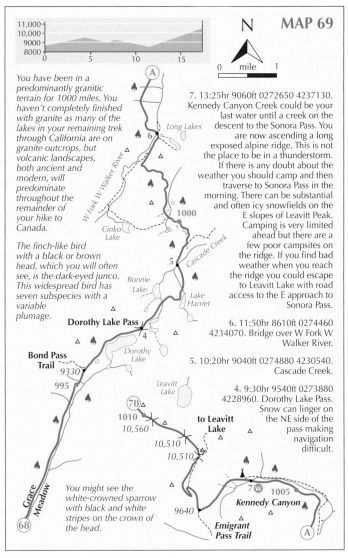

MAP 69

11,000
10,000
9000
8000
0   5   10   15

N

0   mile   1

You have been in a predominantly granitic terrain for 1000 miles. You haven't completely finished with granite as many of the lakes in your remaining trek through California are on granite outcrops, but volcanic landscapes, both ancient and modern, will predominate throughout the remainder of your hike to Canada.

The finch-like bird with a black or brown head, which you will often see, is the dark-eyed junco. This widespread bird has seven subspecies with a variable plumage.

7. 13:25hr 9060ft 0272650 4237130. Kennedy Canyon Creek could be your last water until a creek on the descent to the Sonora Pass. You are now ascending a long exposed alpine ridge. This is not the place to be in a thunderstorm. If there is any doubt about the weather you should camp and then traverse to Sonora Pass in the morning. There can be substantial and often icy snowfields on the E slopes of Leavitt Peak. Camping is very limited ahead but there are a few poor campsites on the ridge. If you find bad weather when you reach the ridge you could escape to Leavitt Lake with road access to the E approach to Sonora Pass.

6. 11:50hr 8610ft 0274460 4234070. Bridge over W Fork W Walker River.

5. 10:20hr 9040ft 0274880 4230540. Cascade Creek.

4. 9:30hr 9540ft 0273880 4228960. Dorothy Lake Pass. Snow can linger on the NE side of the pass making navigation difficult.

Dorothy Lake Pass

Bond Pass Trail 9330

995

1010
10,560

to Leavitt Lake

10,510
10,510

9640

You might see the white-crowned sparrow with black and white stripes on the crown of the head.

7 **W** 1005
Kennedy Canyon

Emigrant Pass Trail

Long Lakes
W Fork W Walker River
Cinko Lake
Bonnie Lake
Lake Harriet
Dorothy Lake
Leavitt Lake
Cascade Creek
Grace Meadow

MAP 70

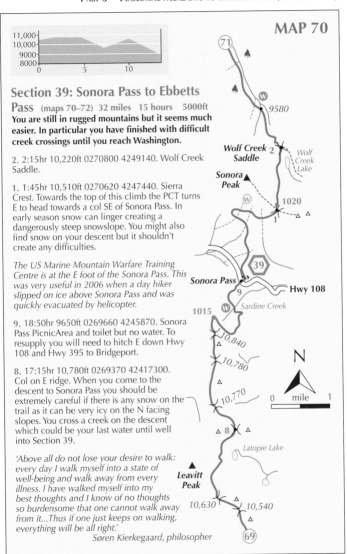

Section 39: Sonora Pass to Ebbetts

Pass (maps 70–72) 32 miles 15 hours 5000ft
You are still in rugged mountains but it seems much easier. In particular you have finished with difficult creek crossings until you reach Washington.

2. 2:15hr 10,220ft 0270800 4249140. Wolf Creek Saddle.

1. 1:45hr 10,510ft 0270620 4247440. Sierra Crest. Towards the top of this climb the PCT turns E to head towards a col SE of Sonora Pass. In early season snow can linger creating a dangerously steep snowslope. You might also find snow on your descent but it shouldn't create any difficulties.

The US Marine Mountain Warfare Training Centre is at the E foot of the Sonora Pass. This was very useful in 2006 when a day hiker slipped on ice above Sonora Pass and was quickly evacuated by helicopter.

9. 18:50hr 9650ft 0269660 4245870. Sonora Pass PicnicArea and toilet but no water. To resupply you will need to hitch E down Hwy 108 and Hwy 395 to Bridgeport.

8. 17:15hr 10,780ft 0269370 42417300. Col on E ridge. When you come to the descent to Sonora Pass you should be extremely careful if there is any snow on the trail as it can be very icy on the N facing slopes. You cross a creek on the descent which could be your last water until well into Section 39.

'Above all do not lose your desire to walk: every day I walk myself into a state of well-being and walk away from every illness. I have walked myself into my best thoughts and I know of no thoughts so burdensome that one cannot walk away from it...Thus if one just keeps on walking, everything will be all right.'
Søren Kierkegaard, philosopher

191

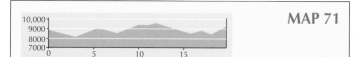

MAP 71

9. 11:10hr 8440ft 0258430 4264720. Wolf Creek Pass Trail. Careful navigation is needed here with a proliferation of small paths. The PCT crosses the outlet of popular Asa Lake before climbing above this small tarn.

8. 9:50hr 8320ft. E Fork Wolf Creek. The first of 3 main tributaries of Wolf Creek.

7. 9:10hr 9080ft 0261750 4262260. Saddle.

6. 7:45hr 9090ft 0262360 4259140. Golden Lake Creek. Golden Lake is more of a marsh than a lake.

5. 6:35hr 8600ft. Boulder Creek.

4. 5:50hr 8570ft 0266120 4257870. Boulder Lake Trail goes W from the saddle.

3. 4:10hr 8150ft. E Fork Carson River Trail. You now cross a tributary and climb steeply out of the canyon.

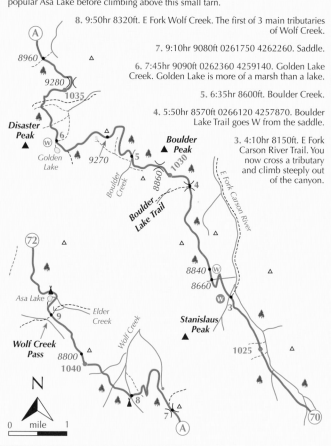

MAP 72

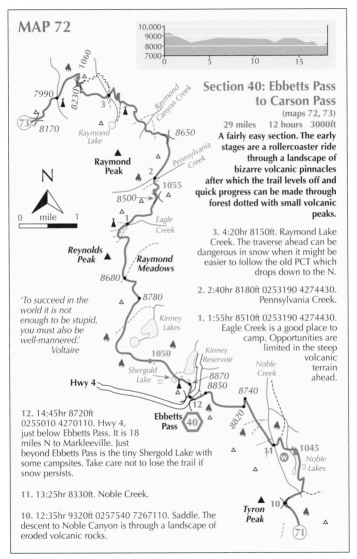

10,000
9000
8000
7000

0   5   10   15

Section 40: Ebbetts Pass to Carson Pass
(maps 72, 73)
29 miles   12 hours   3000ft
A fairly easy section. The early stages are a rollercoaster ride through a landscape of bizarre volcanic pinnacles after which the trail levels off and quick progress can be made through forest dotted with small volcanic peaks.

3. 4:20hr 8150ft. Raymond Lake Creek. The traverse ahead can be dangerous in snow when it might be easier to follow the old PCT which drops down to the N.

2. 2:40hr 8180ft 0253190 4274430. Pennsylvania Creek.

1. 1:55hr 8510ft 0253190 4274430. Eagle Creek is a good place to camp. Opportunities are limited in the steep volcanic terrain ahead.

'To succeed in the world it is not enough to be stupid, you must also be well-mannered.'
Voltaire

12. 14:45hr 8720ft 0255010 4270110. Hwy 4, just below Ebbetts Pass. It is 18 miles N to Markleeville. Just beyond Ebbetts Pass is the tiny Shergold Lake with some campsites. Take care not to lose the trail if snow persists.

11. 13:25hr 8330ft. Noble Creek.

10. 12:35hr 9320ft 0257540 7267110. Saddle. The descent to Noble Canyon is through a landscape of eroded volcanic rocks.

1060
7990
8230
73
8170
3
Raymond Canyon Creek
8650
Raymond Lake
Raymond Peak
Pennsylvania Creek
2
1055
8500
N
0   mile   1
1
Eagle Creek
Reynolds Peak
Raymond Meadows
8680
8780
Kinney Lakes
1050
Kinney Reservoir
Noble Creek
Shergold Lake
8870
8850
Hwy 4
8740
12
Ebbetts Pass 40
8820
Noble Lakes
W
1045
Tyron Peak
10
71

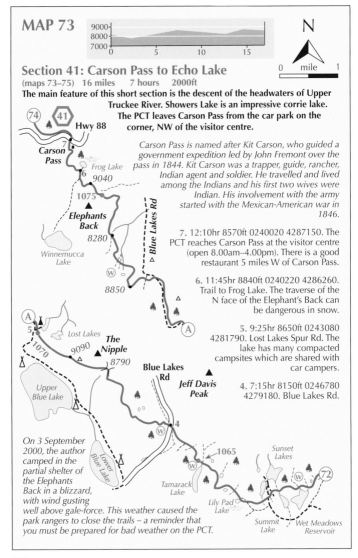

MAP 73

9000
8000
7000
0   5   10   15

N

0 ──── mile ──── 1

Section 41: Carson Pass to Echo Lake

(maps 73–75)   16 miles   7 hours   2000ft

The main feature of this short section is the descent of the headwaters of Upper Truckee River. Showers Lake is an impressive corrie lake. The PCT leaves Carson Pass from the car park on the corner, NW of the visitor centre.

74   41
Hwy 88

7
Carson Pass

Frog Lake
6   9040

1075

▲
Elephants Back
8280

Winnemucca Lake

W
8850

A
5
Lost Lakes
1070   9090
The Nipple
8790

Blue Lakes Rd

▲
Jeff Davis Peak

Upper Blue Lake

Lower Blue Lake

4

Tamarack Lake

1065
W

Lily Pad Lake

Sunset Lakes

W
72

Summit Lake

Wet Meadows Reservoir

Carson Pass is named after Kit Carson, who guided a government expedition led by John Fremont over the pass in 1844. Kit Carson was a trapper, guide, rancher, Indian agent and soldier. He travelled and lived among the Indians and his first two wives were Indian. His involvement with the army started with the Mexican-American war in 1846.

7. 12:10hr 8570ft 0240020 4287150. The PCT reaches Carson Pass at the visitor centre (open 8.00am–4.00pm). There is a good restaurant 5 miles W of Carson Pass.

6. 11:45hr 8840ft 0240220 4286260. Trail to Frog Lake. The traverse of the N face of the Elephant's Back can be dangerous in snow.

5. 9:25hr 8650ft 0243080 4281790. Lost Lakes Spur Rd. The lake has many compacted campsites which are shared with car campers.

4. 7:15hr 8150ft 0246780 4279180. Blue Lakes Rd.

On 3 September 2000, the author camped in the partial shelter of the Elephants Back in a blizzard, with wind gusting well above gale-force. This weather caused the park rangers to close the trails – a reminder that you must be prepared for bad weather on the PCT.

MAP 74

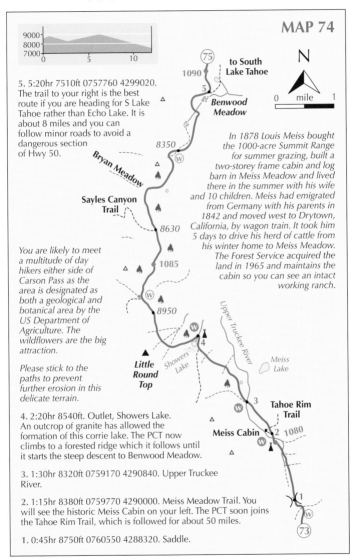

to South
Lake Tahoe

**Benwood
Meadow**

5. 5:20hr 7510ft 0757760 4299020.
The trail to your right is the best
route if you are heading for S Lake
Tahoe rather than Echo Lake. It is
about 8 miles and you can
follow minor roads to avoid a
dangerous section
of Hwy 50.

Bryan Meadow

**Sayles Canyon
Trail**

In 1878 Louis Meiss bought
the 1000-acre Summit Range
for summer grazing, built a
two-storey frame cabin and log
barn in Meiss Meadow and lived
there in the summer with his wife
and 10 children. Meiss had emigrated
from Germany with his parents in
1842 and moved west to Drytown,
California, by wagon train. It took him
5 days to drive his herd of cattle from
his winter home to Meiss Meadow.
The Forest Service acquired the
land in 1965 and maintains the
cabin so you can see an intact
working ranch.

You are likely to meet
a multitude of day
hikers either side of
Carson Pass as the
area is designated as
both a geological and
botanical area by the
US Department of
Agriculture. The
wildflowers are the big
attraction.

Please stick to the
paths to prevent
further erosion in this
delicate terrain.

Upper Truckee River

Meiss
Lake

**Little
Round
Top**

Showers
Lake

Tahoe Rim
Trail

Meiss Cabin

4. 2:20hr 8540ft. Outlet, Showers Lake.
An outcrop of granite has allowed the
formation of this corrie lake. The PCT now
climbs to a forested ridge which it follows until
it starts the steep descent to Benwood Meadow.

3. 1:30hr 8320ft 0759170 4290840. Upper Truckee
River.

2. 1:15hr 8380ft 0759770 4290000. Meiss Meadow Trail. You
will see the historic Meiss Cabin on your left. The PCT soon joins
the Tahoe Rim Trail, which is followed for about 50 miles.

1. 0:45hr 8750ft 0760550 4288320. Saddle.

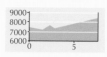

N

0   mile   1

MAP 75

2. 3:45hr 8130ft 0747580 4306930. Here you leave Lake Aloha.

1. 1:55hr 7880ft 0752070 4304010. Tamarack Lake Trail.

8. 6:45hr 7450ft 0756610 4302560. Echo Lake Resort. Once the snowmelt streams have dried up there will be no water until Lake Aloha. Look out for osprey fishing in the lake.

7. Hwy 50. Little Norway has camping or accommodation for hikers.

Lake Tahoe is the biggest natural lake in California and its shores are dotted with big resorts to cater for winter sports and summer visitors. At 514m, it is second only to Crater Lake in depth in the US.

Section 42: Echo Lake to Barker Pass (maps 75–77)
32 miles   15 hours   4000ft

You are heading into Desolation Wilderness, where a large outcrop of granite has resulted in a landscape of lakes and bare rock. This is a special section which is understandably popular with hikers staying in the resorts around Lake Tahoe.

Camping is not allowed until you are clear of Upper Echo Lake.

In 2002, the author met Flying Brian (Brian Robinson) at Echo Lake, taking a day off to perform trail angel duties before a 100-mile mountain race over the weekend. In 2001 he became the first hiker to complete the Triple Crown of the PCT, Continental Divide Trail and Appalachian Trail in one year, a total of about 8000 miles.

▲ **Keiths Dome**

Ⓐ

water taxi to resort

▲ **Echo Peak**

1

1095

Flagpole △ **Peak**

△ *Tamarack Lake*

Echo Lakes

⬡ 42

8P

Talking Mountain ▲

Echo Lake Resort

2   76

Hwy 50

1100

△ *Heather Lake*

△ *Lake Le Conte*

Little Norway

Lake Aloha

△

7

Echo Summit Sno-Park

▲ 74

Meyers Grade

Ⓐ

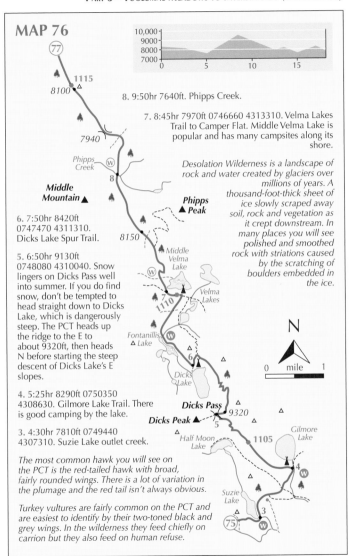

MAP 76

77

1115
8100

7940

Phipps Creek

8

Middle Mountain ▲

8150

Middle Velma Lake

7
1110

Velma Lakes

Fontanillis ▲ *Lake*

6

Dicks Lake

Dicks Pass 9320

Dicks Peak ▲ 5

Half Moon Lake

1105

Gilmore Lake

4

Suzie Lake

3

75

8. 9:50hr 7640ft. Phipps Creek.

7. 8:45hr 7970ft 0746660 4313310. Velma Lakes Trail to Camper Flat. Middle Velma Lake is popular and has many campsites along its shore.

Desolation Wilderness is a landscape of rock and water created by glaciers over millions of years. A thousand-foot-thick sheet of ice slowly scraped away soil, rock and vegetation as it crept downstream. In many places you will see polished and smoothed rock with striations caused by the scratching of boulders embedded in the ice.

Phipps Peak ▲

6. 7:50hr 8420ft 0747470 4311310. Dicks Lake Spur Trail.

5. 6:50hr 9130ft 0748080 4310040. Snow lingers on Dicks Pass well into summer. If you do find snow, don't be tempted to head straight down to Dicks Lake, which is dangerously steep. The PCT heads up the ridge to the E to about 9320ft, then heads N before starting the steep descent of Dicks Lake's E slopes.

4. 5:25hr 8290ft 0750350 4308630. Gilmore Lake Trail. There is good camping by the lake.

3. 4:30hr 7810ft 0749440 4307310. Suzie Lake outlet creek.

The most common hawk you will see on the PCT is the red-tailed hawk with broad, fairly rounded wings. There is a lot of variation in the plumage and the red tail isn't always obvious.

Turkey vultures are fairly common on the PCT and are easiest to identify by their two-toned black and grey wings. In the wilderness they feed chiefly on carrion but they also feed on human refuse.

N

0   mile   1

MAP 77

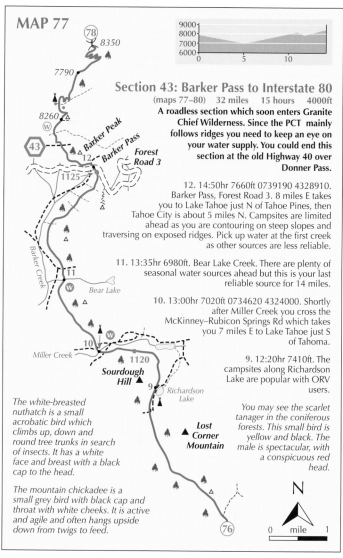

8350

7790

8260

Barker Peak

Barker Pass

43

1125

Forest Road 3

Barker Pass

12

Barker Creek

11

Bear Lake

10

Miller Creek

1120

Sourdough Hill

9

Richardson Lake

Lost Corner Mountain

76

Section 43: Barker Pass to Interstate 80

(maps 77–80)   32 miles   15 hours   4000ft

A roadless section which soon enters Granite Chief Wilderness. Since the PCT mainly follows ridges you need to keep an eye on your water supply. You could end this section at the old Highway 40 over Donner Pass.

12. 14:50hr 7660ft 0739190 4328910. Barker Pass, Forest Road 3. 8 miles E takes you to Lake Tahoe just N of Tahoe Pines, then Tahoe City is about 5 miles N. Campsites are limited ahead as you are contouring on steep slopes and traversing on exposed ridges. Pick up water at the first creek as other sources are less reliable.

11. 13:35hr 6980ft. Bear Lake Creek. There are plenty of seasonal water sources ahead but this is your last reliable source for 14 miles.

10. 13:00hr 7020ft 0734620 4324000. Shortly after Miller Creek you cross the McKinney–Rubicon Springs Rd which takes you 7 miles E to Lake Tahoe just S of Tahoma.

9. 12:20hr 7410ft. The campsites along Richardson Lake are popular with ORV users.

You may see the scarlet tanager in the coniferous forests. This small bird is yellow and black. The male is spectacular, with a conspicuous red head.

The white-breasted nuthatch is a small acrobatic bird which climbs up, down and round tree trunks in search of insects. It has a white face and breast with a black cap to the head.

The mountain chickadee is a small grey bird with black cap and throat with white cheeks. It is active and agile and often hangs upside down from twigs to feed.

N

0   mile   1

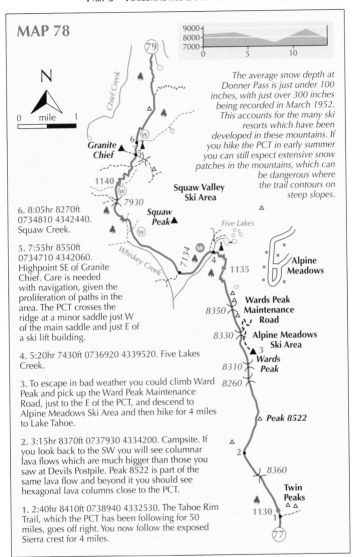

MAP 78

N
0   mile   1

Chief Creek

79

Granite
Chief

1140

6 W

7930 W

**Squaw Valley
Ski Area**

Squaw
Peak▲

W

Whiskey Creek

Five Lakes

7134

W

4

1135

**Alpine
Meadows**

*The average snow depth at
Donner Pass is just under 100
inches, with just over 300 inches
being recorded in March 1952.
This accounts for the many ski
resorts which have been
developed in these mountains. If
you hike the PCT in early summer
you can still expect extensive snow
patches in the mountains, which can
be dangerous where
the trail contours on
steep slopes.*

6. 8:05hr 8270ft
0734810 4342440.
Squaw Creek.

5. 7:55hr 8550ft
0734710 4342060.
Highpoint SE of Granite
Chief. Care is needed
with navigation, given the
proliferation of paths in the
area. The PCT crosses the
ridge at a minor saddle just W
of the main saddle and just E
of a ski lift building.

4. 5:20hr 7430ft 0736920 4339520. Five Lakes
Creek.

3. To escape in bad weather you could climb Ward
Peak and pick up the Ward Peak Maintenance
Road, just to the E of the PCT, and descend to
Alpine Meadows Ski Area and then hike for 4 miles
to Lake Tahoe.

2. 3:15hr 8370ft 0737930 4334200. Campsite. If
you look back to the SW you will see columnar
lava flows which are much bigger than those you
saw at Devils Postpile. Peak 8522 is part of the
same lava flow and beyond it you should see
hexagonal lava columns close to the PCT.

1. 2:40hr 8410ft 0738940 4332530. The Tahoe Rim
Trail, which the PCT has been following for 50
miles, goes off right. You now follow the exposed
Sierra crest for 4 miles.

8350

**Wards Peak
Maintenance
Road**

8330

**Alpine Meadows
Ski Area**

3

*Wards
Peak*

8310

8260

△ **Peak 8522**

2

8360

**Twin
Peaks**

1130

1

77

MAP 79

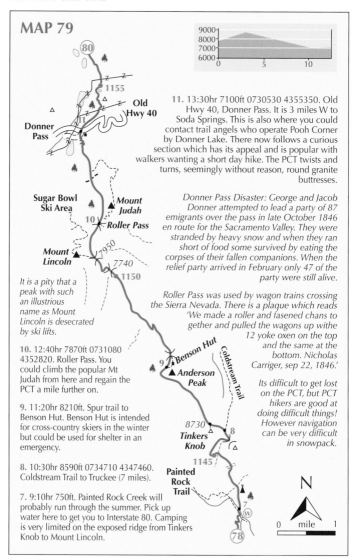

1155

Old Hwy 40

Donner Pass

Sugar Bowl Ski Area

Mount Judah

10 **Roller Pass**

Mount Lincoln

7950

7740

1150

It is a pity that a peak with such an illustrious name as Mount Lincoln is desecrated by ski lifts.

9 **Benson Hut**

▲**Anderson Peak**

Coldstream Trail

8730

Tinkers Knob

8

1145

Painted Rock Trail

7

78

11. 13:30hr 7100ft 0730530 4355350. Old Hwy 40, Donner Pass. It is 3 miles W to Soda Springs. This is also where you could contact trail angels who operate Pooh Corner by Donner Lake. There now follows a curious section which has its appeal and is popular with walkers wanting a short day hike. The PCT twists and turns, seemingly without reason, round granite buttresses.

Donner Pass Disaster: George and Jacob Donner attempted to lead a party of 87 emigrants over the pass in late October 1846 en route for the Sacramento Valley. They were stranded by heavy snow and when they ran short of food some survived by eating the corpses of their fallen companions. When the relief party arrived in February only 47 of the party were still alive.

Roller Pass was used by wagon trains crossing the Sierra Nevada. There is a plaque which reads 'We made a roller and fasened chans to gether and pulled the wagons up withe 12 yoke oxen on the top and the same at the bottom. Nicholas Carriger, sep 22, 1846.'

Its difficult to get lost on the PCT, but PCT hikers are good at doing difficult things! However navigation can be very difficult in snowpack.

10. 12:40hr 7870ft 0731080 4352820. Roller Pass. You could climb the popular Mt Judah from here and regain the PCT a mile further on.

9. 11:20hr 8210ft. Spur trail to Benson Hut. Benson Hut is intended for cross-country skiers in the winter but could be used for shelter in an emergency.

8. 10:30hr 8590ft 0734710 4347460. Coldstream Trail to Truckee (7 miles).

7. 9:10hr 750ft. Painted Rock Creek will probably run through the summer. Pick up water here to get you to Interstate 80. Camping is very limited on the exposed ridge from Tinkers Knob to Mount Lincoln.

N

0   mile   1

MAP 80

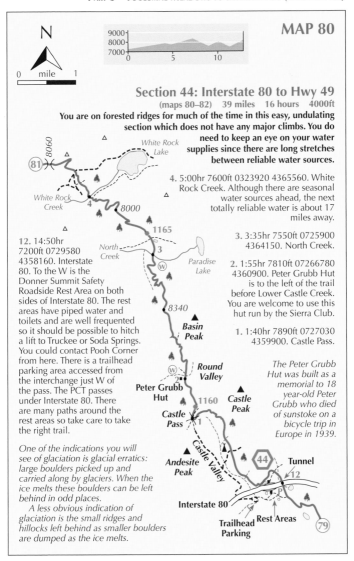

N

0   mile   1

Section 44: Interstate 80 to Hwy 49
(maps 80–82)   39 miles   16 hours   4000ft

You are on forested ridges for much of the time in this easy, undulating section which does not have any major climbs. You do need to keep an eye on your water supplies since there are long stretches between reliable water sources.

4. 5:00hr 7600ft 0323920 4365560. White Rock Creek. Although there are seasonal water sources ahead, the next totally reliable water is about 17 miles away.

3. 3:35hr 7550ft 0725900 4364150. North Creek.

2. 1:55hr 7810ft 07266780 4360900. Peter Grubb Hut is to the left of the trail before Lower Castle Creek. You are welcome to use this hut run by the Sierra Club.

1. 1:40hr 7890ft 0727030 4359900. Castle Pass.

12. 14:50hr 7200ft 0729580 4358160. Interstate 80. To the W is the Donner Summit Safety Roadside Rest Area on both sides of Interstate 80. The rest areas have piped water and toilets and are well frequented so it should be possible to hitch a lift to Truckee or Soda Springs. You could contact Pooh Corner from here. There is a trailhead parking area accessed from the interchange just W of the pass. The PCT passes under Interstate 80. There are many paths around the rest areas so take care to take the right trail.

The Peter Grubb Hut was built as a memorial to 18 year-old Peter Grubb who died of sunstoke on a bicycle trip in Europe in 1939.

One of the indications you will see of glaciation is glacial erratics: large boulders picked up and carried along by glaciers. When the ice melts these boulders can be left behind in odd places.

A less obvious indication of glaciation is the small ridges and hillocks left behind as smaller boulders are dumped as the ice melts.

Boiling Springs Lake (Section 50)

NORTHERN CALIFORNIA

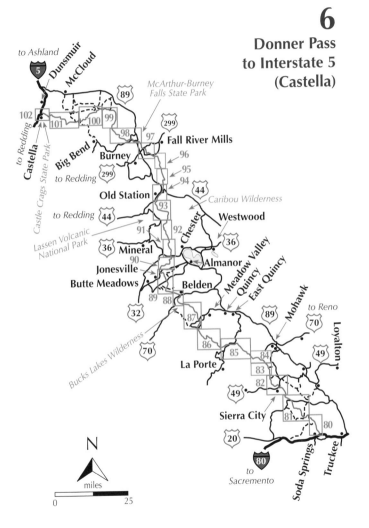

to Ashland

5

Dunsmuir

McCloud

McArthur-Burney
Falls State Park

89

99

98

97

299

Fall River Mills

102

101

100

96

95

94

Big Bend

Burney

Castella

299

to Redding

Castle Crags State Park

44

Old Station

Caribou Wilderness

to Redding

44

93

Westwood

91

92

Chester

Lassen Volcanic
National Park

36

Mineral

36

Jonesville

90

Almanor

Meadow Valley

Quincy

Butte Meadows

Belden

East Quincy

89

88

Mohawk

to Reno

89

89

32

87

70

70

86

85

84

49

Bucks Lakes Wilderness

La Porte

83

Loyalton

82

49

Sierra City

81

80

20

80

Soda Springs

Truckee

N

miles

0   25

to
Sacramento

PART 6: DONNER PASS TO INTERSTATE 5 (CASTELLA)

Section	Distance (miles)	Time (hours)	Ascent (feet)	Maps
44 Interstate 80–Sierra City	39	16	4000	80–82
45 Sierra City–Quincy/LaPorte Rd	38	18	6000	82–85
46 Quincy/LaPorte Rd–Big Creek Rd	29	13	4000	85–87
47 Big Creek Rd–Belden	24	10	2000	87, 88
48 Belden–Humboldt Summit	25	14	6000	88–90
49 Humboldt Summit–Highway 36	20	8	2000	90, 91
50 Highway 36–Hat Creek Resort	42	17	4000	91–94
51 Hat Creek Resort–Road 22	21	8	1000	94–96
52 Road 22–Burney Falls	25	9	700	96–98
53 Burney Falls–Bartle Gap	28	13	4000	98, 99
54 Bartle Gap–McCloud River	25	10	2000	99–101
55 McCloud River–Interstate 5	32	14	4000	101,102
Part total	**348**	**150**	**40,000**	

Much of this long section is along forested hills so there is plenty of shade from the mid-summer sun. There are big climbs as you drop to cross Middle Fork and North Fork Feather Rivers and McCloud River but there are also long flatter sections. As the hiking is primarily now along ridges, sourcing water again becomes a problem and you need to ensure you don't become dehydrated. A few long stretches, along which the forest hasn't recovered from fires and from 20th-century clear felling, are exposed to the sun. Hat Creek Rim is the most notorious but you should appreciate the views as a change from forest hiking. It is in

this section that you enter the Cascade Mountains and encounter Lassen Peak, the first of the big volcanoes that will accompany you to the Canadian border.

Now is the time for thru'-hikers to pick up their pace. If possible, you should arrange to swap your winter sleeping bag and clothing for lightweight summer equipment for Northern California and Oregon.

Best time

July–October. Any time after the snow has melted. Sections 47–55 might be hikeable in June in an average snow year. Thru'-hikers will be pleased to

Bridge over the Middle Fork of the Feather River (Section 46)

know that the remainder of their hike will be at optimum times for the areas through which they are hiking. In a dry summer, seasonal water sources will be sparse and you will have to carry a lot of water later in the season.

Permits

You will need a permit to camp overnight in Section 50 but this won't be required if you organise your schedule so that you can camp at Warner Valley Campground and not in the wilderness in Lassen Volcanic National Park.

Section 50: Lassen Volcanic National Park

Lassen Volcanic National Park, Box 100, Mineral CA96063
(530)-595-4444, www.nps.gov/lavo

Facilities

It is suggested that you resupply at Sierra City, Belden, Hat Creek, Burney Falls and Castella.

Truckee, Soda Springs, Pooh Corner
(from Interstate 80) (Sections 43, 44)
(0 hours)
See Part 5 introduction.

Sierra City (PO, P, G, R, A, C, L, B)
(Sections 44, 45) (16 hours)
Sierra City PO, 215 Main St, Sierra City CA96125
(530)-862-1152. Mon–Fri: 8.30am–11.30am, 12.30pm–4.30pm, Sat: 10.30am–12.30pm
Small town facilities.
www.sierracity.com. Sierra Country Store accepts hiker packages:

Sierra Country Store, 213 Main St,
Sierra City CA96125
(530)-862-1560. 9.00am–8.00pm

Quincy (PO, G, R, A, L, B) (from
Quincy–LaPorte Rd) (Sections 45, 46)
(34 hours) and (from Big Creek Rd)
(Sections 46, 47) (47 hours)
Quincy PO, 222 Lawrence St, Quincy
CA95971
(530)-283-3912.
Mon–Fri: 8.30am–5.00pm
Full town facilities.

LaPorte (small G) (from Quincy–
LaPorte Rd) (Sections 45, 46) (34
hours)

Meadow Valley (PO, small G) (from
Big Creek Rd) (Sections 46, 47) (47
hours)

Meadow Valley PO, 7091 Bucks Lake
Rd, Meadow Valley CA95956
(530)-283-1379. Mon–Fri: 8.30am–
4.30pm, Sat: 12.00noon–1.00pm

Bucks Lake Resort (minimal G, R, A,
C) (from Big Creek Rd) (Sections 46,
47) (47 hours)
www.buckslakelodge.com
The store is in Bucks Lake Lodge.

Belden (PO, small G, R, A, C, L)
(Sections 47, 48) (57 hours)
Belden PO, 1 Belden County Rd,
Belden CA95915
(530)-533-8206.
Mon–Fri: 9.00am–1.00pm
Belden Resort with store and restau-
rant was run down but is now under
new management and could have
improved its service to hikers.

Granite outcrop above Belden (Section 47)

Caribou Crossroads RV Park (minimal G, R, L) (Sections 47, 48) (57 hours)
1½ miles east of the PCT along Highway 70.

Little Haven (P, A, Sh) (Sections 47, 48) (57 hours)
(530)-623-9880, ljbraaten@aol.com
Trail angels Laurie and Brenda Braaten offer a package service, accommodation and local transport in June and July. Hikers can stay one night and packages will be collected from Belden Post Office by prior arrangement.

Chester (PO, G, R, A, B) (from Highway 36) (Sections 49, 50) (79 hours)
Chester PO, 218 Laurel Lane, Chester CA96020
(530)-258-4184.
Mon–Fri: 7.30am–4.00pm
Full town facilities.

Drakesbad Guest Ranch (P, R, L, Sh) (Section 50) (87 hours)
Drakesbad Guest Ranch, End of Warner Valley Rd, Chester CA96020
(866)-999-0914, www.drakesbad. com, Drakesbad@calparksco.com
Drakesbad Guest Ranch offers a package service and use of its restaurant, laundry, showers and pool. Accommodation is likely to be fully booked months in advance and would be expensive. Warner Valley Campground is a quarter-mile to the east.

Hat Creek Resort (PO, G, A, C) (Sections 50, 51) (96 hours)
Old Station PO, 12529 State Highway 44/99, Old Station CA96071
(530)-335-7191.
Mon–Fri: 8.30am–4.30pm
Old Station PO is at Hat Creek Resort, not at Old Station! There is a deli in the store.
www.hatcreekresortrv.com

The Hideaway (C, L, Sh) (Sections 50, 51) (96 hours)
(530)-335-7463,
bobnweav@gmail.com
Trail angels Firewalker and Firefly (Dennis and Georgi), who live near Hat Creek Resort, offer accommodation, meals, showers, laundry and local transport to PCT hikers.

Cassel (PO, small G, C) (from Baum Lake) (Section 52) (107 hours)
Cassel PO, 21594 Cassel Rd, Cassel CA96016
(530)-335-3100.
Mon–Fri: 7.30am–3.30pm

Burney (PO, G, R, A, L, B) (from Highway 299) (Section 52) (110 hours)
Burney PO, 20655 Commerce Way, Burney CA96013
(530)-335-5430.
Mon–Fri: 7.30am–4.00pm
Full town facilities.

Burney Falls Campground (P, small G, C, Sh) (Sections 52, 53) (113 hours)

The entrance to Subway Cave (Section 51)

Burney Falls General Store, 24900, Highway 89, Burney CA96013 (530)-335-5713, www.burney-falls. com. 8.00am–8.00pm
The store offers a package service ($5 fee in 2009). Hot snacks in the store.

Castella (PO, P, G, L, C) (from Interstate 5) (Sections 55, 56) (150 hours)
Castella PO, 20115 Castle Creek Rd, Castella CA96017
(530)-235-4413. Mon–Fri: 8.45am–12.30pm, 1.00pm–4.30pm,
Sat: 8.30am–10.00am

Ammirati's Market, 20107 Castle Creek Rd, Castella CA96017 (530)-235-2676. 7.30am–9.00pm. This well-stocked small store offers a package service.

Dunsmuir (PO, G, R, A, B) (from Interstate 5) (Sections 55, 56) (150 hours)
Dunsmuir PO, 5530 Dunsmuir Avenue, Dunsmuir CA96025
(530)-235-0338.
Mon–Fri: 8.30am–5.00pm
Full town facilities.

MAP 81

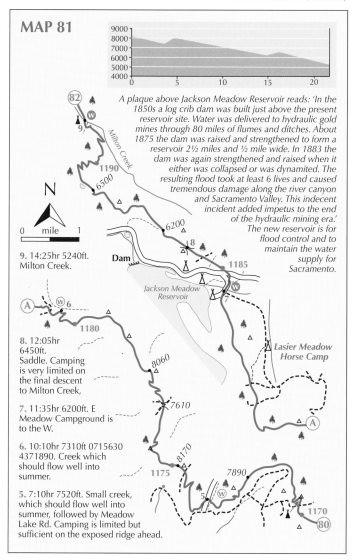

A plaque above Jackson Meadow Reservoir reads: 'In the 1850s a log crib dam was built just above the present reservoir site. Water was delivered to hydraulic gold mines through 80 miles of flumes and ditches. About 1875 the dam was raised and strengthened to form a reservoir 2½ miles and ½ mile wide. In 1883 the dam was again strengthened and raised when it either was collapsed or was dynamited. The resulting flood took at least 6 lives and caused tremendous damage along the river canyon and Sacramento Valley. This indecent incident added impetus to the end of the hydraulic mining era.' The new reservoir is for flood control and to maintain the water supply for Sacramento.

9. 14:25hr 5240ft. Milton Creek.

8. 12:05hr 6450ft. Saddle. Camping is very limited on the final descent to Milton Creek,

7. 11:35hr 6200ft. E Meadow Campground is to the W.

6. 10:10hr 7310ft 0715630 4371890. Creek which should flow well into summer.

5. 7:10hr 7520ft. Small creek, which should flow well into summer, followed by Meadow Lake Rd. Camping is limited but sufficient on the exposed ridge ahead.

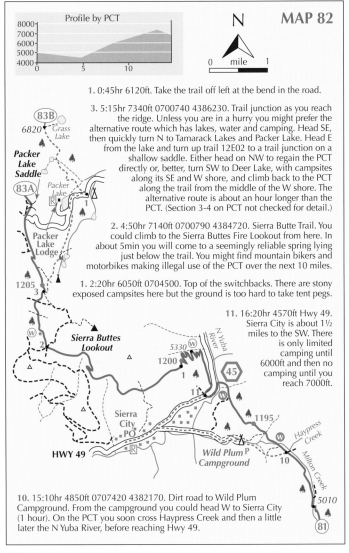

MAP 82

Profile by PCT

N

0   mile   1

1. 0:45hr 6120ft. Take the trail off left at the bend in the road.

3. 5:15hr 7340ft 0700740 4386230. Trail junction as you reach the ridge. Unless you are in a hurry you might prefer the alternative route which has lakes, water and camping. Head SE, then quickly turn N to Tamarack Lakes and Packer Lake. Head E from the lake and turn up trail 12E02 to a trail junction on a shallow saddle. Either head on NW to regain the PCT directly or, better, turn SW to Deer Lake, with campsites along its SE and W shore, and climb back to the PCT along the trail from the middle of the W shore. The alternative route is about an hour longer than the PCT. (Section 3-4 on PCT not checked for detail.)

83B

6820 Grass Lake

Packer Lake Saddle

83A   Packer Lake

1

2. 4:50hr 7140ft 0700790 4384720. Sierra Butte Trail. You could climb to the Sierra Buttes Fire Lookout from here. In about 5min you will come to a seemingly reliable spring lying just below the trail. You might find mountain bikers and motorbikes making illegal use of the PCT over the next 10 miles.

Packer Lake Lodge

1205
3

1. 2:20hr 6050ft 0704500. Top of the switchbacks. There are stony exposed campsites here but the ground is too hard to take tent pegs.

Sierra Buttes Lookout

2

11. 16:20hr 4570ft Hwy 49. Sierra City is about 1½ miles to the SW. There is only limited camping until 6000ft and then no camping until you reach 7000ft.

N Yuba River

5330
1200

45

1

11

Sierra City PO

1195

HWY 49

Wild Plum Campground

Haypress Creek

10

Milton Creek

5010

81

10. 15:10hr 4850ft 0707420 4382170. Dirt road to Wild Plum Campground. From the campground you could head W to Sierra City (1 hour). On the PCT you soon cross Haypress Creek and then a little later the N Yuba River, before reaching Hwy 49.

MAP 83

0   mile   1

8. 9:25hr 7040ft. You could camp by this small pond. Better water is to be found by following the trail E for 200yd.

7. 8:15hr 7280ft. Junction to the shallow Oakland Pond.

6. 7:45hr 7020ft. Junction to the small shallow Summit Lake, which is just behind the ridge.

5. 7:15hr 7340ft. Alternative route rejoins the PCT.

2. 2:05hr 7040ft. Junction to Deer Lake. It would be quicker to go straight on but Deer Lake is the best part of the alternative route. There is a faint trail round the north of the lake, then a dirt road back to the PCT.

4. 7:10hr 7400ft 0699780 4391210. Jeep road to Deer Lake. You can drop 300ft to Deer Lake with camping and swimming on the W shore (the alternative route is 2:40hr).

Hydraulic mining is the method of mining by washing away the soil and loose rock with pressure from giant water hoses. It is very destructive to the environment, causing horrendous erosion. You can see evidence of this mining in all the hills surrounding Sierra City.

Section 45: Hwy 49 to Quincy-LaPorte Road (maps 82–85)

38 miles   18 hours   6000ft ascent

There is a number of sharp climbs and descents in this section, but none is particularly long. The route follows forested ridges for much of the distance so water can be a problem. The route is contorted around the volcanic peaks of Gibraltar, Stafford and Mount Etna. The waterless ascent from Hwy 49 can be very hot.

An alternative route via Packer Lake and Deer Lake is given for those who want to visit some of the lakes on the granite shelf to the E of the PCT.

It is possible that there will be a reroute via Gold Lake at some time in the future.

Should you have the time and energy, the 1400ft climb to the Sierra Buttes Fire Buttes Lookout is worthwhile.

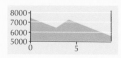

MAP 84

0   mile   1

11. 13:30hr 5950ft. Seasonal Creek. If this is dry, you will have to drop down to Branch Nelson Creek as the creeks ahead are also likely to be dry. The next on-trail water is 24 miles away but there is water close to the trail.

10. 12:10hr 7370ft 0691140. McRae Ridge Saddle. You now descend steep slopes with good views of Gibralter and your first views of Lassen Peak, the first of the active volcanoes, to the N.

9. 11:50hr 6530ft. A-Tree is a multiple road junction. There is a reliable spring a short distance down a jeep track to the SW. Camping is limited but sufficient until you reach Bunker Hill Ridge.

The mile posts you have been seeing for 25 miles seem to be measured from the A-Tree.

It is unlawful to excavate, remove, disturb or destroy any historic or prehistoric building, structure, ruin, site, artefact or object. This law applies to Indian artefacts so you would be breaking the law if you picked up any obsidian chips found on the trail!

It was in Section 44 that Simon Willis, a writer for TGO (The Great Outdoors) Magazine, told me a story that illustrates the difference between the traditional approach to hiking the PCT and the ultra-lightweight approach. 'When Chris Townsend, an author of many books on trekking in N America, thru'-hiked the PCT in the early 1980s, he set off from Kennedy Meadows on 15 May with ice axe, crampons, rope and 23 days' food! At a later date he was hiking with Ray Jardine, the guru of lightweight backpacking and advocate of leaving Kennedy Meadows on 15 June. A storm came in and Chris suggested it was time to stop and put on waterproofs, but Ray suggested it was time to start running. He wasn't carrying any waterproofs!'

You will see many golden-mantled ground squirrels which are often mistaken for a chipmunks. They are relatively tame and you might find them trying to steal your food.

Stellar's jay is a noisy opportunist who frequents mountain recreation areas to take advantage of easy meals from humans. It is dark blue and black with a conspicuous crest.

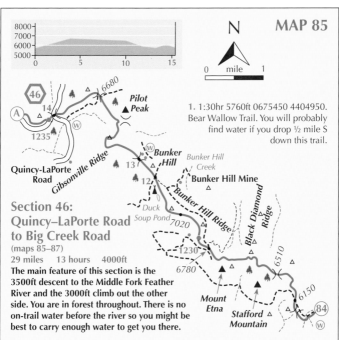

MAP 85

1. 1:30hr 5760ft 0675450 4404950.
Bear Wallow Trail. You will probably
find water if you drop ½ mile S
down this trail.

Section 46:
Quincy–LaPorte Road
to Big Creek Road
(maps 85–87)

29 miles   13 hours   4000ft

The main feature of this section is the
3500ft descent to the Middle Fork Feather
River and the 3000ft climb out the other
side. You are in forest throughout. There is no
on-trail water before the river so you might
be best to carry enough water to get you there.

14. 17:50hr 6470ft 0680530 4405730. Quincy–LaPorte Rd. You could resupply by
hitching (not much traffic) N to Quincy or S to LaPorte. Head SW along this road
for water.

13. 16:40hr 6720ft. Drop down from the saddle and you might find water at 2
seasonal springs in a clear area. The one at the S end of the clearing seems more
reliable, possibly to the end of July (6620ft, 0683140 4404640).

12. 16:30hr 6740ft. Road.

*The distinctive male mountain
bluebird is sky blue above and pale
blue below, with a white belly. The
female is a duller bird.*

213

MAP 86

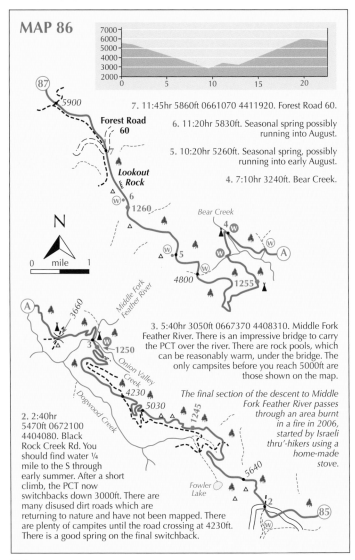

87

5900

Forest Road 60

Lookout Rock

N

0   mile   1

7. 11:45hr 5860ft 0661070 4411920. Forest Road 60.

6. 11:20hr 5830ft. Seasonal spring possibly running into August.

5. 10:20hr 5260ft. Seasonal spring, possibly running into early August.

4. 7:10hr 3240ft. Bear Creek.

Bear Creek

4   w

w   w   A

w   5

4800

w

1255

6

1260

w

3660

Middle Fork Feather River

A

3   w   1250

Onion Valley Creek

4230

5030

1245

Dogwood Creek

3. 5:40hr 3050ft 0667370 4408310. Middle Fork Feather River. There is an impressive bridge to carry the PCT over the river. There are rock pools, which can be reasonably warm, under the bridge. The only campsites before you reach 5000ft are those shown on the map.

The final section of the descent to Middle Fork Feather River passes through an area burnt in a fire in 2006, started by Israeli thru'-hikers using a home-made stove.

2. 2:40hr 5470ft 0672100 4404080. Black Rock Creek Rd. You should find water ¼ mile to the S through early summer. After a short climb, the PCT now switchbacks down 3000ft. There are many disused dirt roads which are returning to nature and have not been mapped. There are plenty of campsites until the road crossing at 4230ft. There is a good spring on the final switchback.

Fowler Lake

5640

2

w

85

MAP 87

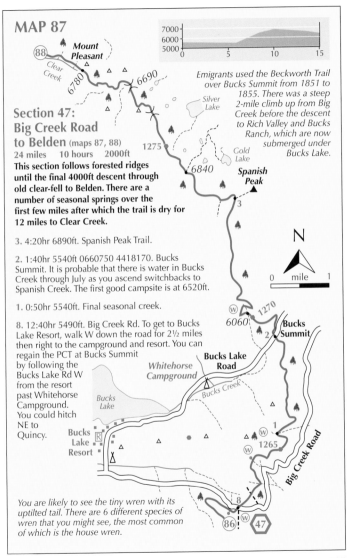

Emigrants used the Beckworth Trail over Bucks Summit from 1851 to 1855. There was a steep 2-mile climb up from Big Creek before the descent to Rich Valley and Bucks Ranch, which are now submerged under Bucks Lake.

Section 47:
Big Creek Road
to Belden (maps 87, 88)
24 miles 10 hours 2000ft

This section follows forested ridges until the final 4000ft descent through old clear-fell to Belden. There are a number of seasonal springs over the first few miles after which the trail is dry for 12 miles to Clear Creek.

3. 4:20hr 6890ft. Spanish Peak Trail.

2. 1:40hr 5540ft 0660750 4418170. Bucks Summit. It is probable that there is water in Bucks Creek through July as you ascend switchbacks to Spanish Creek. The first good campsite is at 6520ft.

1. 0:50hr 5540ft. Final seasonal creek.

8. 12:40hr 5490ft. Big Creek Rd. To get to Bucks Lake Resort, walk W down the road for 2½ miles then right to the campground and resort. You can regain the PCT at Bucks Summit by following the Bucks Lake Rd W from the resort past Whitehorse Campground. You could hitch NE to Quincy.

You are likely to see the tiny wren with its uptilted tail. There are 6 different species of wren that you might see, the most common of which is the house wren.

215

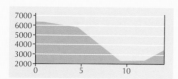

N

MAP 88

0   mile   1

Section 48: Belden to Humboldt Summit

(maps 88–90)

25 miles   14 hours   6000ft

You start the 5000ft climb out of Belden. You need to check up on diversions as the PCT has become impassable due to serious erosion in a gully dropping down into Chips Creek and, at the time of writing, a permanent solution has not been produced. The ascent up the S facing slope, through an area with fire damage can be very hot.

1. 0:25hr 2440ft. Indian Creek.

7. 9:45hr 2330ft. Hwy 70. Belden PO is a little way W along the highway on the right. There is a café and commercial campground 1½ miles E along Hwy 70. There are trail angels in Belden. Check to see if they are still offering a service to hikers. There are no campsites until the site of Williams Cabin (destroyed by fire) at 3700ft.

You might find that the N Fork Feather River is being dredged. This is a remnant of the gold mining industry that used to be a feature of this area. Gold is being separated from the sediment on the riverbed.

6. 9:30hr 2310ft. Western Pacific Railroad. After crossing the railroad you follow the road through Belden Resort, which had been rundown but is now under new management and hopefully will have more to offer the hiker. Continue to Hwy 70.

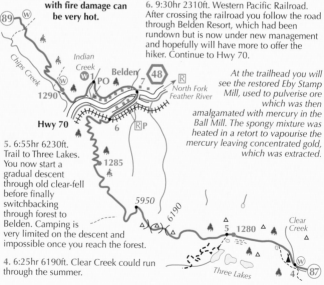

At the trailhead you will see the restored Eby Stamp Mill, used to pulverise ore which was then amalgamated with mercury in the Ball Mill. The spongy mixture was heated in a retort to vapourise the mercury leaving concentrated gold, which was extracted.

Chips Creek

Indian Creek

Belden

North Fork Feather River

1290

Hwy 70

5. 6:55hr 6230ft. Trail to Three Lakes. You now start a gradual descent through old clear-fell before finally switchbacking through forest to Belden. Camping is very limited on the descent and impossible once you reach the forest.

1285

5950

6190

4. 6:25hr 6190ft. Clear Creek could run through the summer.

Three Lakes

5   1280

Clear Creek

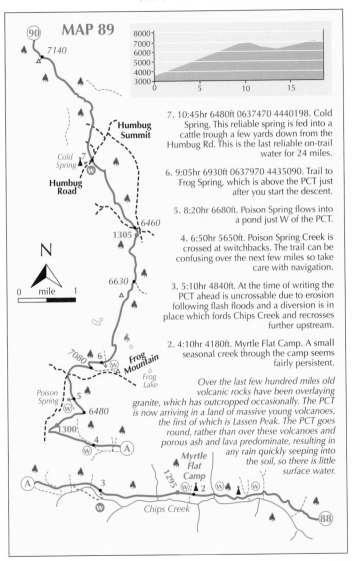

MAP 89

Humbug Summit

Cold Spring

Humbug Road

N

0   mile   1

Frog Mountain

Frog Lake

Poison Spring

Myrtle Flat Camp

Chips Creek

7. 10:45hr 6480ft 0637470 4440198. Cold Spring. This reliable spring is fed into a cattle trough a few yards down from the Humbug Rd. This is the last reliable on-trail water for 24 miles.

6. 9:05hr 6930ft 0637970 4435090. Trail to Frog Spring, which is above the PCT just after you start the descent.

5. 8:20hr 6680ft. Poison Spring flows into a pond just W of the PCT.

4. 6:50hr 5650ft. Poison Spring Creek is crossed at switchbacks. The trail can be confusing over the next few miles so take care with navigation.

3. 5:10hr 4840ft. At the time of writing the PCT ahead is uncrossable due to erosion following flash floods and a diversion is in place which fords Chips Creek and recrosses further upstream.

2. 4:10hr 4180ft. Myrtle Flat Camp. A small seasonal creek through the camp seems fairly persistent.

Over the last few hundred miles old volcanic rocks have been overlaying granite, which has outcropped occasionally. The PCT is now arriving in a land of massive young volcanoes, the first of which is Lassen Peak. The PCT goes round, rather than over these volcanoes and porous ash and lava predominate, resulting in any rain quickly seeping into the soil, so there is little surface water.

217

MAP 90

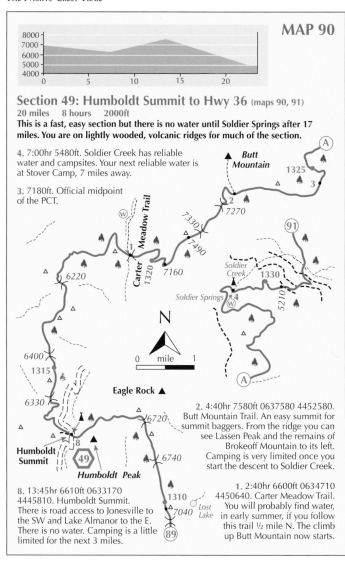

Section 49: Humboldt Summit to Hwy 36 (maps 90, 91)
20 miles   8 hours   2000ft
This is a fast, easy section but there is no water until Soldier Springs after 17 miles. You are on lightly wooded, volcanic ridges for much of the section.

4. 7:00hr 5480ft. Soldier Creek has reliable water and campsites. Your next reliable water is at Stover Camp, 7 miles away.

3. 7180ft. Official midpoint of the PCT.

▲ **Butt Mountain**

1325

△ 3

2 △
7270

91

Carter Meadow Trail

7330

△ 7490

△ 7160

7160

W

△ 6220

Carter Meadow Trail 1320

Soldier Creek **1330**

Soldier Springs **4**
W

5210

N

0   mile   1

Eagle Rock ▲

6400
1315
△

6330

△

△

△

△

△
6720

2. 4:40hr 7580ft 0637580 4452580. Butt Mountain Trail. An easy summit for summit baggers. From the ridge you can see Lassen Peak and the remains of Brokeoff Mountain to its left. Camping is very limited once you start the descent to Soldier Creek.

8
Humboldt Summit

49

Humboldt Peak

6740

8. 13:45hr 6610ft 0633170 4445810. Humboldt Summit. There is road access to Jonesville to the SW and Lake Almanor to the E. There is no water. Camping is a little limited for the next 3 miles.

1310
△ 7040 ○ *Lost Lake*

89

1. 2:40hr 6600ft 0634710 4450640. Carter Meadow Trail. You will probably find water, in early summer, if you follow this trail ½ mile N. The climb up Butt Mountain now starts.

MAP 91

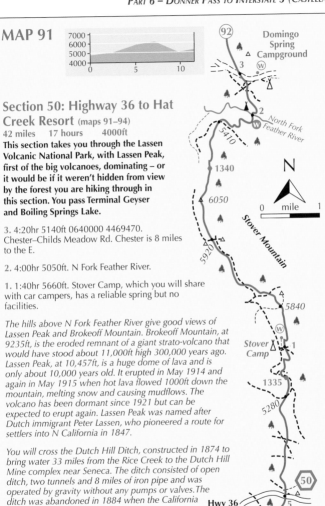

Section 50: Highway 36 to Hat Creek Resort (maps 91–94)

42 miles   17 hours   4000ft

This section takes you through the Lassen Volcanic National Park, with Lassen Peak, first of the big volcanoes, dominating – or it would be if it weren't hidden from view by the forest you are hiking through in this section. You pass Terminal Geyser and Boiling Springs Lake.

3. 4:20hr 5140ft 0640000 4469470. Chester–Childs Meadow Rd. Chester is 8 miles to the E.

2. 4:00hr 5050ft. N Fork Feather River.

1. 1:40hr 5660ft. Stover Camp, which you will share with car campers, has a reliable spring but no facilities.

The hills above N Fork Feather River give good views of Lassen Peak and Brokeoff Mountain. Brokeoff Mountain, at 9235ft, is the eroded remnant of a giant strato-volcano that would have stood about 11,000ft high 300,000 years ago. Lassen Peak, at 10,457ft, is a huge dome of lava and is only about 10,000 years old. It erupted in May 1914 and again in May 1915 when hot lava flowed 1000ft down the mountain, melting snow and causing mudflows. The volcano has been dormant since 1921 but can be expected to erupt again. Lassen Peak was named after Dutch immigrant Peter Lassen, who pioneered a route for settlers into N California in 1847.

You will cross the Dutch Hill Ditch, constructed in 1874 to bring water 33 miles from the Rice Creek to the Dutch Hill Mine complex near Seneca. The ditch consisted of open ditch, two tunnels and 8 miles of iron pipe and was operated by gravity without any pumps or valves. The ditch was abandoned in 1884 when the California Legislature outlawed hydraulic mining.

5. 8:20hr 5090ft. Hwy 36. Chester is 8 miles to the E.

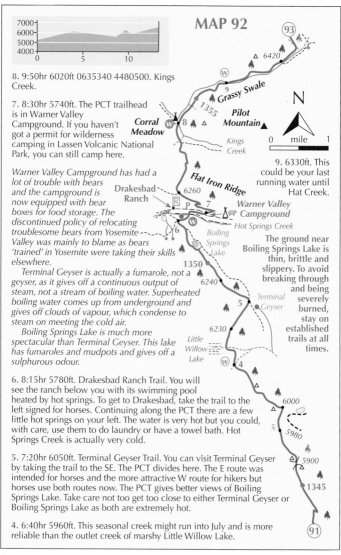

MAP 92

8. 9:50hr 6020ft 0635340 4480500. Kings Creek.

7. 8:30hr 5740ft. The PCT trailhead is in Warner Valley Campground. If you haven't got a permit for wilderness camping in Lassen Volcanic National Park, you can still camp here.

Warner Valley Campground has had a lot of trouble with bears and the campground is now equipped with bear boxes for food storage. The discontinued policy of relocating troublesome bears from Yosemite Valley was mainly to blame as bears 'trained' in Yosemite were taking their skills elsewhere.

Terminal Geyser is actually a fumarole, not a geyser, as it gives off a continuous output of steam, not a stream of boiling water. Superheated boiling water comes up from underground and gives off clouds of vapour, which condense to steam on meeting the cold air.

Boiling Springs Lake is much more spectacular than Terminal Geyser. This lake has fumaroles and mudpots and gives off a sulphurous odour.

9. 6330ft. This could be your last running water until Hat Creek.

The ground near Boiling Springs Lake is thin, brittle and slippery. To avoid breaking through and being severely burned, stay on established trails at all times.

6. 8:15hr 5780ft. Drakesbad Ranch Trail. You will see the ranch below you with its swimming pool heated by hot springs. To get to Drakesbad, take the trail to the left signed for horses. Continuing along the PCT there are a few little hot springs on your left. The water is very hot but you could, with care, use them to do laundry or have a towel bath. Hot Springs Creek is actually very cold.

5. 7:20hr 6050ft. Terminal Geyser Trail. You can visit Terminal Geyser by taking the trail to the SE. The PCT divides here. The E route was intended for horses and the more attractive W route for hikers but horses use both routes now. The PCT gives better views of Boiling Springs Lake. Take care not too get too close to either Terminal Geyser or Boiling Springs Lake as both are extremely hot.

4. 6:40hr 5960ft. This seasonal creek might run into July and is more reliable than the outlet creek of marshy Little Willow Lake.

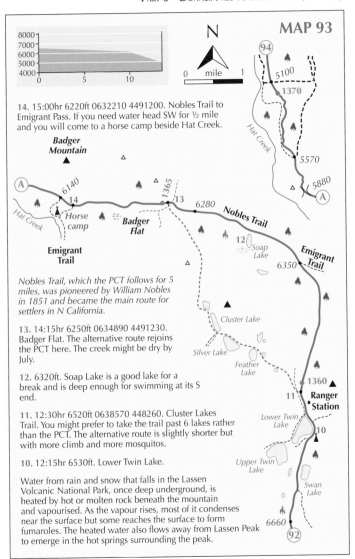

MAP 93

N

0   mile   1

14. 15:00hr 6220ft 0632210 4491200. Nobles Trail to Emigrant Pass. If you need water head SW for ½ mile and you will come to a horse camp beside Hat Creek.

Badger
Mountain

Nobles Trail

Emigrant
Trail

Horse
camp

Badger
Flat

Emigrant
Trail

Hat Creek

Soap
Lake

Cluster Lake

Silver Lake

Feather
Lake

Ranger
Station

Lower Twin
Lake

Upper Twin
Lake

Swan
Lake

Nobles Trail, which the PCT follows for 5 miles, was pioneered by William Nobles in 1851 and became the main route for settlers in N California.

13. 14:15hr 6250ft 0634890 4491230. Badger Flat. The alternative route rejoins the PCT here. The creek might be dry by July.

12. 6320ft. Soap Lake is a good lake for a break and is deep enough for swimming at its S end.

11. 12:30hr 6520ft 0638570 448260. Cluster Lakes Trail. You might prefer to take the trail past 6 lakes rather than the PCT. The alternative route is slightly shorter but with more climb and more mosquitos.

10. 12:15hr 6530ft. Lower Twin Lake.

Water from rain and snow that falls in the Lassen Volcanic National Park, once deep underground, is heated by hot or molten rock beneath the mountain and vapourised. As the vapour rises, most of it condenses near the surface but some reaches the surface to form fumaroles. The heated water also flows away from Lassen Peak to emerge in the hot springs surrounding the peak.

221

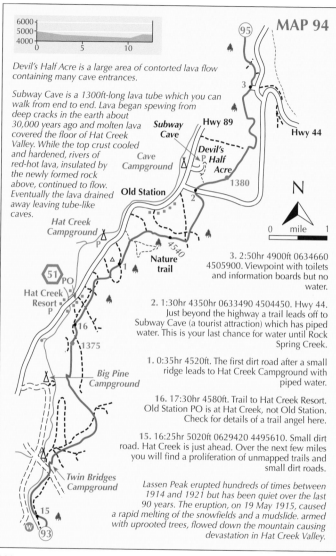

MAP 94

Devil's Half Acre is a large area of contorted lava flow containing many cave entrances.

Subway Cave is a 1300ft-long lava tube which you can walk from end to end. Lava began spewing from deep cracks in the earth about 30,000 years ago and molten lava covered the floor of Hat Creek Valley. While the top crust cooled and hardened, rivers of red-hot lava, insulated by the newly formed rock above, continued to flow. Eventually the lava drained away leaving tube-like caves.

6000
5000
4000
0   5   10

3. 2:50hr 4900ft 0634660 4505900. Viewpoint with toilets and information boards but no water.

2. 1:30hr 4350hr 0633490 4504450. Hwy 44. Just beyond the highway a trail leads off to Subway Cave (a tourist attraction) which has piped water. This is your last chance for water until Rock Spring Creek.

1. 0:35hr 4520ft. The first dirt road after a small ridge leads to Hat Creek Campground with piped water.

16. 17:30hr 4580ft. Trail to Hat Creek Resort. Old Station PO is at Hat Creek, not Old Station. Check for details of a trail angel here.

15. 16:25hr 5020ft 0629420 4495610. Small dirt road. Hat Creek is just ahead. Over the next few miles you will find a proliferation of unmapped trails and small dirt roads.

Lassen Peak erupted hundreds of times between 1914 and 1921 but has been quiet over the last 90 years. The eruption, on 19 May 1915, caused a rapid melting of the snowfields and a mudslide. armed with uprooted trees, flowed down the mountain causing devastation in Hat Creek Valley.

MAP 95

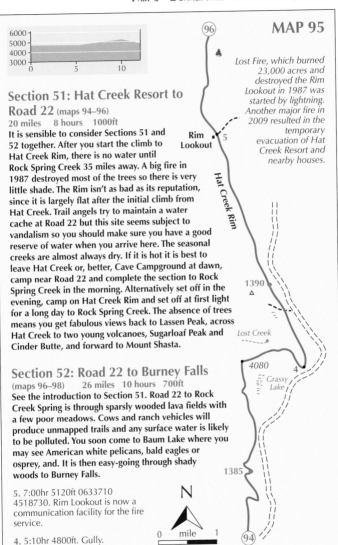

Lost Fire, which burned 23,000 acres and destroyed the Rim Lookout in 1987 was started by lightning. Another major fire in 2009 resulted in the temporary evacuation of Hat Creek Resort and nearby houses.

Section 51: Hat Creek Resort to Road 22 (maps 94–96)

20 miles   8 hours   1000ft

It is sensible to consider Sections 51 and 52 together. After you start the climb to Hat Creek Rim, there is no water until Rock Spring Creek 35 miles away. A big fire in 1987 destroyed most of the trees so there is very little shade. The Rim isn't as bad as its reputation, since it is largely flat after the initial climb from Hat Creek. Trail angels try to maintain a water cache at Road 22 but this site seems subject to vandalism so you should make sure you have a good reserve of water when you arrive here. The seasonal creeks are almost always dry. If it is hot it is best to leave Hat Creek or, better, Cave Campground at dawn, camp near Road 22 and complete the section to Rock Spring Creek in the morning. Alternatively set off in the evening, camp on Hat Creek Rim and set off at first light for a long day to Rock Spring Creek. The absence of trees means you get fabulous views back to Lassen Peak, across Hat Creek to two young volcanoes, Sugarloaf Peak and Cinder Butte, and forward to Mount Shasta.

Section 52: Road 22 to Burney Falls
(maps 96–98)   26 miles   10 hours   700ft

See the introduction to Section 51. Road 22 to Rock Creek Spring is through sparsely wooded lava fields with a few poor meadows. Cows and ranch vehicles will produce unmapped trails and any surface water is likely to be polluted. You soon come to Baum Lake where you may see American white pelicans, bald eagles or osprey, and. It is then easy-going through shady woods to Burney Falls.

5. 7:00hr 5120ft 0633710 4518730. Rim Lookout is now a communication facility for the fire service.

4. 5:10hr 4800ft. Gully.

223

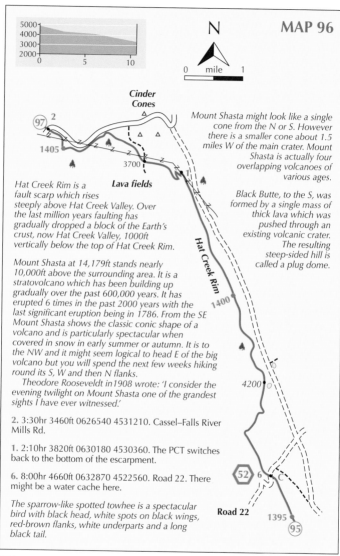

MAP 96

Cinder Cones

Mount Shasta might look like a single cone from the N or S. However there is a smaller cone about 1.5 miles W of the main crater. Mount Shasta is actually four overlapping volcanoes of various ages.

Black Butte, to the S, was formed by a single mass of thick lava which was pushed through an existing volcanic crater. The resulting steep-sided hill is called a plug dome.

Lava fields

Hat Creek Rim is a fault scarp which rises steeply above Hat Creek Valley. Over the last million years faulting has gradually dropped a block of the Earth's crust, now Hat Creek Valley, 1000ft vertically below the top of Hat Creek Rim.

Mount Shasta at 14,179ft stands nearly 10,000ft above the surrounding area. It is a stratovolcano which has been building up gradually over the past 600,000 years. It has erupted 6 times in the past 2000 years with the last significant eruption being in 1786. From the SE Mount Shasta shows the classic conic shape of a volcano and is particularly spectacular when covered in snow in early summer or autumn. It is to the NW and it might seem logical to head E of the big volcano but you will spend the next few weeks hiking round its S, W and then N flanks.

Theodore Rooseveldt in 1908 wrote: 'I consider the evening twilight on Mount Shasta one of the grandest sights I have ever witnessed.'

2. 3:30hr 3460ft 0626540 4531210. Cassel–Falls River Mills Rd.

1. 2:10hr 3820ft 0630180 4530360. The PCT switches back to the bottom of the escarpment.

6. 8:00hr 4660ft 0632870 4522560. Road 22. There might be a water cache here.

The sparrow-like spotted towhee is a spectacular bird with black head, white spots on black wings, red-brown flanks, white underparts and a long black tail.

Road 22

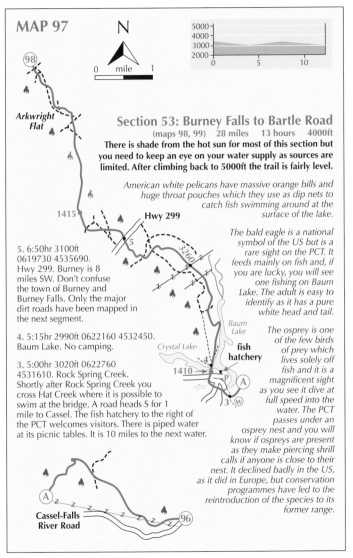

MAP 97

N

0   mile   1

*Arkwright
Flat*

1415

Hwy 299

Section 53: Burney Falls to Bartle Road

(maps 98, 99)   28 miles   13 hours   4000ft

**There is shade from the hot sun for most of this section but
you need to keep an eye on your water supply as sources are
limited. After climbing back to 5000ft the trail is fairly level.**

*American white pelicans have massive orange bills and
huge throat pouches which they use as dip nets to
catch fish swimming around at the
surface of the lake.*

5. 6:50hr 3100ft
0619730 4535690.
Hwy 299. Burney is 8
miles SW. Don't confuse
the town of Burney and
Burney Falls. Only the major
dirt roads have been mapped in
the next segment.

4. 5:15hr 2990ft 0622160 4532450.
Baum Lake. No camping.

3. 5:00hr 3020ft 0622760
4531610. Rock Spring Creek.
Shortly after Rock Spring Creek you
cross Hat Creek where it is possible to
swim at the bridge. A road heads S for 1
mile to Cassel. The fish hatchery to the right of
the PCT welcomes visitors. There is piped water
at its picnic tables. It is 10 miles to the next water.

*The bald eagle is a national
symbol of the US but is a
rare sight on the PCT. It
feeds mainly on fish and, if
you are lucky, you will see
one fishing on Baum
Lake. The adult is easy to
identify as it has a pure
white head and tail.*

*Baum
Lake*

Crystal Lake

**fish
hatchery**

*The osprey is one
of the few birds
of prey which
lives solely off
fish and it is a
magnificent sight
as you see it dive at
full speed into the
water. The PCT
passes under an
osprey nest and you will
know if ospreys are present
as they make piercing shrill
calls if anyone is close to their
nest. It declined badly in the US,
as it did in Europe, but conservation
programmes have led to the
reintroduction of the species to its
former range.*

**Cassel-Falls
River Road**

3260

5

1410

225

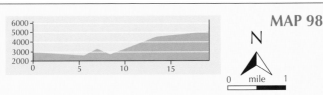

MAP 98

N

0   mile   1

3. 7:00hr 4770ft 0602080 4546150. Peavine Creek is at a complex road junction. You might have to fight your way through brush to get at the water. In the unlikely event that the creek is dry, head N down the road to Rock Creek. For the next 23 miles the PCT goes parallel to and frequently crosses Summit Lake Rd. The next on-trail water is likely to be at Moosehead Springs in Section 54.

2. 2:15hr 2970ft. Rock Creek. It is possible to camp beside the creek but there are better spots in the woods beyond the creek.

1. 0:40hr 2720ft 0611360 4541960. Lake Britton Dam. The PCT climbs steeply from near the N end of the dam.

7. 9:50hr 2950ft. Burney Falls. A bridge takes you to the main Burney Falls Campground which will hold packages for hikers. Return across the bridge to regain the PCT.

6. 9:30hr 3000ft. Hwy 89. You could shortcut down the road to Burney Falls Campground but it is better to follow the PCT or follow the alternative route along the N bank of Burney Creek. Cross the normally dry Burney Creek and follow the PCT through a backpacker campground and on to Burney Falls.

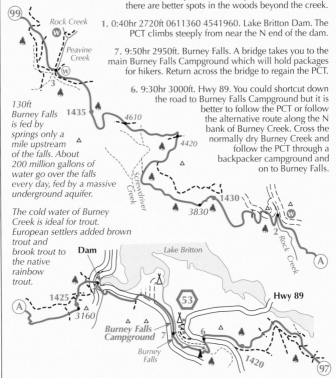

130ft Burney Falls is fed by springs only a mile upstream of the falls. About 200 million gallons of water go over the falls every day, fed by a massive underground aquifer.

The cold water of Burney Creek is ideal for trout. European settlers added brown trout and brook trout to the native rainbow trout.

MAP 99

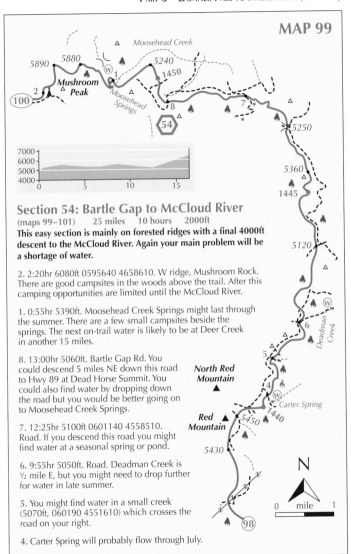

Section 54: Bartle Gap to McCloud River
(maps 99–101)   25 miles   10 hours   2000ft

This easy section is mainly on forested ridges with a final 4000ft descent to the McCloud River. Again your main problem will be a shortage of water.

2. 2:20hr 6080ft 0595640 4658610. W ridge, Mushroom Rock. There are good campsites in the woods above the trail. After this camping opportunities are limited until the McCloud River.

1. 0:55hr 5390ft. Moosehead Creek Springs might last through the summer. There are a few small campsites beside the springs. The next on-trail water is likely to be at Deer Creek in another 15 miles.

8. 13:00hr 5060ft. Bartle Gap Rd. You could descend 5 miles NE down this road to Hwy 89 at Dead Horse Summit. You could also find water by dropping down the road but you would be better going on to Moosehead Creek Springs.

7. 12:25hr 5100ft 0601140 4558510. Road. If you descend this road you might find water at a seasonal spring or pond.

6. 9:55hr 5050ft. Road. Deadman Creek is ½ mile E, but you might need to drop further for water in late summer.

5. You might find water in a small creek (5070ft, 060190 4551610) which crosses the road on your right.

4. Carter Spring will flow through July.

227

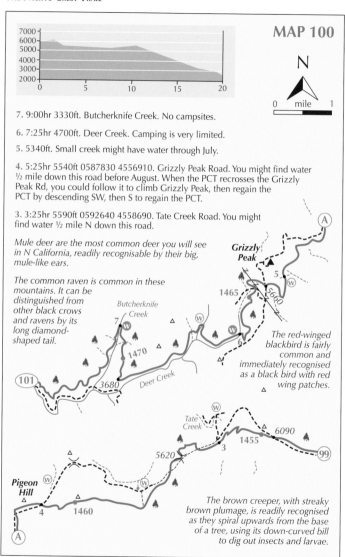

MAP 100

N

0   mile   1

7. 9:00hr 3330ft. Butcherknife Creek. No campsites.

6. 7:25hr 4700ft. Deer Creek. Camping is very limited.

5. 5340ft. Small creek might have water through July.

4. 5:25hr 5540ft 0587830 4556910. Grizzly Peak Road. You might find water ½ mile down this road before August. When the PCT recrosses the Grizzly Peak Rd, you could follow it to climb Grizzly Peak, then regain the PCT by descending SW, then S to regain the PCT.

3. 3:25hr 5590ft 0592640 4558690. Tate Creek Road. You might find water ½ mile N down this road.

Mule deer are the most common deer you will see in N California, readily recognisable by their big, mule-like ears.

The common raven is common in these mountains. It can be distinguished from other black crows and ravens by its long diamond-shaped tail.

Grizzly Peak

The red-winged blackbird is fairly common and immediately recognised as a black bird with red wing patches.

The brown creeper, with streaky brown plumage, is readily recognised as they spiral upwards from the base of a tree, using its down-curved bill to dig out insects and larvae.

Butcherknife Creek

Deer Creek

Tate Creek

Pigeon Hill

101

99

1465

2660

1470

3680

1460

1455

6090

5620

4

3

5

6

7

228

MAP 101

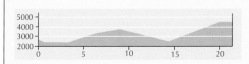

Section 55: McCloud River to Interstate 5 (near Castella)
(maps 101, 102)
30 miles   14 hours   4000ft
You are in forest for most of this section which crosses a couple of ridges before going down to the Sacramento River.

5. 9:50hr 4600ft 0565300 4555530. Girard Ridge Rd. Camping is very limited on the descent.

4. 6:20hr 2580ft 0569680 4554740. Squaw Valley Creek has campsites upstream. There are waterholes for a chilly swim. It is 11 miles to your next reliable water.

1. 0:50hr 2320ft. Fitzhugh Gulch Creek. This creek probably has water but it is safer to fill up at the McCloud River. You soon cross a road going SW to Ah-Di-Na Campground and climb 1500ft before dropping down to Trough Creek.

8. 10:20hr 2390ft. McCloud River. Ash Camp (0578860 4552180) is used by car campers and the ground is too compressed to take tent pegs. This trout stream is famous for its fly fishing. You could hitch 15 miles to McCloud and a further 12 miles W on Hwy 89 to Mt Shasta City. You are unlikely to find campsites ahead except for those marked on the map.

3. 5:00hr 2990ft. Trough Creek. No campsites.

2. 1:34hr 3440ft. Spur. **Skunk Hill**

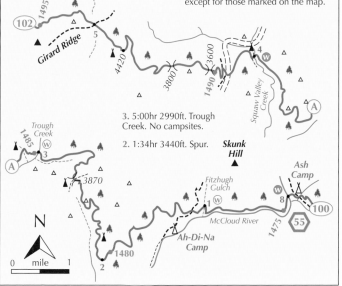

229

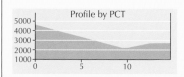

N

MAP 102

0 mile 1

Section 56: Interstate 5 to Parks Creek Road
(maps 102–104)

39 miles   19 hours   7000ft

The PCT gets more demanding as terrain gets more mountainous. This section starts with a long exposed climb with views of Castle Crags, followed by a high-level traverse as you enter the Klamath Mountains. The ascent to the Trinity Divide is only lightly wooded and can be very hot. It is best to climb from Burstarse Creek in the early morning or evening when there is some shade.

Either side of Castella you will see mysterious numbered posts along the PCT which are 1km apart and in Castle Crags State Park you will find signposts in km. These are from the 1970s when the US had a brief flirtation with metrication.

2. 1:40hr 2880ft. Winton Canyon Creek.

1. 1:20hr 2880ft. Rejoin the PCT (1:50hr via Castella).

1. 0:45hr 2090ft 0557290 4555410. Castella. The well-stocked store will hold packages for hikers. From Castella PO, continue up Castle Creek Road and come to the main entrance to Castle Crags State Park with ranger office and campground. Enter and take a paved road NW, signed to Bobs Hat Trail, which becomes a dirt road swinging to the NE. Then turn left, NW again, then a right fork will take you Bobs Hat Trail, which leads to the PCT.

7. 13:35hr 2180ft 0559260 4556630. Sacramento River. Most hikers will want to resupply now. Dunsmuir is 5 miles to the NE. The smaller Castella is the preferred choice of most hikers. If you aren't resupplying, or are starting a section-hike, you will want to follow the PCT. Otherwise the easiest way is to follow the road along the N bank of the Sacramento River. Ignore the unmapped dirt road on your left, unless you want to camp. Cross the railroad and head N briefly before turning left along Frontage Rd, then right at Castle Creek Rd, under Interstate 5 and the PO and store will be on your left.

Major forestry operations might affect this section.

6. 11:30hr 4040ft. Fall Creek might run through the summer.

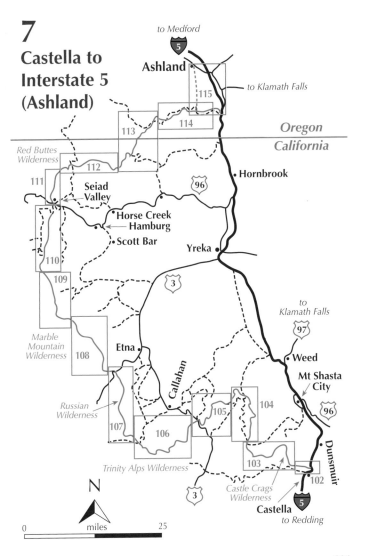

7
Castella to
Interstate 5
(Ashland)

to Medford

5

Ashland

to Klamath Falls

115

114

113

Oregon

California

Red Buttes Wilderness

112

111

Seiad Valley

96

Hornbrook

Horse Creek
Hamburg

Scott Bar

110

109

Yreka

3

to Klamath Falls

97

Marble Mountain Wilderness

108

Etna

Weed

Mt Shasta City

96

Russian Wilderness

Callahan

107

106

105

104

103

102

Dunsmuir

3

Trinity Alps Wilderness

Castle Crags Wilderness

5

Castella
to Redding

N

0   miles   25

PART 7: CASTELLA TO INTERSTATE 5 (ASHLAND)

Section	Distance (miles)	Time (hours)	Ascent (feet)	Maps
56 Castella–Parks Creek Rd	39	19	7000	102–104
57 Parks Creek Rd–Highway 3	21	8	1000	104, 105
58 Highway 3–Carter Meadows Summit	20	9	3000	105, 106
59 Carter Meadows Summit–Etna Summit	20	9	2000	106, 107
60 Etna Summit–Paradise Lake	29	14	4000	107–109
61 Paradise Lake–Seiad Valley	27	10	1000	109–111
62 Seiad Valley–Cook and Green Pass	15	10	5000	111, 112
63 Cook and Green Pass–Wrangle Gap	28	13	4000	112, 113
64 Wrangle Gap–Interstate 5 (Ashland)	21	8	2000	113–115
Part total	**220**	**100**	**28,000**	

In this section you basically hike round three sides of the massive volcano Mount Shasta, heading into the Klamath Mountains which include the Trinity Alps, Russian and Marble Mountain Wilderness Areas before heading east through lower mountains to the Oregon border.

For most of this section you are on ridges, which vary from broad forested ridges to exposed alpine ridges. Water can be a problem and, as many of the springs and creeks are fed by the melting of winter snow, there is only a narrow window between the snow melting and the seasonal creeks drying up.

On exposed ridges you must be aware of the risk of thunderstorms and ensure you don't get caught out high in a storm.

A major diversion is suggested in Section 64 to finish the section at Ashland rather than Interstate 5.

Best time

July–October. Any time after the snow has melted. This section would be very difficult in snowpack.

Permits

Permits are required for Sections 58 and 60.

Section 58: Trinity Alps Wilderness

Shasta-Trinity National Forests, 3644 Avtech Parkway, Redding CA96002 (530)-226-2500, www.fs.fed.us/r5/shastatrinity

PCT near Beardog Spring (Section 63)

Section 60: Marble Mountain Wilderness
Klamath National Forest, 1312 Fairlane Rd, Yreka CA96097
(530)-842-6131,
www.r5.fed.us/klamath

Facilities
It is suggested that you resupply at Etna, Seiad Valley and Ashland.

Castella (PO, P, G, L, C) (from Interstate 5) (Sections 55, 56) (0 hours)
See Part 6 introduction.

Etna (P, PO, G, R, A, B) (from Etna Summit) (Sections 59, 60) (45 hours)
Etna PO, 119 Diggles St, Etna CA96027
(530)-467-3981. Mon–Fri: 8.30am–5.00pm
Etna has small town facilities including a good store.
Etna Deli, 449 Main Street, Etna CA96027
(530)-467-3429, las@sisqtel.net
Mon–Thur: 9.00am–5.00pm,
Fri: 9.00am–9.00pm,
Sat 10.00am–9.00pm
Etna Deli will hold packages for hikers.
Alderbrook B&B (P, A, L, Sh) 836, Sawyers Bar, Etna CA96027
(530)-467-3917, www.alderbrook manor.com, Harrison@sisqtel.net
Alderbrook has a Hikers' Hut ($25 a night in 2009) and offers a package service for those staying there.

Seiad Valley (PO, P, G, R, C, L, Sh) (Sections 61, 62) (70 hours)
Seiad Valley PO, 44717 State Highway 96, Seiad Valley CA96086
(530)-496-3211. Mon–Fri: 8.00am–11.00am, 11.30am–4.00pm, Sat: 12.00noon–1.30pm
Mid River RV Park, 44701 State Highway 96, Seiad Valley CA96086
The RV park, next to the post office, the well-stocked store and café,

233

has an area set aside for hikers. Staff will hold parcels for hikers ($5 in 2009, $10 including camping) and offer use of showers and laundry. Store 7.00am–7.00pm, cafe 7.00am–2.00pm

Ashland (PO, G, R, A, L, O, B) (from Interstate 5) (Sections 64, 65) (99 hours)
Ashland PO, 120N 1st St, Ashland OR97520
(541)-552-1622.
Mon–Fri: 9.00am–5.00pm
Ashland is a tourist town, the main attraction being its Oregon Shakespeare Festival, which runs most of the year. Ashland Hostel (150 N Main St) welcomes hikers. Ashland Outdoor Store is the best outdoor equipment shop on the PCT:
Ashland Outdoor Store, 37N, Third St, Ashland OR97520
(541)-488-1202, www.outdoorstore. com, info@outdoorstore.com

From the PCT roadhead on Highway 99, Callahan's Lodge is 1000 yards north and Ashland is a further 12 miles to the north-west. Either hitch nine miles down Interstate 5 to the Highway 66 Interchange and follow Highway 66 into Ashland or go northeast down Highway 273 to its junction with Highway 66, past Ashland KOA Campground (small G, C) to Ashland. To rejoin the PCT from Ashland head out on Highway 66, then hitch up Interstate 5 to Mount Ashland Interchange or follow Highway 273.

Callahan's Lodge (P, R, A, L, Sh, C) (Sections 64, 65) (99 hours)
Callahan's Lodge, 7100 Old Highway 99 South, Ashland OR97520
(800)-286-0507 (toll free), info@callahanslodge.com
Restaurant: Fri–Mon: 8.00am–9.00pm, Thur: 4.00pm–9.00pm (in 2009)
Callahan's Lodge will hold packages for hikers. You can camp in the grounds and use facilities at a reasonable cost.

The ridge north of Etna Summit (Section 60)

MAP 103

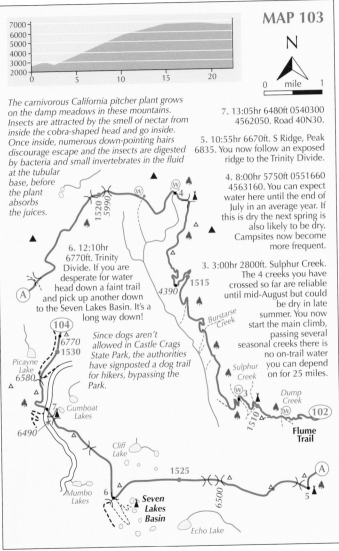

The carnivorous California pitcher plant grows on the damp meadows in these mountains. Insects are attracted by the smell of nectar from inside the cobra-shaped head and go inside. Once inside, numerous down-pointing hairs discourage escape and the insects are digested by bacteria and small invertebrates in the fluid at the tubular base, before the plant absorbs the juices.

7. 13:05hr 6480ft 0540300 4562050. Road 40N30.

5. 10:55hr 6670ft. S Ridge, Peak 6835. You now follow an exposed ridge to the Trinity Divide.

4. 8:00hr 5750ft 0551660 4563160. You can expect water here until the end of July in an average year. If this is dry the next spring is also likely to be dry. Campsites now become more frequent.

3. 3:00hr 2800ft. Sulphur Creek. The 4 creeks you have crossed so far are reliable until mid-August but could be dry in late summer. You now start the main climb, passing several seasonal creeks there is no on-trail water you can depend on for 25 miles.

6. 12:10hr 6770ft. Trinity Divide. If you are desperate for water head down a faint trail and pick up another down to the Seven Lakes Basin. It's a long way down!

Since dogs aren't allowed in Castle Crags State Park, the authorities have signposted a dog trail for hikers, bypassing the Park.

235

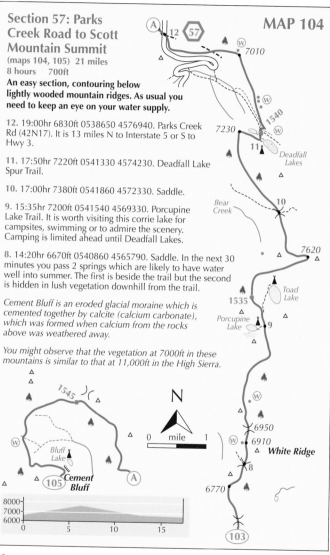

Section 57: Parks Creek Road to Scott Mountain Summit

(maps 104, 105) 21 miles
8 hours   700ft

An easy section, contouring below lightly wooded mountain ridges. As usual you need to keep an eye on your water supply.

12. 19:00hr 6830ft 0538650 4576940. Parks Creek Rd (42N17). It is 13 miles N to Interstate 5 or S to Hwy 3.

11. 17:50hr 7220ft 0541330 4574230. Deadfall Lake Spur Trail.

10. 17:00hr 7380ft 0541860 4572330. Saddle.

9. 15:35hr 7200ft 0541540 4569330. Porcupine Lake Trail. It is worth visiting this corrie lake for campsites, swimming or to admire the scenery. Camping is limited ahead until Deadfall Lakes.

8. 14:20hr 6670ft 0540860 4565790. Saddle. In the next 30 minutes you pass 2 springs which are likely to have water well into summer. The first is beside the trail but the second is hidden in lush vegetation downhill from the trail.

Cement Bluff is an eroded glacial moraine which is cemented together by calcite (calcium carbonate), which was formed when calcium from the rocks above was weathered away.

You might observe that the vegetation at 7000ft in these mountains is similar to that at 11,000ft in the High Sierra.

MAP 104

57

7010

1540

7230

11

Deadfall Lakes

Bear Creek

10

7620

Toad Lake

1535

Porcupine Lake

9

1545

Bluff Lake

Cement Bluff

105

A

N

0   mile   1

6950

6910   White Ridge

8

6770

103

8000
7000
6000
0   5   10   15

MAP 105

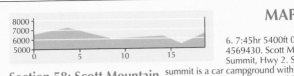

Section 58: Scott Mountain Summit to Carter Meadows Summit (maps 105, 106)

20 miles   9 hours   3000ft

After an initial climb, the PCT makes every effort to maintain altitude on this easy forested section with some sparsely forested mountain ridges. Water is again a problem. The PCT leaves Scott Mountain Summit at the back of the parking area with a multitude of unmapped tracks.

When the author was caught in a hailstorm at Bull Lake in August 2002, there were hailstones as big as golf balls and a couple of inches of hail covered the ground.

6. 7:45hr 5400ft 0525290 4569430. Scott Mountain Summit, Hwy 2. S of the summit is a car campground with unreliable piped water. You could drop down S to get water from Scott Mountain Creek.

5. Small springs probably run through July.

4. 5:20hr 6080ft 0529510. Two small springs might be running through July.

3. Take care as the PCT forks left while the main trail continues to the right.

2. 3:10hr 7090ft 0533590 474140. Bull Lake Saddle. If you are visiting Bull Lake, go cross-country as soon as you see the lake to save unnecessary ascent.

1. 2:10hr 6670ft 0535420 4575480. Chilcott Creek Spring is likely to have water into August.

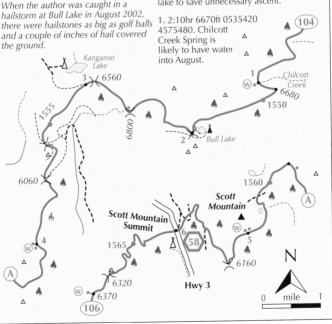

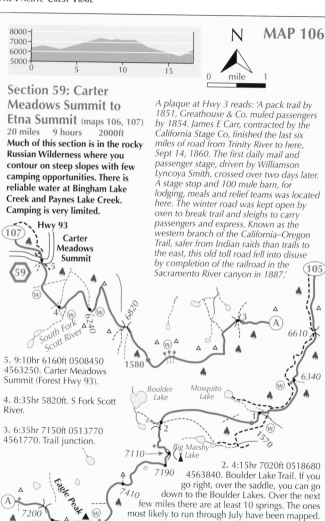

MAP 106

Section 59: Carter Meadows Summit to Etna Summit (maps 106, 107)

20 miles   9 hours   2000ft

Much of this section is in the rocky Russian Wilderness where you contour on steep slopes with few camping opportunities. There is reliable water at Bingham Lake Creek and Paynes Lake Creek. Camping is very limited.

A plaque at Hwy 3 reads: 'A pack trail by 1851, Greathouse & Co. muled passengers by 1854. James E Carr, contracted by the California Stage Co, finished the last six miles of road from Trinity River to here, Sept 14, 1860. The first daily mail and passenger stage, driven by Williamson Lyncoya Smith, crossed over two days later. A stage stop and 100 mule barn, for lodging, meals and relief teams was located here. The winter road was kept open by oxen to break trail and sleighs to carry passengers and express. Known as the western branch of the California–Oregon Trail, safer from Indian raids than trails to the east, this old toll road fell into disuse by completion of the railroad in the Sacramento River canyon in 1887.'

5. 9:10hr 6160ft 0508450 4563250. Carter Meadows Summit (Forest Hwy 93).

4. 8:35hr 5820ft. S Fork Scott River.

3. 6:35hr 7150ft 0513770 4561770. Trail junction.

2. 4:15hr 7020ft 0518680 4563840. Boulder Lake Trail. If you go right, over the saddle, you can go down to the Boulder Lakes. Over the next few miles there are at least 10 springs. The ones most likely to run through July have been mapped.

1. 3:00 6270ft 0521330 4564110. Mosquito Lake Creek can be expected to flow through the summer.

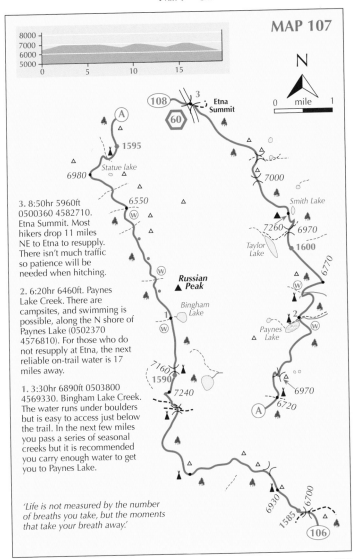

MAP 107

N

0 _____ mile _____ 1

(108)
3 ╱ Etna Summit
(60)

(A)
△
△ **1595**

Statue lake
6980 △

3. 8:50hr 5960ft
0500360 4582710.
Etna Summit. Most
hikers drop 11 miles
NE to Etna to resupply.
There isn't much traffic
so patience will be
needed when hitching.

6550
(W) △
△

7000

Smith Lake
▲
7260 6970
1600

Taylor
Lake

6770

Russian Peak ▲

(W)

Bingham Lake

2. 6:20hr 6460ft. Paynes
Lake Creek. There are
campsites, and swimming is
possible, along the N shore of
Paynes Lake (0502370
4576810). For those who do
not resupply at Etna, the next
reliable on-trail water is 17
miles away.

1
(W)

2
(W)
Paynes
Lake
△

1. 3:30hr 6890ft 0503800
4569330. Bingham Lake Creek.
The water runs under boulders
but is easy to access just below
the trail. In the next few miles
you pass a series of seasonal
creeks but it is recommended
you carry enough water to get
you to Paynes Lake.

7160
1590
7240

6970
(A) 6720

'Life is not measured by the number
of breaths you take, but the moments
that take your breath away.'

6930 6700
1585 (106)

239

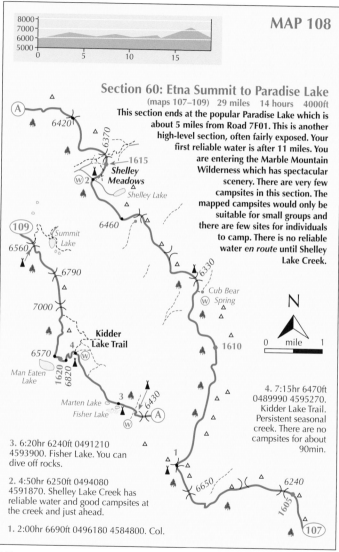

MAP 108

8000
7000
6000
5000

0   5   10   15

Section 60: Etna Summit to Paradise Lake
(maps 107–109)   29 miles   14 hours   4000ft

This section ends at the popular Paradise Lake which is about 5 miles from Road 7F01. This is another high-level section, often fairly exposed. Your first reliable water is after 11 miles. You are entering the Marble Mountain Wilderness which has spectacular scenery. There are very few campsites in this section. The mapped campsites would only be suitable for small groups and there are few sites for individuals to camp. There is no reliable water *en route* until Shelley Lake Creek.

A
6420

6370

1615
Shelley Meadows
W 2
Shelley Lake

109
Summit Lake
6560
6460

6790

7000

Kidder Lake Trail
6570
4 W
1620
6820
Man Eaten Lake

Marten Lake
Fisher Lake
3
6430
W
A

6330

Cub Bear
W Spring

1610

N

0   mile   1

4. 7:15hr 6470ft 0489990 4595270. Kidder Lake Trail. Persistent seasonal creek. There are no campsites for about 90min.

3. 6:20hr 6240ft 0491210 4593900. Fisher Lake. You can dive off rocks.

2. 4:50hr 6250ft 0494080 4591870. Shelley Lake Creek has reliable water and good campsites at the creek and just ahead.

1. 2:00hr 6690ft 0496180 4584800. Col.

1
6650
6240
1605
107

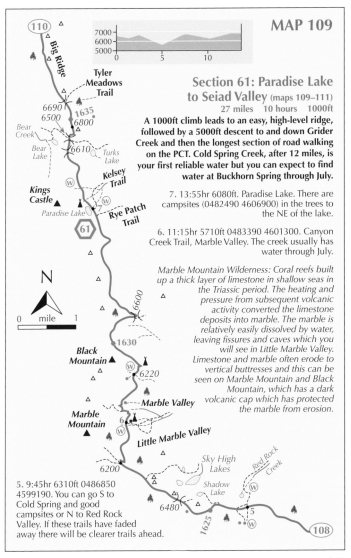

110

Big Ridge

7000
6000
5000

0   5   10

MAP 109

Tyler
Meadows
Trail

6690
6500   1635
            6800

Bear
Creek

Bear
Lake

6610   Turks
                    Lake

W

Kelsey
Trail

Kings
Castle

Paradise Lake

Rye Patch
Trail

61

N

0   mile   1

6600

1630

Black
Mountain

W   6220

Marble Valley

Marble
Mountain

W

Little Marble Valley

6200

Sky High
Lakes

Red Rock Creek

Shadow
Lake

6480

W

1625   5

W

108

Section 61: Paradise Lake to Seiad Valley (maps 109–111)
27 miles   10 hours   1000ft

A 1000ft climb leads to an easy, high-level ridge, followed by a 5000ft descent to and down Grider Creek and then the longest section of road walking on the PCT. Cold Spring Creek, after 12 miles, is your first reliable water but you can expect to find water at Buckhorn Spring through July.

7. 13:55hr 6080ft. Paradise Lake. There are campsites (0482490 4606900) in the trees to the NE of the lake.

6. 11:15hr 5710ft 0483390 4601300. Canyon Creek Trail, Marble Valley. The creek usually has water through July.

Marble Mountain Wilderness: Coral reefs built up a thick layer of limestone in shallow seas in the Triassic period. The heating and pressure from subsequent volcanic activity converted the limestone deposits into marble. The marble is relatively easily dissolved by water, leaving fissures and caves which you will see in Little Marble Valley. Limestone and marble often erode to vertical buttresses and this can be seen on Marble Mountain and Black Mountain, which has a dark volcanic cap which has protected the marble from erosion.

5. 9:45hr 6310ft 0486850 4599190. You can go S to Cold Spring and good campsites or N to Red Rock Valley. If these trails have faded away there will be clearer trails ahead.

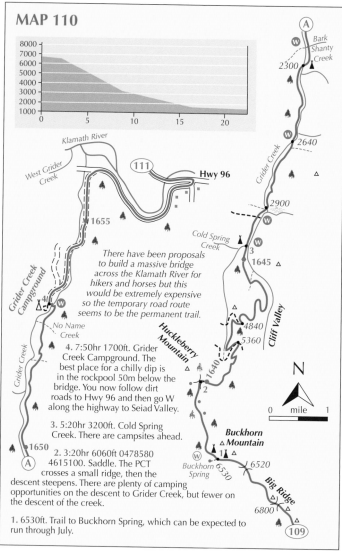

MAP 110

8000
7000
6000
5000
4000
3000
2000
1000

0   5   10   15   20

Klamath River

West Grider Creek

111

Hwy 96

1655

Cold Spring Creek

3
1645

There have been proposals to build a massive bridge across the Klamath River for hikers and horses but this would be extremely expensive so the temporary road route seems to be the permanent trail.

Grider Creek Campground

4840

5360

Huckleberry Mountain

1640

Cliff Valley

No Name Creek

4. 7:50hr 1700ft. Grider Creek Campground. The best place for a chilly dip is in the rockpool 50m below the bridge. You now follow dirt roads to Hwy 96 and then go W along the highway to Seiad Valley.

3. 5:20hr 3200ft. Cold Spring Creek. There are campsites ahead.

Grider Creek

1650

2. 3:20hr 6060ft 0478580 4615100. Saddle. The PCT crosses a small ridge, then the descent steepens. There are plenty of camping opportunities on the descent to Grider Creek, but fewer on the descent of the creek.

2

Buckhorn Mountain

Buckhorn Spring

6530

6520

Big Ridge

1. 6530ft. Trail to Buckhorn Spring, which can be expected to run through July.

6800

109

N

0   mile   1

A
Bark Shanty Creek
2300

2640

Grider Creek

2900

MAP 111

Section 62: Seiad Valley to Cook and Green Pass

(maps 111, 112) 15 miles 10 hours 5000ft

This short section starts with a 4500ft ascent up S facing slopes. Campsites on the climb are very limited so the best strategy is to camp overnight at the RV park or at Fern Spring and leave at dawn in the morning, doing the bulk of the climb before it gets too hot. Fern Spring might be dry by the end of July but, amazingly, Lookout Spring on Devil's Peak seems to be pretty persistent.

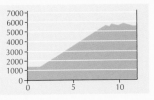

2. 7:15hr 5940ft 0483340 4640010. Boundary Trail. You now drop down to a basin containing Kangaroo Springs, where you can expect to find campsites and water of dubious quality. You then circle above Lily Pad Lake and cross a jeep track E of Red Butte. You can usually find water into August about 100yd before the road. You could camp on some exposed campsites on the flat ridge below the trail.

1. 5:00hr 4900ft 0483090 4636160. Lookout Spring Trail. Just before you reach Lower Devils Peak, with the remains of a lookout tower, a trail goes 40yd on your left to Lookout Spring, which seems to run into August but you need an emergency reserve of water in case it is dry.

5. 10:00hr 1360ft 0483750 4632240. Seiad Valley. There is a swimming hole under the bridge just W of the store. From the store head W along the highway until the second left-hand bend where the PCT is clearly signed.

Seiad Valley Café is the location of the infamous Pancake Challenge. The challenge is to eat just 5 of the chef's pancakes in under an hour. This seems easy until you see the pancakes which are about ½in thick and fill the plate. The few young men who have succeeded get their money back. The author ordered 2 pancakes for breakfast and failed halfway through the second!

The thru'-hiker passes through N California and Oregon at the height of the fire season. In 2002, 2 firemen died fighting the Titus Ridge Fire in Seiad Valley. You might find sections of the PCT closed by fire and will often see the smoke from forest fires.

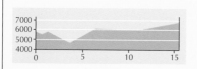

MAP 112

N

0   mile   1

Section 63: Cook and Green Pass to Wrangle Gap
(maps 112, 113)   28 miles   13 hours   4000ft
An easy section with adequate water sources but this is cattle country so they
could be polluted. The main feature for the thru'-hiker is the Oregon border, after
1700 miles in California. You start with a climb to Copper Butte. There are plenty
of campsites throughout this section.

Section 64: Wrangle Gap to Interstate 5
(maps 113–115)   21 miles   8 hours   2000ft
This is an easy section but there is no reliable water on the trail. Virtually all
thru'-hikers resupply and take a break at Ashland. Rather than hitching the 13
miles to Ashland from the end of the section you might prefer to descend directly
to Ashland from Bull Gap but there is no good hiking route back from Ashland to
the PCT.

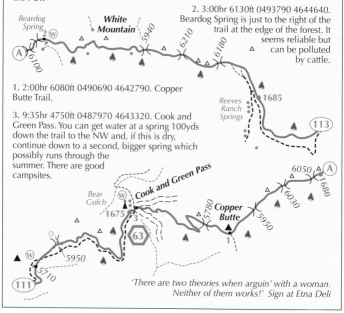

Beardog Spring

White Mountain

2. 3:00hr 6130ft 0493790 4644640.
Beardog Spring is just to the right of the
trail at the edge of the forest. It
seems reliable but
can be polluted
by cattle.

1. 2:00hr 6080ft 0490690 4642790. Copper
Butte Trail.

3. 9:35hr 4750ft 0487970 4643320. Cook and
Green Pass. You can get water at a spring 100yds
down the trail to the NW and, if this is dry,
continue down to a second, bigger spring which
possibly runs through the
summer. There are good
campsites.

Reeves Ranch Springs   ●1685

113

Bear Gulch   **Cook and Green Pass**

Copper Butte

6050   A

6030

1680

5780

5950

1675   3

63

1

5950

111   5710

*'There are two theories when arguin' with a woman.
Neither of them works!' Sign at Etna Deli*

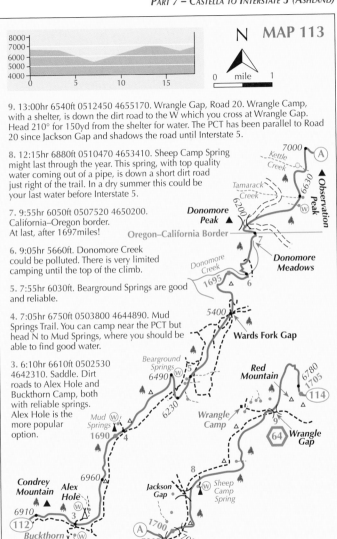

9. 13:00hr 6540ft 0512450 4655170. Wrangle Gap, Road 20. Wrangle Camp, with a shelter, is down the dirt road to the W which you cross at Wrangle Gap. Head 210° for 150yd from the shelter for water. The PCT has been parallel to Road 20 since Jackson Gap and shadows the road until Interstate 5.

8. 12:15hr 6880ft 0510470 4653410. Sheep Camp Spring might last through the year. This spring, with top quality water coming out of a pipe, is down a short dirt road just right of the trail. In a dry summer this could be your last water before Interstate 5.

7. 9:55hr 6050ft 0507520 4650200. California–Oregon border. At last, after 1697miles!

6. 9:05hr 5660ft. Donomore Creek could be polluted. There is very limited camping until the top of the climb.

5. 7:55hr 6030ft. Beargroround Springs are good and reliable.

4. 7:05hr 6750ft 0503800 4644890. Mud Springs Trail. You can camp near the PCT but head N to Mud Springs, where you should be able to find good water.

3. 6:10hr 6610ft 0502530 4642310. Saddle. Dirt roads to Alex Hole and Buckthorn Camp, both with reliable springs. Alex Hole is the more popular option.

245

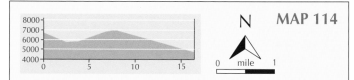

MAP 114

5. 6:25hr 5490ft. Ashland Inn offers bed and breakfast. Piped water is available at the picnic table.

3. 5:15hr 6550ft. Access to Mount Ashland Campground, a small campground with toilet. You might be able to get water at a spring fed gully.

4. 5:55hr 6060ft. Road 2080. The alternative route to Ashland descends from here. Take Road 2080 N to Bull Gap then take Road 200 N and it rejoins Road 2080 after 3 miles. Follow Road 2080 down to Glenview Drive in Ashland and descend N, then down Fork St to Pioneer St and C St.

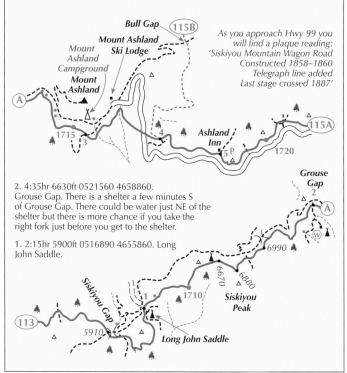

As you approach Hwy 99 you will find a plaque reading: 'Siskiyou Mountain Wagon Road Constructed 1858–1860 Telegraph line added Last stage crossed 1887'

2. 4:35hr 6630ft 0521560 4658860. Grouse Gap. There is a shelter a few minutes S of Grouse Gap. There could be water just NE of the shelter but there is more chance if you take the right fork just before you get to the shelter.

1. 2:15hr 5900ft 0516890 4655860. Long John Saddle.

246

MAP 115 Section 65: Interstate 5 to Hyatt Lake Road
(maps 115–117)   23 miles   10 hours   3000ft

Pilot Rock dominates the first part of this section after which it is just a matter of making good time to get to the more interesting sections ahead. The first water is likely to be after 10 miles.

Ashland

Hwy 99

Glenview Drive

Morton Street

Lamb Saddle

Reeder Reservoir

Ashland Loop

East Fork Ashland Creek

Ashland Loop

Ashland Loop Road

Road 2060

Road 200

1. 0:10hr 4400ft 0532890 4656350. PCT trailhead. Camping is rather limited for the first few hours but you should be able to find somewhere to pitch a tent.

8. 8:20hr 4240ft 0532850 4657220. Old Hwy 99. The interchange on Interstate 5 with Callahan's Lodge is 10 minutes to the N and Ashland is a further 12 miles to the NW.

7. A shortcut to Callahan's Lodge might be waymarked from here.

6. 7:40hr 4880ft. Three spring-fed gullies could be flowing into August. Pay attention over the final descent to Hwy 99 as the route can be confusing. After crossing several dirt roads the PCT follows an abandoned segment of old Hwy 99 for a couple of minutes and the PCT goes off left to arrive at Hwy 99 just N of where Hwy 99 goes under Interstate 5. If you lose the PCT this is where you should aim for. Head S along Hwy 99 under Interstate 5 and the PCT goes off on your left just after a bend.

If you take the Callahan diversion you will pass the site of the last great train robbery in the West. This occurred at the 3000ft Tunnel 13 on the railroad when the D'Autremont brothers held up a train rumoured to hold half million dollars in gold on 11 October, 1923. They didn't find any money or gold but they did murder four railroad workers. It wasn't until 1927 that the brothers were captured.

Interstate 5

Hwy 273

Callahan's

(114A)

6 (W)

7

(R)

8

(65)

(116)

Hwy 99

N

0   mile   1

Profile by PCT

6000
5000
4000
3000
0   4

(114B)

247

OREGON

Russell Creek (Section 78)

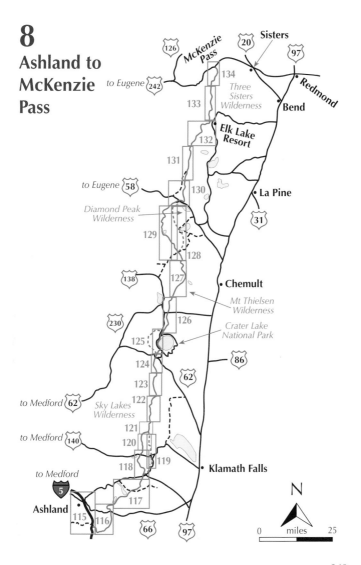

8
Ashland to McKenzie Pass

to Eugene {242}

{126} McKenzie Pass

{20} Sisters

{97}

Redmond

134

Three Sisters Wilderness

133

Bend

Elk Lake Resort

132

131

to Eugene {58}

130

La Pine

Diamond Peak Wilderness

{31}

129

128

{138}

127

{230}

126

Chemult

Mt Thielsen Wilderness

125

Crater Lake National Park

124

{86}

123

122

{62}

to Medford {62}

Sky Lakes Wilderness

121

120

to Medford {140}

118   119

Klamath Falls

to Medford

5

117

Ashland

115   116

{66}   {97}

N

0   miles   25

PART 8: ASHLAND TO MCKENZIE PASS

Section	Distance (miles)	Time (hours)	Ascent (feet)	Maps
65 Interstate 5–Hyatt Lake	24	10	3000	116–117
66 Hyatt Lake–Dead Indian Rd	19	8	3000	117, 118
67A Dead Indian Rd–Red Lake Trail by PCT	25	10	2000	119–120
67B Dead Indian Rd–Red Lake Trail by OST	21	8	1000	118–121
68A Red Lake Trail–Sevenmile Trail by PCT	18	7	2000	121–123
68B Red Lake Trail–Sevenmile Trail by OST	21	9	2000	121–123
69 Sevenmile Trail–Highway 62	17	8	2000	123, 124
70 Highway 62–Highway 138	23	9	2000	124–126
71 Highway 138–Windigo Pass	31	12	3000	126–128
72A Windigo Pass–Williamette Pass by PCT	30	12	3000	128–130
72B Windigo Pass–Williamette Pass by OST	24	9	2000	128–130
73 Williamette Pass–Irish Lake	23	10	3000	130, 131
74 Irish Lake–Horse Lake Trail (Elk Lake)	23	9	2000	131, 132
75 Horse Lake Trail–McKenzie Pass	30	13	3000	132–134
Part total (by PCT)	**263**	**108**	**28,000**	

The PCT in Oregon has been designed to minimise the environmental impact of the trail. In particular, it seems designed to keep horses away from lakes and popular areas. That means it misses some of the most interesting parts of Oregon and there are long waterless sections. In its early years the PCT temporarily followed the excellent

Oregon Skyline Trail (OST) until the present PCT was constructed. Many hikers, understandably, prefer the old OST and hike this instead of the official PCT. In Part 8 it is suggested that you make three major diversions from the PCT (Sections 67, 68 and 72) along the old OST. Sections of the OST have been given local names.

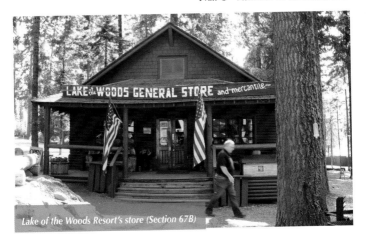
Lake of the Woods Resort's store (Section 67B)

You are hiking through a young volcanic environment with volcanoes towering above a landscape of volcanic ash and lava. The PCT is mainly through forest, where it has managed to get established. A number of large reservoirs in the early sections are succeeded by many natural lakes, if you follow the recommended variations. There is relatively little ascent so you can make rapid progress.

The section's highlight is Crater Lake, one of the wonders of the natural world. The Three Sisters volcanoes would be a worthy highlight of any hike.

On his 2009 hike to check the details of the guidebook, the author hiked the alternative routes in Sections 68 and 72, so the detail on the PCT has not been checked and corrected since 2006.

Best time

Mid-July–September. The best time to tackle this section is as soon as the snow has melted and before the springs start to dry up. By September you might have to carry more water.

Permits

A permit is needed to camp in the wilderness in Crater Lake National Park (Sections 69, 70) but if you camp at Mazama Campground you should be able to manage without.

A Northwest Forest Pass, available from ranger offices, local stores or at the trailhead, is needed for parking at some of the trailheads.

Sections 69 & 70: Crater Lake National Park

Crater Lake National Park, PO Box 7, Crater Lake OR97604
(541)-594-3000, www.nps.gov/crla

Facilities

It is suggested that you resupply at Fish Lake Resort (or Lake of the Woods Resort if you follow the alternative route rather than the PCT), Mazama Campground, Shelter Cove Resort and Elk Lake Resort.

Ashland (PO, G, R, A, L, O, B) and Callahan's Lodge (from Interstate 5) (Sections 64, 65) (0 hours)
See Part 7 introduction.

Hyatt Lake Resort (P, small G, R, A, C, L) (Sections 65, 66) (10 hours)
Hyatt Lake Resort, 7979 Hyatt Prairie Lake Rd, Ashland OR97520
(541)-482-3331,
www.hyattlakeresorts.com,
info@hyattlakes.com
The package service is UPS only.

Lake of the Woods Resort (P, small G, R, A, C, L, Sh) (Section 67B) (21 hours)
Lake of the Woods Resort, 950 Harriman route, Klamath Falls OR97601 (541)-949-8300,
www.lakeofthewoodsresort.com,
lowoffice@aol.com
The package service is UPS only.

Fish Lake Resort (P, small G, R, C, L, Sh) (Section 67A) (22 hours)
Fish Lake Resort, Highway 140, mile marker 30, Medford OR97501
(541)-949-8500, www.fishlakeresort.net, fishlakeresort@aol.com
Mon–Wed: 9.00am–7.00pm,
Thur–Sat: 8.00am–8.00pm,
Sun: 8.00am–7.00pm
The package service ($5 in 2009) is UPS only.

Crater Lake

There are facilities at Mazama village, Crater Lake Headquarters and Rim Village.
www.craterlakelodges.com or

Crescent Lake (Section 72B)

1-888-774-2728 for details of accommodation and campsites.

Mazama Campground (P, G, R, A, C, L, Sh, B) (Sections 69, 70) (43 hours)
Mazama Village Store, 569 Mazama Village Dr, Crater Lake OR97604
Campground: (541)-594-2255.
Store: Mon–Sun: 7.00am–9.00pm.
Restaurant: Mon–Sun: 8.00am–8.00pm
The package service operates from the store.

Crater Lake National Park Headquarters (PO) (Section 70) (45 hours)
Crater Lake PO, 1 Sager Building, Crater Lake OR97604
(541)-594-3115. Mon–Sat: 9.00am–3.00pm
The PO is inside the visitor centre (open 9.00am–5.00pm).

Rim Village (P, R, A) (Section 70) (45 hours)
Café and gift shop:
Mon–Sun: 9.00am–8.00pm
Crater Lake Lodge, 400 Rim Village Drive, Crater Lake OR97604
(541)-830-8700
The lodge offers a package service (UPS only) and has a restaurant which you might prefer to the café.

Diamond Lake Resort (PO, small G, R, A, C, L, Sh) (from Highway 138) (Sections 70, 71) (52 hours)
(541)-793-3333, www.diamondlake.net, info@diamondlake.net

Diamond Lake PO, 350 Resort Dr, Chemult OR97731
(541)-365-4411. Mon–Fri: 8.30am–4.30pm, Sat: 8.30am–12.00noon
The campground is at the southern end of Diamond Lake, the resort at the northern end.

Shelter Cove Resort (P, small G, A, C, B) (Section 72) (75 hours)
Shelter Cove Resort, W Odell Lake Rd, Highway 58, Crescent Lake OR97733
(541)-433-2548,
www.sheltercoveresort.com
The package service is UPS only. Hot snacks. Store: 7.00am–7.00pm

Elk Lake Resort (P, minimal G, A, R, C, L, Sh) (Sections 74, 75) (93 hours)
Elk Lake Resort, 60000 Century Dr, Bend OR97701
(541)-480-7378, www.elklakeresort.net, jwalsh@elklakeresort.net
Mon–Sun: 8.00am–8.00pm
Package service address as above ($5 fee in 2008) for UPS or Fed-Ex. USPS (at least two weeks in advance) to: Elk Lake Resort, PO Box 698, Bend 97709.

Sisters (PO, G, R, A, B) (from McKenzie Pass) (Sections 75, 76) (106 hours)
Sisters PO, 160 S Fir St, Sisters OR97759
(541)-549-0412.
Mon–Fri: 8.30am–5.00pm
Small town facilities.

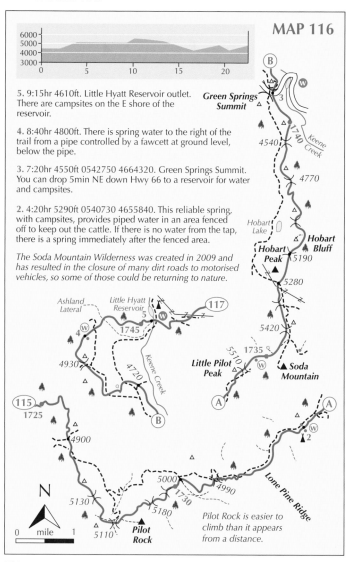

MAP 116

5. 9:15hr 4610ft. Little Hyatt Reservoir outlet. There are campsites on the E shore of the reservoir.

4. 8:40hr 4800ft. There is spring water to the right of the trail from a pipe controlled by a fawcett at ground level, below the pipe.

3. 7:20hr 4550ft 0542750 4664320. Green Springs Summit. You can drop 5min NE down Hwy 66 to a reservoir for water and campsites.

2. 4:20hr 5290ft 0540730 4655840. This reliable spring, with campsites, provides piped water in an area fenced off to keep out the cattle. If there is no water from the tap, there is a spring immediately after the fenced area.

The Soda Mountain Wilderness was created in 2009 and has resulted in the closure of many dirt roads to motorised vehicles, so some of those could be returning to nature.

Pilot Rock is easier to climb than it appears from a distance.

254

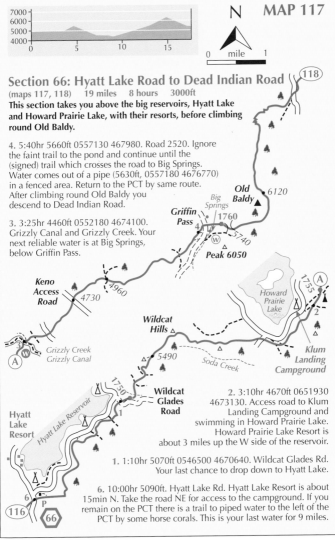

N   MAP 117

0   mile   1

Section 66: Hyatt Lake Road to Dead Indian Road
(maps 117, 118)   19 miles   8 hours   3000ft

This section takes you above the big reservoirs, Hyatt Lake and Howard Prairie Lake, with their resorts, before climbing round Old Baldy.

4. 5:40hr 5660ft 0557130 467980. Road 2520. Ignore the faint trail to the pond and continue until the (signed) trail which crosses the road to Big Springs. Water comes out of a pipe (5630ft, 0557180 4676770) in a fenced area. Return to the PCT by same route. After climbing round Old Baldy you descend to Dead Indian Road.

3. 3:25hr 4460ft 0552180 4674100. Grizzly Canal and Grizzly Creek. Your next reliable water is at Big Springs, below Griffin Pass.

Old Baldy ▲ 6120

Big Springs

Griffin Pass 1760

Peak 6050

Keno Access Road 4730

4960

Howard Prairie Lake

1755 A

Wildcat Hills △

Soda Creek

Klum Landing Campground

5490

Grizzly Creek
Grizzly Canal

Hyatt Lake Reservoir

1750

Wildcat Glades Road

Hyatt Lake Resort

2. 3:10hr 4670ft 0651930 4673130. Access road to Klum Landing Campground and swimming in Howard Prairie Lake. Howard Prairie Lake Resort is about 3 miles up the W side of the reservoir.

1. 1:10hr 5070ft 0546500 4670640. Wildcat Glades Rd. Your last chance to drop down to Hyatt Lake.

6. 10:00hr 5090ft. Hyatt Lake Rd. Hyatt Lake Resort is about 15min N. Take the road NE for access to the campground. If you remain on the PCT there is a trail to piped water to the left of the PCT by some horse corals. This is your last water for 9 miles.

116   66

255

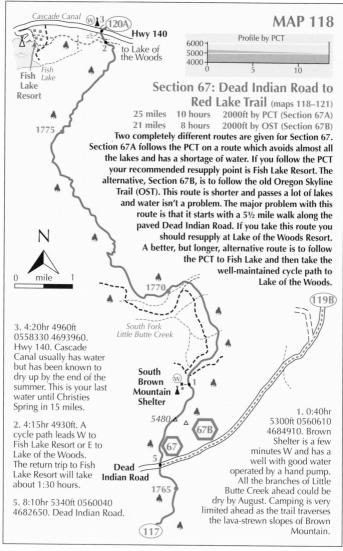

MAP 118

Profile by PCT

Section 67: Dead Indian Road to Red Lake Trail (maps 118–121)

25 miles 10 hours 2000ft by PCT (Section 67A)
21 miles 8 hours 2000ft by OST (Section 67B)

Two completely different routes are given for Section 67. Section 67A follows the PCT on a route which avoids almost all the lakes and has a shortage of water. If you follow the PCT your recommended resupply point is Fish Lake Resort. The alternative, Section 67B, is to follow the old Oregon Skyline Trail (OST). This route is shorter and passes a lot of lakes and water isn't a problem. The major problem with this route is that it starts with a 5½ mile walk along the paved Dead Indian Road. If you take this route you should resupply at Lake of the Woods Resort. A better, but longer, alternative route is to follow the PCT to Fish Lake and then take the well-maintained cycle path to Lake of the Woods.

3. 4:20hr 4960ft 0558330 4693960. Hwy 140. Cascade Canal usually has water but has been known to dry up by the end of the summer. This is your last water until Christies Spring in 15 miles.

2. 4:15hr 4930ft. A cycle path leads W to Fish Lake Resort or E to Lake of the Woods. The return trip to Fish Lake Resort will take about 1:30 hours.

5. 8:10hr 5340ft 0560040 4682650. Dead Indian Road.

South Fork Little Butte Creek

South Brown Mountain Shelter

5480

Dead Indian Road

1. 0:40hr 5300ft 0560610 4684910. Brown Shelter is a few minutes W and has a well with good water operated by a hand pump. All the branches of Little Butte Creek ahead could be dry by August. Camping is very limited ahead as the trail traverses the lava-strewn slopes of Brown Mountain.

256

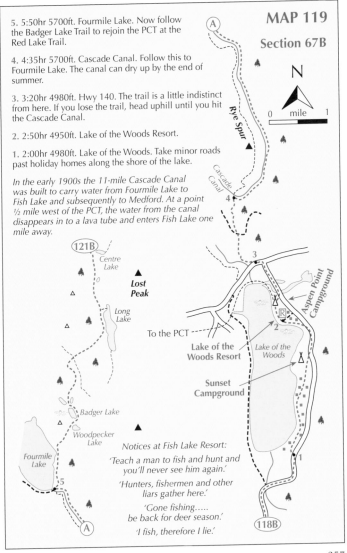

MAP 119

Section 67B

N

0   mile   1

5. 5:50hr 5700ft. Fourmile Lake. Now follow the Badger Lake Trail to rejoin the PCT at the Red Lake Trail.

4. 4:35hr 5700ft. Cascade Canal. Follow this to Fourmile Lake. The canal can dry up by the end of summer.

3. 3:20hr 4980ft. Hwy 140. The trail is a little indistinct from here. If you lose the trail, head uphill until you hit the Cascade Canal.

2. 2:50hr 4950ft. Lake of the Woods Resort.

1. 2:00hr 4980ft. Lake of the Woods. Take minor roads past holiday homes along the shore of the lake.

In the early 1900s the 11-mile Cascade Canal was built to carry water from Fourmile Lake to Fish Lake and subsequently to Medford. At a point ½ mile west of the PCT, the water from the canal disappears in to a lava tube and enters Fish Lake one mile away.

Rye Spur

Cascade Canal

121B

Centre Lake

Lost Peak

Long Lake

To the PCT

Lake of the Woods Resort

Aspen Point Campground

Lake of the Woods

Sunset Campground

Badger Lake

Woodpecker Lake

Notices at Fish Lake Resort:

'Teach a man to fish and hunt and you'll never see him again.'

'Hunters, fishermen and other liars gather here.'

'Gone fishing.....
be back for deer season.'

'I fish, therefore I lie.'

Fourmile Lake

118B

MAP 120

Section 68: Red Lake Trail to Sevenmile Trail (maps 121–123)

18 miles 7 hours 2000ft
by PCT (Section 68A)
21 miles 9 hours 2000ft
by OST (Section 68B)

Immediately after the alternative route rejoins the PCT you have a choice of following the mainly forested, high-level, waterless route taken by the PCT or taking the suggested alternative routes, consisting of 3 main diversions from the PCT. These routes pass a multitude of lakes and are more scenic. If you take all the alternative routes it will take about an hour longer than following the PCT.

The first diversion follows the Red Lake Trail past Island Lake, Red Lake and a number of smaller lakes.

The second diversion follows the Sky Lakes Trail. This has a number of variations. If you want a swim you should take the Isherwood Trail where you can dive off rocks into Isherwood Lake. You could return to the PCT once you reach Margarette Lake but it seems natural to continue up the Snow Lakes Trail and rejoin the PCT S of Shale Butte.

The third diversion is from the NE ridge of Lucifer. Rather than go over Devils Peak you could take the Devils Peak Trail W and then rejoin the PCT through the Seven Lakes Basin. Cliff Lake is best for swimming. In early season this route might be best to avoid steep snow on the descent from Devils Peak.

6. 8:15hr 5850ft 0559180 4702420. Twin Peaks Trail. You could get water from lakes either NW or SE.

5. 6:45hr 6220ft. Mt McLoughlin Trail. If you have time it is worth following this trail to the summit of 9495ft Mt McLoughlin.

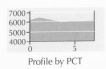

Profile by PCT

N

0   mile   1

MAP 121

About 7700 years ago you would have had a magnificent view of Mazama volcano to the N from Lucifer and Devils Peak. Mazama Volcano started developing about 500,000 years ago and had built up to 12,000ft. Then, about 5700BC, it erupted with a cataclysmic explosion, about 40x bigger than that of Mount St Helens on 18 May, 1980. The immediate landscape was buried under pumice, and ash was scattered over a wide area. (About 3in of ash reached Mount Rainier, 300 miles to the N.) The explosion almost emptied the magma chamber and the remains of the mountain collapsed into the resulting depression. All that was left was the crater rim, 7000–8000ft high, together with a huge caldera (hole) which filled with water over the next 1000 years to form Crater Lake.

2. 1:15hr 6150ft. The recommended Sky Lakes Trail, to the NE, will take about an hour longer than the PCT.

1. 0:55hr 6080ft. PCT and Red Lake Trail rejoin (1:10hr by Red Lake Trail).

8. 10:15hr 6030ft 05632220. Red Lake Trail. The alternative route rejoins the PCT (8:05hr). Either follow the PCT or the Red Lake Trail.

7. 9:40hr 6280ft 0561340 4706170. Trail to Christies Spring, which might flow through the summer.

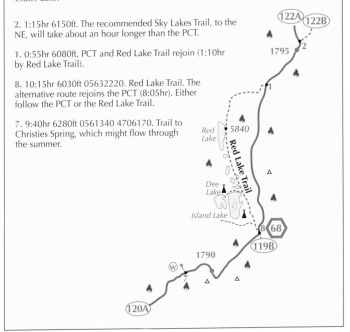

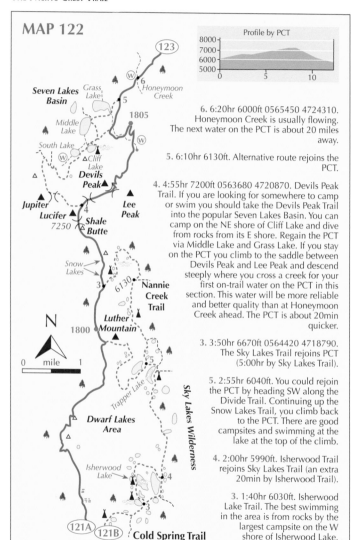

MAP 122

Profile by PCT

Seven Lakes Basin
Grass Lake
Honeymoon Creek
Middle Lake
1805
South Lake
Cliff Lake
Devils Peak
Jupiter
Lucifer
7250
Lee Peak
Shale Butte
Snow Lakes
6130
Nannie Creek Trail
Luther Mountain
1800
5
Trapper Lake
Sky Lakes Wilderness
N
0   mile   1
Dwarf Lakes Area
Isherwood Lake
4
121A   121B   Cold Spring Trail

6. 6:20hr 6000ft 0565450 4724310.
Honeymoon Creek is usually flowing.
The next water on the PCT is about 20 miles
away.

5. 6:10hr 6130ft. Alternative route rejoins the
PCT.

4. 4:55hr 7200ft 0563680 4720870. Devils Peak
Trail. If you are looking for somewhere to camp
or swim you should take the Devils Peak Trail
into the popular Seven Lakes Basin. You can
camp on the NE shore of Cliff Lake and dive
from rocks from its E shore. Regain the PCT
via Middle Lake and Grass Lake. If you stay
on the PCT you climb to the saddle between
Devils Peak and Lee Peak and descend
steeply where you cross a creek for your
first on-trail water on the PCT in this
section. This water will be more reliable
and better quality than at Honeymoon
Creek ahead. The PCT is about 20min
quicker.

3. 3:50hr 6670ft 0564420 4718790.
The Sky Lakes Trail rejoins PCT
(5:00hr by Sky Lakes Trail).

5. 2:55hr 6040ft. You could rejoin
the PCT by heading SW along the
Divide Trail. Continuing up the
Snow Lakes Trail, you climb back
to the PCT. There are good
campsites and swimming at the
lake at the top of the climb.

4. 2:00hr 5990ft. Isherwood Trail
rejoins Sky Lakes Trail (an extra
20min by Isherwood Trail).

3. 1:40hr 6030ft. Isherwood
Lake Trail. The best swimming
in the area is from rocks by the
largest campsite on the W
shore of Isherwood Lake.

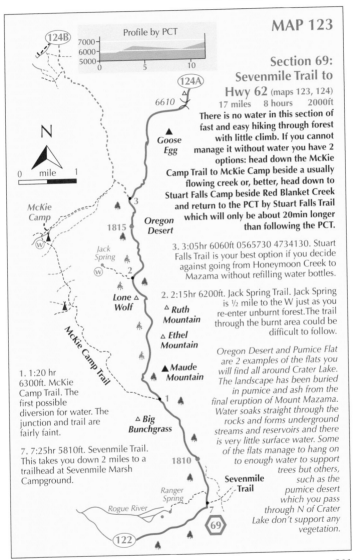

MAP 123

Section 69: Sevenmile Trail to Hwy 62 (maps 123, 124)

17 miles   8 hours   2000ft

There is no water in this section of fast and easy hiking through forest with little climb. If you cannot manage it without water you have 2 options: head down the McKie Camp Trail to McKie Camp beside a usually flowing creek or, better, head down to Stuart Falls Camp beside Red Blanket Creek and return to the PCT by Stuart Falls Trail which will only be about 20min longer than following the PCT.

3. 3:05hr 6060ft 0565730 4734130. Stuart Falls Trail is your best option if you decide against going from Honeymoon Creek to Mazama without refilling water bottles.

2. 2:15hr 6200ft. Jack Spring Trail. Jack Spring is ½ mile to the W just as you re-enter unburnt forest. The trail through the burnt area could be difficult to follow.

Oregon Desert and Pumice Flat are 2 examples of the flats you will find all around Crater Lake. The landscape has been buried in pumice and ash from the final eruption of Mount Mazama. Water soaks straight through the rocks and forms underground streams and reservoirs and there is very little surface water. Some of the flats manage to hang on to enough water to support trees but others, such as the pumice desert which you pass through N of Crater Lake don't support any vegetation.

Profile by PCT

7000
6000
5000
0   5   10

124B

124A

6610

▲ Goose Egg

N

0   mile   1

McKie Camp

W

3

1815

Oregon Desert

Jack Spring

W

2

▲ Lone Wolf

△ Ruth Mountain

△ Ethel Mountain

▲ Maude Mountain

McKie Camp Trail

1

△ Big Bunchgrass

1810

Ranger Spring

Rogue River

Sevenmile Trail

7

69

122

1. 1:20 hr 6300ft. McKie Camp Trail. The first possible diversion for water. The junction and trail are fairly faint.

7. 7:25hr 5810ft. Sevenmile Trail. This takes you down 2 miles to a trailhead at Sevenmile Marsh Campground.

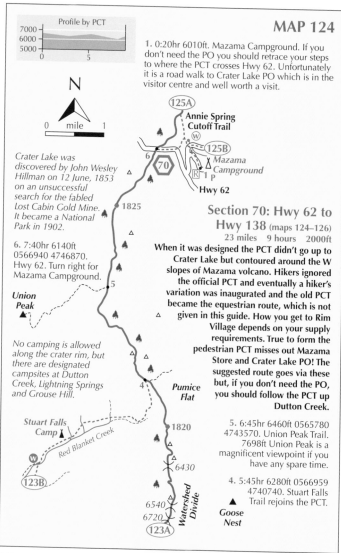

Profile by PCT

7000
6000
5000

0   5

MAP 124

1. 0:20hr 6010ft. Mazama Campground. If you don't need the PO you should retrace your steps to where the PCT crosses Hwy 62. Unfortunately it is a road walk to Crater Lake PO which is in the visitor centre and well worth a visit.

125A

Annie Spring
Cutoff Trail

125B

Mazama
Campground

Hwy 62

Crater Lake was discovered by John Wesley Hillman on 12 June, 1853 on an unsuccessful search for the fabled Lost Cabin Gold Mine. It became a National Park in 1902.

1825

6. 7:40hr 6140ft 0566940 4746870. Hwy 62. Turn right for Mazama Campground.

Union Peak ▲

No camping is allowed along the crater rim, but there are designated campsites at Dutton Creek, Lightning Springs and Grouse Hill.

Stuart Falls Camp ▲

Red Blanket Creek

123B

Section 70: Hwy 62 to Hwy 138 (maps 124–126)

23 miles   9 hours   2000ft

When it was designed the PCT didn't go up to Crater Lake but contoured around the W slopes of Mazama volcano. Hikers ignored the official PCT and eventually a hiker's variation was inaugurated and the old PCT became the equestrian route, which is not given in this guide. How you get to Rim Village depends on your supply requirements. True to form the pedestrian PCT misses out Mazama Store and Crater Lake PO! The suggested route goes via these but, if you don't need the PO, you should follow the PCT up Dutton Creek.

5. 6:45hr 6460ft 0565780 4743570. Union Peak Trail. 7698ft Union Peak is a magnificent viewpoint if you have any spare time.

4. 5:45hr 6280ft 0566959 4740740. Stuart Falls Trail rejoins the PCT.

Goose Nest

Pumice Flat

1820

6430

6540
6720

123A

Watershed Divide

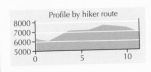

Profile by hiker route

MAP 125

2. 4:55hr 7270ft 0569250 4757410. North Junction, Rim Drive. Here you leave Crater Lake.

Crater Lake is 6 miles across and the intensely blue lake, at 1940ft, is the deepest lake in the US and the seventh deepest in the world. There is no outlet to the lake but there is a balance between rainfall into the caldera and evaporation from the lake. Before the volcano settled down several outbreaks volcanic cones inside the crater and one of these, Wizard Island, rises above the water.

Crater Lake National Park gets an average of 533in – more than 44ft! – of snow a year.

The Clark's nutcracker, a grey crow with black wings, is frequently seen around the rim of Crater Lake. It feeds almost exclusively on the seeds of the whitebark pine. It gathers the seeds and hides some to eat later, helping the tree to disperse its seeds. Forgotten seeds could grow into new whitebark pines.

1. 2:15hr 7060ft 0569580 4751400. Rim Village will be crowded with tourists. The hike round the Crater Rim is possibly the most awe-inspiring part of the PCT. You soon lose the crowd as you follow the trail along the rim. Note that camping is not allowed along the rim. The next water is 26 miles away! Get water from the soda fountain at the café or from outside the visitor centre (3:00hr via alternative route).

2. 1:50hr 6410ft 0570660 4749810. Crater Lake PO and Visitor Centre. Continue up the road to Rim Village.

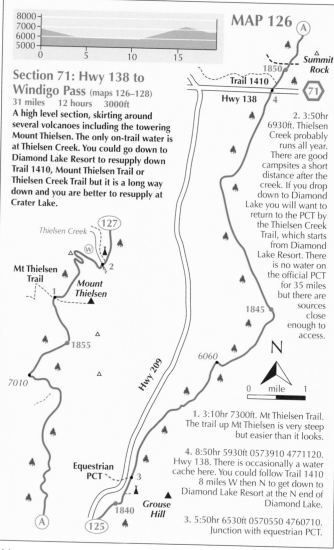

MAP 126

Ⓐ

△ Summit Rock

1850

Trail 1410

Hwy 138   71   4

Section 71: Hwy 138 to Windigo Pass (maps 126–128)
31 miles   12 hours   3000ft

A high level section, skirting around several volcanoes including the towering Mount Thielsen. The only on-trail water is at Thielsen Creek. You could go down to Diamond Lake Resort to resupply down Trail 1410, Mount Thielsen Trail or Thielsen Creek Trail but it is a long way down and you are better to resupply at Crater Lake.

2. 3:50hr 6930ft. Thielsen Creek probably runs all year. There are good campsites a short distance after the creek. If you drop down to Diamond Lake you will want to return to the PCT by the Thielsen Creek Trail, which starts from Diamond Lake Resort. There is no water on the official PCT for 35 miles but there are sources close enough to access.

127

Thielsen Creek

Ⓦ

△   2

Mt Thielsen Trail   1

Mount Thielsen ▲

△ 1855

7010

Hwy 209

1845

6060

N

0   mile   1

1. 3:10hr 7300ft. Mt Thielsen Trail. The trail up Mt Thielsen is very steep but easier than it looks.

4. 8:50hr 5930ft 0573910 4771120. Hwy 138. There is occasionally a water cache here. You could follow Trail 1410 8 miles W then N to get down to Diamond Lake Resort at the N end of Diamond Lake.

Equestrian PCT   3

1840   *Grouse Hill* ▲

Ⓐ   125

3. 5:50hr 6530ft 0570550 4760710. Junction with equestrian PCT.

MAP 127

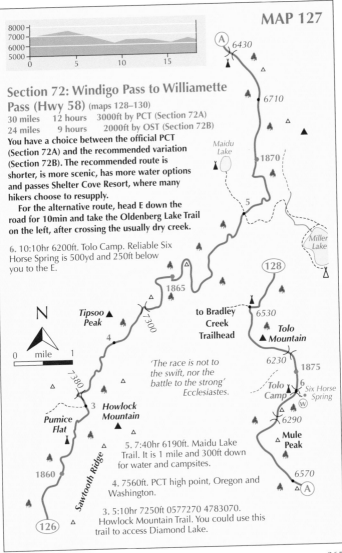

Section 72: Windigo Pass to Williamette Pass (Hwy 58) (maps 128–130)

30 miles 12 hours 3000ft by PCT (Section 72A)
24 miles 9 hours 2000ft by OST (Section 72B)

You have a choice between the official PCT (Section 72A) and the recommended variation (Section 72B). The recommended route is shorter, is more scenic, has more water options and passes Shelter Cove Resort, where many hikers choose to resupply.

For the alternative route, head E down the road for 10min and take the Oldenberg Lake Trail on the left, after crossing the usually dry creek.

6. 10:10hr 6200ft. Tolo Camp. Reliable Six Horse Spring is 500yd and 250ft below you to the E.

'The race is not to the swift, nor the battle to the strong'
Ecclesiastes.

5. 7:40hr 6190ft. Maidu Lake Trail. It is 1 mile and 300ft down for water and campsites.

4. 7560ft. PCT high point, Oregon and Washington.

3. 5:10hr 7250ft 0577270 4783070. Howlock Mountain Trail. You could use this trail to access Diamond Lake.

to Bradley Creek Trailhead

265

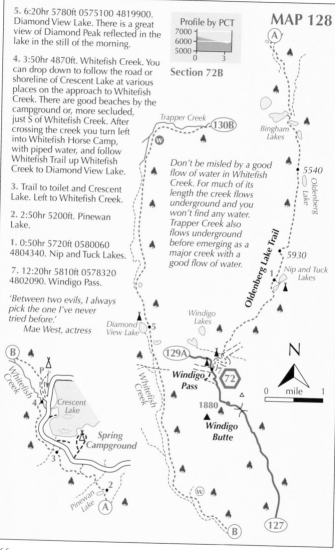

5. 6:20hr 5780ft 0575100 4819900. Diamond View Lake. There is a great view of Diamond Peak reflected in the lake in the still of the morning.

4. 3:50hr 4870ft. Whitefish Creek. You can drop down to follow the road or shoreline of Crescent Lake at various places on the approach to Whitefish Creek. There are good beaches by the campground or, more secluded, just S of Whitefish Creek. After crossing the creek you turn left into Whitefish Horse Camp, with piped water, and follow Whitefish Trail up Whitefish Creek to Diamond View Lake.

3. Trail to toilet and Crescent Lake. Left to Whitefish Creek.

2. 2:50hr 5200ft. Pinewan Lake.

1. 0:50hr 5720ft 0580060 4804340. Nip and Tuck Lakes.

7. 12:20hr 5810ft 0578320 4802090. Windigo Pass.

'Between two evils, I always pick the one I've never tried before.'
Mae West, actress

Profile by PCT

MAP 128

Section 72B

Don't be misled by a good flow of water in Whitefish Creek. For much of its length the creek flows underground and you won't find any water. Trapper Creek also flows underground before emerging as a major creek with a good flow of water.

Trapper Creek

130B

Bingham Lakes

5540

Oldenberg Lake

Oldenberg Lake Trail

5930

Nip and Tuck Lakes

1

Windigo Lakes

Diamond View Lake   5

129A

Windigo Pass

72

N

0   mile   1

1880

Windigo Butte

B

Whitefish Creek

P

4

Crescent Lake

Spring Campground

3

2

Pinewan Lake

A

A

B

127

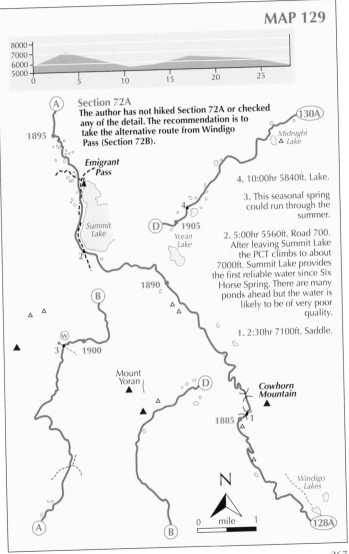

MAP 129

Section 72A

The author has not hiked Section 72A or checked any of the detail. The recommendation is to take the alternative route from Windigo Pass (Section 72B).

4. 10:00hr 5840ft. Lake.

3. This seasonal spring could run through the summer.

2. 5:00hr 5560ft. Road 700. After leaving Summit Lake the PCT climbs to about 7000ft. Summit Lake provides the first reliable water since Six Horse Spring. There are many ponds ahead but the water is likely to be of very poor quality.

1. 2:30hr 7100ft. Saddle.

Emigrant Pass

Summit Lake

Midnight Lake

Yoran Lake

Mount Yoran

Cowhorn Mountain

Windigo Lakes

N

0   mile   1

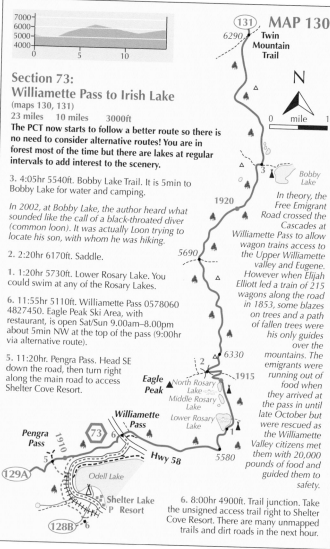

131 6290 **MAP 130**

Twin Mountain Trail

N

0   mile   1

Section 73: Willamette Pass to Irish Lake

(maps 130, 131)

23 miles   10 miles   3000ft

The PCT now starts to follow a better route so there is no need to consider alternative routes! You are in forest most of the time but there are lakes at regular intervals to add interest to the scenery.

3. 4:05hr 5540ft. Bobby Lake Trail. It is 5min to Bobby Lake for water and camping.

In 2002, at Bobby Lake, the author heard what sounded like the call of a black-throated diver (common loon). It was actually Loon trying to locate his son, with whom he was hiking.

2. 2:20hr 6170ft. Saddle.

1. 1:20hr 5730ft. Lower Rosary Lake. You could swim at any of the Rosary Lakes.

6. 11:55hr 5110ft. Williamette Pass 0578060 4827450. Eagle Peak Ski Area, with restaurant, is open Sat/Sun 9.00am–8.00pm about 5min NW at the top of the pass (9:00hr via alternative route).

5. 11:20hr. Pengra Pass. Head SE down the road, then turn right along the main road to access Shelter Cove Resort.

3   *Bobby Lake*

1920

5690

6330

2

1915

Eagle Peak

North Rosary Lake

Middle Rosary Lake

Lower Rosary Lake

1

5580

Williamette Pass

Pengra Pass

1910

73

6

5

129A

Odell Lake

Hwy 58

Shelter Lake P Resort

128B   6

In theory, the Free Emigrant Road crossed the Cascades at Williamette Pass to allow wagon trains access to the Upper Williamette valley and Eugene. However when Elijah Elliott led a train of 215 wagons along the road in 1853, some blazes on trees and a path of fallen trees were his only guides over the mountains. The emigrants were running out of food when they arrived at the pass in until late October but were rescued as the Williamette Valley citizens met them with 20,000 pounds of food and guided them to safety.

6. 8:00hr 4900ft. Trail junction. Take the unsigned access trail right to Shelter Cove Resort. There are many unmapped trails and dirt roads in the next hour.

MAP 131

Between Charlton Lake and Taylor Lake you are walking through an area damaged by a big fire in about 2000. In a serious fire the trees are destroyed but left standing. These are known as ghost trees. They are much weakened and storms usually break off the tops of the trees. After a few years they are further weakened and blow over, causing obstructions across the trail.

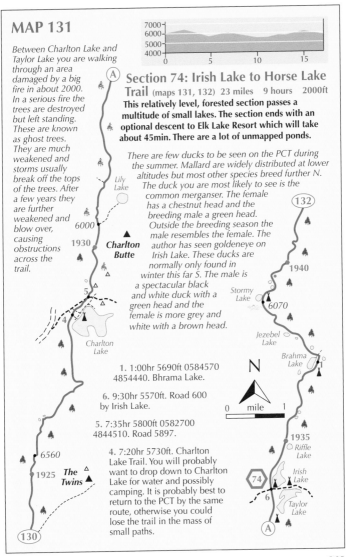

Section 74: Irish Lake to Horse Lake Trail (maps 131, 132) 23 miles 9 hours 2000ft

This relatively level, forested section passes a multitude of small lakes. The section ends with an optional descent to Elk Lake Resort which will take about 45min. There are a lot of unmapped ponds.

There are few ducks to be seen on the PCT during the summer. Mallard are widely distributed at lower altitudes but most other species breed further N. The duck you are most likely to see is the common merganser. The female has a chestnut head and the breeding male a green head. Outside the breeding season the male resembles the female. The author has seen goldeneye on Irish Lake. These ducks are normally only found in winter this far S. The male is a spectacular black and white duck with a green head and the female is more grey and white with a brown head.

1. 1:00hr 5690ft 0584570 4854440. Bhrama Lake.

6. 9:30hr 5570ft. Road 600 by Irish Lake.

5. 7:35hr 5800ft 0582700 4844510. Road 5897.

4. 7:20hr 5730ft. Charlton Lake Trail. You will probably want to drop down to Charlton Lake for water and possibly camping. It is probably best to return to the PCT by the same route, otherwise you could lose the trail in the mass of small paths.

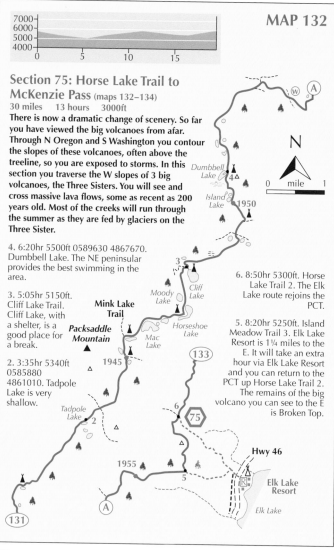

MAP 132

Section 75: Horse Lake Trail to McKenzie Pass (maps 132–134)
30 miles   13 hours   3000ft

There is now a dramatic change of scenery. So far you have viewed the big volcanoes from afar. Through N Oregon and S Washington you contour the slopes of these volcanoes, often above the treeline, so you are exposed to storms. In this section you traverse the W slopes of 3 big volcanoes, the Three Sisters. You will see and cross massive lava flows, some as recent as 200 years old. Most of the creeks will run through the summer as they are fed by glaciers on the Three Sister.

4. 6:20hr 5500ft 0589630 4867670. Dumbbell Lake. The NE peninsular provides the best swimming in the area.

3. 5:05hr 5150ft. Cliff Lake Trail. Cliff Lake, with a shelter, is a good place for a break.

2. 3:35hr 5340ft 0585880 4861010. Tadpole Lake is very shallow.

6. 8:50hr 5300ft. Horse Lake Trail 2. The Elk Lake route rejoins the PCT.

5. 8:20hr 5250ft. Island Meadow Trail 3. Elk Lake Resort is 1¼ miles to the E. It will take an extra hour via Elk Lake Resort and you can return to the PCT up Horse Lake Trail 2. The remains of the big volcano you can see to the E is Broken Top.

270

MAP 133

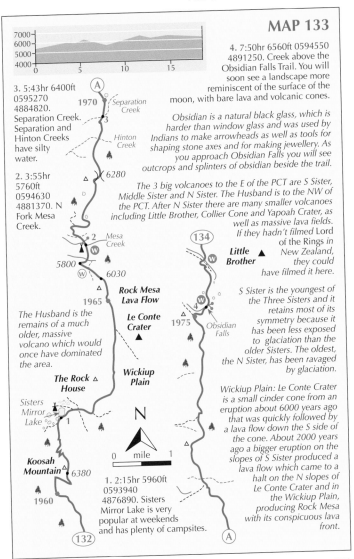

4. 7:50hr 6560ft 0594550 4891250. Creek above the Obsidian Falls Trail. You will soon see a landscape more reminiscent of the surface of the moon, with bare lava and volcanic cones.

Obsidian is a natural black glass, which is harder than window glass and was used by Indians to make arrowheads as well as tools for shaping stone axes and for making jewellery. As you approach Obsidian Falls you will see outcrops and splinters of obsidian beside the trail.

The 3 big volcanoes to the E of the PCT are S Sister, Middle Sister and N Sister. The Husband is to the NW of the PCT. After N Sister there are many smaller volcanoes including Little Brother, Collier Cone and Yapoah Crater, as well as massive lava fields. If they hadn't filmed Lord of the Rings in New Zealand, they could have filmed it here.

S Sister is the youngest of the Three Sisters and it retains most of its symmetry because it has been less exposed to glaciation than the older Sisters. The oldest, the N Sister, has been ravaged by glaciation.

Wickiup Plain: Le Conte Crater is a small cinder cone from an eruption about 6000 years ago that was quickly followed by a lava flow down the S side of the cone. About 2000 years ago a bigger eruption on the slopes of S Sister produced a lava flow which came to a halt on the N slopes of Le Conte Crater and in the Wickiup Plain, producing Rock Mesa with its conspicuous lava front.

3. 5:43hr 6400ft 0595270 4884820. Separation Creek. Separation and Hinton Creeks have silty water.

2. 3:55hr 5760ft 0594630 4881370. N Fork Mesa Creek.

The Husband is the remains of a much older, massive volcano which would once have dominated the area.

1. 2:15hr 5960ft 0593940 4876890. Sisters Mirror Lake is very popular at weekends and has plenty of campsites.

7000
6000
5000
4000
0   5   10   15

1970
Separation Creek
Hinton Creek
6280
1965
6280
1970
3
Separation Creek

2 *Mesa Creek*
5800
6030
1965
Rock Mesa Lava Flow
Le Conte Crater
Wickiup Plain

The Rock House

Sisters Mirror Lake
1
Koosah Mountain 6380
1960

134
Little Brother
Obsidian Falls
1975
4

N
0   mile   1

132
A

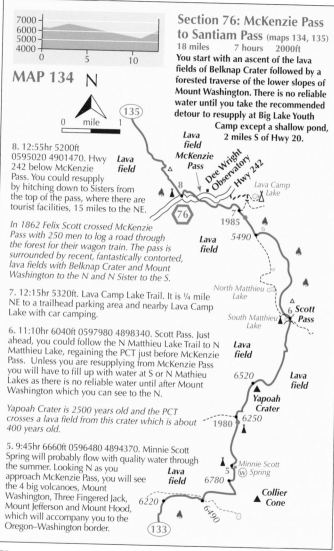

Section 76: McKenzie Pass to Santiam Pass (maps 134, 135)

18 miles   7 hours   2000ft

You start with an ascent of the lava fields of Belknap Crater followed by a forested traverse of the lower slopes of Mount Washington. There is no reliable water until you take the recommended detour to resupply at Big Lake Youth Camp except a shallow pond, 2 miles S of Hwy 20.

MAP 134 N

0   mile   1

8. 12:55hr 5200ft 0595020 4901470. Hwy 242 below McKenzie Pass. You could resupply by hitching down to Sisters from the top of the pass, where there are tourist facilities, 15 miles to the NE.

In 1862 Felix Scott crossed McKenzie Pass with 250 men to log a road through the forest for their wagon train. The pass is surrounded by recent, fantastically contorted, lava fields with Belknap Crater and Mount Washington to the N and N Sister to the S.

7. 12:15hr 5320ft. Lava Camp Lake Trail. It is ¼ mile NE to a trailhead parking area and nearby Lava Camp Lake with car camping.

6. 11:10hr 6040ft 0597980 4898340. Scott Pass. Just ahead, you could follow the N Matthieu Lake Trail to N Matthieu Lake, regaining the PCT just before McKenzie Pass. Unless you are resupplying from McKenzie Pass you will have to fill up with water at S or N Mathieu Lakes as there is no reliable water until after Mount Washington which you can see to the N.

Yapoah Crater is 2500 years old and the PCT crosses a lava field from this crater which is about 400 years old.

5. 9:45hr 6660ft 0596480 4894370. Minnie Scott Spring will probably flow with quality water through the summer. Looking N as you approach McKenzie Pass, you will see the 4 big volcanoes, Mount Washington, Three Fingered Jack, Mount Jefferson and Mount Hood, which will accompany you to the Oregon–Washington border.

Lava field
McKenzie Pass
Dee Wright Observatory
Hwy 242
Lava Camp Lake
Lava field
1985
5490
North Matthieu Lake
Scott Pass
South Matthieu Lake
Lava field
6520
Lava field
Yapoah Crater
1980   6250
Minnie Scott Spring
Lava field
6780
Collier Cone
6220
6490
133
135
76
8

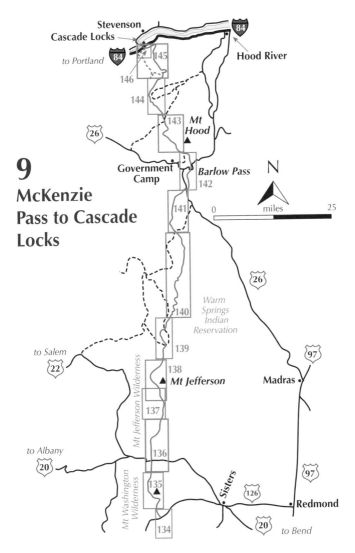

Stevenson

Cascade Locks

to Portland

84

145

146

144

143 *Mt Hood*

26

Government Camp

Barlow Pass

142

141

N

0 miles 25

Warm Springs Indian Reservation

26

to Salem

22

139

138

▲ *Mt Jefferson*

137

136

140

Mt Jefferson Wilderness

to Albany

20

Mt Washington Wilderness

135

134

Sisters

126

97

Madras

Redmond

97

20 to Bend

84

Hood River

PART 9: MCKENZIE PASS TO CASCADE LOCKS

Section	Distance (miles)	Time (hours)	Ascent (feet)	Maps
76 McKenzie Pass–Santiam Pass	18	7	2000	134, 135
77A Santiam Pass–Milk Creek by PCT	28	12	3000	135–138
77B Santiam Pass–Milk Creek by OST	26	12	3000	135–138
78 Milk Creek–Breitenbush Lake	12	6	3000	138, 139
79 Breitenbush Lake–Road 42	36	14	3000	139–141
80 Road 42–Barlow Pass	19	7	2000	141, 142
81 Barlow Pass–Lolo Pass	22	11	5000	142, 143
82 Lolo Pass–Wahtum Lake	16	7	2000	143–145
83A Wahtum Lake–Cascade Locks by PCT	16	6	1000	145, 146
83B Wahtum Lake–Cascade Locks by Eagle Creek	16	6	400	145, 146
Part total	**167**	**70**	**21,000**	

Northern Oregon is dominated by four giant volcanoes: Mount Washington, Three Fingered Jack and Mount Jefferson follow in quick succession. A forested interlude follows before a high level traverse on the flanks of Mount Hood. Virtually all hikers end the section with the dramatic descent down Eagle Creek rather than following the PCT. This is another section with relatively little ascent in which you can make rapid progress.

A lower level diversion given for Section 77, along the Oregon Skyline Trail, should probably be looked on as a bad weather alternative route.

Once you are clear of McKenzie Pass, the volcanic landscape is older than that of Southern Oregon and the huge volcanoes show more erosion from ice age glaciation. As you travel further north the volcanoes' glaciers increase in number and size. The view of Mount Jefferson from Jefferson Park is particularly spectacular.

Best time
Mid-July to September. Any time after the snow has melted.

Permits
No permits are required in this section. A Northwest Forest Pass is needed for parking at some of the trailheads (see Part 8).

Facilities

It is suggested you resupply at Big Lake Youth Camp, Olallie Lake Resort, Timberline Lodge and Cascade Locks. You should be aware that post offices close down completely over Labour Day weekend at the beginning of September, the peak time for thru'-hikers arriving at Cascade Locks.

Sisters (PO, G, R, A, B) (from McKenzie Pass) (Sections 75, 76) (0 hours)
See Part 8 introduction.

Seventh Day Adventists Big Lake Youth Camp (P, C, L, R, Sh) (Section 76) (5 hours)
13100, Highway 20, Sisters OR97759 (503)-850-3583 (winter), 503-805-2267 (summer), www.biglake.org.
9.00am–7.00pm

This hiker friendly establishment offers a package service, showers and laundry, and you can have a meal with them.

Hoodoo Ski Area (minimal G, Sh) (Section 76) (5 hours)
9.00am–4.00pm. Hoodoo Ski Area, shown on Map 21, is between Big Lake and Highway 20. Its store has snacks and very limited backpacking supplies.

Olallie Lake Resort (P, small G, A, C) (Section 79) (28 hours)
503-871-7035,
www.olallielakeresort.com
Olallie Lake Resort came under new ownership in 2009 and was being completely reconstructed. Visit the website to see what services are currently being offered to hikers.

Volcanic area north of North Sister (Section 75)

Mount Hood (Section 82)

Government Camp (PO, G, R, A, L, B) (Section 80, 81) (46 hours)
Government Camp PO, 88331E Government Camp Loop, Government Camp OR97028
(503)-272-3238. Mon–Fri: 7.30am–12.00noon, 1.00pm–4.30pm

Timberline Lodge (P, R, A, B) (Section 81) (49 hours)
Timberline Ski Area, Wy'East Store, Timberline Lodge OR97028
(503)-272-3311 (store), www.timberlinelodge.com
Mon–Sun: 7.00am–7.00pm

The store, which operates the package service ($4 in 2009), and the café are in the lower building. Timberline Lodge, with a reasonably priced restaurant, is a premier mountain hotel.

Cascade Locks (PO, G, R, A, C, L, Sh, B) (Sections 83, 84) (70 hours)
Cascade Locks PO, 461 NW Wanopa St, Cascade Locks OR97014
(541)-374-5026. Mon–Fri: 8.30am–1.00pm, 2.00pm–5.00pm
Cascade Locks has good facilities for a small town, with free camping next to the port.

MAP 135

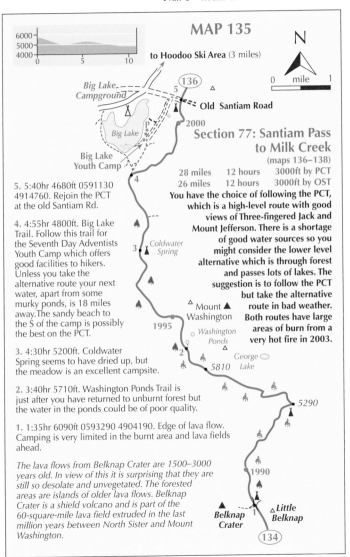

to Hoodoo Ski Area (3 miles)

N

0   mile   1

136

Big Lake Campground

5

Old Santiam Road

2000

Big Lake

P

Big Lake Youth Camp

4

3 ✕ *Coldwater Spring*

△ Mount ▲ **Washington**

1995

Washington Ponds

2 ⛺

5810

George ◯ Lake

5290

1990

▲ **Belknap Crater**

1 ✕ △ *Little Belknap*

134

Section 77: Santiam Pass to Milk Creek

(maps 136–138)

28 miles	12 hours	3000ft by PCT
26 miles	12 hours	3000ft by OST

You have the choice of following the PCT, which is a high-level route with good views of Three-fingered Jack and Mount Jefferson. There is a shortage of good water sources so you might consider the lower level alternative which is through forest and passes lots of lakes. The suggestion is to follow the PCT but take the alternative route in bad weather. Both routes have large areas of burn from a very hot fire in 2003.

5. 5:40hr 4680ft 0591130 4914760. Rejoin the PCT at the old Santiam Rd.

4. 4:55hr 4800ft. Big Lake Trail. Follow this trail for the Seventh Day Adventists Youth Camp which offers good facilities to hikers. Unless you take the alternative route your next water, apart from some murky ponds, is 18 miles away. The sandy beach to the S of the camp is possibly the best on the PCT.

3. 4:30hr 5200ft. Coldwater Spring seems to have dried up, but the meadow is an excellent campsite.

2. 3:40hr 5710ft. Washington Ponds Trail is just after you have returned to unburnt forest but the water in the ponds could be of poor quality.

1. 1:35hr 6090ft 0593290 4904190. Edge of lava flow. Camping is very limited in the burnt area and lava fields ahead.

The lava flows from Belknap Crater are 1500–3000 years old. In view of this it is surprising that they are still so desolate and unvegetated. The forested areas are islands of older lava flows. Belknap Crater is a shield volcano and is part of the 60-square-mile lava field extruded in the last million years between North Sister and Mount Washington.

277

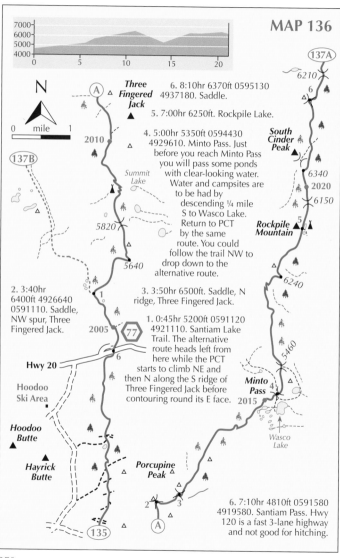

MAP 136

7000
6000
5000
4000

0   5   10   15   20

N

0   mile   1

(A)

Three Fingered Jack

2010

Summit Lake

5820

5640

2. 3:40hr 6400ft 4926640 0591110. Saddle, NW spur, Three Fingered Jack.

2005

(137B)

(77)

Hwy 20

Hoodoo Ski Area

Hoodoo Butte

Hayrick Butte

6. 8:10hr 6370ft 0595130 4937180. Saddle.

5. 7:00hr 6250ft. Rockpile Lake.

4. 5:00hr 5350ft 0594430 4929610. Minto Pass. Just before you reach Minto Pass you will pass some ponds with clear-looking water. Water and campsites are to be had by descending ¼ mile S to Wasco Lake. Return to PCT by the same route. You could follow the trail NW to drop down to the alternative route.

3. 3:50hr 6500ft. Saddle, N ridge, Three Fingered Jack.

1. 0:45hr 5200ft 0591120 4921110. Santiam Lake Trail. The alternative route heads left from here while the PCT starts to climb NE and then N along the S ridge of Three Fingered Jack before contouring round its E face.

(137A)

6210

6

South Cinder Peak

6340

2020

6150

Rockpile Mountain 5

6240

5460

Minto Pass 4
2015

Wasco Lake

Porcupine Peak

2   3

(A)

6. 7:10hr 4810ft 0591580 4919580. Santiam Pass. Hwy 120 is a fast 3-lane highway and not good for hitching.

(135)

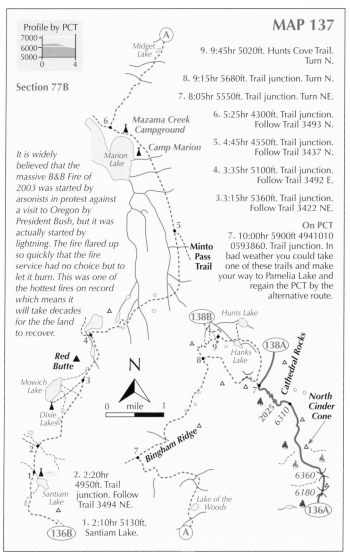

Profile by PCT

Section 77B

MAP 137

9. 9:45hr 5020ft. Hunts Cove Trail. Turn N.

8. 9:15hr 5680ft. Trail junction. Turn N.

7. 8:05hr 5550ft. Trail junction. Turn NE.

6. 5:25hr 4300ft. Trail junction. Follow Trail 3493 N.

5. 4:45hr 4550ft. Trail junction. Follow Trail 3437 N.

4. 3:35hr 5100ft. Trail junction. Follow Trail 3492 E.

3. 3:15hr 5360ft. Trail junction. Follow Trail 3422 NE.

On PCT

7. 10:00hr 5900ft 4941010 0593860. Trail junction. In bad weather you could take one of these trails and make your way to Pamelia Lake and regain the PCT by the alternative route.

It is widely believed that the massive B&B Fire of 2003 was started by arsonists in protest against a visit to Oregon by President Bush, but it was actually started by lightning. The fire flared up so quickly that the fire service had no choice but to let it burn. This was one of the hottest fires on record which means it will take decades for the the land to recover.

Midget Lake

Mazama Creek Campground

Marion Lake

Camp Marion

Minto Pass Trail

Hunts Lake

138B

Hanks Lake

138A

Cathedral Rocks

North Cinder Cone

2025

6310

Red Butte

Mowich Lake

Dixie Lakes

N

0   mile   1

Bingham Ridge

6360

6180

136A

2. 2:20hr 4950ft. Trail junction. Follow Trail 3494 NE.

Santiam Lake

Lake of the Woods

1. 2:10hr 5130ft. Santiam Lake.

136B

A

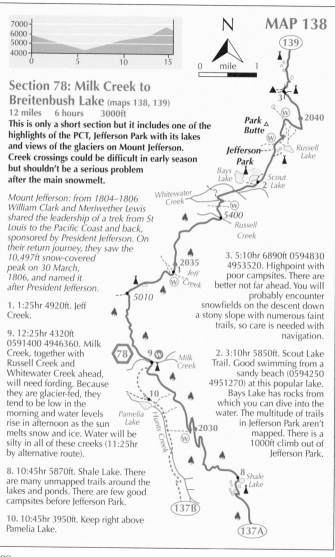

MAP 138

Section 78: Milk Creek to Breitenbush Lake (maps 138, 139)
12 miles   6 hours   3000ft

This is only a short section but it includes one of the highlights of the PCT, Jefferson Park with its lakes and views of the glaciers on Mount Jefferson. Creek crossings could be difficult in early season but shouldn't be a serious problem after the main snowmelt.

Mount Jefferson: from 1804–1806 William Clark and Meriwether Lewis shared the leadership of a trek from St Louis to the Pacific Coast and back, sponsored by President Jefferson. On their return journey, they saw the 10,497ft snow-covered peak on 30 March, 1806, and named it after President Jefferson.

1. 1:25hr 4920ft. Jeff Creek.

9. 12:25hr 4320ft 0591400 4946360. Milk Creek, together with Russell Creek and Whitewater Creek ahead, will need fording. Because they are glacier-fed, they tend to be low in the morning and water levels rise in afternoon as the sun melts snow and ice. Water will be silty in all of these creeks (11:25hr by alternative route).

8. 10:45hr 5870ft. Shale Lake. There are many unmapped trails around the lakes and ponds. There are few good campsites before Jefferson Park.

10. 10:45hr 3950ft. Keep right above Pamelia Lake.

3. 5:10hr 6890ft 0594830 4953520. Highpoint with poor campsites. There are better not far ahead. You will probably encounter snowfields on the descent down a stony slope with numerous faint trails, so care is needed with navigation.

2. 3:10hr 5850ft. Scout Lake Trail. Good swimming from a sandy beach (0594250 4951270) at this popular lake. Bays Lake has rocks from which you can dive into the water. The multitude of trails in Jefferson Park aren't mapped. There is a 1000ft climb out of Jefferson Park.

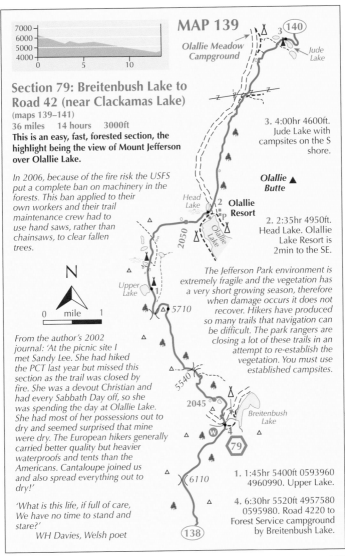

MAP 139

Olallie Meadow Campground

Section 79: Breitenbush Lake to Road 42 (near Clackamas Lake)
(maps 139–141)

36 miles   14 hours   3000ft

This is an easy, fast, forested section, the highlight being the view of Mount Jefferson over Olallie Lake.

In 2006, because of the fire risk the USFS put a complete ban on machinery in the forests. This ban applied to their own workers and their trail maintenance crew had to use hand saws, rather than chainsaws, to clear fallen trees.

3. 4:00hr 4600ft. Jude Lake with campsites on the S shore.

Olallie ▲ Butte

2. 2:35hr 4950ft. Head Lake. Olallie Lake Resort is 2min to the SE.

Head Lake

Olallie Resort

The Jefferson Park environment is extremely fragile and the vegetation has a very short growing season, therefore when damage occurs it does not recover. Hikers have produced so many trails that navigation can be difficult. The park rangers are closing a lot of these trails in an attempt to re-establish the vegetation. You must use established campsites.

Upper Lake

5710

From the author's 2002 journal: 'At the picnic site I met Sandy Lee. She had hiked the PCT last year but missed this section as the trail was closed by fire. She was a devout Christian and had every Sabbath Day off, so she was spending the day at Olallie Lake. She had most of her possessions out to dry and seemed surprised that mine were dry. The European hikers generally carried better quality but heavier waterproofs and tents than the Americans. Cantaloupe joined us and also spread everything out to dry!'

5540

2045

Breitenbush Lake

79

'What is this life, if full of care, We have no time to stand and stare?'
    WH Davies, Welsh poet

6110

138

1. 1:45hr 5400ft 0593960 4960990. Upper Lake.

4. 6:30hr 5520ft 4957580 0595980. Road 4220 to Forest Service campground by Breitenbush Lake.

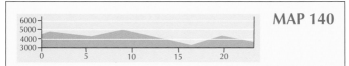

MAP 140

7. 13:10hr 3570ft 0600620 4992320. Road S549.

6. 10:20hr 3300ft. Warm Springs River. Your next water will be 8 miles away.

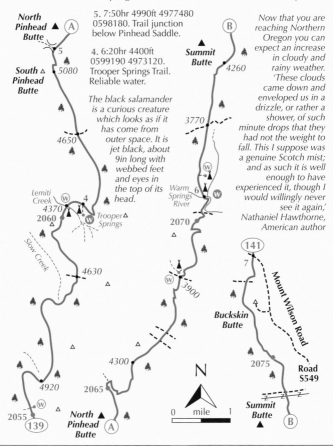

5. 7:50hr 4990ft 4977480 0598180. Trail junction below Pinhead Saddle.

4. 6:20hr 4400ft 0599190 4973120. Trooper Springs Trail. Reliable water.

The black salamander is a curious creature which looks as if it has come from outer space. It is jet black, about 9in long with webbed feet and eyes in the top of its head.

Now that you are reaching Northern Oregon you can expect an increase in cloudy and rainy weather. 'These clouds came down and enveloped us in a drizzle, or rather a shower, of such minute drops that they had not the weight to fall. This I suppose was a genuine Scotch mist; and as such it is well enough to have experienced it, though I would willingly never see it again,' Nathaniel Hawthorne, American author

MAP 141

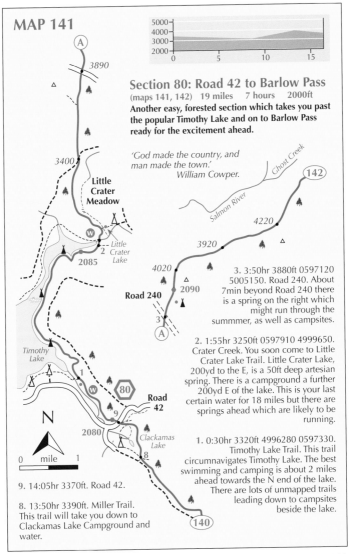

3890

3400

Little Crater Meadow

ⓦ

Little Crater Lake

2

2085

Timothy Lake

1

ⓦ

⑧⓪

Road 42

9

2080

Clackamas Lake

8

N

0 ——— mile ——— 1

Section 80: Road 42 to Barlow Pass
(maps 141, 142)   19 miles   7 hours   2000ft
Another easy, forested section which takes you past the popular Timothy Lake and on to Barlow Pass ready for the excitement ahead.

'God made the country, and man made the town.'
William Cowper.

Ghost Creek

142

Salmon River

4220

3920

4020

2090

Road 240

3

Ⓐ

3. 3:50hr 3880ft 0597120 5005150. Road 240. About 7min beyond Road 240 there is a spring on the right which might run through the summer, as well as campsites.

2. 1:55hr 3250ft 0597910 4999650. Crater Creek. You soon come to Little Crater Lake Trail. Little Crater Lake, 200yd to the E, is a 50ft deep artesian spring. There is a campground a further 200yd E of the lake. This is your last certain water for 18 miles but there are springs ahead which are likely to be running.

1. 0:30hr 3320ft 4996280 0597330. Timothy Lake Trail. This trail circumnavigates Timothy Lake. The best swimming and camping is about 2 miles ahead towards the N end of the lake. There are lots of unmapped trails leading down to campsites beside the lake.

9. 14:05hr 3370ft. Road 42.

8. 13:50hr 3390ft. Miller Trail. This trail will take you down to Clackamas Lake Campground and water.

140

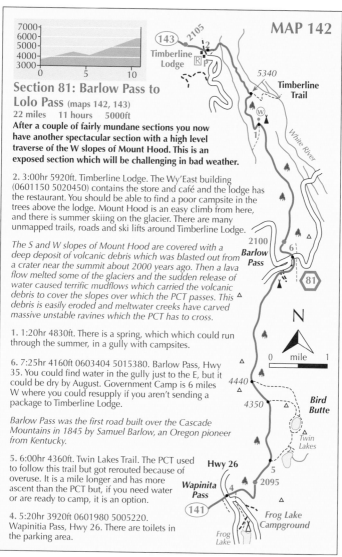

MAP 142

Section 81: Barlow Pass to Lolo Pass (maps 142, 143)

22 miles   11 hours   5000ft

After a couple of fairly mundane sections you now have another spectacular section with a high level traverse of the W slopes of Mount Hood. This is an exposed section which will be challenging in bad weather.

2. 3:00hr 5920ft. Timberline Lodge. The Wy'East building (0601150 5020450) contains the store and café and the lodge has the restaurant. You should be able to find a poor campsite in the trees above the lodge. Mount Hood is an easy climb from here, and there is summer skiing on the glacier. There are many unmapped trails, roads and ski lifts around Timberline Lodge.

The S and W slopes of Mount Hood are covered with a deep deposit of volcanic debris which was blasted out from a crater near the summit about 2000 years ago. Then a lava flow melted some of the glaciers and the sudden release of water caused terrific mudflows which carried the volcanic debris to cover the slopes over which the PCT passes. This debris is easily eroded and meltwater creeks have carved massive unstable ravines which the PCT has to cross.

1. 1:20hr 4830ft. There is a spring, which which could run through the summer, in a gully with campsites.

6. 7:25hr 4160ft 0603404 5015380. Barlow Pass, Hwy 35. You could find water in the gully just to the E, but it could be dry by August. Government Camp is 6 miles W where you could resupply if you aren't sending a package to Timberline Lodge.

Barlow Pass was the first road built over the Cascade Mountains in 1845 by Samuel Barlow, an Oregon pioneer from Kentucky.

5. 6:00hr 4360ft. Twin Lakes Trail. The PCT used to follow this trail but got rerouted because of overuse. It is a mile longer and has more ascent than the PCT but, if you need water or are ready to camp, it is an option.

4. 5:20hr 3920ft 0601980 5005220. Wapinitia Pass, Hwy 26. There are toilets in the parking area.

284

MAP 143

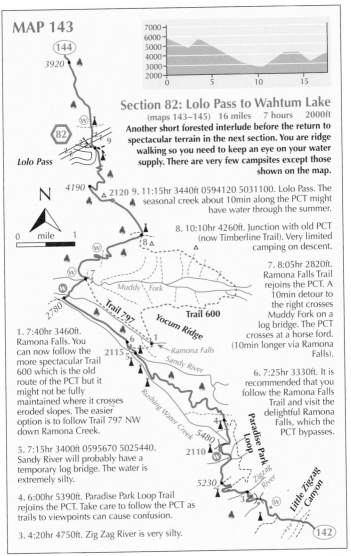

(144)
3920

(82)

Lolo Pass

N

0 — mile — 1

4190

△ *2120* 9.

2780

Trail 797

Muddy Fork

Trail 600

Yocum Ridge

6
2115 5

Ramona Falls

Sandy River

Rushing Water Creek

4
5480

2110

5230

Zigzag River

Paradise Park Loop

Little Zigzag Canyon

3

(142)

Section 82: Lolo Pass to Wahtum Lake
(maps 143–145) 16 miles 7 hours 2000ft

Another short forested interlude before the return to spectacular terrain in the next section. You are ridge walking so you need to keep an eye on your water supply. There are very few campsites except those shown on the map.

9. 11:15hr 3440ft 0594120 5031100. Lolo Pass. The seasonal creek about 10min along the PCT might have water through the summer.

8. 10:10hr 4260ft. Junction with old PCT (now Timberline Trail). Very limited camping on descent.

7. 8:05hr 2820ft. Ramona Falls Trail rejoins the PCT. A 10min detour to the right crosses Muddy Fork on a log bridge. The PCT crosses at a horse ford. (10min longer via Ramona Falls).

6. 7:25hr 3330ft. It is recommended that you follow the Ramona Falls Trail and visit the delightful Ramona Falls, which the PCT bypasses.

1. 7:40hr 3460ft. Ramona Falls. You can now follow the more spectacular Trail 600 which is the old route of the PCT but it might not be fully maintained where it crosses eroded slopes. The easier option is to follow Trail 797 NW down Ramona Creek.

5. 7:15hr 3400ft 0595670 5025440. Sandy River will probably have a temporary log bridge. The water is extremely silty.

4. 6:00hr 5390ft. Paradise Park Loop Trail rejoins the PCT. Take care to follow the PCT as trails to viewpoints can cause confusion.

3. 4:20hr 4750ft. Zig Zag River is very silty.

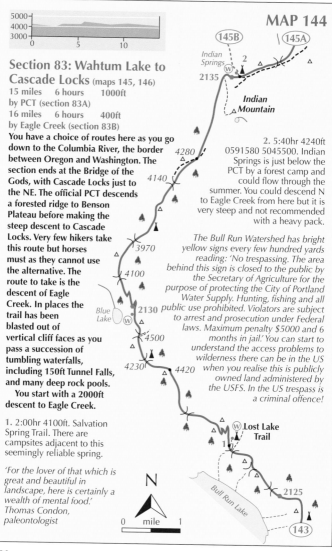

MAP 144

145B   145A

Indian Springs   2
W
2135

Indian Mountain

4280

4140

3970

4100

Blue Lake
W   2130

4500

4230   4420

Section 83: Wahtum Lake to Cascade Locks (maps 145, 146)

15 miles   6 hours   1000ft
by PCT (section 83A)
16 miles   6 hours   400ft
by Eagle Creek (section 83B)

You have a choice of routes here as you go down to the Columbia River, the border between Oregon and Washington. The section ends at the Bridge of the Gods, with Cascade Locks just to the NE. The official PCT descends a forested ridge to Benson Plateau before making the steep descent to Cascade Locks. Very few hikers take this route but horses must as they cannot use the alternative. The route to take is the descent of Eagle Creek. In places the trail has been blasted out of vertical cliff faces as you pass a succession of tumbling waterfalls, including 150ft Tunnel Falls, and many deep rock pools. You start with a 2000ft descent to Eagle Creek.

1. 2:00hr 4100ft. Salvation Spring Trail. There are campsites adjacent to this seemingly reliable spring.

'For the lover of that which is great and beautiful in landscape, here is certainly a wealth of mental food.'
Thomas Condon,
paleontologist

2. 5:40hr 4240ft 0591580 5045500. Indian Springs is just below the PCT by a forest camp and could flow through the summer. You could descend N to Eagle Creek from here but it is very steep and not recommended with a heavy pack.

The Bull Run Watershed has bright yellow signs every few hundred yards reading: 'No trespassing. The area behind this sign is closed to the public by the Secretary of Agriculture for the purpose of protecting the City of Portland Water Supply. Hunting, fishing and all public use prohibited. Violators are subject to arrest and prosecution under Federal laws. Maximum penalty $5000 and 6 months in jail.' You can start to understand the access problems to wilderness there can be in the US when you realise this is publicly owned land administered by the USFS. In the US trespass is a criminal offence!

W **Lost Lake Trail**
1

N

0   mile   1

Bull Run Lake

2125

143

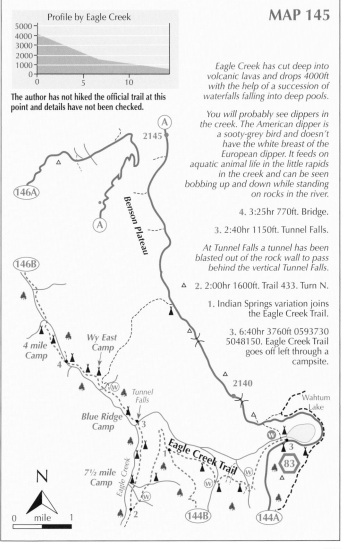

Profile by Eagle Creek

5000
4000
3000
2000
1000
0
0   5   10

The author has not hiked the official trail at this point and details have not been checked.

MAP 145

Eagle Creek has cut deep into volcanic lavas and drops 4000ft with the help of a succession of waterfalls falling into deep pools.

You will probably see dippers in the creek. The American dipper is a sooty-grey bird and doesn't have the white breast of the European dipper. It feeds on aquatic animal life in the little rapids in the creek and can be seen bobbing up and down while standing on rocks in the river.

4. 3:25hr 770ft. Bridge.

3. 2:40hr 1150ft. Tunnel Falls.

At Tunnel Falls a tunnel has been blasted out of the rock wall to pass behind the vertical Tunnel Falls.

2. 2:00hr 1600ft. Trail 433. Turn N.

1. Indian Springs variation joins the Eagle Creek Trail.

3. 6:40hr 3760ft 0593730 5048150. Eagle Creek Trail goes off left through a campsite.

(A)
2145

(146A)

Benson Plateau

(A)

(146B)

Wy East Camp

4 mile Camp
4

Tunnel Falls

Blue Ridge Camp
3

Eagle Creek Trail

7½ mile Camp
2

Eagle Creek

N

0   mile   1

2140

Wahtum Lake

(w)

3

(83)

(w)

(w)

(w)

(144B)

(144A)

287

MAP 146

Profile by
Eagle Creek

Section 84: Cascade Locks to Wind River Road (maps 146–148)

34 miles   16 hours   6000ft

You now enter Washington across the **Bridge of the Gods. This is really a hilly rather than a mountainous section but there is a lot of climb. You need to climb 3000ft out of the Columbia Gorge before descending to 1400ft, back to 3000ft before descending to 900ft.**

Take care crossing the Bridge of the Gods as there is no sidewalk for pedestrians.

The River People inhabited the Columbia Gorge at least 11,000 years ago and are the ancestors of today's NW Indian tribes.

Bridge of the Gods

147

84

Columbia River

Trail 400

Old Columbia Highway

Ruckel Creek

P

5

N

0   mile   1

145B

W

Cascade Locks

145A

2150

6. 5:50hr 200ft 0585870 5057080. Bridge of the Gods. You will want to visit Cascade Locks, which has good facilities for hikers.

The Bridge of the Gods was named after an Indian legend of a Bridge of the Gods at this point where a giant landslide is believed to have fallen from the unstable N wall of the Columbia Gorge, temporarily damming the river. There is evidence that there was a natural dam about 6000 years ago.

The sheer cliffs on Table Mountain and Greenleaf Peak across the gorge were formed about 800 years ago by the Bonneville Slide, a giant slide which dumped about 4 billion cubic yards of debris, temporarily damming the Columbia River before the water broke through to form the Cascade Rapids.

Cascade Locks was built in 1896 to allow ships to travel upriver beyond Columbia River's Cascade Rapids where there was a drop of 50ft in 6 miles. This was before the damming of the river in the 1930s.

5. 4:55hr 150ft. Eagle Creek Trailhead with piped water and toilets. This is the lowest point on the PCT. Follow the road for 5min, then take the paved road right through a picnic area. Cross the campground road and follow Gorge Trail 400 to the Old Columbia Highway. Continue on the highway when it passes under Interstate 84. The highway then becomes a paved trail which takes you to the Bridge of the Gods.

The old Columbia Highway was one of the first paved highways in the Pacific NW and was a marvel of modern engineering when it was built in the 1920s. It has since been replaced by Interstate 84.

WASHINGTON

Coon Lake (Section 98)

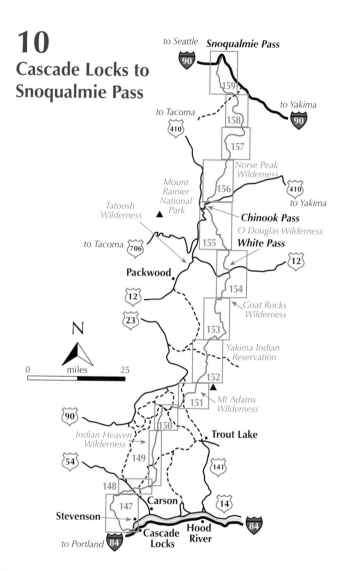

10
Cascade Locks to Snoqualmie Pass

to Seattle **Snoqualmie Pass**

to Yakima

to Tacoma

Chinook Pass

Norse Peak Wilderness

Mount Rainier National Park ▲

Tatoosh Wilderness

to Yakima

O Douglas Wilderness

White Pass

to Tacoma

Packwood

Goat Rocks Wilderness

Yakima Indian Reservation

N

0 miles 25

▲ *Mt Adams Wilderness*

Trout Lake

Indian Heaven Wilderness

Carson

Stevenson

to Portland

Cascade Locks

Hood River

290

PART 10: CASCADE LOCKS TO SNOQUALMIE PASS

Section	Distance (miles)	Time (hours)	Ascent (feet)	Maps
84 Cascade Locks–Wind River Rd	34	16	6000	146–148
85 Wind River Rd–Road 24	34	16	5000	148–150
86 Road 24–Road 23	15	6	2000	150, 151
87 Road 23–Road 5603	22	10	3000	151, 152
88 Road 5603–White Pass	44	21	6000	152–154
89 White Pass–Chinook Pass	30	15	4000	154, 155
90 Chinook Pass–Road 784	32	14	3000	155–157
91 Road 784–Stampede Pass	19	8	2000	157, 158
92 Stampede Pass–Snoqualmie Pass	19	8	2000	158–159
Part total	**249**	**114**	**33,000**	

Part 10 starts at the lowest point of the PCT and, after a very hilly first section, you aren't much higher than when you started. You then climb Huckleberry Mountain after which the section is relatively flat as you traverse the slopes of Mount Adams and return to alpine ridges in the spectacular Goats Rock Wilderness. The majestic Mount Rainier, covered in glaciers, is passed on its east side. While much of the route is in forest, you reach alpine and sub-alpine sections often enough to maintain interest.

Washington has a reputation for rain that is rather unfair. It is rainy compared with the mountains of California but in summer you can expect many hot sunny days. You must, however, be prepared for rainy days, possibly a succession of them. Thru'-hikers in September must be prepared for snow showers and cold nights.

Best time
Late July to early October. Any time after the snow has melted. Snowpack in Goats Rock Wilderness would make the PCT extremely difficult.

Permits
No permits are required. A Northwest Forest Pass is needed for parking at some of the trailheads (see Part 8).

Facilities
Resupply in this section is difficult and you will be carrying a heavy

pack. It is suggested you resupply at Stabler Store, Trout Lake, White Pass and Snoqualmie Pass.

Cascade Locks (PO, G, R, A, C, L, Sh, B) (Sections 83, 84) (0 hours)
See Part 9 introduction.

Hood River (from Cascade Locks) (Sections 83, 84) (0 hours)
Hood River is a major town and shopping should be easier than in Portland.

Stabler (P, small G) (Section 84, 85) (16 hours)
Stabler Country Store, 22 Hemlock Y Rd, Carson WA98610
(509)-427-2717.
Mon–Sun: 7.00am–7.00pm
The store sells hot snacks and will hold packages for hikers.

Carson (PO, G, R, B) (from Wind River Rd) (Sections 84, 85) (16 hours)
Carson PO, 1182 Wind River Rd, Carson WA98610
(509)-427-5051. Mon–Fri: 8.30am–1.00pm, 2.00pm–5.00pm
Carson is a small town. Wind River Market (open 5.00am–10.00pm) is well-stocked and serves hot snacks.

Trout Lake (P, PO, G, R, A, B) (from Road 23) (Sections 86, 87) (38 hours)
Trout Lake Grocery, 2383 Highway 141, Trout Lake WA98650
(509)-395-2777, www.troutlake.org. 8.00am–8.00pm
Trout Lake Grocery is well-stocked and will hold packages for hikers (UPS or Fedex).

White Pass (PO, small G, A, L, C, B) (Sections 88, 89) (69 hours)

Split boulder, Goat Rocks Wilderness (Section 88)

Mount Rainier (Section 89)

White Pass PO, Kracker Barrel Store, 48851 US Highway 12, Naches WA98937
(509)-653-2467 (PO), (509)-672-3105 (store). 8.00am–6.00pm
The post office is situated inside the store and you can pick up packages during store opening hours. You cannot send parcels from the post office. The store sells hot snacks, has a laundry and an area to socialise. The Village Inn, with accommodation, is adjacent and the campground is north-east of Leech Lake.
www.skiwhitepass.com

Packwood (PO, G, R, A, B) (from White Pass) (Sections 88, 89) (69 hours)
Packwood PO, 111 Smith Rd, Packwood WA98361
(360)-494-6311. Mon–Fri: 8.00am–12.00noon, 1.00pm–4.45pm

Packwood is a small town, 20 miles from White Pass

Snoqualmie Pass (P, PO, G, R, A, B) (Sections 92, 93) (114 hours)
Snoqualmie Pass PO, Snoqualmie Pass WA98068
Mon–Sat: 10.00am–12.00noon
The post office is located inside the gas station store, which is reasonably well-stocked for a small store. You can only send out flat-rate parcels from the post office. It is are unlikely to have customs forms so you will need to provide these if you want to post parcels abroad. The Summit Inn has a reasonable value restaurant and will accept packages ($10 fee in 2009 for those not staying at the hotel):
Summit Inn, 603, State Route 906, PO Box 163, Snoqualmie Pass WA98068
(425)-434-6300, www.snoqualmie summitlodge.com

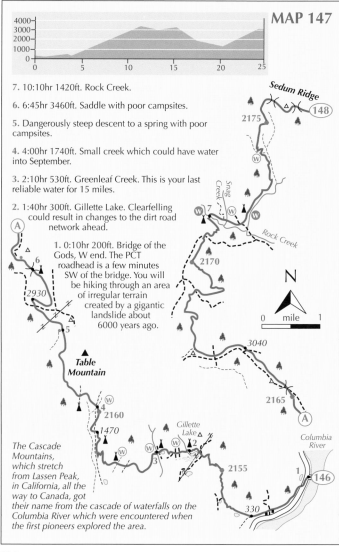

MAP 147

7. 10:10hr 1420ft. Rock Creek.

6. 6:45hr 3460ft. Saddle with poor campsites.

5. Dangerously steep descent to a spring with poor campsites.

4. 4:00hr 1740ft. Small creek which could have water into September.

3. 2:10hr 530ft. Greenleaf Creek. This is your last reliable water for 15 miles.

2. 1:40hr 300ft. Gillette Lake. Clearfelling could result in changes to the dirt road network ahead.

1. 0:10hr 200ft. Bridge of the Gods, W end. The PCT roadhead is a few minutes SW of the bridge. You will be hiking through an area of irregular terrain created by a gigantic landslide about 6000 years ago.

Table Mountain

Sedum Ridge

Snag Creek

Rock Creek

Gillette Lake

Columbia River

The Cascade Mountains, which stretch from Lassen Peak, in California, all the way to Canada, got their name from the cascade of waterfalls on the Columbia River which were encountered when the first pioneers explored the area.

MAP 148

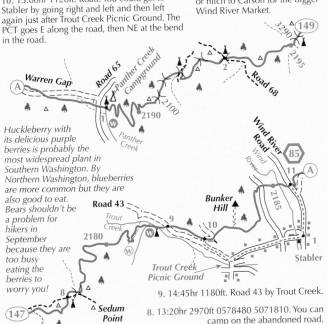

Section 85: Wind River Road to Road 22 (maps 148–150)

34 miles   16 hours   5000ft

You now climb 3000ft and follow a long ridge to Big Huckleberry Mountain before reaching terrain with many small lakes in this forested section.

1. 950ft. Stabler Store has a limited stock but does accept hikers' packages and has hot snacks.

10. 15:00hr 1120ft. Road. You could get to Stabler by going right and left and then left again just after Trout Creek Picnic Ground. The PCT goes E along the road, then NE at the bend in the road.

Huckleberry with its delicious purple berries is probably the most widespread plant in Southern Washington. By Northern Washington, blueberries are more common but they are also good to eat. Bears shouldn't be a problem for hikers in September because they are too busy eating the berries to worry you!

2. 4:00hr 2810ft 5075600 0590410. Road 68.

1. 0:55hr 900ft. Panther Creek. Panther Creek Campground is to the N. Fill up with water. You have a fairly reliable spring in 10 uphill miles but you need a reserve in case it is dry.

11. 15:55hr 1020ft. You could access Stabler Store from here or hitch to Carson for the bigger Wind River Market.

9. 14:45hr 1180ft. Road 43 by Trout Creek.

8. 13:20hr 2970ft 0578480 5071810. You can camp on the abandoned road.

MAP 149

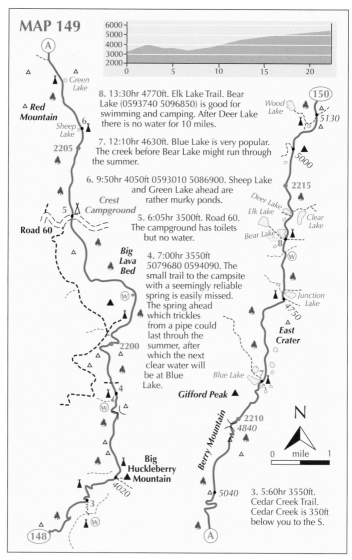

△ Green
Lake

△ **Red
Mountain**

*Sheep
Lake*

2205

*Crest
Campground*

Road 60

**Big
Lava
Bed**

2200

4

**Big
Huckleberry
Mountain**

4020

3

(148)

Wood
Lake

(150)

△ 5130

5000

2215

Deer Lake

Elk Lake

*Clear
Lake*

Bear Lake

8

Junction
Lake

4150

**East
Crater**

Blue Lake

7

Gifford Peak ▲

Berry Mountain

2210
4840

△ 5040

N

0   mile   1

8. 13:30hr 4770ft. Elk Lake Trail. Bear Lake (0593740 5096850) is good for swimming and camping. After Deer Lake there is no water for 10 miles.

7. 12:10hr 4630ft. Blue Lake is very popular. The creek before Bear Lake might run through the summer.

6. 9:50hr 4050ft 0593010 5086900. Sheep Lake and Green Lake ahead are rather murky ponds.

5. 6:05hr 3500ft. Road 60. The campground has toilets but no water.

4. 7:00hr 3550ft 5079680 0594090. The small trail to the campsite with a seemingly reliable spring is easily missed. The spring ahead which trickles from a pipe could last throuh the summer, after which the next clear water will be at Blue Lake.

3. 5:60hr 3550ft. Cedar Creek Trail. Cedar Creek is 350ft below you to the S.

MAP 150

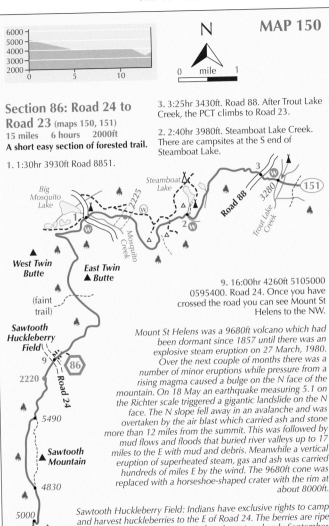

Section 86: Road 24 to Road 23 (maps 150, 151)
15 miles   6 hours   2000ft
A short easy section of forested trail.

1. 1:30hr 3930ft Road 8851.

3. 3:25hr 3430ft. Road 88. After Trout Lake Creek, the PCT climbs to Road 23.

2. 2:40hr 3980ft. Steamboat Lake Creek. There are campsites at the S end of Steamboat Lake.

9. 16:00hr 4260ft 5105000 0595400. Road 24. Once you have crossed the road you can see Mount St Helens to the NW.

Mount St Helens was a 9680ft volcano which had been dormant since 1857 until there was an explosive steam eruption on 27 March, 1980. Over the next couple of months there was a number of minor eruptions while pressure from a rising magma caused a bulge on the N face of the mountain. On 18 May an earthquake measuring 5.1 on the Richter scale triggered a gigantic landslide on the N face. The N slope fell away in an avalanche and was overtaken by the air blast which carried ash and stone more than 12 miles from the summit. This was followed by mud flows and floods that buried river valleys up to 17 miles to the E with mud and debris. Meanwhile a vertical eruption of superheated steam, gas and ash was carried hundreds of miles E by the wind. The 9680ft cone was replaced with a horseshoe-shaped crater with the rim at about 8000ft.

Sawtooth Huckleberry Field: Indians have exclusive rights to camp and harvest huckleberries to the E of Road 24. The berries are ripe in late August and early September.

MAP 151

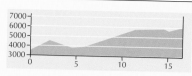

Section 87: Road 23 to Road 5603 (maps 151, 152)
22 miles   10 hours   3000ft

After an initial climb this section contours the slopes of Mount Adams at the treeline, giving magnificent views of the W face of Mount Adams with its glaciers as well as Mount Rainier to the N.

3. 5:20hr 5770ft 0610450 5118730. Riley Creek is a little silty, as are all the permanent creeks until Adams Creek, but has good campsites. Sheep Lake might be little more than a muddy pond by the end of a dry summer.

The last eruptions on Mount Adams were between 1000–2000 years ago but in May 1921 magma rose near enough to the surface for its heat to start a massive snow slide which eradicated much of the forest on the western slopes. The PCT crosses a number of lava flows from the most recent eruptions. To the N of Adams Glacier the rocks look yellow and in the 1930s sulphur was mined and carried down the mountain by mule train but it wasn't an economic success.

In 2006 there appeared to be steam coming from the Pinnacle Glacier area.

2. 3:45hr 5870ft 0610470 5115010. Trail 9 junction. Horseshoe Meadow Creek will probably be dry.

1. 0:35hr 4010ft. Swampy Creek. Fill up with water here as as the seasonal water sources on the climb could be dry.

5. 6:15hr 3830ft 0605640 5112890. Road 23. Trout Lake is about 13 miles S.

4. 4:50hr 4120ft 0603390 5109720. Road 8810. You could shortcut along this dirt road with good views of Mt Adams to the N. It will save you about 25min.

MAP 152

2. 3:00hr 5220ft 5139188 0616440. Junction with Trail 121 at switchback.

1. 0:55hr 4690ft. Midway Creek should flow through the summer. You pass some murky ponds ahead and a few early season creeks, but it might be better not to depend on them for water. The next certain running water is at Walupt Creek.

Section 88: Road 5603 to White Pass
(maps 152–154)

44 miles   21 hours   6000ft

This long traverse of the Goat Rocks Wilderness is one of the most interesting sections of the PCT, with exposed alpine ridges in mountains sprinkled with glaciers. This is not a route to traverse in bad weather and snowfields could make the route very difficult in early season.

Adams Glacier has an icefall that would do justice to a much higher mountain. Adams Creek flows through a 330yd swath of bouldery glacial deposits left behind by the retreat of the Adams Glacier after the last ice age. Adams Creek could be difficult to cross in early season.

7. 10:20hr 4750ft 0615000 5131300. Road 5603.

6. 9:35hr 4510ft 0614130 5129020. Lava Spring. The water from this spring is filtered through a lava field producing possibly the best spring water on the PCT.

5. 9:15hr 4740ft. Muddy Fork.

4. 7:50hr 5920ft 0613920 5123490. Killeen Creek.

You may see blacktail deer in this section. They are readily identified by the black fur on their rump.

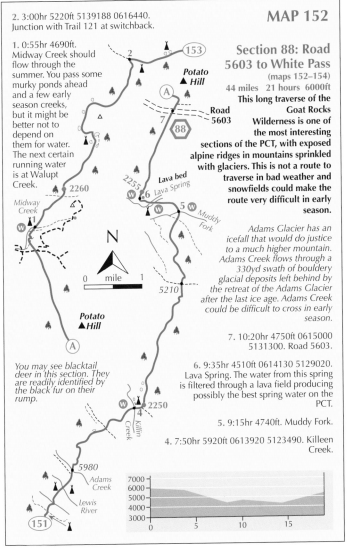

299

MAP 153

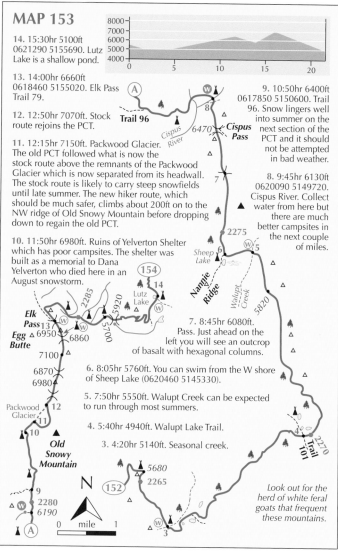

14. 15:30hr 5100ft 0621290 5155690. Lutz Lake is a shallow pond.

13. 14:00hr 6660ft 0618460 5155020. Elk Pass Trail 79.

12. 12:50hr 7070ft. Stock route rejoins the PCT.

11. 12:15hr 7150ft. Packwood Glacier. The old PCT followed what is now the stock route above the remnants of the Packwood Glacier which is now separated from its headwall. The stock route is likely to carry steep snowfields until late summer. The new hiker route, which should be much safer, climbs about 200ft on to the NW ridge of Old Snowy Mountain before dropping down to regain the old PCT.

10. 11:50hr 6980ft. Ruins of Yelverton Shelter which has poor campsites. The shelter was built as a memorial to Dana Yelverton who died here in an August snowstorm.

9. 10:50hr 6400ft 0617850 5150600. Trail 96. Snow lingers well into summer on the next section of the PCT and it should not be attempted in bad weather.

8. 9:45hr 6130ft 0620090 5149720. Cispus River. Collect water from here but there are much better campsites in the next couple of miles.

7. 8:45hr 6080ft. Pass. Just ahead on the left you will see an outcrop of basalt with hexagonal columns.

6. 8:05hr 5760ft. You can swim from the W shore of Sheep Lake (0620460 5145330).

5. 7:50hr 5550ft. Walupt Creek can be expected to run through most summers.

4. 5:40hr 4940ft. Walupt Lake Trail.

3. 4:20hr 5140ft. Seasonal creek.

Look out for the herd of white feral goats that frequent these mountains.

300

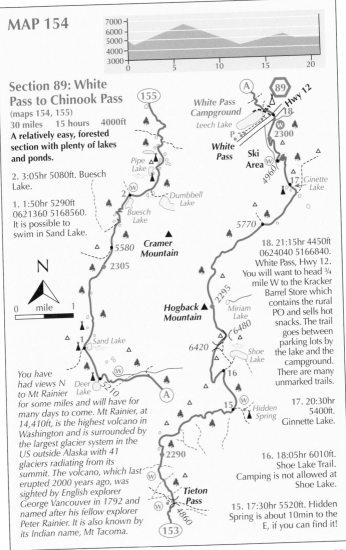

MAP 154

Section 89: White Pass to Chinook Pass
(maps 154, 155)
30 miles   15 hours   4000ft
A relatively easy, forested section with plenty of lakes and ponds.

2. 3:05hr 5080ft. Buesch Lake.

1. 1:50hr 5290ft 0621360 5168560. It is possible to swim in Sand Lake.

You have had views N to Mt Rainier for some miles and will have for many days to come. Mt Rainier, at 14,410ft, is the highest volcano in Washington and is surrounded by the largest glacier system in the US outside Alaska with 41 glaciers radiating from its summit. The volcano, which last erupted 2000 years ago, was sighted by English explorer George Vancouver in 1792 and named after his fellow explorer Peter Rainier. It is also known by its Indian name, Mt Tacoma.

White Pass Campground
Leech Lake

White Pass

Ski Area

18. 21:15hr 4450ft 0624040 5166840. White Pass, Hwy 12. You will want to head ¾ mile W to the Kracker Barrel Store which contains the rural PO and sells hot snacks. The trail goes between parking lots by the lake and the campground. There are many unmarked trails.

17. 20:30hr 5400ft. Ginnette Lake.

16. 18:05hr 6010ft. Shoe Lake Trail. Camping is not allowed at Shoe Lake.

15. 17:30hr 5520ft. Hidden Spring is about 10min to the E, if you can find it!

Pipe Lake

Dumbbell Lake

Buesch Lake

Cramer Mountain

Hogback Mountain

Miriam Lake

Shoe Lake

Hidden Spring

Sand Lake

Deer Lake

Tieton Pass

N

0   mile   1

MAP 155

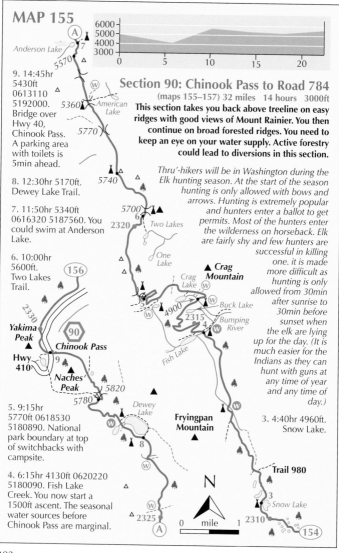

Section 90: Chinook Pass to Road 784

(maps 155–157) 32 miles   14 hours   3000ft

This section takes you back above treeline on easy ridges with good views of Mount Rainier. You then continue on broad forested ridges. You need to keep an eye on your water supply. Active forestry could lead to diversions in this section.

Thru'-hikers will be in Washington during the Elk hunting season. At the start of the season hunting is only allowed with bows and arrows. Hunting is extremely popular and hunters enter a ballot to get permits. Most of the hunters enter the wilderness on horseback. Elk are fairly shy and few hunters are successful in killing one. it is made more difficult as hunting is only allowed from 30min after sunrise to 30min before sunset when the elk are lying up for the day. (It is much easier for the Indians as they can hunt with guns at any time of year and any time of day.)

9. 14:45hr 5430ft 0613110 5192000. Bridge over Hwy 40, Chinook Pass. A parking area with toilets is 5min ahead.

8. 12:30hr 5170ft. Dewey Lake Trail.

7. 11:50hr 5340ft 0616320 5187560. You could swim at Anderson Lake.

6. 10:00hr 5600ft. Two Lakes Trail.

5. 9:15hr 5770ft 0618530 5180890. National park boundary at top of switchbacks with campsite.

4. 6:15hr 4130ft 0620220 5180090. Fish Lake Creek. You now start a 1500ft ascent. The seasonal water sources before Chinook Pass are marginal.

3. 4:40hr 4960ft. Snow Lake.

Anderson Lake

5570

5360

American Lake

5770

5740

5700

2320   Two Lakes

One Lake

156

2330

Yakima Peak

90

Chinook Pass

Hwy 410

Naches Peak   5820

5780

Dewey Lake

8

2325

Crag Lake

▲ **Crag Mountain**

4900

2315   Buck Lake

Bumping River

Fish Lake

Fryingpan Mountain

Trail 980

3

Snow Lake   2310

154

N

0   mile   1

6000
5000
4000
3000

0   5   10   15   20

MAP 156

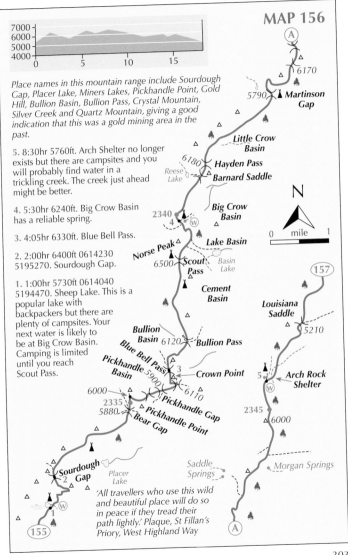

Place names in this mountain range include Sourdough Gap, Placer Lake, Miners Lakes, Pickhandle Point, Gold Hill, Bullion Basin, Bullion Pass, Crystal Mountain, Silver Creek and Quartz Mountain, giving a good indication that this was a gold mining area in the past.

5. 8:30hr 5760ft. Arch Shelter no longer exists but there are campsites and you will probably find water in a trickling creek. The creek just ahead might be better.

4. 5:30hr 6240ft. Big Crow Basin has a reliable spring.

3. 4:05hr 6330ft. Blue Bell Pass.

2. 2:00hr 6400ft 0614230 5195270. Sourdough Gap.

1. 1:00hr 5730ft 0614040 5194470. Sheep Lake. This is a popular lake with backpackers but there are plenty of campsites. Your next water is likely to be at Big Crow Basin. Camping is limited until you reach Scout Pass.

'All travellers who use this wild and beautiful place will do so in peace if they tread their path lightly.' Plaque, St Fillan's Priory, West Highland Way

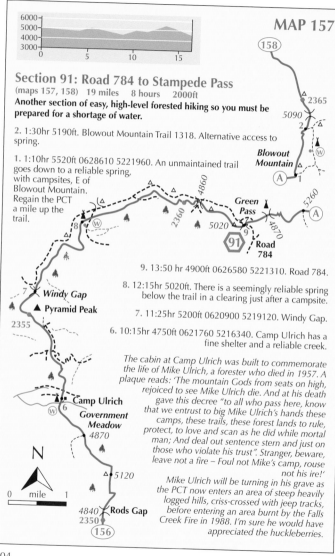

MAP 157

Section 91: Road 784 to Stampede Pass
(maps 157, 158)   19 miles   8 hours   2000ft

Another section of easy, high-level forested hiking so you must be prepared for a shortage of water.

2. 1:30hr 5190ft. Blowout Mountain Trail 1318. Alternative access to spring.

1. 1:10hr 5520ft 0628610 5221960. An unmaintained trail goes down to a reliable spring, with campsites, E of Blowout Mountain. Regain the PCT a mile up the trail.

9. 13:50 hr 4900ft 0626580 5221310. Road 784.

8. 12:15hr 5020ft. There is a seemingly reliable spring below the trail in a clearing just after a campsite.

7. 11:25hr 5200ft 0620900 5219120. Windy Gap.

6. 10:15hr 4750ft 0621760 5216340. Camp Ulrich has a fine shelter and a reliable creek.

The cabin at Camp Ulrich was built to commemorate the life of Mike Ulrich, a forester who died in 1957. A plaque reads: 'The mountain Gods from seats on high, rejoiced to see Mike Ulrich die. And at his death gave this decree "to all who pass here, know that we entrust to big Mike Ulrich's hands these camps, these trails, these forest lands to rule, protect, to love and scan as he did while mortal man; And deal out sentence stern and just on those who violate his trust". Stranger, beware, leave not a fire – Foul not Mike's camp, rouse not his ire!'

Mike Ulrich will be turning in his grave as the PCT now enters an area of steep heavily logged hills, criss-crossed with jeep tracks, before entering an area burnt by the Falls Creek Fire in 1988. I'm sure he would have appreciated the huckleberries.

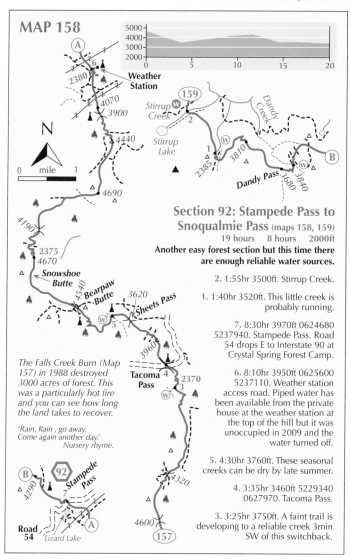

MAP 158

Weather Station

N

0   mile   1

Snowshoe Butte

Bearpaw Butte

Sheets Pass

Tacoma Pass

The Falls Creek Burn (Map 157) in 1988 destroyed 3000 acres of forest. This was a particularly hot fire and you can see how long the land takes to recover.

'Rain, Rain, go away, Come again another day.'
  Nursery rhyme.

Stampede Pass

Road 54   *Lizard Lake*

Section 92: Stampede Pass to Snoqualmie Pass (maps 158, 159)
19 hours   8 hours   2000ft
Another easy forest section but this time there are enough reliable water sources.

2. 1:55hr 3500ft. Stirrup Creek.

1. 1:40hr 3520ft. This little creek is probably running.

7. 8:30hr 3970ft 0624680 5237940. Stampede Pass. Road 54 drops E to Interstate 90 at Crystal Spring Forest Camp.

6. 8:10hr 3950ft 0625600 5237110. Weather station access road. Piped water has been available from the private house at the weather station at the top of the hill but it was unoccupied in 2009 and the water turned off.

5. 4:30hr 3760ft. These seasonal creeks can be dry by late summer.

4. 3:35hr 3460ft 5229340 0627970. Tacoma Pass.

3. 3:25hr 3750ft. A faint trail is developing to a reliable creek 3min SW of this switchback.

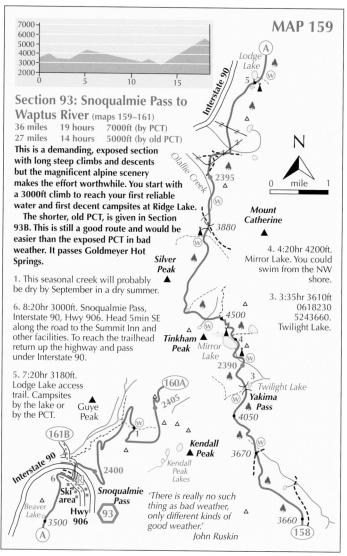

MAP 159

Section 93: Snoqualmie Pass to Waptus River (maps 159–161)

36 miles   19 hours   7000ft (by PCT)
27 miles   14 hours   5000ft (by old PCT)

This is a demanding, exposed section with long steep climbs and descents but the magnificent alpine scenery makes the effort worthwhile. You start with a 3000ft climb to reach your first reliable water and first decent campsites at Ridge Lake.

The shorter, old PCT, is given in Section 93B. This is still a good route and would be easier than the exposed PCT in bad weather. It passes Goldmeyer Hot Springs.

1. This seasonal creek will probably be dry by September in a dry summer.

6. 8:20hr 3000ft. Snoqualmie Pass, Interstate 90, Hwy 906. Head 5min SE along the road to the Summit Inn and other facilities. To reach the trailhead return up the highway and pass under Interstate 90.

5. 7:20hr 3180ft. Lodge Lake access trail. Campsites by the lake or by the PCT.

4. 4:20hr 4200ft. Mirror Lake. You could swim from the NW shore.

3. 3:35hr 3610ft 0618230 5243660. Twilight Lake.

'There is really no such thing as bad weather, only different kinds of good weather.'
John Ruskin

11

Snoqualmie Pass to Manning Park

Manning Provincial Park

to Vancouver

Manning Park

174

CANADA

USA

173

Pasayten Wilderness

Pasayten Wilderness

172

20

North Cascades National Park

171

Rainy Pass

170

Mazama

to Winthrop

Lake Chelan National Recreational Area

169

Glacier Peak Wilderness

Stehekin

167

168

Lake Chelan

166

Henry M Jackson Wilderness

165

164

2

to Leavenworth

to Skykomish

Stevens Pass

163

Alpine Lakes Wilderness

162

161

160

to Seattle

Snoqualmie Pass

159

90

N

0   miles   25

PART 11: SNOQUALMIE PASS TO MANNING PARK

Section	Distance (miles)	Time (hours)	Ascent (feet)	Maps
93A Snoqualmie Pass–Waptus River (by PCT)	36	19	7000	159, 161
93B Snoqualmie Pass–Waptus River (by alternative route)	27	14	5000	159–161
94 Waptus River–Stevens Pass	38	20	8000	160–164
95 Stevens Pass–Indian Pass	33	17	7000	164, 165
96 Indian Pass–Suiattle River	40	21	8000	165–167
97 Suiattle River–Stehekin River	26	13	4000	167–169
98 Stehekin River–Rainy Pass	20	9	4000	169, 170
99 Rainy Pass–Harts Pass	31	15	5000	170–172
100 Harts Pass–US/Canada border	31	14	4000	172–174
101 US/Canada border–Manning Park	9	4	1000	174
Part total	**264**	**132**	**48,000**	

After the easy going in Oregon and Southern Washington, the final section of the PCT comes as a bit of a shock. You again encounter long steep climbs and cannot expect to average much more than two miles per hour. Thru'-hikers will probably hike this section in late September and will find fewer hours of daylight so it would be wise to schedule conservatively for this section.

After you pass through the spectacular Alpine Lakes Wilderness, Glacier Peak dominates the landscape and gives you some hard days before you get to an easier although still very scenic run to the Canadian border.

There are very few highways so resupply is a problem in this section, making it a difficult proposition for weekend hikers. The fit thru'-hiker can expect to better the times given for this section but they are realistic times for section-hikers.

You must be prepared for bad weather but, hopefully, you will get plenty of sunny days. Thru'-hikers in September can expect a period of snow showers and cold weather but you are unlikely to get the first of the heavy winter snowfalls until October.

Best time

August or September. Don't go too early in July. The PCT in Northern Washington was not designed to be hiked until the snow has melted. This is a big problem for the north-to-south hiker. In a low snow year you could go in July.

Permits

Permits are required for camping in North Cascades National Park, where you are required to use designated trailside campsites. You also need a permit as well as your passport to enter Canada via the PCT (see Documentation).

A Northwest Forest Pass is needed for parking at some of the trailheads (see Part 8).

Section 98: North Cascades National Park

North Cascades National Park Complex, 810 State Route 20, Sedro-Woolley WA98284
(360)-856-5700, www.nps.gov/noca

Facilities

There are no resupply possibilities near the PCT. It is suggested you resupply at Skykomish and Stehekin.

Snoqualmie Pass (PO, G, R, A)
(Sections 92, 93) (0 hours)
See Part 10 introduction.

Skykomish (PO, G, R, A, B) (from Stevens Pass, Sections 94, 95) (38 hours)
Skykomish PO, 114 N 5th St, Skykomish WA98288

Lake Sally Ann (Section 95)

Campground, Harts Pass (Section 99/100)

(360)-677-2241. Mon–Fri: 8.00am–
11.30pm, 12.00noon–3.45pm

Dinsmores' Hiker Haven (P, L, Sh, C,
A) (from Stevens Pass, Sections 94,
95) (38 hours)
Dinsmores Hiker Haven, PO Box
374, Skykomish WA98288. UPS
parcels should be addressed to:
Dinsmores' Hiker Haven, 63330
NE197th Place, Baring WA98224.
(360)-677-1237, www.dinsmores
hikerhaven.com, andrea@
dinsmoreshikerhaven.com
Trail angels Jerry and Andrea
Dinsmore have offered hospitality
to hikers at Hiker Haven, Baring,
eight miles west of Skykomish. Hitch
to Skykomish, or preferably Baring.
Hiker Haven is at the end of 197th
St across the railway, just past Baring

Store. Check their website to see if
they are still offering services.

Stehekin (PO, minimal G, R, A, L, C,
Sh) (from Stehekin River) (Sections
97, 98) (88 hours)
Stehekin PO, 31 Defacto Lane,
Stehekin WA98852
(509)-682-2625. Mon, Wed, Fri:
8.00am–12.00noon, 1.30pm–
4.00pm, Tue, Thur: 9.00am–3.00pm
There is a daily bus service to
Stehekin from the High Bridge Ranger
Station, where the PCT crosses the
Stehekin River:
High Bridge–Stehekin: 9.00am,
12.00noon, 3.00pm, 4.15pm
Stehekin–High Bridge: 8.00am,
11.15am, 2.00pm, 5.30pm
(in 2009; contact the North Cascades
National Park for latest details)

Stehekin Bakery is several miles upstream from Stehekin.

Mazama (small G, A, C, B) (from Rainy Pass) (Sections 98, 99) (98 hours)
The small store serves hot snacks.

Winthrop (PO, G, R, A, B) (from Rainy Pass) (Sections 98, 99) (98 hours)
Winthrop PO, 1110 State Route 20, Winthrop WA98862
(509)-996-2282. Mon–Fri: 9.00am–4.30pm
Winthrop is a small tourist town with buildings all in the style of the Wild West in the late 19th century.

Marblemount (PO, small G, R, A, C, L, B) (from Rainy Pass) (Sections 98, 99) (97 hours)
Marblemount PO, 60096 State Route 20, Marblemount WA98267
(360)-873-2125. Mon–Fri: 7.30am–11.30am, 12.00noon–3.30pm

Manning Park (small G, R, A, C) (Section 101) (137 hours)
A Greyhound bus service runs from Manning Park to Vancouver BC (see Getting to the PCT section).

The author at the US/Canada border (Section 100/101)

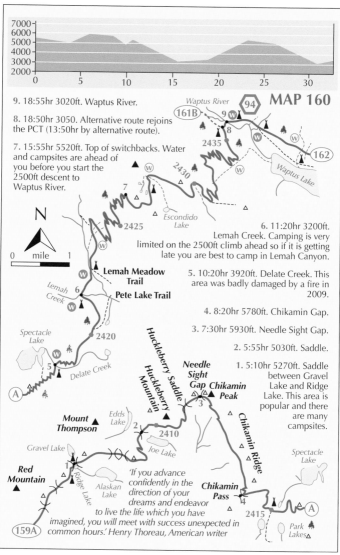

9. 18:55hr 3020ft. Waptus River.

8. 18:50hr 3050. Alternative route rejoins the PCT (13:50hr by alternative route).

7. 15:55hr 5520ft. Top of switchbacks. Water and campsites are ahead of you before you start the 2500ft descent to Waptus River.

Waptus River
161B
94
MAP 160
9
8
2435
162
Waptus Lake
2430
7
2425
Escondido Lake

6. 11:20hr 3200ft. Lemah Creek. Camping is very limited on the 2500ft climb ahead so if it is getting late you are best to camp in Lemah Canyon.

5. 10:20hr 3920ft. Delate Creek. This area was badly damaged by a fire in 2009.

4. 8:20hr 5780ft. Chikamin Gap.

3. 7:30hr 5930ft. Needle Sight Gap.

2. 5:55hr 5030ft. Saddle.

1. 5:10hr 5270ft. Saddle between Gravel Lake and Ridge Lake. This area is popular and there are many campsites.

N
0 mile 1

Lemah Meadow Trail
Lemah Creek
6
Pete Lake Trail
2420
Spectacle Lake
5
A
Delate Creek

Needle Sight Gap
Chikamin Peak
3
Huckleberry Saddle
Huckleberry Mountain
Mount Thompson
Edds Lake
2
2410
Joe Lake
Chikamin Ridge
Spectacle Lake
Chikamin Pass
4
2415
Park Lakes
A

Gravel Lake
1
Ridge Lake
Red Mountain
Alaskan Lake
159A

'If you advance confidently in the direction of your dreams and endeavor to live the life which you have imagined, you will meet with success unexpected in common hours.' Henry Thoreau, American writer

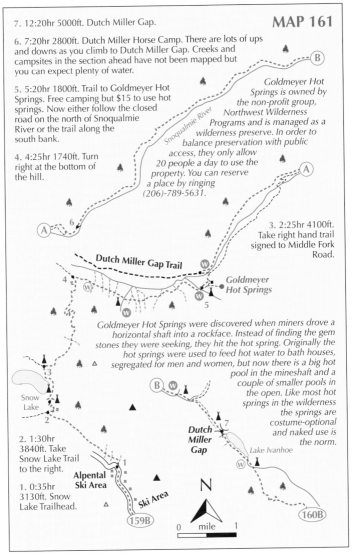

MAP 161

7. 12:20hr 5000ft. Dutch Miller Gap.

6. 7:20hr 2800ft. Dutch Miller Horse Camp. There are lots of ups and downs as you climb to Dutch Miller Gap. Creeks and campsites in the section ahead have not been mapped but you can expect plenty of water.

5. 5:20hr 1800ft. Trail to Goldmeyer Hot Springs. Free camping but $15 to use hot springs. Now either follow the closed road on the north of Snoqualmie River or the trail along the south bank.

4. 4:25hr 1740ft. Turn right at the bottom of the hill.

Goldmeyer Hot Springs is owned by the non-profit group, Northwest Wilderness Programs and is managed as a wilderness preserve. In order to balance preservation with public access, they only allow 20 people a day to use the property. You can reserve a place by ringing (206)-789-5631.

Snoqualmie River

3. 2:25hr 4100ft. Take right hand trail signed to Middle Fork Road.

Dutch Miller Gap Trail

Goldmeyer Hot Springs

Goldmeyer Hot Springs were discovered when miners drove a horizontal shaft into a rockface. Instead of finding the gem stones they were seeking, they hit the hot spring. Originally the hot springs were used to feed hot water to bath houses, segregated for men and women, but now there is a big hot pool in the mineshaft and a couple of smaller pools in the open. Like most hot springs in the wilderness the springs are costume-optional and naked use is the norm.

Snow Lake

2. 1:30hr 3840ft. Take Snow Lake Trail to the right.

1. 0:35hr 3130ft. Snow Lake Trailhead.

Alpental Ski Area

Ski Area

Dutch Miller Gap

Lake Ivanhoe

N

0   mile   1

MAP 162

Section 94: Waptus River to Stevens Pass (maps 160–164)
38 miles   20 hours   8000ft

This is a section of short, sharp climbs and descents. You are in forest for much of the time but get good views as you cross the ridges. Water shouldn't be a problem. The section starts with a 2500ft ascent to Cathedral Pass via Deep Lake.

Notice at Cathedral Pass in 2002:
'Attention, Wildfire Danger. A lightning-caused wildland fire is currently burning in an area beneath Cathedral Rock, downslope of the Pacific Crest Trail, one quarter mile northeast of Cathedral Pass.

'The Wilderness Act of 1964 emphasizes that natural forces continue to shape the wilderness ecosystem. The fire (named the Peggy Fire) is being monitored by the fire managers for such resource benefit. Suppression action will be initiated if the fire exceeds defined parameters, established boundaries, or if weather conditions cause an unacceptable increase in fire activity.

'All travellers in the area must exercise extreme caution when passing the fire on Cathedral Pass Trail. Study the fire behaviour and do not pass if the fire appears active and dangerous. Turbulent smoke, active flames or tree torching, loud crackling sounds, or spreading ground fire are indicators that it is unsafe to approach.'

The suppression of fires in the 20th century that resulted in the build up of combustibles (such as fallen branches) below the trees and fires now get quickly out of control. The USFS is now happy to see these small fires burning to control the underbrush and to help build up firebreaks to slow down major fires.

2. 5:50hr 5600ft 0640630 5268060. Cathedral Pass. There are lots of campsites as you begin the descent. Take care with route finding as there are many little trails to campsites and viewpoints over the next few miles. In early season you might prefer to take the longer alternative route via Hyas Lake to avoid a difficult creek crossing ahead.

1. 3:50hr 4380ft 0640030 5266890. Deep Lake Trail. The best campsites are by the PCT or on the W or NW shore of Deep Lake.

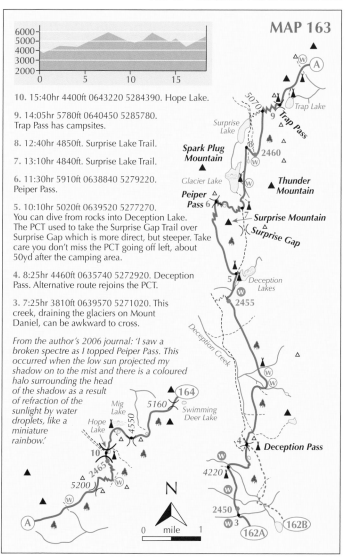

MAP 163

10. 15:40hr 4400ft 0643220 5284390. Hope Lake.

9. 14:05hr 5780ft 0640450 5285780.
Trap Pass has campsites.

8. 12:40hr 4850ft. Surprise Lake Trail.

7. 13:10hr 4840ft. Surprise Lake Trail.

6. 11:30hr 5910ft 0638840 5279220.
Peiper Pass.

5. 10:10hr 5020ft 0639520 5277270.
You can dive from rocks into Deception Lake.
The PCT used to take the Surprise Gap Trail over
Surprise Gap which is more direct, but steeper. Take
care you don't miss the PCT going off left, about
50yd after the camping area.

4. 8:25hr 4460ft 0635740 5272920. Deception
Pass. Alternative route rejoins the PCT.

3. 7:25hr 3810ft 0639570 5271020. This
creek, draining the glaciers on Mount
Daniel, can be awkward to cross.

*From the author's 2006 journal: 'I saw a
broken spectre as I topped Peiper Pass. This
occurred when the low sun projected my
shadow on to the mist and there is a coloured
halo surrounding the head
of the shadow as a result
of refraction of the
sunlight by water
droplets, like a
miniature
rainbow.'*

315

MAP 164

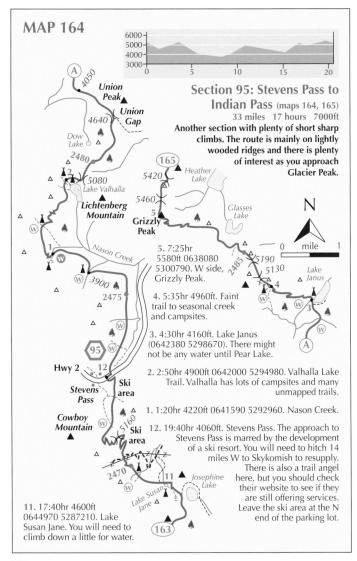

6000
5000
4000
3000

0   5   10   15   20

Section 95: Stevens Pass to Indian Pass (maps 164, 165)

33 miles   17 hours   7000ft

Another section with plenty of short sharp climbs. The route is mainly on lightly wooded ridges and there is plenty of interest as you approach Glacier Peak.

A 4050
Union Peak
Union Gap
4640
Dow Lake
2480
5080
Lake Valhalla
Lichtenberg Mountain
Nason Creek
3900
2475

165
5420
Heather Lake
5460
Grizzly Peak
5
Glasses Lake
5190
2485
5130
Lake Janus
A

N

0   mile   1

5. 7:25hr 5580ft 0638080 5300790. W side, Grizzly Peak.

4. 5:35hr 4960ft. Faint trail to seasonal creek and campsites.

3. 4:30hr 4160ft. Lake Janus (0642380 5298670). There might not be any water until Pear Lake.

95
Hwy 2   12
Stevens Pass
Ski area
Cowboy Mountain
5160
Ski area
2470
11
Josephine Lake
Lake Susan Jane
163

2. 2:50hr 4900ft 0642000 5294980. Valhalla Lake Trail. Valhalla has lots of campsites and many unmapped trails.

1. 1:20hr 4220ft 0641590 5292960. Nason Creek.

12. 19:40hr 4060ft. Stevens Pass. The approach to Stevens Pass is marred by the development of a ski resort. You will need to hitch 14 miles W to Skykomish to resupply. There is also a trail angel here, but you should check their website to see if they are still offering services. Leave the ski area at the N end of the parking lot.

11. 17:40hr 4600ft 0644970 5287210. Lake Susan Jane. You will need to climb down a little for water.

316

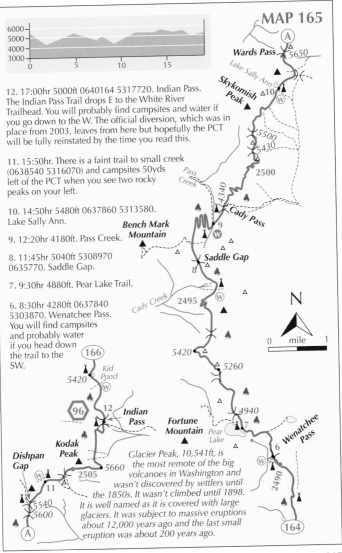

MAP 165

12. 17:00hr 5000ft 0640164 5317720. Indian Pass. The Indian Pass Trail drops E to the White River Trailhead. You will probably find campsites and water if you go down to the W. The official diversion, which was in place from 2003, leaves from here but hopefully the PCT will be fully reinstated by the time you read this.

11. 15:50hr. There is a faint trail to small creek (0638540 5316070) and campsites 50yds left of the PCT when you see two rocky peaks on your left.

10. 14:50hr 5480ft 0637860 5313580. Lake Sally Ann.

9. 12:20hr 4180ft. Pass Creek.

8. 11:45hr 5040ft 5308970 0635770. Saddle Gap.

7. 9:30hr 4880ft. Pear Lake Trail.

6. 8:30hr 4280ft 0637840 5303870. Wenatchee Pass. You will find campsites and probably water if you head down the trail to the SW.

Glacier Peak, 10,541ft, is the most remote of the big volcanoes in Washington and wasn't discovered by settlers until the 1850s. It wasn't climbed until 1898. It is well named as it is covered with large glaciers. It was subject to massive eruptions about 12,000 years ago and the last small eruption was about 200 years ago.

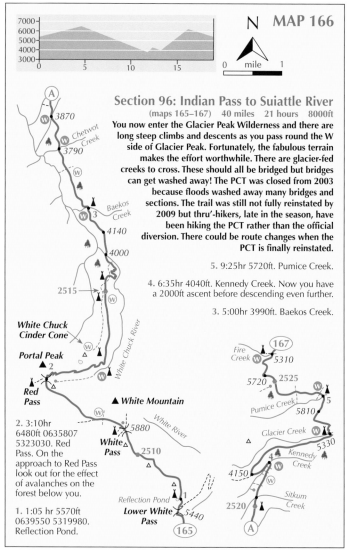

N MAP 166

Section 96: Indian Pass to Suiattle River

(maps 165–167)   40 miles   21 hours   8000ft

You now enter the Glacier Peak Wilderness and there are long steep climbs and descents as you pass round the W side of Glacier Peak. Fortunately, the fabulous terrain makes the effort worthwhile. There are glacier-fed creeks to cross. These should all be bridged but bridges can get washed away! The PCT was closed from 2003 because floods washed away many bridges and sections. The trail was still not fully reinstated by 2009 but thru'-hikers, late in the season, have been hiking the PCT rather than the official diversion. There could be route changes when the PCT is finally reinstated.

5. 9:25hr 5720ft. Pumice Creek.

4. 6:35hr 4040ft. Kennedy Creek. Now you have a 2000ft ascent before descending even further.

3. 5:00hr 3990ft. Baekos Creek.

3870

Chetwot Creek
3790

Baekos Creek
3
4140
4000

2515

White Chuck Cinder Cone

Portal Peak
▲ 2

Red Pass

White Mountain ▲

White Chuck River

White River

2. 3:10hr 6480ft 0635807 5323030. Red Pass. On the approach to Red Pass look out for the effect of avalanches on the forest below you.

5880
White Pass △
2510

△

Reflection Pond

1. 1:05 hr 5570ft 0639550 5319980. Reflection Pond.

Lower White Pass
5440
1

165

Fire Creek
167
5310

5720   2525

Pumice Creek
5810
5

Glacier Creek
5330

4150
Kennedy Creek
4

2520

Sitkum Creek

A

MAP 167

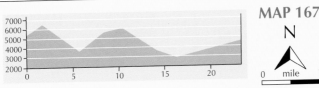

N

0   mile   1

Section 97: Suiattle River to Stehekin River

(maps 167–169)

26 miles   13 hours   4000ft

At last an easy section although it does start with a 3000ft climb to Suiattle Pass! This is followed by a long gentle descent to the Stehekin River. If you have time to spare you might like to start the section with a detour to Image Lake with good camping and magnificent views of Glacier Peak.

2. 3:00hr 4540ft. Miners Creek.

1. 2:45hr 4600ft. Official diversion rejoins the PCT.

10. 20:45hr 2860ft. Suiattle River was still not bridged in 2009. There could be a realignment of the trail as any bridge built here will be vulnerable to flooding. If there is no bridge, hopefully you can cross on fallen logs as fording the river would be dangerous.

9. 19:50hr 2880ft Vista Creek.

8. 17:20hr 5760ft. E Fork Milk Creek.

7. 13:30hr 3400ft Milk Creek. There is a new bridge downstream from the bridge marked on old maps.

Image Lake

Miners Ridge

Plummer Mountain

Miners Creek Trail

Suiattle River

Vista Creek

Miners Creek

2 168

2550

3670 **Middle Ridge**

9

10

3040

2545

Gamma Creek

97

East Fork Milk Creek

Dolly Vista Campsite

Dolly Creek

Vista Ridge

A

2535

5530

5900

3680

5430

Mica Lake

2530

7

Milk Creek

2540

Vista Creek

6 **Fire Creek Pass**

8

6000

6. 11:15hr 6340ft 0636510 5335580. Fire Creek Pass.

166

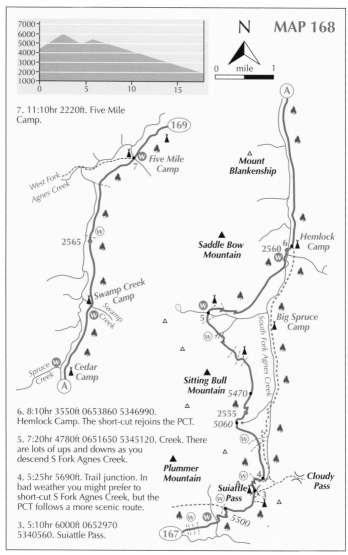

MAP 168

7000
6000
5000
4000
3000
2000
1000

0   5   10   15

7. 11:10hr 2220ft. Five Mile Camp.

Five Mile Camp

West Fork Agnes Creek

Mount Blankenship

Saddle Bow Mountain

Hemlock Camp

2565

Swamp Creek Camp

Swamp Creek

Big Spruce Camp

South Fork Agnes Creek

Cedar Camp
Spruce Creek

Sitting Bull Mountain
5470

2555
5060

6. 8:10hr 3550ft 0653860 5346990. Hemlock Camp. The short-cut rejoins the PCT.

5. 7:20hr 4780ft 0651650 5345120. Creek. There are lots of ups and downs as you descend S Fork Agnes Creek.

Plummer Mountain

Cloudy Pass

4. 5:25hr 5690ft. Trail junction. In bad weather you might prefer to short-cut S Fork Agnes Creek, but the PCT follows a more scenic route.

Suiattle Pass

5500

3. 5:10hr 6000ft 0652970 5340560. Suiattle Pass.

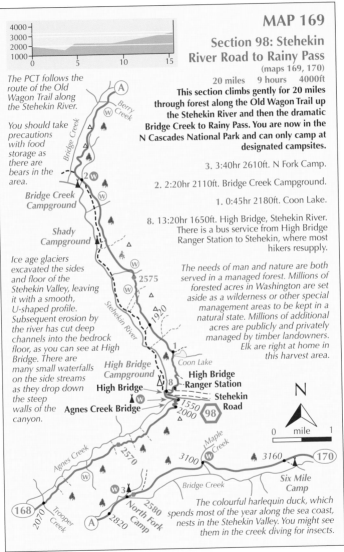

MAP 169

Section 98: Stehekin River Road to Rainy Pass
(maps 169, 170)

20 miles   9 hours   4000ft

This section climbs gently for 20 miles through forest along the Old Wagon Trail up the Stehekin River and then the dramatic Bridge Creek to Rainy Pass. You are now in the N Cascades National Park and can only camp at designated campsites.

3. 3:40hr 2610ft. N Fork Camp.

2. 2:20hr 2110ft. Bridge Creek Campground.

1. 0:45hr 2180ft. Coon Lake.

8. 13:20hr 1650ft. High Bridge, Stehekin River. There is a bus service from High Bridge Ranger Station to Stehekin, where most hikers resupply.

The PCT follows the route of the Old Wagon Trail along the Stehekin River.

You should take precautions with food storage as there are bears in the area.

Bridge Creek Campground

Shady Campground

Ice age glaciers excavated the sides and floor of the Stehekin Valley, leaving it with a smooth, U-shaped profile. Subsequent erosion by the river has cut deep channels into the bedrock floor, as you can see at High Bridge. There are many small waterfalls on the side streams as they drop down the steep walls of the canyon.

The needs of man and nature are both served in a managed forest. Millions of forested acres in Washington are set aside as a wilderness or other special management areas to be kept in a natural state. Millions of additional acres are publicly and privately managed by timber landowners. Elk are right at home in this harvest area.

High Bridge Campground

High Bridge

Agnes Creek Bridge

High Bridge Ranger Station

Stehekin Road

N

0 — mile — 1

Six Mile Camp

North Fork Camp

The colourful harlequin duck, which spends most of its life along the sea coast, nests in the Stehekin Valley. You might see them in the creek diving for insects.

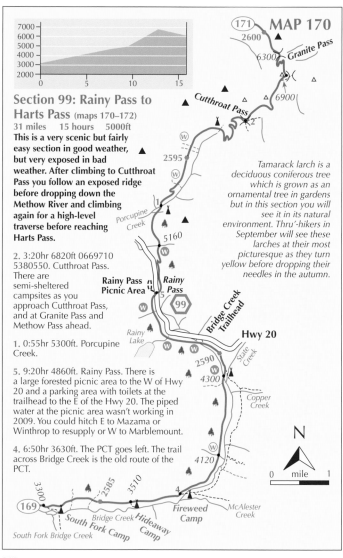

Section 99: Rainy Pass to Harts Pass (maps 170–172)

31 miles   15 hours   5000ft

This is a very scenic but fairly easy section in good weather, but fairly exposed in bad weather. After climbing to Cutthroat Pass you follow an exposed ridge before dropping down the Methow River and climbing again for a high-level traverse before reaching Harts Pass.

2. 3:20hr 6820ft 0669710 5380550. Cutthroat Pass. There are semi-sheltered campsites as you approach Cutthroat Pass, and at Granite Pass and Methow Pass ahead.

1. 0:55hr 5300ft. Porcupine Creek.

5. 9:20hr 4860ft. Rainy Pass. There is a large forested picnic area to the W of Hwy 20 and a parking area with toilets at the trailhead to the E of the Hwy 20. The piped water at the picnic area wasn't working in 2009. You could hitch E to Mazama or Winthrop to resupply or W to Marblemount.

4. 6:50hr 3630ft. The PCT goes left. The trail across Bridge Creek is the old route of the PCT.

Tamarack larch is a deciduous coniferous tree which is grown as an ornamental tree in gardens but in this section you will see it in its natural environment. Thru'-hikers in September will see these larches at their most picturesque as they turn yellow before dropping their needles in the autumn.

MAP 170

Granite Pass

Cutthroat Pass

Porcupine Creek

Rainy Pass Picnic Area

Rainy Pass

Bridge Creek Trailhead

Hwy 20

Rainy Lake

State Creek

Copper Creek

McAlester Creek

Fireweed Camp

Bridge Creek Hideaway Camp

South Fork Camp

South Fork Bridge Creek

N

0   mile   1

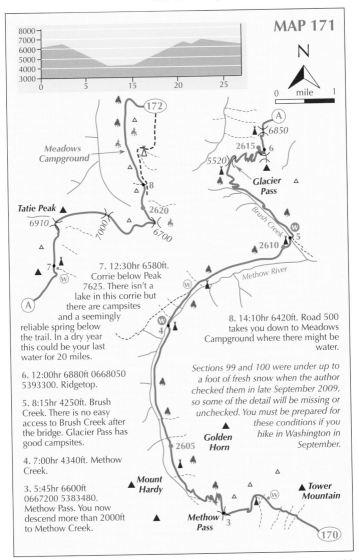

MAP 171

N

0 ——— mile ——— 1

Meadows Campground

Tatie Peak ▲
6910

7000

172

6850
2615
5520

Glacier Pass

Brush Creek

2620
6700

2610

5

7. 12:30hr 6580ft. Corrie below Peak 7625. There isn't a lake in this corrie but there are campsites and a seemingly reliable spring below the trail. In a dry year this could be your last water for 20 miles.

Methow River

8. 14:10hr 6420ft. Road 500 takes you down to Meadows Campground where there might be water.

6. 12:00hr 6880ft 0668050 5393300. Ridgetop.

5. 8:15hr 4250ft. Brush Creek. There is no easy access to Brush Creek after the bridge. Glacier Pass has good campsites.

4. 7:00hr 4340ft. Methow Creek.

3. 5:45hr 6600ft 0667200 5383480. Methow Pass. You now descend more than 2000ft to Methow Creek.

Sections 99 and 100 were under up to a foot of fresh snow when the author checked them in late September 2009, so some of the detail will be missing or unchecked. You must be prepared for these conditions if you hike in Washington in September.

Golden Horn

2605

Mount Hardy

Tower Mountain

Methow Pass
3

170

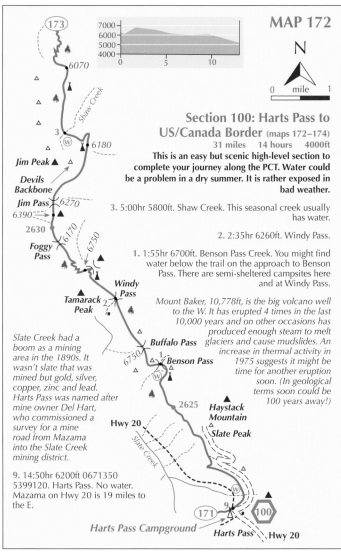

(173)

6070

Shaw Creek

3

(W) 6180

Jim Peak ▲

Devils Backbone

Jim Pass 6270
6390
2630

Foggy Pass 6170 6750

Windy Pass

Tamarack Peak 2

MAP 172

7000
6000
5000
4000

0   5   10

N

0   mile   1

Section 100: Harts Pass to US/Canada Border (maps 172–174)
31 miles   14 hours   4000ft
This is an easy but scenic high-level section to complete your journey along the PCT. Water could be a problem in a dry summer. It is rather exposed in bad weather.

3. 5:00hr 5800ft. Shaw Creek. This seasonal creek usually has water.

2. 2:35hr 6260ft. Windy Pass.

1. 1:55hr 6700ft. Benson Pass Creek. You might find water below the trail on the approach to Benson Pass. There are semi-sheltered campsites here and at Windy Pass.

Mount Baker, 10,778ft, is the big volcano well to the W. It has erupted 4 times in the last 10,000 years and on other occasions has produced enough steam to melt glaciers and cause mudslides. An increase in thermal activity in 1975 suggests it might be time for another eruption soon. (In geological terms soon could be 100 years away!)

Buffalo Pass
6750 1
Benson Pass
(W)

2625

▲ **Haystack Mountain**

Slate Peak

Hwy 20

Slate Creek

Slate Creek had a boom as a mining area in the 1890s. It wasn't slate that was mined but gold, silver, copper, zinc and lead. Harts Pass was named after mine owner Del Hart, who commissioned a survey for a mine road from Mazama into the Slate Creek mining district.

9. 14:50hr 6200ft 0671350 5399120. Harts Pass. No water. Mazama on Hwy 20 is 19 miles to the E.

(W)

9
(171)

(100)

Harts Pass Campground

Harts Pass ... **Hwy 20**

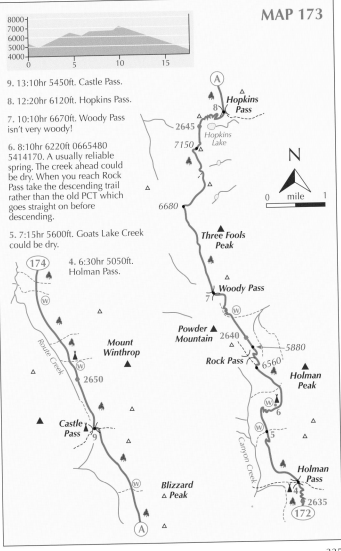

MAP 173

9. 13:10hr 5450ft. Castle Pass.

8. 12:20hr 6120ft. Hopkins Pass.

7. 10:10hr 6670ft. Woody Pass isn't very woody!

6. 8:10hr 6220ft 0665480 5414170. A usually reliable spring. The creek ahead could be dry. When you reach Rock Pass take the descending trail rather than the old PCT which goes straight on before descending.

5. 7:15hr 5600ft. Goats Lake Creek could be dry.

4. 6:30hr 5050ft. Holman Pass.

Hopkins Pass

2645

Hopkins Lake

7150

6680

Three Fools Peak

Woody Pass

Powder Mountain 2640

Rock Pass 6560 5880

Holman Peak

6

5

Holman Pass 2635

174

Route Creek

Mount Winthrop

2650

Castle Pass 9

Blizzard Peak

Canyon Creek

172

A

N

0   mile   1

MAP 174

Section 101: US/Canada Border to Manning Park (map 174)

9 miles   4 hours   1000ft

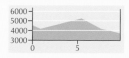

If you have the permit to enter Canada along the PCT, continue along an extension of the PCT by an easy, forested trail to Manning Park in Canada. Otherwise turn around and head back to Harts Pass campground (where you should be able to hitch down to Highway 20).

4. 4:00hr 3880ft 0661770 5436860. Manning Park Lodge. There is a campground just over a mile to the NW.

The border is marked by a forest ride about 10yd wide. A little different to the security fence where you started the PCT 2700 miles away. There is a monument (a scaled down version of the Washington Monument) commemorating the treaty of 1848 by which the 49th parallel was agreed as the border between the US and Canada. There is a trail register inside this monument. There is also a copy of the PCT monument that you saw at the Mexican border and a sign welcoming you to Canada.

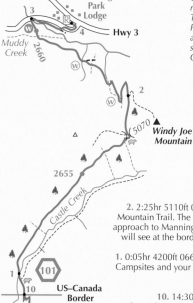

3. 3:40hr 3900ft 5436900 0660870. Road.

2. 2:25hr 5110ft 0663360 5435152. Windy Joe Mountain Trail. The PCT has been rerouted on the approach to Manning Park since the trail maps you will see at the border and ahead were produced.

1. 0:05hr 4200ft 0660660 5430060. Castle Creek. Campsites and your first 100% reliable water for a very long way.

10. 14:30hr 4240ft. US/Canada Border. The end! However, you've still got to get home.

APPENDIX A
Local information and conversions

Emergency telephone number
911

Sales tax
Prices shown in shops are not the prices you pay for goods. The state sales tax needs to be added.

Federal holidays
Most federal employees will be on holiday on the following dates during the hiking season. Post offices will be closed and mail will not be moved or sorted so can be disrupted for several days.

- Last Monday in May: Memorial Day

- July 4: Independence Day (or July 3 or 5 if July 4 falls during a weekend)

- First Monday in September: Labour Day

- Second Monday in October: Columbus Day

American units
1 mile = 1.6km
1000ft = 305m
1ft = 30.5cm
1in = 2.5cm
1 pint (US) = 0.5 litre
1 quart (US) = 1 litre
1 gallon (US) = 4 litres
1 pound (lb) = 0.45kg
32°F = 0°C
70°F = 21°C
100°F = 38°C
Americans tend to use feet rather than yards for distance (1yd = 3ft).
The instructions with some freeze-dried foods give quantities in terms of cups (1 cup = 240ml).

Telephone dialling codes
The US and Canada have an integrated telephone system. To call the US or Canada from most European countries dial 001 followed by the local telephone number. To call abroad from the US or Canada, dial 011 followed by the country code. Country code for United Kingdom: 44

APPENDIX B
Useful addresses

Pacific Crest Trail Association
1331, Garden Highway, Sacramento
CA95833
(916)-285-1846, www.pcta.org
The association's website has application forms for PCT thru'-hike permits, Mount Whitney permits and permits for entry to Canada along the PCT.

Canada Border Services Agency
2 Sumas Way, Abbotsford, BC V2S
8B7, Canada
(604)-504-4690

Useful websites
www.pct77.org/adz
Annual Day Zero PCT Kick Off and a good source of information

www.trailjournals.com
Journals from PCT hikers

www.fire.ca.gov
Fire information in California and California fire permits

www.4jeffrey.net/pct
PCT water reports

www.fs.fed.us/pct
US government's PCT website

www.pctmap.net
PCT maps and GPS waymarks. These are the best maps for the trail.

http://postholer.com
Snow reports and Google map with PCT superimposed

www.hikertrash.net
www.nationalforeststore.com
PCT maps

www.morethanamile.com/pctaorg
PCT information including maps on a CD-ROM

http://maps.nationalgeographic.com/topo
CD-ROM of USGS topographic maps

www.trailquest.net/PCTtrlsvcs.html
Trail town information

Pct-L@mailman.backcountry.net
PCT forum

www.tarptent.com
Tarp-tents

www.gossamergear.com
www.sixmoondesigns.com
www.golite.com
www.ula-equipment.com
Lightweight gear

APPENDIX C
Other publications

If you are going to hike the PCT in snowpack you will need more detailed maps than those featured in this guidebook. You could purchase US Forest Service maps, CD-ROMs or download maps from the websites in Appendix B.

Other guidebooks and handbooks
The John Muir Trail Guide, Alan Castle (Cicerone, 2004, updated 2010)
Covers Yosemite Valley to Whitney Portal.
www.cicerone.co.uk

The Pacific Crest Trail (three volumes), Ben Schirfin, Thomas Winnett, Jeffrey Schaffer, Ruby Johnson Jenkins and Andy Selters (Wilderness Press, 1973, updated 2003)
A comprehensive guidebook in three heavy volumes with black and white 1:50,000 maps.

Pacific Crest Trail Data Book, Benedict 'Gentle Ben' Go (Wilderness Press, 1997, updated 2005)
Summarises the information in the guidebooks.
www.wildernesspress.com

The PCT Hiker's Handbook, Ray Jardine (AdventureLore Press, 1992)
Advice on hiking the PCT with an emphasis on ultra-lightweight hiking and high daily mileages.

Trail Life: Ray Jardine's Lightweight Backpacking, Ray Jardine (AdventureLore, 2009)
The latest incarnation of Jardine's PCT Hiker's Handbook benefits from the experience of thousands of additional trail miles.
www.adventurelore.com

Yogi's PCT Handbook, Jackie 'Yogi' McDonnell (self-published)
Provides the most comprehensive information on towns as well as other trail information (no maps).
www.pcthandbook.com

Pacific Crest Trail Atlas, Erik Asorson (Blackwoods Press, second edition, 2010)
A set of PCT maps in five expensive volumes with brief notes on the route.
www.pctatlas.com

Pocket PCT, Paul Bodnar (self-published, 2009)
Elevation guide to the PCT in three small volumes, with limited water and resupply information.
http://hikethru.com

John Muir Trail Map-Pack (Tom Harrison, 2009)
13 A4 topographic trekking maps, with relief shading and contour intervals at 80m, covering the John Muir and Pacific Crest Trails between Yosemite Valley and Mount Whitney.

Crater Mountain (Section 31)

Natural History

The Laws Field Guide to the Sierra Nevada, John Muir Laws (Heyday Books, 2007)
A superb guide to the fauna and flora of the Sierra Nevada.

Sierra Birds: A Hiker's Guide, John Muir Laws (Heyday Books, 2004)
www.johnmuirlaws.com

National Geographic Field Guide to the Birds of North America, Jon L. Dunn and Jonathan Alderfer (National Geographic Society, 2006)

National Geographic Field Guide to the Trees of North America, Charles Hollis and Keith Rushforth (National Geographic Society, 2006)
http://shop.nationalgeographic.com

Books by PCT hikers

A Thru-Hiker's Heart, 'No Way Ray' Echols (Tuolumne Press, 2009)
A collection of tales from the PCT.

Zero Days, Barbara Egbert (Wilderness Press, 2008)
Tells the story of the thru'-hike by 10-year-old Mary 'Scrambler' Chambers, with her parents Barbara Egbert and Gary Chambers

Soul, Sweat and Survival on the Pacific Crest Trail, Bob Holtel (Essence Publishing, 2007)
Tells the story of his solo run of the PCT, over three summers.

Along the Pacific Crest Trail, Karen Berger and Bart Smith (Westcliffe Publishers, 1998)
A coffee-table book with superb photographs from a PCT hike.

A Blistered Kind of Love: One Couple's Trial by Trail, Angela and Duffy Ballard (Mountaineers Books, 2003)
A humorous account of a young couple's PCT hike.

Walking Down a Dream: Mexico to Canada on Foot, Natasha Carver (self-published, 2003)
A humorous account of a PCT thru'-hike.

APPENDIX D
Schedules for 110 to 180-day thru'-hikes

The tables show the number of hiking hours between resupply points (third column) as well as the cumulative number of hiking hours from the start of the trail (fourth column). For each suggested schedule, the latest advisable departure date for each point is given, both as the number of days into your hike and the date.

Note These schedules are based on hiking in an average snow year with the aim of leaving Kennedy Meadows on June 15. In a low snow year it would be sensible to leave Kennedy Meadows earlier if you intend to use one of the slower schedules.

A rainbow in waterfalls on the Tuolumne River (Section 37)

Part	Resupply point	hrs	cumulative hrs	110 days		120 days		130 days		140 days	
				day	date	day	date	day	date	day	date
1	Campo	0	0	1	May 16	1	May 13	1	May 10	1	May 7
	Mount Laguna	19	19	3	May 18	3	May 15	3	May 12	3	May 9
	Warner Springs	26	45	5	May 20	6	May 18	7	May 16	7	May 13
	Paradise Corner	19	64	7	May 22	8	May 20	9	May 18	9	May 15
	San Gorgonio Pass	27	91	10	May 25	11	May 23	12	May 21	12	May 18
2	Van Dusen Canyon	31	122	13	May 28	14	May 26	15	May 24	16	May 22
	Wrightwood	38	160	16	May 31	18	May 30	19	May 28	21	May 27
3	Agua Dulce	42	202	20	Jun 4	22	Jun 3	24	Jun 2	26	Jun 1
	Neenach	28	230	23	Jun 7	25	Jun 6	28	Jun 6	30	Jun 5
	Willows Spring Road	17	247	25	Jun 9	27	Jun 8	30	Jun 8	32	Jun 7
4	Onyx	42	289	29	Jun 13	31	Jun 12	34	Jun 12	37	Jun 12
	Kennedy Meadows	24	313	31	Jun 15	34	Jun 15	37	Jun 15	40	Jun 15
	Onion Valley	57	370	36	Jun 20	39	Jun 20	42	Jun 20	46	Jun 21
	VVR	53	423	40	Jun 24	43	Jun 24	47	Jun 25	51	Jun 26
5	Tuolumne Meadows	29	452	43	Jun 27	47	Jun 28	51	Jun 29	55	Jun 30
	Sonora Pass	38	490	47	Jul 1	51	Jul 2	55	Jul 3	60	Jul 5
	Echo Lakes	34	524	50	Jul 4	55	Jul 6	59	Jul 7	64	Jul 8
	Donner Pass	28	552	53	Jul 7	58	Jul 9	63	Jul 11	68	Jul 13

Table 1 Schedules for 110, 120, 130 and 140-day thru-hikes

Sec	Location		Mile							
6	Sierra City	18	570	55 Jul 9	60 Jul 11	65 Jul 13	70 Jul 15
	Belden	41	611	58 Jul 12	63 Jul 14	69 Jul 17	74 Jul 19
	Hat Creek Resort	39	650	61 Jul 15	66 Jul 17	72 Jul 20	78 Jul 23
	Burney Falls	17	667	63 Jul 17	68 Jul 19	74 Jul 22	80 Jul 25
	Castella	37	704	66 Jul 20	72 Jul 23	78 Jul 26	84 Jul 29
7	Etna Summit	45	749	70 Jul 24	76 Jul 27	83 Jul 31	89 Aug 3
	Seiad Valley	24	773	72 Jul 26	79 Jul 30	86 Aug 3	92 Aug 6
	Interstate 5	31	804	75 Jul 29	82 Aug 2	89 Aug 6	96 Aug 10
8	Fish Lake Resort	23	827	77 Jul 31	83 Aug 3	91 Aug 8	98 Aug 12
	Mazama	20	847	79 Aug 2	85 Aug 5	93 Aug 10	100 Aug 14
	Shelter Cove	32	879	81 Aug 4	87 Aug 7	95 Aug 12	103 Aug 17
	Elk Lake	20	899	83 Aug 6	89 Aug 9	97 Aug 14	105 Aug 19
	Big Lake YC	18	917	84 Aug 7	91 Aug 11	99 Aug 16	107 Aug 21
9	Olallie	23	940	86 Aug 9	93 Aug 13	101 Aug 18	110 Aug 24
	Timberline Lodge	22	962	88 Aug 11	95 Aug 15	103 Aug 20	112 Aug 26
	Cascade Locks	21	983	90 Aug 13	97 Aug 17	105 Aug 22	114 Aug 28
10	Stabler Store	16	999	91 Aug 14	99 Aug 19	107 Aug 24	116 Aug 30
	White Pass	53	1052	95 Aug 18	103 Aug 23	112 Aug 29	121 Sep 4
	Snoqualmie Pass	45	1097	98 Aug 21	107 Aug 27	116 Sep 2	126 Sep 9
11	Stevens Pass	39	1136	102 Aug 25	111 Aug 31	121 Sep 7	131 Sep 14
	Stehekin River	51	1187	107 Aug 30	117 Sep 6	127 Sep 13	137 Sep 20
	Manning Park	42	1229	110 Sep 2	120 Sep 9	130 Sep 16	140 Sep 23

Table 2 Schedules for 150, 160, 170 and 180-day thru'-hikes

Part	Resupply point	hrs	cumulative hrs	150 days		160 days		170 days		180 days	
				day	date	day	date	day	date	day	date
1	Campo	0	0	1	May 4	1	May 1	1	Apr 28	1	Apr 25
	Mount Laguna	19	19	3	May 6	3	May 3	3	Apr 30	4	Apr 28
	Warner Springs	26	45	7	May 10	7	May 7	7	May 4	8	May 2
	Paradise Corner	19	64	10	May 13	10	May 10	10	May 7	11	May 5
	San Gorgonio Pass	27	91	13	May 16	14	May 14	14	May 11	15	May 9
	Van Dusen Canyon	31	122	17	May 20	18	May 18	19	May 16	20	May 14
2	Wrightwood	38	160	22	May 25	23	May 23	25	May 22	27	May 21
3	Agua Dulce	42	202	28	May 31	30	May 30	32	May 29	34	May 28
	Neenach	28	230	32	Jun 4	34	Jun 3	36	Jun 2	38	Jun 1
	Willows Spring Road	17	247	34	Jun 6	36	Jun 5	39	Jun 5	41	Jun 4
	Onyx	42	389	39	Jun 11	42	Jun 11	45	Jun 11	47	Jun 10
4	Kennedy Meadows	24	313	43	Jun 15	46	Jun 15	49	Jun 15	52	Jun 15
	Onion Valley	57	370	49	Jun 21	53	Jun 22	56	Jun 22	60	Jun 23
	VVR	53	423	55	Jun 27	59	Jun 28	63	Jun 29	67	Jun 30
	Tuolumne Meadows	29	452	59	Jul 1	64	Jul 3	68	Jul 4	73	Jul 6
5	Sonora Pass	38	490	64	Jul 6	69	Jul 8	74	Jul 10	79	Jul 12
	Echo Lakes	34	524	68	Jul 10	74	Jul 13	79	Jul 15	83	Jul 16
	Donner Pass	28	552	72	Jul 14	78	Jul 17	83	Jul 19	88	Jul 21

				74	Jul 16	80	Jul 19	85	Jul 21	90	Jul 23
6	Sierra City	18	570	74	Jul 16	80	Jul 19	85	Jul 21	90	Jul 23
	Belden	41	611	79	Jul 21	85	Jul 24	91	Jul 27	96	Jul 29
	Hat Creek Resort	39	650	84	Jul 26	90	Jul 29	96	Aug 1	102	Aug 4
	Burney Falls	17	667	86	Jul 28	92	Jul 31	98	Aug 3	104	Aug 6
	Castella	37	704	90	Aug 1	96	Aug 4	102	Aug 7	108	Aug 10
7	Etna Summit	45	749	96	Aug 7	102	Aug 10	109	Aug 14	115	Aug 17
	Seiad Valley	24	773	99	Aug 10	105	Aug 13	112	Aug 17	119	Aug 21
	Interstate 5	31	804	103	Aug 14	110	Aug 18	117	Aug 22	124	Aug 26
8	Fish Lake Resort	23	827	105	Aug 16	112	Aug 20	119	Aug 24	126	Aug 28
	Mazama	20	847	108	Aug 19	115	Aug 23	122	Aug 27	130	Sep 1
	Shelter Cove	32	879	111	Aug 22	118	Aug 26	125	Aug 31	134	Sep 5
	Elk Lake	20	899	113	Aug 24	121	Aug 29	129	Sep 3	137	Sep 8
	Big Lake YC	18	917	115	Aug 26	123	Aug 31	131	Sep 5	139	Sep 10
9	Olallie	23	940	118	Aug 29	126	Sep 3	134	Sep 8	142	Sep 13
	Timberline Lodge	22	962	120	Aug 31	129	Sep 6	137	Sep 11	145	Sep 16
	Cascade Locks	21	983	122	Sep 2	131	Sep 8	140	Sep 14	148	Sep 19
10	Stabler Store	16	999	124	Sep 4	133	Sep 10	142	Sep 16	150	Sep 21
	White Pass	53	1052	130	Sep 10	139	Sep 16	148	Sep 22	157	Sep 28
	Snoqualmie Pass	45	1097	135	Sep 15	144	Sep 21	153	Sep 27	163	Oct 4
11	Stevens Pass	39	1136	140	Sep 20	149	Sep 26	159	Oct 3	169	Oct 10
	Stehekin River	51	1187	146	Sep 26	156	Oct 3	166	Oct 10	176	Oct 17
	Manning Park	42	1229	150	Sep 30	160	Oct 7	170	Oct 14	180	Oct 21

APPENDIX E

Summaries of Ancient Brit's schedules

The table below summarises Ancient Brit's successful 2002 and 2006 thru'-hikes and his theoretical 180-day schedule (set out in full in Appendix G).

Notes

- Ancient Brit was an out-of-training 50+ year-old.
- 2006 was a record snow year and Ancient Brit set off much too early! The times in the High Sierra reflect heavy snowpack.
- Trail closures, because of fire and flood, resulted in lower mileages in 2006.
- 2002 was a continuous hike from Campo to Manning Park.
- On each trip, Ancient Brit took two zero days in Southern California, a 7-day break between Southern California and the High Sierra and another week-long break between Northern California and Oregon.
- The 180-day schedule includes suggested diversions.
- Only in Washington are there significant differences between the theoretical 180-day schedule and Ancient Brit's hiking schedules. Only in areas which involve much ascent can a fit hiker expect to gain significantly on the 180-day schedule.
- Miles/day and hours/day are for walking days and exclude zero days

Sunset from the ridge north of Etna Summit (Section 60)

	Southern California			High Sierra			Northern California			Oregon			Washington			Overall		
	2002	2006	180	2002	2006	180	2002	2006	180	2002	2006	180	2002	2006	180	2002	2006	180
miles	707	699	725	467	407	473	570	571	573	422	397	421	512	495	511	2678	2569	2703
hours	306	298	320	225	230	228	233	239	256	169	153	174	230	212	243	1171	1132	1220
mph	2.31	2.35	2.26	2.07	1.77	2.07	2.45	2.39	2.27	2.50	2.60	2.42	2.26	2.27	2.10	2.29	2.27	2.21
miles/day	15	17	15	15	15	14	19	19	16	19	18	18	17	16	16	17	17	16
hours/day	6.5	7.1	6.7	7.8	8.2	6.5	7.8	7.7	7.3	7.7	7.0	7.2	7.7	6.8	7.6	7.5	7.5	7.0
hiking days	47	42	48	29	28	35	30	30	35	22	22	24	30	31	32	158	153	174
zero days																16	16	6

APPENDIX F
Ancient Brit's 2002 (160-day) schedule

This schedule, successfully hiked by the author in 2002, can be used as the basis for a 160-day thru'-hike. His continuous hike included some of the variants recommended in this guidebook. An early start meant significant snow remained on the High Sierra passes. The schedule allows for only two zero days – you will need to get ahead of the schedule if you want to take others.

Day	Camp	Miles	Hours	Section
1	Hauser Mountain	8.8	3:51	1
2	Cottonwood Creek	16.9	7:01	2
3	Lower Morris Meadow	13.5	6:11	2
4	Resupply Laguna Store, Oriflamme Canyon	12.3	4:52	3
5	Rodriguez Canyon	16.9	6:42	3
6	San Felipe Hills	17.5	7:49	4
7	Barrel Spring	14.3	6:16	4
8	Resupply Warner Springs PO, Agua Caliente Creek	14.8	5:32	5
9	Combs Peak	12.0	6:12	6
10	Kamp Anza (resupply) (alternative route)	13.9	5:19	6
11	Kamp Anza (slack pack to Hwy 74)	16.7	6:12	6
12	Cedar Springs	16.9	6:42	7
13	Apple Canyon Saddle	9.1	5:21	7
14	Strawberry Junction Camp	11.8	6:28	8
15	Snow Canyon	19.3	8:15	8
16	Resupply San Gorgonio Valley N Teulang Canyon	15.6	6:34	9
17	Fork Springs	15.7	7:48	9
18	Road 1N96	11.9	6:45	9
19	Road 2N02	17.0	6:50	10
20	Resupply Big Bear City, Van Dusen Canyon	11.6	4:52	11
21	Holcomb Creek Crossing	17.8	7:00	11
22	Deep Creek Hot Springs	13.5	5:30	11
	Injury break (2 days)	0	0	
23	Resupply Summit Valley Cleghorn Picnic Site	20.0	7:40	12
24	Crowder Canyon	13.4	5:14	13
25	Gobblers Knob	15.9	7:44	14
26	Resupply (cache), Vincent Gap	15.3	6:37	15
27	Little Jimmy Trail Camp	11.1	6:03	15
28	Camp Glenwood	15.5	7:45	16

Day	Camp	Miles	Hours	Section
29	Gleason Road	17.2	6:59	17
30	Mattox Canyon	19.2	7:35	18
31	Resupply Agua Dulce	15.0	6:10	18
32	Spunky Canyon Road	17.0	7:44	19
33	Maxwell Truck Trail	18.2	7:44	19
34	Oakland Canyon	20.6	8:31	20
35	Resupply Neenach, Aqueduct Road	16.9	6:35	21
36	Gamble Spring Canyon	18.7	7:57	22
37	Cameron Ridge	16.5	7:37	22
38	Resupply Mojave, Peak 6253	12.6	5:58	23
39	Joshua Canyon	16.6	7:47	23
40	Piute Mountain Road	16.7	6:50	23
41	Road SC47	18.1	7:15	24
42	McIvers Hut	17.3	8:30	25
43	Walker Pass	7.7	2:47	25
	Resupply break (7 days)	0	0	
44	Morris Peak	3.3	1:54	26
45	Spanish Needle Creek	14.5	7:19	26
46	Peak 8226	15.8	7:32	27
47	Resupply Kennedy Meadows, S Fork Kern River	21.0	8:34	28
48	Cow Creek	13.7	7:03	28
49	Crestline Saddle	14.8	7:26	28
50	Siberia Trail Junction	21.0	8:57	29
51	Bighorn Plateau	18.6	8:19	30
52	Vidette Meadow	14.3	7:33	30
53	Resupply Kearsarge Lakes (cache), Rae Lakes	10.8	7:03	31
54	Mount Wynne	11.4	7:02	31
55	Upper Palisade Lake	13.7	9:00	32
56	Middle Fork Kings River	15.0	8:19	32
57	Evolution Meadow	15.2	9:05	33
58	Resupply Muir Trail Ranch, Sally Keyes Lake	15.8	8:45	34
59	Mono Creek	15.2	8:14	35
60	Cascade Valley (alternative route)	13.0	7:26	35
61	Cold Creek (alternative route)	12.4	6:26	35
62	Badger Lake	19.9	8:57	36
63	Lyell Canyon	16.1	8:44	36
64	Resupply Tuolumne Meadows Glen Aulin	11.4	4:36	37
65	Wilson Creek	17.1	8:33	37
66	Stubblefield Canyon	16.9	9:28	38
67	W Walker Trail Junction	18.1	8:51	38
68	Resupply (cache) Sonora Pass	17.3	8:25	38
69	Golden Lake	16.5	8:29	39
70	Raymond Meadows Lake	19.1	8:54	40
71	Lost Lakes	18.0	8:16	40

Day	Camp	Miles	Hours	Section
72	Benwood Meadow Creek	17.6	7:34	41
73	Resupply Echo Lake, Gilmore Lake	16.5	7:25	42
74	Barker Creek	20.1	8:48	42
75	Painted Rock Trail	21.2	8:45	43
76	Resupply Pooh Corner, Interstate 80	12.2	4:36	43
77	Peak 8166	20.0	8:00	44
78	Resupply Sierra City, Sierra Butte	20.8	8:46	45
79	Jamison Lake	15.7	7:00	45
80	Saddle 6510	20.3	8:33	46
81	Bear Creek	22.9	8:42	46
82	Three Lakes	23.2	9:07	47
83	Resupply Belden, Myrtle Flat Camp	15.3	6:52	48
84	Humboldt Summit	19.0	8:36	49
85	Resupply (cache), Highway 36	20.6	8:04	50
86	Flatiron Ridge	19.3	8:46	50
87	Hat Creek	18.4	7:00	50
88	Resupply Hat Creek Resort, Hat Creek Rim	15.6	6:07	51
89	Baum Lake	23.1	8:31	52
90	Rock Creek	17.2	6:40	53
91	Peak 5432	18.3	7:43	53
92	Deer Creek	24.2	9:46	54
93	Squaw Valley Creek	18.4	7:46	55
94	Resupply (cache, Interstate 5), Kettlebelly Ridge	18.7	7:37	56
95	Castle Crags	12.4	6:44	56
96	Toad Lake	19.6	8:33	56
97	Peak 6610	21.8	8:33	57
98	Mavis Lake	19.0	8:16	58
99	Statue Lake	17.1	8:07	59
100	Resupply (cache Etna summit), Kidder Creek Saddle	16.8	7:45	60
101	Black Mountain	17.8	9:05	60
102	Grider Creek	21.1	8:59	61
103	Resupply Seiad Valley, Devils Peak	16.3	7:32	62
104	Condrey Mountain	19.0	8:59	63
105	Long John Saddle	22.4	8:47	64
106	Interstate 5	15.7	6:00	64
	Resupply break (7 days)	0	0	
107	Keene Creek	17.6	7:22	65
108	Old Baldy	19.5	7:51	66
109	Resupply Lake of the Woods (alternative route), Cascade Canal (alternative route)	21.2	7:52	67
110	Upper Snow Lakes (alternative route)	18.3	7:27	68
111	Trail 1078	22.6	8:39	69
112	Resupply Mazama, Crater Lake Rim	19.6	7:30	70
113	Thielsen Creek Camp	19.8	7:34	71

Day	Camp	Miles	Hours	Section
114	Tolo Mountain	20.3	7:34	71
115	Diamond View Lake (alternative route)	18.4	7:10	72
116	Resupply Shelter Cove, Bobby Lake	16.6	6:56	73
117	Cougar Flat	19.6	8:43	74
118	Sisters Mirror Lake	18.1	7:05	75
119	S Mattieu Lake	20.7	8:20	75
120	Resupply Big Lake, Highway 20	20.1	8:10	76
121	Trail 3493 (alternative route)	19.4	9:03	77
122	Breitenbush Lake	19.6	8:42	78
123	Resupply Olallie Resort			
	Trooper Springs	19.0	6:56	79
124	Timothy Lake	23.4	8:29	80
125	Mount Hood	17.9	7:01	81
126	Resupply, Timberline Lodge,			
	Muddy Fork (alternative route)	14.7	8:00	81
127	Wahtum Lake	20.0	9:16	82
128	Rock Creek (alternative route)	24.4	8:40	83
129	Trout Creek	16.1	7:08	84
130	Resupply Stabler Store			
	Gayles Brook Camp	15.5	6:59	85
131	Sawtooth Mountain	20.6	8:13	85
132	Mount Adams	21.2	8:33	87
133	Midway Creek	19.1	7:59	88
134	Cispus Creek	18.6	8:08	88
135	Hogback Mountain	15.1	8:01	88
136	Resupply White Pass, Trail 43	20.0	8:08	89
137	Sheep Lake	18.4	9:14	90
138	Arch Rock Shelter	15.7	7:30	90
139	Blowout Mountain	17.2	7:22	91
140	Dandy Creek	19.1	8:29	92
141	Lodge Lake	14.2	6:19	92
142	Resupply Snowqualmie Pass,			
	Ridge Lake	9.5	5:03	93
143	Escondido Ridge	18.6	8:53	93
144	Deep Lake	18.5	7:57	94
145	Trap Pass	18.7	8:46	94
146	Resupply cache, Stephens Pass,			
	Nason Creek	15.4	7:13	95
147	Pear Lake	14.5	7:24	95
148	ReflectionPond	16.8	8:18	96
149	Kennedy Hot Springs (alternative route)	12.9	5:09	96
150	Above Milk Creek	15.8	8:08	96
151	Resupply cache Suiattle River,			
	Image Lake (alternative route)	16.9	8:31	97
152	Agnes Creek	21.5	8:21	97
153	Hideaway Camp	15.7	6:26	98
154	Snowy Lakes	16.0	7:17	99
155	Tatie Peak	15.2	6:45	99

APPENDIX G

Schedule for a 180-day thru'-hike

This is an example of the type of schedule I recommend that you prepare before undertaking a thru'-hike. At 180 leisurely days, it is the longest feasible time for tackling the entire PCT in one hiking season. It assumes that you will start your thru'-hike on a Monday, that you will arrive in towns during the mornings and leave in the evenings, and that you will be camping throughout.

Most hikers will want to travel faster and it is suggested that they start with this schedule, then adopt a faster one (see Appendix D) on reaching Agua Dulce, Kennedy Meadows or Donner Pass.

Designed to enable you to arrive in towns when post offices are open, this schedule allows for resupplying by buying food at stores and sending packages to post offices, resorts and trail angels at other times. Times given in brackets in the resupply information indicate the number of hiking hours until the next resupply opportunity.

The schedule includes very few zero days but does feature many short or half-days. You could easily earn extra zero days by getting ahead of the schedule. The hiking hours are those given in the guidebook and, once fit, you should be able to beat them by between 10 and 20 per cent.

Day		Camp	Miles	Hours	Section
0		Send supply package to Warner Springs PO (19hr) and Paradise Corner Café (27hr)			
1	Mon	Supplies (19hr), Hauser Mountain	12	5	1
2	Tue	Cottonwood Creek	12	6	2
3	Wed	Lower Morris Meadow	15	7	2
4	Thur	Resupply at Mt Laguna Store (26hr), Pioneer Mail Trailhead	13	5	3
5	Fri	Rodriguez Spur Truck Trail	17	6	3
6	Sat	San Felipe Hills	18	7	4
7	Sun	Barrel Spring	15	6	4
8	Mon	Pick up package Warner Springs PO, Agua Caliente Creek	14	5	5
9	Tue	Combs Peak	15	7	6
10	Wed	W of Table Mountain	18	7	6
11	Thur	Pick up package Paradise Corner Café Cedar Spring	18	8	7

Day		Camp	Miles	Hours	Section
12	Fri	Little Tarquitz Valley	15	8	7
13	Sat	Fuller Ridge Trailhead Campground	14	7	8
14	Sun	Tamarack Road, hitch to Cabazon	19	6	8
15	Mon	Resupply at Cabazon (31hr), hitch back to PCT, Teutang Canyon	6	4	9
16	Tue	Fork Springs	17	8	9
17	Wed	Coon Creek Jump-off	15	8	10
18	Thur	Highway 18	19	8	10
19	Fri	Van Dusen Canyon, hike to Big Bear City, resupply at store, 31hr return to Van Dusen Canyon	18	7	10
20	Sat	Holcomb Crossing Trail Camp	19	7	11
21	Sun	Deep Creek Hot Springs	14	5	11
22	Mon	Zero day (or take at Wrightwood)	0	0	
23	Tue	Silverwood Lake	20	7	12
24	Wed	Cajon Pass. Top up supplies	19	7	13
25	Thur	Gobblers Knob	15	8	14
26	Fri	Resupply at Wrightwood (45hr), send resupply package to Hikertown (17hr), Wrightwood	11	5	14
27	Sat	Blue Ridge Campground	9	5	15
28	Sun	Little Jimmy Campground	17	9	15
29	Mon	Cooper Canyon Trail Camp	12	6	16
30	Tue	Mill Creek Summit	23	9	17
31	Wed	Mattox Canyon	21	9	18
32	Thur	Agua Dulce, resupply at store (28hr)	15	6	18
33	Fri	Zero day at Hiker Heaven	0	0	
34	Sat	Spunky Canyon Road	18	9	19
35	Sun	Elizabeth Canyon Road	14	6	19
36	Mon	Bear Campground	19	9	20
37	Tue	Pick up package Hikertown, Hwy 138	13	6	20
38	Wed	Cottonwood Creek	18	6	21
39	Thur	Headwaters, Burnham Canyon	16	8	22
40	Fri	Willow Springs Road, hitch to Mojave, resupply at store (41hr), send resupply packages to Onyx PO (24hr), Kennedy Meadows Store (57hr), Independence PO (53hr), VVR (29hr)	8	3	22
41	Sat	Hitch back to PCT, Waterfall Canyon, Tehachapi Pass	10	4	23
42	Sun	Golden Oaks Spring	15	8	23
43	Mon	Robin Bird Spring	19	8	23
44	Tue	Willow Spring Road	20	8	24

Day		Camp	Miles	Hours	Section
45	Wed	Lower Jack Spring Trail	15	7	25
46	Thur	Walker Pass campground. Hitch to Onyx to pick up package, return to PCT	14	5	25
47	Fri	Spanish Needle Creek	17	8	26
48	Sat	Canebrake Road Campground	13	6	26
49	Sun	Rockhouse Basin	13	7	27
50	Mon	Pick up package Kennedy Meadows Store	10	3	27
51	Tue	Zero day	0	0	
52	Wed	Cow Creek	18	8	28
53	Thur	Crestline Saddle	15	9	28
54	Fri	Chicken Spring Lake	17	7	29
55	Sat	Crabtree Meadow	16	7	29
56	Sun	Climb Mt Whitney (or zero day)	17	9	29
57	Mon	Below Forester Pass	12	7	30
58	Tue	Kearsarge Lakes	14	7	30
59	Wed	Onion Valley Trailhead, hitch to Independence, pick up package	7	3	30
60	Thur	Return to PCT, Kearsarge Lakes	7	5	30
61	Fri	Woods Creek Bridge	13	6	31
62	Sat	S Fork Kings River	13	8	32
63	Sun	Middle Fork Kings River	16	8	32
64	Mon	Evolution Creek	15	9	33
65	Tue	Senger Creek	20	8	34
66	Wed	Bear Ridge Trail (or continue to VVR)	13	7	35
67	Thur	Pick up package Vermillion Valley Resort, return to PCT at Mono Creek	13	5	35
68	Fri	Cascade Valley (alternative route)	15	7	35
69	Sat	Iva Bell Hot Springs (alternative route)	5	2	35
70	Sun	Top up supplies at Reds Meadow, Upper Soda Springs Campground	17	7	36
71	Mon	Rush Creek	15	8	36
72	Tue	Resupply from Tuolumne Meadows Store (38hr)	17	7	36
73	Wed	Glen Aulin Campground	6	2	37
74	Thur	Wilson Creek	17	9	37
75	Fri	Kerrick Canyon	15	6	37
76	Sat	Grace Meadow	13	7	38
77	Sun	Kennedy Canyon	14	6	38
78	Mon	Sonora Pass, hitch to Bridgeport to resupply (34hr)	12	6	38
79	Tue	Return to PCT, E Carson Trail	9	4	39

Day		Camp	Miles	Hours	Section
80	Wed	Noble Lakes	19	9	39
81	Thur	Lily Pond Lake	19	8	40
82	Fri	Showers Lake	19	8	41
83	Sat	Resupply at Echo Lake Resort (28hr), Lake Margery	16	7	42
84	Sun	Phipps Creek	15	7	42
85	Mon	N Fork Blackwood Creek	15	7	43
86	Tue	Painted Rock Trail	17	7	43
87	Wed	Donner Pass. Resupply at Truckee (18hr), send resupply package to Belden PO (39hr) and Burney Falls Campground (37 hr)	12	4	43
88	Thur	Meadow Lake Road	19	9	44
89	Fri	Wild Plum Campground	21	8	44
90	Sat	Resupply Sierra City (41hr), Packer Lake (alternative route)	15	7	45
91	Sun	W Branch Nelson Creek	18	8	45
92	Mon	Black Rock Creek Rd	17	7	46
93	Tue	Top of climb	19	9	46
94	Wed	Clear Creek	19	8	47
95	Thur	Pick up package from Belden PO	9	3	47
96	Fri	Myrtle Flat Camp	7	4	48
97	Sat	Cold Spring	12	7	48
98	Sun	Soldier Creek Springs	22	10	49
99	Mon	N Fork Feather River	13	5	50
100	Tue	Lower Twin Lake	17	8	50
101	Wed	Resupply at Hat Creek Resort (17hr)	17	6	50
102	Thur	Road 22	20	8	51
103	Fri	Burney Falls (backpacker camp)	26	10	52
104	Sat	Pick up package from Burney Falls, Peavine Creek	14	7	53
105	Sun	W Ridge Mushroom Rock	18	8	54
106	Mon	Ah-da-nah Campground	24	9	55
107	Tue	Girard Ridge	16	9	55
108	Wed	Resupply at Castella (45hr), Winton Canyon Creek	15	6	56
109	Thur	Saddle	11	6	56
110	Fri	Porcupine Lake	17	7	56
111	Sat	Bull Lake	17	7	57
112	Sun	Mosquito Lake Creek	18	7	58
113	Mon	S Fork Scott River	13	6	58
114	Tue	Etna Summit, hitch to Etna	21	9	59

Day		Camp	Miles	Hours	Section
115	Wed	Resupply at store (24hr), return to Etna Summit, saddle	4	2	60
116	Thur	Marble Valley	20	9	60
117	Fri	Cold Spring Creek	17	8	61
118	Sat	Seiad Valley, resupply at store (31hr)	15	5	61
119	Sun	E ridge Red Butte	12	8	62
120	Mon	Mud Springs Road	18	9	63
121	Tue	Long John Saddle	19	8	64
122	Wed	Highway 99, hitch to Ashland	16	6	64
123	Thur	Zero day, resupply at store (43hr), send packages to Shelter Cove Resort (20hr), Elk Lake Resort (18hr), Big Lake Youth Camp (23hr), Olallie Resort (22hr), Timberline Lodge (21hr), Stabler Store (53hr)	0	0	
124	Fri	Hitch back to PCT, Green Springs Summit	18	7	65
125	Sat	Griffin Pass Road	19	8	66
126	Sun	Top up supplies from Lake of the Woods Store, Cascade Canal (alternative route)	17	8	67
127	Mon	Isherwood Lake (alternative route)	15	6	68
128	Tue	Honeymoon Creek	14	6	68
129	Wed	Resupply at Mazama Campground (32hr)	20	9	69
130	Thur	Grouse Hill	13	7	70
131	Fri	Thielsen Creek	18	7	71
132	Sat	Tolo Camp (above spring)	17	6	71
133	Sun	Diamond View Lake (alternative route)	21	9	72
134	Mon	Pick up package Shelter Cove, Bobby Lake	17	7	73
135	Tue	Stormy Lake	18	7	74
136	Wed	Pick up package Elk Lake Resort	18	7	74
137	Thur	Obsidian Falls	20	8	75
138	Fri	Belknap Crater	16	7	76
139	Sat	Pick up package Big Lake Youth Camp, Wasco Lake	21	10	76
140	Sun	Milk Creek	17	7	77
141	Mon	Breitenbush Campground	13	6	78
142	Tue	Pick up package Olallie Lake, Trooper Spring	16	6	79
143	Wed	Clackamas Lake Campground	19	8	79
144	Thur	Barlow Pass	20	8	80
145	Fri	Pick up package Timberline Lodge, Ramona Falls	16	8	81

Day		Camp	Miles	Hours	Section
146	Sat	Indian Springs Campground	20	10	82
147	Sun	Cascade Locks (by Eagle Creek)	19	7	83
148	Mon	Resupply at store (16hr), send package to White Pass (45hr), Snoqualmie Pass (39hr), Skykomish (51hr) Stehekin (42hr), Gillette Lake	4	2	84
149	Tue	Rock Creek	16	9	84
150	Wed	Pick up package Stabler Store, Panther Creek	15	7	85
151	Thur	Sheep Lake	17	9	85
152	Fri	Steamboat Lake Creek	22	9	86
153	Sat	Riley Creek	18	9	87
154	Sun	Midway Creek	14	6	88
155	Mon	Trail 96	20	9	88
156	Tue	Ginette Lake	19	10	88
157	Wed	Pick up package White Pass, Fish Lake Creek	17	7	89
158	Thur	Sheep Lake	17	9	90
159	Fri	Camp Ulrich	21	9	90
160	Sat	Tarn below Blowout Mountain	11	5	91
161	Sun	Stirrup Creek	22	9	92
162	Mon	Pick up package Snoqualmie Pass	14	6	92
163	Tue	Ridge Lake	8	5	93
164	Wed	N Fork Lemah Creek	15	6	93
165	Thur	N of Waptus Lake	16	8	94
166	Fri	Cle Elum Creek	13	7	94
167	Sat	Hope Lake	16	8	94
168	Sun	Stevens Pass, hitch to Skykomish	9	4	94
169	Mon	Resupply Skykomish, return to PCT, Lake Janus	10	4	95
170	Tue	Pass Creek	15	8	95
171	Wed	White Chuck River	19	9	96
172	Thur	Milk Creek	16	9	96
173	Fri	Miners Creek	18	10	97
174	Sat	High Bridge, Stehekin River	22	10	97
175	Sun	Take shuttle bus to Stehekin	0	0	
176	Mon	Pick up package, return to PCT, Hideaway Camp	14	7	98
177	Tue	Creek before Methow Pass	16	8	99
178	Wed	Harts Pass Campground	20	9	99
179	Thur	Creek before Woody Pass	20	10	100
180	Fri	Manning Park	20	9	101

APPENDIX H

Schedule for a super-slow start

Those who are extremely unfit might like to start a little earlier and adopt a gentle schedule for the first few weeks. This slow start is designed to maximise use of water sources. No zero days are given but you shouldn't need them. If you then pick up the 180-day schedule from Big Bear City, a starting date of April 18 would get you to Kennedy Meadows on June 13.

day	camp	miles	hours	section
1	Hauser Mountain	9	4	1
2	Lake Morena Campground	12	5	1
3	Cottonwood Creek	5	2	2
4	Long Canyon Creek	12	6	2
5	Mount Laguna	5	2½	2
6	Pioneer Mail Trailhead	10	4	3
7	Rodriguez Spur Truck Trail	16	6½	3
8	San Felipe Creek	9	3½	3
9	San Felipe Hills	14	6	4
10	Barrel Spring	10	4	4
11	Warner Springs	8	3½	4
12	Lost Valley Road (near spring)	10	4½	5
13	Tule Canyon Spring	17	7	6
14	Highway 74	15	7	6
15	Cedar Spring	12	6	7
16	Apache Spring	9	5	7
17	Idyllwild (from Saddle Junction)	14	6½	7
18	Fuller Ridge Campground	12	7½	8
19	Snow Canyon	15	5	8
20	Tamarack Road (for Cabazon)	4	1½	8
21	Whitewater River	11	5½	9
22	Fork Springs	15	6	9
23	Coon Creek Jump-off	14	7½	9
24	Arrastre Trail Camp	10	4	10
25	Van Dusen Canyon	18	7½	10
26	Resupply form Big Bear Canyon, return to Van Dusen Canyon	8	3	

LISTING OF CICERONE GUIDES

BRITISH ISLES CHALLENGES, COLLECTIONS AND ACTIVITIES

The End to End Trail
The Mountains of England and Wales
  Vol 1: Wales
  Vol 2: England
The National Trails
The Relative Hills of Britain
The Ridges of England, Wales and Ireland
The UK Trailwalker's Handbook
Three Peaks, Ten Tors
Unjustifiable Risk? A social history of climbing
World Mountain Ranges: Scotland

NORTHERN ENGLAND TRAILS

A Northern Coast to Coast Walk
Backpacker's Britain: Northern England
Hadrian's Wall Path
The Dales Way
The Pennine Way
The Spirit of Hadrian's Wall

LAKE DISTRICT

An Atlas of the English Lakes
Coniston Copper Mines
Great Mountain Days in the Lake District
Lake District Winter Climbs
Roads and Tracks of the Lake District
Rocky Rambler's Wild Walks
Scrambles in the Lake District North & South
Short Walks in Lakeland
  Book 1: South Lakeland
  Book 2: North Lakeland
  Book 3: West Lakeland
The Central Fells
The Cumbria Coastal Way
The Cumbria Way and the Allerdale Ramble
The Lake District Anglers' Guide
The Mid-Western Fells
The Near Eastern Fells
The Southern Fells
The Tarns of Lakeland
  Vol 1: West
  Vol 2: East
Tour of the Lake District

NORTH WEST ENGLAND AND THE ISLE OF MAN

A Walker's Guide to the Lancaster Canal
Historic Walks in Cheshire
Isle of Man Coastal Path
The Isle of Man
The Ribble Way
Walking in Lancashire
Walking in the Forest of Bowland and Pendle
Walking on the West Pennine Moors
Walks in Lancashire Witch Country
Walks in Ribble Country
Walks in Silverdale and Arnside
Walks in The Forest of Bowland

NORTH EAST ENGLAND, YORKSHIRE DALES AND PENNINES

Historic Walks in North Yorkshire
South Pennine Walks
The Cleveland Way and the Yorkshire Wolds Way
The North York Moors
The Reivers Way
The Teesdale Way
The Yorkshire Dales Angler's Guide
The Yorkshire Dales:
  North and East
  South and West
Walking in County Durham
Walking in Northumberland
Walking in the North Pennines
Walking in the Wolds
Walks in Dales Country
Walks in the Yorkshire Dales
Walks on the North York Moors
  Books 1 & 2

DERBYSHIRE, PEAK DISTRICT AND MIDLANDS

High Peak Walks
Historic Walks in Derbyshire
The Star Family Walks
Walking in Derbyshire
White Peak Walks:
  The Northern Dales
  The Southern Dales

SOUTHERN ENGLAND

A Walker's Guide to the Isle of Wight
London: The Definitive Walking Guide
The Cotswold Way
The Greater Ridgeway
The Lea Valley Walk
The North Downs Way
The South Downs Way
The South West Coast Path
The Thames Path
Walking in Bedfordshire
Walking in Berkshire
Walking in Buckinghamshire
Walking in Kent
Walking in Sussex
Walking in the Isles of Scilly
Walking in the Thames Valley
Walking on Dartmoor

WALES AND WELSH BORDERS

Backpacker's Britain: Wales
Glyndwr's Way
Great Mountain Days in Snowdonia
Hillwalking in Snowdonia
Hillwalking in Wales
  Vols 1 & 2
Offa's Dyke Path
Ridges of Snowdonia
Scrambles in Snowdonia
The Ascent of Snowdon
The Lleyn Peninsula Coastal Path
The Pembrokeshire Coastal Path
The Shropshire Hills
The Spirit Paths of Wales
Walking in Pembrokeshire
Walking on the Brecon Beacons
Welsh Winter Climbs

SCOTLAND

Backpacker's Britain:
  Central and Southern Scottish Highlands
  Northern Scotland
Ben Nevis and Glen Coe
Border Pubs and Inns
North to the Cape
Not the West Highland Way
Scotland's Best Small Mountains

IRELAND

Irish Coastal Walks
The Irish Coast to Coast Walk
The Mountains of Ireland

ITALY

Central Apennines of Italy
Gran Paradiso
Italian Rock
Italy's Sibillini National Park
Shorter Walks in the Dolomites
Through the Italian Alps
Trekking in the Apennines
Treks in the Dolomites
Via Ferratas of the Italian Dolomites: Vols 1 & 2
Walking in Sicily
Walking in the Central Italian Alps
Walking in the Dolomites
Walking in Tuscany
Walking on the Amalfi Coast

MEDITERRANEAN

Jordan – Walks, Treks, Caves, Climbs and Canyons
The Ala Dag
The High Mountains of Crete
The Mountains of Greece
Treks & Climbs in Wadi Rum, Jordan
Walking in Malta
Western Crete

NORTH AMERICA

British Columbia
The Grand Canyon
The John Muir Trail
The Pacific Crest Trail

SOUTH AMERICA

Aconcagua and the Southern Andes
Torres del Paine

SCANDINAVIA

Trekking in Greenland
Walking in Norway

SLOVENIA, CROATIA AND MONTENEGRO

The Julian Alps of Slovenia
The Mountains of Montenegro
Trekking in Slovenia
Walking in Croatia

SPAIN AND PORTUGAL

Costa Blanca Walks
Vol 1: West
Vol 2: East
Mountain Walking in Southern Catalunya
The Mountains of Central Spain
Trekking through Mallorca
Via de la Plata
Walking in Madeira
Walking in Mallorca
Walking in the Algarve
Walking in the Canary Islands Vol 2: East
Walking in the Cordillera Cantabrica
Walking in the Sierra Nevada
Walking the GR7 in Andalucia
Walks and Climbs in the Picos de Europa

SWITZERLAND

Alpine Pass Route
Central Switzerland
The Bernese Alps
Tour of the Jungfrau Region
Walking in the Valais
Walking in Ticino
Walks in the Engadine

EUROPEAN CYCLING

Cycle Touring in France
Cycle Touring in Ireland
Cycle Touring in Spain
Cycle Touring in Switzerland
Cycling in the French Alps
Cycling the Canal du Midi
Cycling the River Loire
The Danube Cycleway
The Grand Traverse of the Massif Central
The Way of St James Cyclist Guide

TECHNIQUES

Indoor Climbing
Map and Compass
Mountain Weather
Moveable Feasts
Outdoor Photography
Rock Climbing
Snow and Ice Techniques
Sport Climbing
The Book of the Bivvy
The Hillwalker's Guide to Mountaineering
The Hillwalker's Manual

MINI GUIDES

Avalanche!
Navigating with a GPS
Navigation
Pocket First Aid and Wilderness Medicine
Snow

For full and up-to-date information on our ever-expanding list of guides, visit our website: **www.cicerone.co.uk**.

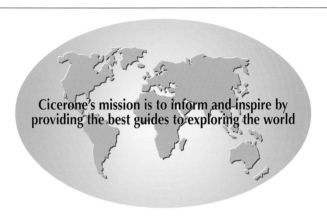

Cicerone's mission is to inform and inspire by providing the best guides to exploring the world

Since its foundation 40 years ago, Cicerone has specialised in publishing guidebooks and has built a reputation for quality and reliability. It now publishes nearly 300 guides to the major destinations for outdoor enthusiasts, including Europe, UK and the rest of the world.

Written by leading and committed specialists, Cicerone guides are recognised as the most authoritative. They are full of information, maps and illustrations so that the user can plan and complete a successful and safe trip or expedition – be it a long face climb, a walk over Lakeland fells, an alpine cycling tour, a Himalayan trek or a ramble in the countryside.

With a thorough introduction to assist planning, clear diagrams, maps and colour photographs to illustrate the terrain and route, and accurate and detailed text, Cicerone guides are designed for ease of use and access to the information.

If the facts on the ground change, or there is any aspect of a guide that you think we can improve, we are always delighted to hear from you.

Cicerone Press
2 Police Square Milnthorpe Cumbria LA7 7PY
Tel: 015395 62069 Fax: 015395 63417
info@cicerone.co.uk www.cicerone.co.uk

CICERONE

Symbols used on the overview maps

7	area covered by map 7
(15) ————	interstate highway
(14) ————	state highway
- - - - - - -	mountain road
· · · · · · · ·	trail
•	town or city

Abbreviations used in the facilities information for each part

PO	post office
P	package service
G	groceries (store or supermarket)
R	restaurant or café
A	accommodation (hotel, motel, hostel or chalets)
C	campground
L	laundry
Sh	showers
O	outdoor store
B	bank or ATM